13/02/2024

ALAN TITCHMARSH
HOW TO BE A
SUPERGARDENER

ALAN TITCHMARSH
HOW TO BE A
SUPERGARDENER

WARD LOCK

A WARD LOCK BOOK

A Cassell Imprint
Wellington House
125 Strand
London
WC2R 0BB

First published 1983
Second edition 1988
Third edition 1993
First paperback edition 1994
Second paperback edition, revised 1997

Distributed in the United States
by Sterling Publishing Co., Inc.
387 Park Avenue South, New York, NY 10016-8810

A British Library Cataloguing in Publication Data block for
this book may be obtained from the British Library

ISBN 0-7063-7725-7 Paperback
ISBN 0-7063-7729-X Hardback

Typeset by Business ColorPrint, Welshpool, Powys, Wales
Printed and bound in Spain

Contents

DEDICATION

For my Mother
who bought me my first packet of seeds;
And my Father
who was relieved to hand over the spade

Preface to First Edition

'The man who could call a spade a spade should be compelled to use one. It is the only thing he is fit for', said Oscar Wilde. So it is that gardeners have acquired a reputation as down-to-earth dullards who possess most of nature's secrets and few social graces. But the days of the crumbling conservatory presided over by a grumbling gardener have long since gone. The mystery of supposed 'green fingers' certainly lingers on, but folk who tackle the land with a handful of common sense as well as a bucketful of manure, will find that this oldest of crafts offers satisfaction and excitement as well as frustration and fury.

Don't believe that all expert gardeners have the patience of Job. Some of them are itching for their seeds to come up and grow into cabbages overnight; others want a mature garden in a matter of weeks. But all of them, if they have a feeling for the soil and for plants, will curb their impatience and learn that there's no rushing nature, though occasionally she'll let you cheat a bit.

I started gardening when I left school—having shown singular lack of success in any subject remotely academic. Off I plodded to the local nursery where I was astounded to find that someone would pay me to grow plants; something that I'd been doing in my spare time for the previous five years. Gardening doesn't grab everybody this way. Lots of folk look upon it as a chore that has to be done on a Sunday after the car has been washed. And it's easy to see why. They find that everything that shouldn't grow fast does—weeds, the hedge and the lawn—and everything that should be bursting into leaf and flower doesn't—the hastily planted tree, the summer bedding and the bulbs.

The secret of success is to adopt the right attitude to your garden. For a start, stop worrying about it, and stop worrying about what the neighbours will say if you don't cut the lawn or the hedge with monotonous regularity. Look upon your garden as a haven where you can escape the high-speed living of today; then the fact that things move slowly within its leafy confines will soon be welcomed as a positive advantage.

Hopefully *Supergardener* will give you a bit of inspiration as well as practical, down-to-earth advice. Everybody considers that their garden is a problem plot, so there are suggestions of plants that will put up with all sorts of soils and situations. If you've never lifted a spade before, you should still be able to understand what I'm rambling on about. Above all, remember that this is one man's choice of plants, and one man's way of growing them, though both plants and techniques have been filched from other gardeners during the couple of decades that count as my apprenticeship in the craft.

I've had to garden, so far, on heavy clay in the north, on dust-like sand and now on chalk, clay and flints in the south, so I know that time spent tending the earth is not always rewarded with bumper crops and a bounty of blooms. But the failures make the successes that much more enjoyable. If the book makes gardening seem faintly interesting and even encourages you to grow just one plant to perfection then I'll be well pleased. I hope you will be too.

'*Woodroyd*'
Beech

A.T.

Introduction

It's great when a book takes off! *Supergardener* first thrust itself on an unsuspecting public 14 years ago and, I'm delighted to say, has gone on selling well ever since. But even in the pastoral world of gardening things move on – albeit rather slowly. New varieties are introduced, and some of them are reliable enough to oust previous favourites. In this edition I've included the best of the new ones, but only those that have proved themselves.

We are fortunately much more conservation conscious than we were 14 years ago. Peat is something we reckon should be substituted with other organic matter so that natural peat resources are not depleted and unique forms of wildlife endangered. I've endeavoured to use other materials wherever possible, though the oft recommended coir fibre has still some way to go before it's the panacea some folk seem to think.

Like many people, in my own garden I now use no chemical spray because I value the balance of nature that exists there – the masses of birds, insects and animals (from deer to voles) and I'd rather not upset them. I also find that plants supplied with plenty of soil enrichment in the form of garden compost, well-rotted manure and organic fertilizer do seem to resist epidemics. Yes, of course I have greenfly on my roses and caterpillars on my cabbages. But nowadays (old softie that I am) I'd rather squirt them off with a hosepipe or pick them off by hand.

The result is a garden that gives me more pleasure than it has ever done, and which makes me feel certain that all those years ago I picked the right job.

With any luck *Supergardener* will continue to offer inspiration and answer those niggling questions that pop up from time to time.

Alan Titchmarsh

Acknowledgements

The publishers gratefully acknowledge the following for granting permission to reproduce colour photographs: Bob Challinor (pp.93 top and lower right, 94 lower left and right, 95 top left and right, 129, 132 lower), Alan Titchmarsh (pp.25, 93 lower left, 181). The remainder of the colour photographs are by Bob Challinor (pp. 26, 27 top left, 95 lower, 96 top, 132 top, 182 top and lower left, 183 lower) and Michael Stead (pp. 27 top right and lower, 28, 94 top, 96 lower, 130, 131, 182 lower right, 183 top, 184).

The following line drawings are by Pamela Dowson: Figs. 1, 10, 12–15, 17–26, 28–32, 34, 35, 37–42 and 47–65. The following line dawings are by Nils Solberg: Figs. 2–9, 11, 16, 27, 43–6, 66–80 and 86–8.

Figs. 1, 12, 14, 15, 28a, 29, 46 and 48 are after drawings on pp. 12, 30, 48 (Figs. 14 and 15), 25, 30, 63 and 71 respectively in *Gardening Techniques*, Alan Titchmarsh published by Mitchell Beazley/Royal Horticultural Society, 1981; Figs. 3, 4, 6, 8, 32, 56, 58, 59, 60, 61, 62, 63, 64, 65, 78 and 87 are after drawings on pp. 19, 18, 14, 27, 93, 114, 32-3, 45, 46, 53, 70, 80, 93, 102, 108, 25 and 38 respectively in *The Allotment Gardener's Handbook*, Alan Titchmarsh, published by Severn House, 1982; Figs. 21, 22 and 23 are after drawings on pp.81, 91 and 94 respectively in *The Rose Expert*, D.G. Hessayon, published by Pan Britannica Industries Ltd, 1981; Figs 30 and 31 are after drawings on pp.82 and 80 respectively in *Textbook of Botany*, J.M. Lowson, published by University Tutorial Press Ltd, 1949; Fig. 39 is after the drawing on p.327 in *Reader's Digest New Illustrated Guide to Gardening*, 1979; Fig. 43 is after drawings on pp.16-17 in *Lawns, Ground Cover and Weed Control*, David Pycraft, published by Mitchell Beazley/Royal Horticultural Society, 1980; Figs. 51, 52, 53, 54 and 55 are after drawings on pp.8, 53, 61, 56 and 90 respectively in *Fruit*, Harry Barker, published by Mitchell Beazley/Royal Horticultural Society, 1980; Figs.66, 67, 68, 69 and 70 are after drawings on pp.9 (Figs. 66 and 67), 10 (Figs.68 and 69) and 11 respectively in *Gardening under Cover*, Alan Titchmarsh, published by Hamlyn, 1979; Fig. 74 is after drawings on p. 170 in *Hausbuch der Zimmerpflanzen*, K. Jacobi and on p.46 in *Mehr Blumenfreude durch Hydrokultur*, M. Schubert, both published by BLV, Munich, in 1981 and 1979 respectively; Figs. 7b-d and 9 are after drawings appearing in Bentleys Catalogue 1983; and Fig. 7a is after an illustration appearing in the Wilkinson Sword Catalogue.

1 How to start

It's a daunting prospect but an irresistible challenge—a weed-infested patch of earth from which must be sculpted a garden. So what should you do first? Most experts are united in their opinions on this: you must draw up a plan.

PLANNING YOUR PATCH

Say the word 'plan' to an architect and he'll immediately take out his pencil and a sheet of graph paper. The pencil will be of use to you; the graph paper is not essential. Certainly it's a good idea to consult with all members of the family so that you know just what they want of a garden: somewhere to sit (in sun or shade?), somewhere to play football, somewhere to put a swing or a sandpit, in fact it might seem at times as if there will be no room for plants. But don't make the mistake of thinking that gardens are planned on paper; I reckon the best ones are planned on soil. Get out there with an armful of bamboo canes and a hosepipe and draw patterns and shapes on the earth.

I'm not going to tell you much about the elements of garden design; there are a lot of them and they've been covered in depth in many books on garden planning. What I will say is that your garden should be both practical and pleasing to look at. If you want a formal plot (all circles and squares) then have one, but most folk like an informal scheme that utilizes gentle curves that are easy on the eye, sympathetic to plants, and totally divorced from the symmetry of motorways, traffic roundabouts and office layouts.

With your list of desirable attributes to hand you'll have fun plotting the shape of your potential garden. View it from all angles—both on the ground and from upstairs windows—and use your imagination to tell you that a bamboo cane will, in time, be a tree of sizeable proportions. Avoid fiddly corners on lawns (they'll be difficult to mow) and in beds (they'll be difficult to plant up), but make sure that one or two parts of the garden are invisible as you walk down it—that way you'll be drawn to explore the hidden nooks and crannies.

There are not many rules in gardening, but there are a few that will prevent disasters in garden design:

1 Make sure you know the aspect of your garden—a tall row of conifers planted on the south side will cast heavy shade over most of the plot. Find out where north is and plant with the sun's path in mind.

2 Garden features that need sun (a pond, a vegetable plot or a greenhouse) must be sited in the open.

3 Make sure that your soil is well drained and in good shape before you plant anything.

4 Be nosey. Look at gardens in your area and take note of plants that do well and those that don't. Avoid the poor 'doers' and save yourself some money.

5 Use trees and shrubs as the backbone of your planting scheme. Make sure some of them are evergreens, and try to ensure that there's something to look at all the year round.

6 If you can't afford the time or money to plant all your garden at once (and few of us can), start in one corner and work slowly outwards. If you start near the house you'll always have something to take your mind off the squalor that lies beyond.

7 Make it simple, sweeping and bold, even if the plot is small. Lots of twiddly bits will drive you nuts.

8 Remember that plant foliage is more important and more enduring than flowers. The predominant foliage colour should be green (too many purples and greys will be overpowering), and each plant should be put next to a neighbour which in some way contrasts with or complements its shape, form or colour. It sounds a bit pretentious but it makes for much more impact than a jumbled scheme of assorted flowers.

Whatever design you settle on, don't make the mistake of thinking that one day your garden will be finished. No garden is a museum (those that are preserved as such invariably go downhill) and constant adjustment of shapes and replanting can be carried out when you tire of your original plantings. Mind you, the trees will appreciate being left alone.

LAND CLEARANCE

I'm afraid there's no magic formula—it's basically hard graft. For a start, all tall weeds, brambles and seedling trees should be hacked down as close to ground level as possible with a sickle, scythe or powered 'strimmer', and the compostable greenstuff stacked on the compost heap (see p. 12). Woody stems can be burned, but dry them off a bit first so that they don't smoke out the neighbours.

I don't like using weedkillers much, but if the plot is vast then you might feel it's essential. They act best in spring and summer on growing weeds. For full details and the right way to use them see Chapter 22.

Whether you kill off the weeds or not the soil will still have to be turned, and I can't get out of the habit of pulling out thick weed roots, even if they are supposed to be dead, thanks to a herbicide. It's tempting to use a rotavator to turn over the soil. Do so if you're really short of time and energy, but remember that weed roots which are not dead will be chopped up by the blades, and each small piece will make a new plant. Added to this it is difficult to incorporate organic soil enrichment with a rotavator, and the soil is seldom cultivated as deeply as it is with a spade. Pay your money and take your choice.

When soil has once been cleared and dug, keep an eye on it and deal quickly with any weeds that emerge. Better still, mulch it immediately with a 5–8 cm (2–3 in) thick layer of organic matter such as leafmould, pulverized bark, compost or manure to prevent weed emergence. Neglect it and you'll have to do the whole job again—it's heartbreaking.

Don't overdo the hard work. A little slog every couple of days is better than one back-breaking blitz.

SOIL IMPROVEMENT

Soil is pretty boring stuff on the face of it, but it is the staff of life as far as your plants are concerned. Remember—what goes in must come up—you only get out of your soil what you put into it.

Drainage

If soil drainage is poor you'll know about it: pools of water may lie on the surface, or the ground may be like a paddy field in wet weather. Where drainage problems are severe, some kind of piped, underground drainage system will have to be invested in, but such cases are, thank goodness, rare. More often than not, poor drainage is caused either by the fact that the soil is almost pure clay, or because the surface has been compacted by heavy traffic, or because there is a hard and impenetrable layer in the subsoil. The way to deal with these problems is as follows:

1 Clay soil is easy to identify: it is rock-hard when dry and very plastic when wet. Rub it between your finger and thumb and it has a polished sheen. Improve its drainage by working in as much sharp sand, grit and organic matter as you can lay your spade on. All these materials will break up the clay and prevent the individual particles from adhering quite so firmly to one another. Winter digging allows frost to shatter clay but the effect is only temporary.

2 If the surface of the soil refuses to allow water to drain away, fork or dig over the area. If this is not possible (on a lawn for instance) spike the area deeply with a special aerator or a garden fork. Work grit and organic matter into the soil to prevent a recurrence of the problem.

3 If a 'subsoil pan' (a hard, impervious layer below the topsoil) is causing poor drainage, break up the stiff or rocky layer with a pick or a crowbar to allow water through. In large gardens the job might have to be done with a tractor attachment.

Soil types

The ideal garden soil is something called a medium loam. It exists but I don't know anyone who's got it! It consists of a mixture of sand, clay and rotted organic matter known as 'humus'. It doesn't become too sticky when wet nor too dusty when dry.

Sandy soils are 'light' and easy to work but they tend to be lacking in nutrients (which are rapidly washed through) and quick to dry in summer.

Clay soils dry like rock and become squidgy when wet. They are difficult to cultivate whatever the time of year. They are slow to warm up in spring, too.

Stony soils may be sandy or they may have a high proportion of clay.

Peaty soils are good to work, moisture retentive in summer but inclined to be too acidic for certain plants.

Soil enrichment

Whatever your soil, the chances are that it needs improving. Sandy, stony or clay soil will be much easier to cultivate, and more conducive to plant growth, if some organic nourishment is added, not just at the start of cultivation but regularly over the years. Manure and compost (well-rotted) are best, but leafmould and composted bark will do wonders too if they can be supplemented with a sprinkling of general fertilizer (they lack the nutrients contained in compost and manure which will fuel both beneficial soil bacteria and plants). A bucketful to the square metre (yard) will do for all.

Dig in bulky enrichment like this during autumn and winter. Clay soils can be broken down and 'opened up' if plenty of grit and sharp sand is dug in. This stuff has a longer-lasting effect than organic matter, but will not have the same effect on soil fertility as good old muck—use both if you can.

Stones you will have to live with. Don't try to dig them all out—you'll be at it for ever. Instead, work in plenty of enrichment and let the plants' roots find their way around obstructions.

Sharp sand and grit can be added to peaty soils and liming may also be necessary (see below).

Compost There's real mystery attached to compost making, which is a shame because it puts a lot of people off. Don't be intimidated. Make yourself a couple of post and wire-netting enclosures 1·2 m (4 ft) square (or buy a proprietary bin if you haven't the space for these) and start from there (Fig. 1). Line the first netting bin with newspaper (to prevent the sides of the heap from drying) and start off your heap. Tip into it anything organic (except waste food such as bread, meat and the like, which can tempt the odd rat or two). Grass clippings, vegetable tops, potato

a

b

Fig. 1 (*a*) Make compost in a 1·2 m (4 ft) square post and wire netting bin. Use all kinds of vegetable waste but make sure all the materials are well mixed together.

(*b*) Scatter sulphate of ammonia or compost activator over each 23 cm (9 in) layer and water the heap in dry weather. Throw a piece of old carpet over the top.

peelings, annual weeds, dead flowers, crushed egg-shells, tea leaves and even a few torn up newspapers can be put into the bin, but make sure they are mixed together well. Trample the heap every time you add more. Concentrations of any one substance can slow down rotting. Over every 23 cm (9 in) layer sprinkle a little compost activator or sulphate of ammonia, and keep the top of the heap covered with a bit of carpet or sacking. Pour on a canful or two of water if the surface looks dry. Unfirmed and dry compost heaps don't rot. When the first bin is full, start to fill the second one. Some compost buffs claim to have their stuff ready to use in a matter of weeks; I'd give it three to six months if I were you. Then it will be fairly brown, fairly crumbly and just the thing for any plant in any soil.

Autumn leaves are a pain, but you can make them work for you too. Avoid the evergreen types, but put all others in black polythene dustbin liners which have been perforated at intervals to allow a little air circulation. Tread the leaves firm as the bag fills up (to expel air pockets), then seal the top. The leaves should be moist or rotting will not take place, and remember, it's fungi that break down dead leaves rather than bacteria, so the sulphated ammonia won't help much.

Stack the bags in an out-of-the-way corner and crumbly leafmould, ideal for a mulch, should be yours within about three months. Oak, beech and other small leaves are best; horse chestnut, plane and other toughies can be slower to rot down.

Don't start to worry about this complicated chemical state of affairs. Certainly it will affect the type of plants you can grow, but there is an easy way to discover the lime content—or pH value—of your soil if you feel that you want to know it. There are now plenty of soil testing kits which allow a small sample of soil to be put in a test tube, treated with a special solution and checked against a colour chart which will tell you its pH value. Lots of gardeners get by without ever knowing the pH of their soil, but it's fun to find out and it can save you a lot of time.

The desirable pH for most plants is a reading of between 6·0 and 6·5 on the pH scale. This is a slightly acid soil. Readings between 4·0 and 6·0 are very acid; and those between 6·5 and 8·0 are very alkaline (and probably very chalky). What does all this mean to you? Well, if your soil is very acid, rhododendrons, heathers and many woodland plants will be blissfully happy, and almost all plants will grow well in a soil that is slightly acid. In alkaline or chalky soil these real lime haters will not thrive, but many, many plants will. Choose those which can cope with your conditions, rather than trying to change the status quo. I've indicated right through the book which plants are suitable for which conditions.

Making a chalky soil more acidic is not really practical in the long term, but acid ground can be ameliorated by the addition of ground limestone or chalk. Only on the vegetable plot is such adjustment made on a regular basis, when lime is applied in autumn several weeks after manuring (if you do the two jobs at the same time undesirable chemical reactions can take place). Brassicas (members of the cabbage family) in particular are best on a soil that is not too acid, and liming also discourages clubroot, that deadly disease which distorts the roots.

The kit you use to test your soil will indicate how much lime is necessary to bring an acid soil into a more hospitable state. If you can't be bothered with all this palaver, stick your nose over the fence and see what grows well in your neighbour's garden.

Fertilizers

Cast your eye along the fertilizer shelf in a garden centre or hardware shop and you'll be surprised just how many different concoctions there are. Most of them you can happily do without, but a few of them at your elbow will make sure that you always have a tonic ready for your plants. These are the fertilizers that are most useful.

Sulphate of ammonia is high in nitrogen which boosts plant growth. Leafy crops will enjoy a light dusting over the surrounding soil in spring and summer. Apply it very sparingly at the rate of half a clenched handful to the square metre (yard) and use it only between March and August when plants are actively growing. It's useful to keep bacteria fuelled within the compost heap.

Blood, bone and fishmeal is a general fertilizer that supplies the three most important plant foods—nitrogen for leaf and shoot growth; phosphates for root development, and potassium for flower and fruit production. Use it at the rate of one or two handfuls to the square metre (yard) during the growing season and one week before sowing or planting. It is an organic fertilizer which encourages bacterial activity within the soil. Inorganic fertilizers supply more concentrated nutrition which the plant can utilize more rapidly, but they make beneficial soil bacteria (which would otherwise break down the stuff) redundant. Use inorganic fertilizers (such as sulphate of ammonia) to give crops a rapid boost, and organic fertilizers to improve fertility.

Growmore is a granular general fertilizer that's inorganic. It is readily available and reasonably priced but I find that blood, bone and fishmeal is more effective and a better tonic for the soil.

Bonemeal is high in phosphates, but to be fair, most of them are held on to so tightly by the soil that few are made available to plants. Bonemeal is always recommended as a suitable fertilizer to dust around the hole when you're planting trees and shrubs, but in reality the plants probably see little benefit. Use it if it makes you feel better—I don't bother any more!

Rose fertilizer is just the job for getting plants to flower and fruit well, thanks to its high potash and magnesium content. Use it on plants that are well established and coming into flower or fruit—toma-

toes, dahlias and other greedy types. Half a clenched handful to the square metre (yard) is ample.

Tomato fertilizer in liquid form is high in potash and can be diluted and used on *all* flowers and fruits. It's invaluable and quick-acting.

Foliar feeds are useful where growing crops need a quick boost. They are diluted in water and sprayed on to the foliage, preferably on a dull day. The leaves rapidly absorb the nutrients which perk up the plant. The effect is not so long-lasting as when fertilizers are applied to the soil.

Many gardeners are mean to their plants. Don't be. They need regular feeding just as we do. Give anything a dusting of general fertilizer every spring, and again in summer if you can.

WATERING

There are more old wives' tales about watering than anything else. Forget them all and remember a few simple rules:

1 Water any newly planted tree, shrub or border plant thoroughly during its first season whenever the soil looks dry on the surface.

2 Water established ornamental plants thoroughly when they show signs of wilting.

3 Don't wait for vegetable or fruit crops to wilt before you water.

4 Don't use a watering can or an open-ended hosepipe to water garden plants. Invest in a sprinkler which can be attached to the end of the hosepipe and leave it running over one patch of earth for at least two hours. That way the plants will be thoroughly soaked. Damping down the soil surface does more harm than good.

A well-nourished soil that's been mulched is less likely to dry out than poor, unmulched earth and as a result it will grow better plants. If you can possibly afford to mulch your beds and borders then do so. The job might cost you a few pounds but it will save you both labour and plants.

PLANT NAMES

I've no space to go into detail on plant names, but as I've used those terrifying Latin ones throughout I suppose I'd better make my excuses. They're a real mouthful but, unlike common names, they are standard wherever you might be. Even in China or Russia you could ask for *Alcea rosea* and get it; but they'd look puzzled if you asked for a hollyhock. The problem is almost as bad in Britain—common names vary from county to county and some plants have no common name at all—so I've classified the plants under their botanical names and given their common ones alongside, and in the index.

2 The toolshed

You might think that the best place to find a good set of garden tools is the garden centre or the local hardware shop, and sure enough that's where you'll come face to face with a showcase that rivals Blackpool illuminations for brilliance. But how do you tell which tools are the best buy, and how do you know which are just expensive gimmicks that will end up gathering dust after their first disastrous try-out?

I reckon you'd do far better delaying a visit to the shop and going first to the garage or toolshed of an aged member of the family whose gardening days are numbered. There you might find a set of basic tools that have not only stood the test of time but which have been 'run in' for you. Bright new spades and forks are all very well but they don't half take some breaking in. Until the blades and prongs have been honed to perfection by the soil they are often difficult and exhausting to work with.

Should your aged relative decide that the tools cannot be parted with, then cast your eye round local auction sales or second-hand shops for spades, forks, rakes and hoes that are well worn. Just make sure that in spite of their age the implements are still strong and that the handles have not cracked or become loose in their sockets. Years of use should have polished the shafts to a silken smoothness, but any splinters can easily be rubbed off with sandpaper. When all attempts at finding second-hand tools fail, then you can visit the local emporium, but beware of being bamboozled into buying something you don't need.

Here's my list of basic essentials that most gardeners can't do without. Buy them one at a time as you need them.

SPADE

However lazy you are you'll have to dig sooner or later, even if you're only digging a hole for a tree or shrub. Here the spade is essential, but if your soil is really stony a fork is much easier to use for general digging over. The spade has the advantage of being able to skim off surface weed growth before digging starts, and you can also use it for mixing composts and for edging the lawn (if, like me, you're too mean to buy one of those special 'half moon' edging tools).

You'll find that there are three sizes of spade: the standard digging spade has a blade measuring 29 by 19 cm (11½ by 7½ in); the ladies' spade 25 by 16·5 cm (10 by 6½ in); and the border spade 23 by 14 cm (9 by 5½ in). Forget the 'he-man' image you're trying to project and pick the spade that's most comfortable to use. Even if you're in a shop, hold it as if you were about to dig, and go through the motions to see if it's well balanced and feels comfortable. The shaft should be smooth and splinter free, the socket should be gently cranked to make for better leverage and any rivets should have smooth heads that do not chafe your hands. The handle at the top may be 'T', 'D', or 'YD' shaped (Fig. 2). Choose whichever feels the most comfortable, and be warned that the 'T' shape can be more blister-making if you have tender skin. If your soil is very heavy, look for a spade with flattened treads on the upper edges of the blade—they'll be

Fig. 2 A spade (here with a 'D'-shaped handle); a digging fork ('YD' handle), and a border fork ('T' handle) for folk who like to take their digging at a steady pace.

15

more easy going on your feet. You'd also be well advised to go for a medium-sized spade on very heavy soil, just to guard against strained muscles.

Most spade shafts are wooden, but some are made from tubular steel or alloy coated with polypropylene. The latter are likely to be more expensive. Nearly all spades and forks now have plastic handles at the top, and in spite of their appearance they are usually comfortable and long lasting. Which spade you choose will depend on the size of your pocket as well as the size of your physique. The most expensive tools are always made from stainless steel, but they're not essential (and they can be rather heavy to work with). A well-made, well-balanced spade that doesn't feel 'numb' or clumsy will probably outlast you, so use your common sense when buying and come away with a well-made yet reasonably priced implement.

How to dig

A lot of folk are appalled at the thought of digging, but tackled a little at a time it's a grand way of getting a bit of exercise. Once you're into the rhythm of the job you'll really enjoy seeing the fresh soil appearing in your wake. But until you've passed the pain barrier it's a real slog, so take it slowly and dig for just half an hour a day until you're ready for more.

But before you start, consider why digging is necessary. First of all it relieves compaction of the soil, so allowing plant roots to penetrate the soil more easily. It allows in air which is as vital to plants as water, even around the roots. It improves surface drainage, allows weeds to be removed and organic enrichment such as muck and compost to be worked in. And dug soil looks good too!

There are those who advocate the 'no-dig' technique, in which the ground is never cultivated. Instead a layer of muck or compost is spread over the surface of the soil where it keeps down weeds, keeps in moisture and is incorporated by the worms. This is a fine system to adopt after an initial digging over if you have unlimited supplies of organic matter. Once any border or bed has been planted up it works a treat. On previously uncultivated ground and on the vegetable plot I'm not convinced of its usefulness, except in avoiding work. For me, digging is essential, but I'm all for short cuts where possible.

There are two main methods of digging: single digging and double digging. Cynics assume that double digging is so called because it's twice as tiring as single digging. That's absolutely true. But the term was originally used to indicate that in double digging the soil is cultivated to a depth of two 'spits' or spade blades, while in single digging it's worked to a depth of just one spit.

Now there is really no need to double dig ground unless it's packed hard 30 m (1 ft) down and hasn't been cultivated for donkey's years. Even then I'd get out of double digging it if I possibly could. Only

Fig. 3 Double digging (*a*) Dig a trench one spit deep and 60 cm (2 ft) wide at one end of the plot and barrow the soil to the opposite end.

when trees and shrubs are to be established on really hard soil is double digging worthwhile (unless you aim to be a prize parsnip grower, in which case you can double dig your vegetable plot—but not every year, please!).

If you're pining for exercise or feel that you genuinely have to double dig, this is how to proceed:

Double digging (Fig. 3)

1 Excavate a trench one spit deep and 60 cm (2 ft) wide at one end of the plot to be dug. Barrow the soil

Fig. 4 Single digging (*a*) Dig a trench one spit deep and 45 cm (18 in) wide at one end of the plot and barrow the soil to the opposite end.

(*b*) Fork over the base of the trench to the full depth of the tines, working in manure.

(*c*) Dig up, invert, and throw forwards the soil immediately in front of the trench to create another one. Fill the last trench with soil removed from the first.

to the other end of the plot.

2 Fork over the base of the trench to the full depth of the tines of the fork—that way the soil is cultivated in two spits. Work in some compost or manure to perk up the earth.

3 Dig up, spadeful by spadeful, the soil immediately in front of the trench and throw it forwards into the trench, turning it upside down as you do so. This will bury any short-lived weeds such as groundsel and chickweed, but thick-rooted weeds should be pulled out or they will re-emerge later. When the

original trench has been filled, another of the same size will have been created and can again be forked over and enriched.

4 This system proceeds until the end of the plot is reached and the soil removed from the first trench is used to fill the last.

If the plot is quite wide it can be divided in two down the centre and the first trench taken out at the end of one half only. Dump the soil at the same end of the other half of the plot and then dig down one side

(*b*) Throw plenty of well-rotted compost, manure or other organic material into the base of the trench. The more you can put in the better.

(*c*) Dig up, invert and throw forward the soil immediately in front of the trench, pulling out any perennial weed roots. Repeat until the last trench is filled.

and back up the other, using the soil to fill the last trench. This will save you barrowing the soil at all—you can simply throw it to the end of the adjacent strip. The line drawings should make the operation crystal clear, if no easier on your back muscles.

Single digging (Fig. 4)

1 Excavate a trench one spit deep and 45 cm (18 in) wide at one end of the plot to be dug. Barrow the soil to the other end of the plot (or leave it at the same end if you are dividing the plot in two).

2 Scatter manure or compost in the bottom of the trench.

3 Dig up the soil immediately in front of the trench and throw it forward, inverting it and removing thick-rooted weeds. When the second trench has been created, repeat the operation until the entire plot has been dug.

4 Replace the soil in the final trench.

Cheat's digging (Fig. 5)

I use this system all the time.

1 Instead of taking out a trench, simply start to dig across one end of the strip to be cultivated—lift up each spadeful of soil, invert it and throw it forward a little so that a slight 'V'-shaped trench is created. Remove any thick-rooted weeds.

2 Spread compost or manure along the sloping side of soil facing you.

3 Turn over another spadeful of soil across the strip and repeat the process.

4 At the end of the plot only a slight depression will be left and this can be filled in when the soil is trampled immediately before planting or sowing.

This method saves the onerous job of barrowing soil around and it allows manure to be spread easily in the upper soil where roots can get at it quickly.

Fig. 5 Cheat's digging (*a*) Start at one end of the plot, digging up a row of soil, inverting it and throwing it forward slightly. Remove any thick-rooted perennial weeds.

(*b*) Throw well-rotted compost or manure over the sloping bank of soil that now faces you; this will put the organic matter within easy reach of plant roots.

(*c*) Turn over another strip of soil immediately in front of the first, removing perennial weed roots and spreading well-rotted manure as before.

(*d*) Continue until the plot is dug. You will be left with a slight ridge at one end and a hollow at the other but both will even out with later cultivations.

There's another system of digging in which the soil is cultivated to a depth of three spits. I can't believe that anyone would ever want to do it, but for the benefit of masochists it's described in my book *Gardening Techniques* (Mitchell Beazley, 1981).

FORK

For digging stony or heavy soil the fork is a better bet than the spade, and for pricking over cultivated soil in beds and borders it's essential. Use it, too, for moving compost and manure and for spiking the surface of the lawn to let in air in spring and autumn. When soil has been rough-dug, use the back of the fork rather like a carpet beater to smash up the clods. This action will produce a fine-textured surface or 'tilth' without bringing stones to the surface—always a problem if you use a rake for the job.

As to construction, the same general rules apply as for the spade, but two sizes are generally available: the digging fork has a head 30 by 19 cm (12 by 7½ in) and the border fork measures 23 by 14 cm (9 by 5½ in). Both have prongs or tines that are square in cross section. The potato fork has flattened prongs, supposedly to prevent damage to your spuds when they're being lifted, but I still manage to spear a few of mine whichever fork I use. Again, pick a fork that feels comfortable and not too heavy in your hands.

RAKE

I reckon the rake is most over-used tool in the garden. True enough, it's vital for levelling soil before seed sowing, and it's helpful in clearing up leaves and debris, but it can produce unwanted results if it is used to break down the soil to a fine texture. It brings every available stone to the surface and causes the soil to cake in the first shower of rain. Use the back of the fork for breaking down the soil, and use the rake sparingly in long, sweeping motions to level the surface.

Your average rake has a handle about 1·5 m (5 ft) long and a 30 cm (1 ft) wide head equipped with 5 cm (2 in) teeth. Make sure the handle is smooth and splinter free if it is wooden, and that the head is securely attached. Rakes with plastic-coated alloy handles are easiest to use for they are light and less likely to dig up stones. They are also more expensive.

The wire-toothed 'springbok' rake is the best tool for clearing up leaves and lawn mowings and for ripping the 'thatch', or dead grass, from lawns. It's not too expensive to buy and if you've a lot of grass (or plenty of leaves in autumn) I'd invest in one. Don't fall for the bamboo-toothed kind which will hardly last for a season if you've powerful biceps.

HOE

You can get by with just one hoe—the Dutch hoe. This is the type that has a long handle and a head shaped like a horse-shoe with a band of metal across the open end (Fig. 6). There's nothing nicer than standing behind a sharp Dutch hoe as it smoothly chops through weeds in the flower border or between vegetable rows. Used properly (and kept sharp with a file) it makes light work of weed control—the secret is to use it regularly every week or so and to let it skim over the surface of the soil, rather than holding it at an angle so that it digs deeply. That way it's not half so effective at separating the weeds from their roots and they'll probably perk up after the next shower of rain. When you use the Dutch hoe you'll be working backwards so that the soil is left untrampled, but with the draw hoe (the flat-bladed hoe whose blade is held

Fig. 6. The draw hoe (*above*) and the Dutch hoe (*below*) can both be used to excavate seed drills on the vegetable plot, but the Dutch hoe is the better weeder.

at right angles to the shaft) you'll have to walk over the ground you've just scraped over. Both hoes can be used for drawing drills for seeds (those little channels that are taken out against a taut garden line). As with other long-handled tools, a smooth shaft and a secure head are the things to look for, plus a feeling of balance in the implement as a whole. If you're a keen potato and celery grower you'll find the draw hoe useful when it comes to earthing up.

Although it's not strictly a hoe, I'll include the hand cultivator here because it's useful for perking up the soil between all manner of plants. Its head is claw-shaped, usually with three spikes, and it is pulled through the soil with jerky motions to break up the surface crust. Choose a small, lightweight version and you'll find it really comfortable to use.

TROWEL

There are some very poor trowels on the market that bend as soon as you show them a tough bit of ground. They'll drive you mad if you have to live with them. Play safe—lash out and buy a stainless steel trowel—it's the only stainless steel tool I possess but I wouldn't be without it (Fig. 7a). Make sure the handle is smooth and that it fits your hand well and you'll not have to worry a jot about the blade—it will stay clean and sturdy whatever your soil. Short-handled trowels are much easier to use than the long-handled versions which tend to wobble around. You'll need a trowel for planting everything from bedding plants to young vegetables, and it's a useful weeder in confined spaces.

SECATEURS

A good pair of pruning shears will help you with all cutting operations from flower gathering and 'dead heading' to snipping out dead stems up to finger thickness. Don't try to cut fatter stems than this or you'll sprain the secateurs and render them useless. There are several different designs, but the two basic kinds are those with a scissor action and those with what is described as an anvil mechanism (Fig. 7b). The first type cut with a slicing motion and the second with a sharp blade that comes down against a flat metal surface. Both are reliable, but the anvil type in particular must be kept razor sharp if stems are not to be crushed and disease admitted. I've used a pair of Rolcut anvil secateurs for years and have found them very durable—sharpening is simple either with emery paper or a whetstone. Some secateurs must be returned to the manufacturer for sharpening, and those that look very glossy and chrome plated are best avoided—they can't keep an edge for half an hour.

By far the best secateurs (if you can afford them) are the type manufactured by Felco. They are superbly made and serviced free for life—not a bad recommendation! Avoid at all costs those very cheap secateurs that look as if they are made of cast iron. They cut very badly, if at all, and are extremely uncomfortable to hold—trapping your fingers more times than not.

Stems thicker than your finger are best cut with loppers—those long-handled pruners that have tougher blades than secateurs and which can produce more torque. If you've a garden full of shrubs and roses a pair of loppers is a must.

Fig. 7 Invest in a short-handled stainless steel trowel. Rolcut 'anvil' type secateurs are very durable; so is a good budding knife. Shears should be lightweight and comfortable.

With all pruning shears remember always to cut back to a point immediately above a bud or a leaf to prevent die-back. Leave a finger of budless stem and it will rot back, probably allowing fungus diseases to enter.

KNIFE

When I first went to work I was told by the foreman that my pocket should always contain a sharp knife, a piece of string and sixpence. The knife was used for taking cuttings, the string to hold my trousers up when all else failed, and the sixpence was for the foreman himself! The knife I always had but the other two were often missing.

Buy a good knife and it will last for ages—I still use the one I was given on my first day at work, and even then it wasn't new—the propagator decided he'd purloin the one sent for me and I could have his old one. I found I'd got the better of the deal for his was nicely sharpened and well run in. The types sold as budding or grafting knives are good for general purpose work and not too heavy. Do make sure you buy a knife that's specifically made for garden use (Fig. 7c), but not one of those with a blade you can see your face in—it will be the very devil to keep sharp. A good tempered steel blade is what you should look for in a gardening knife—not a stainless steel blade that's more at home on the dinner table. Always keep your knife sharp on a whetstone and keep it in your pocket (with or without the string and two-and-a-half new pence).

SHEARS

A pair of general-purpose garden shears is always handy, whether it's for hedge clipping or for slicing off those tufts of grass that refuse to give in to the lawn mower. Wooden, polypropylene or tubular steel handles can all be comfortable, but check that your wrists are not jarred by the snipping action—rubber buffers between the blades are a help here. Go for carbon steel blades and find a pair of shears that possesses a notch at the base of each blade to allow individual thicker stems to be cut (Fig. 7d).

I try to avoid creating bare edges to lawns in the interests of saving labour, but if your garden is full of them you'll find that edging-shears save a lot of time. They have long handles fitted with blades that are set at right angles, and they save you bending down to snip off overhanging grass. When you're buying a pair, the same considerations apply as for ordinary shears. When you're using them, try to get into the way of holding the left hand still and moving just the right hand (which controls the upper blade). That way you'll achieve a more even cut faster and with less exertion (not that this is the most exhausting job in the garden!).

Rub the blades of your shears with emery paper

after use—this will clear them of dried sap and keep them cutting cleanly. (See Chapter 5 for details of electric trimmers.)

ROD AND LINE

Not a quick dissertation on fishing, just a note on two pieces of equipment that can be made at home. Two metal spikes (or lengths of broomhandle) linked with 10 yards of stout nylon or hemp twine is just what you need to mark the position of drills being drawn on the vegetable plot, and for cutting straight edges on the lawn. Keep the line free of knots (which will throw the drill-drawing hoe off course) and wrap it up after use to prevent it from being tangled by children or animals. The line should always be kept as taut as possible when it's being used, and it should rest on the ground to prevent it from moving too much.

I do all my planting both in the flower garden and on the vegetable plot by eye, but if you don't know what 15 cm (6 in) or 30 cm (1 ft) looks like, make yourself a measuring rod from a piece of 5 by 2·5 cm (2 by 1 in) timber marked with shallow saw-cuts at the appropriate distances—a little notch every 15 cm (6 in) and a larger one every 30 cm (1 ft).

DIBBER

The dibber is perhaps the most traditional tool in the ancient gardener's armoury, but it's still valuable today. For transplanting or 'pricking out' seedlings into trays there's no finer dibber than a pencil. For transplanting cabbages and the like on the vegetable plot, an old spade or fork handle is what is needed (if you've not broken a spade handle in years, go out and buy a new handle to use as a dibber).

With both kinds of dibber, the method of using the tool (Fig. 8) is the same: wiggle it around in the soil to make a hole; lower the roots into place and push back the soil with the point of the dibber, firming it as you do so.

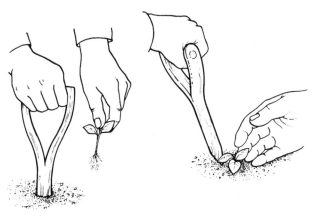

Fig. 8 An old spade handle makes a handy dibber. Push it in to make a hole; lower in the seedling and firm back the soil. Water well.

WHEELBARROW

Not always essential in a small garden, the wheelbarrow is nevertheless a must where soil, leaves, lawn mowings and rubbish have to be carted any distance. There are all sorts of barrows made of all sorts of materials, but the vital thing about any barrow is that it should be easy to push when full. Look for one that has its wheel tucked well under the body so that the weight is carried by the wheel and not by you. Ball-shaped wheels will travel over soft ground more easily than narrower types, but plastic bodies and wheels will not be so durable as those of steel, even though they have the advantage of being lightweight.

Buy a barrow that's large enough for your needs but small enough to go through your gate, and always store it under cover or tipped up so that water does not collect in the body.

WATERING EQUIPMENT

After years of using galvanized watering cans, most gardeners have switched to plastic. True enough, the plastic cans cannot be repaired easily, but they are much cheaper and lighter in weight than their metal counterparts and more economical even if thrown away as soon as leaks develop. Long-spouted cans are always easiest to use, and a 9·1 litre (2 gal) capacity can is best for general watering, though I'd plump for a 4·55 litre (1 gal) can in the greenhouse for its ease of manoeuvrability. The sprinkler heads on the end of the spout are known as 'roses' and brass ones are by far the best.

Use the can for watering anything, and fix the rose to the spout when watering in newly planted seedlings or plants. Use a second can for applying weed-killers and label it as such. Don't be tempted to use such a can for watering garden plants—herbicide residues hang about in them and can decimate cultivated crops.

When you tire of using a can it's time you invested in a hosepipe. Only you will know how long a hose you need, but let me persuade you to buy one that's reinforced with nylon thread—it will last far longer than a plain plastic one even though it costs more at the outset. It will also be less likely to kink. Always coil up the hose when you've finished with it and store it out of full sun. If it's left tangled it will drive you batty every time you come to use it, and where kinks are formed the hose may eventually rupture.

In the interests of spending more time in your deckchair and less time holding on to a hosepipe or watering can, invest in a garden sprinkler which will do the watering while you stare at it. There are two types—the rotating sprinkler (which soaks a circle of ground) and the oscillating type (which moves back and forth to soak a square or rectangle)—Fig. 9. As most gardens are square or rectangular, rather than circular, the oscillating sprinkler is more useful (its back and forth motion is also quite soporific if you're

Fig. 9 The oscillating sprinkler (*above*) can be adjusted to cover a variable square or rectangular area. The rotary sprinkler (*below*) always waters a circular patch.

trying to doze). Added to this the oscillating type can usually be adjusted to cover only half the rectangle or square.

Both types of sprinkler apply water more effectively than any hosepipe because they create a fine rain that penetrates the soil very efficiently—getting the moisture to the plant's roots rather than caking the surface of the earth.

Some gardeners are frightened of watering plants in the garden, believing the old wives' tale that if you do the roots come up to the surface. This is rubbish. They will only come to the surface if you constantly keep the surface moist and allow the lower part of the soil to dry out. Give the ground a thorough soak with a sprinkler for two hours when necessary and you'll do the plants nothing but good. Plants hate drought—it stops them from growing, reduces their flowering and fruiting capabilities and may even kill them. So if it hasn't rained for a week or more in summer, and your soil is dry 5 cm (2 in) down when you scoop out a hole with a trowel, turn on the sprinkler. Your plants will show their appreciation while those of your superstitious friends peg out.

On a practical note, remember that you'll need to apply to the water board for a permit to use a hosepipe (which will cost a few pounds extra on your water rates) and you may also require permission to use a

sprinkler. Check first to avoid costly embarrassment later.

SPRAYER

Whether it's for perking up your house plants with a drop of fresh water, or for boosting them with a foliar feed, a small trigger-action hand sprayer is a useful bit of equipment. A 0.5 litre or 1 litre capacity sprayer (roughly 1 pint or 2 pints) is sufficient for most gardens (and many insecticides are being made to dilute in such small quantities of water nowadays) but a larger pump-up 4.55 litre (1 gal) version may be more suited to your needs if you have rolling acres of roses or vegetables. Whichever size you use, wash it out thoroughly after use to rid it of damaging residues. Don't keep made-up spray in the vessel for more than a couple of days—it may 'go off'.

POWERED CULTIVATOR

The rotavator is thought of by many gardeners as the only way of cultivating soil. Certainly it's quick and (even though it may pull your arms out of their sockets occasionally) it's easy to use. But it won't rid your ground of weeds, and it doesn't work in organic matter very efficiently, so don't think that it replaces the spade completely.

Used too regularly at the same depth it will cause a 'pan' or hard, impenetrable layer in the subsoil, so it is best used considerately, where its advantages outweigh its disadvantages.

Use it for turning over the vegetable plot in winter, or for cultivating ground that has been treated with a herbicide to kill off weeds. It's seldom worth buying a rotavator unless you plan to use it at least once a week—hire it instead and let somebody else worry about the maintenance and storage. If you prepare all the patches of land you want cultivated in advance, you'll be able to romp away with the machine on the day it arrives.

All rotavated land becomes well aerated but rather 'fluffy', so trample it well before you sow or plant to rid it of large air pockets.

CARE OF TOOLS

The longest-lasting tools are those which are cared for. Try to get into the habit of scraping off mud and rubbing all metal parts with an oily rag after use. I know it's a real fag but it does make the implements easier to use next time you take them out. The cutting edges of spades and hoes benefit from an occasional honing up with a file so that they cut through soil and weeds quickly, saving your energy.

Store your tools in a dry place—a shed or garage—where rust will not be a problem. Good tools are not cheap, but taken care of they'll last a lifetime.

3 Trees

Why is it that many folk with small gardens are terrified of trees? I'll tell you why; it's because they've previously been in gardens where badly chosen trees have dominated the scene—casting shade over most of the plot, moving foundations with their roots, dripping water and leaves everywhere in autumn and threatening to fall on to the house in the first gale of winter. But if only the right tree had been planted in the first place the story would be different, and the little job of leaf sweeping in autumn would be a modest price to pay for colour and form during the rest of the year.

So if you're faced with a treeless plot, let me cajole you into planting a tree that will not foster your neurosis. You own the air space right up to the sky and there really is no need to worry when the tree rises beyond head height. Provided it's one of the kinds I've recommended it will not endanger life and limb when planted in the right place.

There's much confusion between trees and shrubs, and some shrubs are often referred to as trees simply because they grow quite tall. But, strictly speaking, a tree is a plant which can reach a height of 15 to 20 ft on a single woody stem. If your favourite tree is missing from my selection, take a look at the shrub chapter to see if it belongs there instead.

HOW TO USE TREES
In a small garden there's only one way to use a tree and that is as a single eye-catching specimen around which the rest of the garden revolves. Such a tree takes a lot of choosing: it should be of interest for as much of the year as possible; its shape should be desirable; it should not outgrow its situation and it should be able to tolerate your garden conditions.

If you can fit in several trees, use them to carry the eye around the garden and lift your gaze from flatter plantings below, and try to have at least one tree under which you can sit.

In larger gardens, trees can be used as windbreaks and screens (on smaller plots their place will have to be taken by hedges, shrubs and fences), and as tall backgrounds to plantings of shrubs and border plants.

WHAT TO LOOK FOR
When it comes to choosing a particular tree for a particular spot, there are quite a few considerations to

bear in mind. Uppermost in your mind should be the ultimate height and spread of the tree. Work out how much space you have to spare and select a tree that will fit the bill with a few feet to spare—do this and you won't have to worry about pruning in the future.

Consider the shape and 'habit' of the tree and whether or not it will look right in your chosen spot. Do you want an upright, columnar tree; a weeping tree; a round-headed tree, or one with branches that spread horizontally?

If you're planting just one tree, tick off its attributes and make sure that it offers as many features as possible. The ideal tree will have attractive foliage, colourful flowers followed by bright fruits, and bark that is good to look at in winter. All right, so your choice may not have all these characteristics, but unless it is exceptional in any one area you should always plump for a tree that offers at least two seasons of interest.

Will the tree be happy in your soil and in the spot you've chosen for it? Check with the nurseryman and cast an eye round local gardens to get some idea of what grows well in your locality. If yours is an area of biting winds it's no good choosing a tree with tender foliage that will be ripped to shreds in the first strong breeze. If your soil is chalky, don't plant a lime hater. The table at the end of the chapter will help you to find the right tree for the right spot.

Finally, even though it's a good idea to be guided by what succeeds in your area, try to plant something a little out of the ordinary. Not necessarily a tree that is difficult to grow, but one that doesn't crop up on every street corner. If you've room for only one tree it seems a shame to plant a laburnum or a flowering cherry that can be seen in greater glory in a public park.

When you're choosing the tree at the nursery (and you should always be able to pick the particular plant you want) go for one that has a strong central shoot or 'leader'—this will ensure that the tree will make a shapely specimen when it starts to grow away—and go for a youngster.

Young trees always establish themselves far more easily than tall, old ones; they don't need staking and their roots receive little check during transplanting. Sometimes it's not possible to obtain a youngster and you'll have to settle for an older plant of greater stature (as I did with the one illustrated on p. 26). You might think you've got a better deal at the outset, but during its first year the mighty specimen will grow slowly and can often be overtaken by a youngster which may well develop a better shape and a better root system. What's more, youngsters are a darned sight cheaper than their older relations.

WHEN TO PLANT

Trees growing in containers can be planted at any time of year provided the soil is in a workable condition. Don't plant them when the ground is so wet that it sticks to your wellies, when it is frosted hard, or when it is dust dry in the heart of summer. Container-grown trees will be quite happy to wait until soil conditions are right.

Trees lifted from rows in the nursery are sold as 'bare-root' plants, because precious little soil is left clinging to their roots. The planting season for deciduous bare-root trees (those that lose their leaves in winter) is in the dormant season from November to March. Evergreens are usually sold with their roots and surrounding soil wrapped in a piece of hessian. They are described as being 'balled' and are best planted in April and May when they can grow away actively, rather than in winter when they will sit sulkily in wet soil and drying wind.

HOW TO PLANT

With the right tree selected for the right spot you can think about planting. But remember the general rules: the site should not be overshadowed; there should be plenty of room for growth; shelter should be provided from strong winds (in the early stages of growth), and the tree should be at least 4·5 m (15 ft) from any building. No tree should be planted on waterlogged soil, though *Salix*, *Metasequoia* and *Alnus* are all tolerant of poor drainage if you're stuck with a bog.

You can usually arrange a convenient delivery date with the nurseryman, who will ship the plants to you in good condition (if he's worth his salt). Any bare roots should have been wrapped in damp hessian or straw and polythene, and the branches should be tied together to prevent them from becoming damaged. Remove the ties and any straw from the branches, but leave the wrapping in place around the roots until you are ready to plant (if this can be accomplished within a day or two of their arrival). Stand the trees in an unheated garage or shed.

If the weather turns nasty and you can't plant for a few days, heel the trees in on a spare patch of ground. All this involves is digging out a hole, freeing the roots of any wrappings and packings and pushing them into the hole. Replace the soil and the roots will be kept moist until you are ready to plant. Don't position the trees upright—instead lay them on the ground, or at an angle of 45° so that they offer less wind resistance. I've left trees heeled in for far longer than I should (up to four months) and they've come to no harm.

Trees bought from garden centres, rather than nurseries, will usually have to be collected. As most of them will be container grown the heeling-in precautions are not necessary.

With a bit of luck, any tree is going to be with you for a long time, so it's important to prepare the soil well so that it establishes itself quickly.

With both bare-root and container-grown trees, dig a hole one spit (spade blade) deep and 30 cm (1 ft) wider all round than the roots or the rootball (the combination of roots and compost within the pot). Fork over the base of the hole and work in a bucketful of well-rotted manure, garden compost, or leafmould dusted with a general fertilizer such as blood, bone and fishmeal. Mix some of this organic enrichment with the soil removed from the hole to perk that up, too.

I like to bung the roots of all bare-root trees and shrubs in a bucket of water for an hour prior to planting so that they don't have a chance to dry out. Cover the roots with damp sacking when you carry the trees to the planting site.

If the tree needs staking, now is the time to knock the stake into the hole—do it later and the roots will be disturbed. At least 60 cm (2 ft) of stake should be buried below ground level for stability, and the top of the stake should finish below the lowest branch of the tree. Stakes for trees should be about 5 cm (2 in) in diameter but they need not be treated with preservative; if the preservative is fresh it may harm the roots, and after two or three years the tree will be able to support itself anyway—a stake which rots after a year or two is a positive advantage for it can be removed with little disturbance to the tree.

The current trend is for a short stake, emerging only about 30 cm (1 ft) out of the ground. The theory is that this anchors the bare roots or rootball, while allowing the top growth to flex in the wind and so encourage rapid establishment to new roots below. Where children are at large a long stake offers more protection

With the stake in position and the hole properly prepared, all that remains to be done now is to remove the protective covering from a bare-root tree and examine the roots. Trim off with sharp secateurs any thick roots that are more than 30 cm (1 ft) long, and any roots that are torn or damaged. Snip off any broken shoots from the branch framework, making all cuts just above a bud. Forget to prune the branches and you may have to find a step ladder once the tree is planted.

From this point on another pair of hands will be helpful.

Stand the tree in the hole and check that when it is planted the old soil mark on the stem will rest just below the new soil level. Add or subtract soil until

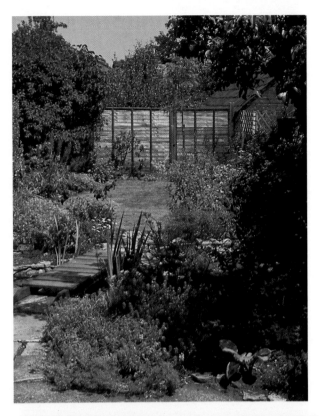

Left: Pocket-handkerchief plots can be transformed with amazing speed. When we inherited our first garden we also took on a tumbledown chickenhouse, half a ton of broken bricks and a network of ash paths – all in a patch just 4.5 m (15 ft) by 12 m (40 ft). Here it is after four months' work. The lawn has been sown and the borders carved out of the dusty earth. Nothing yet masks the dreary fence.

Below: Three-and-a-half years later it looked like this. *Robinia pseudoacacia* 'Frisia' makes a brilliant focal point at the end of the garden, and tucked among the undergrowth at the sides are a shed and a greenhouse. *Rosa* 'Complicata' is the pink-flowered beauty on the left, and a patchwork of foliage and flowers fills the two tiny borders. I like overcrowded gardens; I'd much rather spend time pruning out vigorous stems of cultivated plants than pulling up weeds. Here there's no room for them.

1. Tree planting Excavate a hole that's amply big enough for the roots, knock in the stake and fork well-rotted manure or garden compost into the hole.

2. Trim off any damaged roots and make sure that when the tree is lowered into the hole the roots are able to spread out unrestricted.

3. Replace the soil, mixing it with extra compost or manure as you do so. Shake the tree up and down and firm back the soil with your foot.

4. Replace the rest of the soil and check that when planting is complete the old soil mark on the stem is level with the surface of the soil.

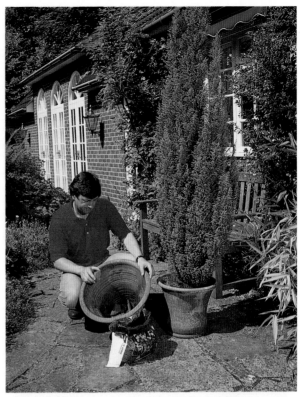

5. Staked and tied for stability, this is the same tree three months later. Water the roots in dry spells and slacken the tie as the trunk expands.

1. **Potting on patio plants** This container-grown conifer has outgrown its pot. Choose a larger container, and put crocks in the base to assist drainage.

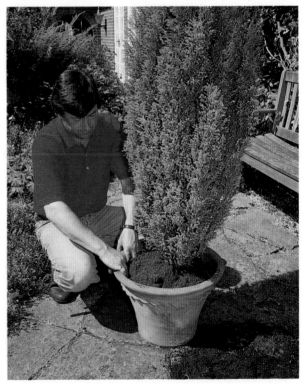

2. Knock the conifer out of its old pot and tease away some of the old compost to make more room for the new.

3. Add suitable compost to the pot and insert the conifer. Feed in compost around the rootball and firm in. The compost should finish below the rim of the pot.

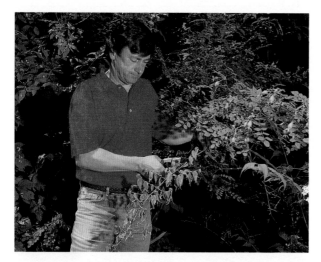

Stems that have died back should be snipped out – make the cut back into healthy wood.

Birch trees which need their canopies raised should have lower branches removed in late summer.

Long-arm pruners can reach where secateurs and loppers are too short in the handle.

Summer-prune cordon apple trees by shortening side shoots to three or four buds in summer.

Trees such as limes can be pleached to form an alley. Hard prune in winter, shorten long growths in summer.

When clipping a hedge, ensure a straight line by stretching a length of string between two canes.

you are happy with the result. Spread out the roots so that they are not all squashed together.

A container-grown plant should be watered well an hour before planting, and the pot tapped or cut off carefully at planting time. Any thick roots which are obviously growing inwards can be teased out very gently—if just a fibrous rootball exists, leave it intact. Now replace the soil gradually, adding compost or manure as you do so. The second pair of hands should be enlisted to hold the tree upright and to jar it up and down occasionally so that the soil particles are shaken down around the roots.

Firm the soil into place with your welly-booted foot—not daintily, but really hard so that no air pockets are left to cause root drying. When planting is completed, leave a slight depression in the soil around the tree trunk so that water can be applied if necessary in dry weather.

Now fasten the tree to the stake. I prefer proprietary tree ties (plastic affairs with buckles) because they can be slackened when necessary, but if funds are short you can use rope cushioned with cloth, or even old tights. Position one tie about 30 cm (1 ft)

Fig. 10 When a long stake *is* used to protect trees exposed to children and ball games, position one tie just below the top of the stake and the other 30 cm (1 ft) above soil level.

above ground level and another 2·5 cm (1 in) below the top of the stake (Fig. 10). Ideally the stake should be on the windward side of the tree (south-westerlies are the prevailing winds in Britain) but I honestly don't think that the life or death of your tree will depend on this.

Immediately after planting, and while the soil is nicely moist, spread an 8 cm (3 in) mulch of garden compost, manure or pulverized bark over the soil around the tree—a 90 cm (3 ft) diameter circle will be sufficient. Trees planted between April and October will almost always need to be watered in before this mulch is laid. Leave a hosepipe running on the soil at the foot of the tree for an hour, or give it at least three 9 litre (2 gal) cans of water.

AFTERCARE

Check the tree ties every month or so to see that they are not constricting the stem. Slacken them if they look too tight.

Do make sure that the tree doesn't run short of water, especially during its first spring and summer. If the roots are allowed to dry out you stand to lose a lot of money and a whole season's growth.

Trees that are bought as large specimens will often grow very slowly during their first few years. Some gardeners believe that they become 'bark bound'— the bark is so dry and hard that it refuses to allow the trunk to expand and grow. If you think that this is the case after a couple of years, try running a penknife down the length of the trunk so that the bark is split— the old hands swear that this gives the tree a chance.

PRUNING

I'm not a great tree pruner—if a tree needs pruning when it's more than a few years old then the chances are it's been planted in the wrong place. But in its formative years a young tree will need pruning to produce that bare stem and a good head of branches.

In the first two or three years of its life the tree is best left intact—the shoots that arise low down on the stem will encourage it to thicken and support the branches higher up. A tree with such a collection of lower branches is said to be 'feathered'.

If you want a tree that's furnished with leaves to ground level it's still best to remove the lowest branches so that those above can hang down a little. If this is the case the tree will look good and yet still have a strong trunk that may offer winter colour. As soon as your tree is about 2·5 or 3 m (roughly 8 or 10 ft) high, make sure that the lower 90 cm (3 ft) of stem is cleared of shoots – cut them off almost flush with the trunk. As the tree grows trim off more shoots until you have the length of bare stem you require. Trees bought as 'standards' or 'half standards' should have their trunks trimmed of any emerging shoots. 'Standard' trees are those with about 1·8 m (6 ft) of bare trunk; 'half standards' have about 1·2 m of trunk.

As with all rules there are exceptions. Trees with an upright, columnar habit will never trail their branches to cover the trunk and you may prefer to let them retain all their stems right down to ground level.

Any shoots which arise from below ground level are called suckers and they should be pulled or cut away from the roots at their point of origin. If you let them remain (or cut them off flush with the soil) they'll develop into a disfiguring thicket. Suckers are an especial problem with some ornamental plums and cherries. Here the upper flowering growth has been grafted on to a rootstock which has no ornamental value but which forms a healthy root system governing the vigour of the tree. If you leave suckers to develop on such trees, the upper portion may go into decline.

The only regular pruning needed on most ornamental trees will be to remove dead wood. This is easiest to see in summer and can be cut off at that time, as can suckers. The removal of badly placed or dangerous branches may occasionally be necessary and this is done in the dormant season—November to March—when the sap is not rising.

Tree surgery

This grand-sounding term is usually applied to any kind of tree pruning. On a small scale you can do it yourself, but when large trees are creating a real problem then a reputable firm of tree surgeons should be called in to advise. Don't agree to let any bunch of cowboys tackle your trees. The sort of 'firm' that knocks on your door asking if you want your trees pruned is not the type to employ. True enough, they may be cheaper than a skilled firm of tree surgeons (which can be found in your Yellow Pages) but they'll leave you heartbroken if you care about trees.

Anyway, on smaller trees where just the odd branch needs to be removed you can make a good job of it yourself. A second pair of hands is always helpful when you're mucking about with a tree—whether it's to hold the ladder steady or to pass the saw. Small branches can be cut off in one go, but anything with a bit of weight to it should be dismantled from the tip inwards (Fig. 11). Tie a rope to each section of branch that's being removed before you saw through the stem. Then the wood can be slowly lowered to the ground by your mate on the other end of the rope. That way no damage will be done to the lower branches by falling timber.

If you've a lot of trees you might be tempted by a chain saw, but I always use a bow saw for tree pruning—it is, by far, a much safer option than a chain saw. If you have to remove any branches larger than about 15 cm (6 in) in diameter, a professional tree surgeon is a safer option. Trees have a natural defence mechanism to prevent wound infection. It is situated at the branch collar (a slight swelling where the branch joins the trunk). The tree will heal itself, without the need for wound paints, if you don't cut into this collar. When you're left with a foot-long stump, make a clean cut at a slight angle away from the trunk. You can find the correct line for the cut by finding the ridge of bark on the trunk, which starts in the crotch where the branch joins the trunk. If you make the cut on the branch at

Fig. 11 (a) Cut off heavy branches in stages. Support the weight of the one to be removed by running a rope from it and over a higher, sturdy branch. (b) Saw through the branch at least 30 cm (1 ft) away from its junction with the trunk. That way you'll remove most of the weight before the final cut is made. (c) Undercut the stump, flush with the trunk, then cut through from above to meet it. Neaten the surface with a knife and seal it with wound paint.

an equal and opposite angle to that made by this ridge, you won't breach the collar that provides the tree's main defence against infection by fungi and other wood-rotting organisms. Undercut the stump first to prevent the bark tearing when the main cut is made.

PROPAGATION

The propagation methods used for increasing trees are exactly the same as for increasing shrubs. Details of the techniques involved are given in Chapter 20.

A–Z OF GARDEN TREES

This is a selection of what I consider to be some of the best garden trees. I've left out the real giants—the oaks, beeches and cedars—and concentrated on those trees that are at home in gardens of modest size. They are not all dwarfs (such trees tend to be lacking in grace) but few of them should present any major problems provided they are planted in the right place. Table 1 (p. 35) will help you to find the tree you want for a particular spot or for a particular effect.

The height and spread of each tree will depend entirely on the situation in which it is planted—the figures I have given are a rough idea of the ultimate sizes to help you discover if the tree will fit in your garden. Height is the first figure; spread the second.

Acer griseum   Paperbark Maple
6 × 4·5 m (20 × 15 ft)
A maple renowned for its glorious peeling bark of coppery bronze. The three-lobed leaves are orange-tinged on opening, later becoming green, and taking on fiery tints of scarlet in autumn.

Acer japonicum 'Vitifolium'   Downy Japanese Maple   4·5 × 4·5 m (15 × 15 ft)
This and its more shrub-like relation *A. japonicum* 'Aconitifolium' are two of the very best autumn-colouring plants in any garden. The leaves are deep-cut into seven or more lobes and are softly downy. They seem to catch fire in autumn, turning to shades of yellow, pink, orange and bright crimson.

Acer negundo 'Variegatum'   Box Elder
6 × 4·5 m (20 × 15 ft)
A maple whose foliage is striking in summer rather than autumn. The leaves are pinnate (like those of the rose) and edged with creamy white variegation. The whole effect is delicate and graceful. Occasional all-green shoots will arise and these should be cut out. There's a form called 'Flamingo' which has pink variegation. It's a real beauty, but bad weather can cause leaf browning. This form is probably best grown as a shrub, pruned hard each spring.

Acer pseudoplatanus 'Brilliantissimum'
6 × 4·5 m (20 × 15 ft)
A slow-growing beauty, this is a spectacular form of the sycamore whose leaves are shrimp-pink on opening, gradually turning yellow, then creamy white until they are eventually suffused with green. In spring and early summer it's a sparkling sight. Young specimens may burn a little in brilliant sunlight until their roots are well established.

Alnus glutinosa 'Aurea'   Golden Alder
4·5 × 3 m (15 × 10 ft)
The yellow-leaved form of the common alder is not so widely planted as it should be. It is modest-sized and keeps the yellow colouring of its leaves until late summer in a sunny, sheltered spot.

Arbutus unedo   Strawberry Tree   4·5 × 4·5 m (15 × 15 ft)
This superb evergreen is a slow grower but offers a number of attractive features. The bark is dark brown and peeling; white urn-shaped flowers are carried in clusters in autumn, and these are followed the next autumn by rough-skinned spherical fruits of bright red so that flowers and fruits are carried at the same time. The fruits are edible but tart—don't make a pie of them!

Betula ermanii   Erman's Birch
6 × 4·5 m (20 × 15 ft)
Anyone who plants the deformed Young's weeping birch is obviously unaware of the three beautiful species mentioned here. This one makes a broad cone of growth and has bark that is white when young, pink-flushed as it ages. The young stems are orange brown.

Betula papyrifera   Paper-bark Birch
10·5 × 4·5 m (35 × 15 ft)
A good 'peeler', this species has white bark marked with orange, pink or dark brown. Pure yellow autumn colour.

Betula pendula 'Laciniata' (syn. 'Dalecarlica')
Swedish Birch   10·5 × 4·5 m (35 × 15 ft)
Superb finely cut foliage carried on weeping stems and a good, white bark make this species an excellent choice where a bit of space is available.

Betula utilis var. **jacquemontii**   Kashmir Birch
6 × 4·5 m (20 × 15 ft)
The main branches and trunk are bright white or cream and the saw-edged leaves turn warm yellow before falling in autumn.

Cercis siliquastrum   Judas Tree   4·5 × 4·5 m (15 × 15 ft)
Slow growing and often seen as a shrub rather than a tree, cercis is a fascinating plant. Its leaves are rounded and smooth, but before they emerge the stems and even the old branches are smothered in rich pink pea flowers during May. These are followed in autumn by flattened pods of crimson purple. It often grows rather lop-sided but is still charming. Give it a sunny, sheltered spot and allow it a few years to settle in before expecting flowers—birds can eat the buds so

beware! Reputedly the tree on which Judas hanged himself.

Chamaecyparis lawsoniana   Lawson Cypress
9 × 3 m (30 × 10 ft)

Don't plant the boring ordinary species, but go for one of its varieties such as 'Columnaris', upright and blue grey; 'Ellwoodii', a rich green; 'Green Pillar', erect green 'fans' of growth; 'Lane' (syn. 'Lanei'), the best yellow form; 'Pembury Blue', rich blue grey. All these conifers are especially valuable for brightening the winter garden.

Crataegus oxyacantha 'Paul's Scarlet'   Paul's Scarlet Thorn   4·5 × 2·4 m (15 × 8 ft)

A welcome sight every spring, this hawthorn wreathes its branches in clusters of double pink blossoms. Plant it near shrubs that will please the eye later in the season when it's not much to look at.

Cunninghamia lanceolata   Chinese Fir
9 × 3 m (30 × 10 ft)

This is an unusual conifer that deserves greater popularity. It produces masses of narrow leaves, arranged rather like those of yew but with an exceptionally shiny texture that's almost metallic. They turn bronzy in autumn and persist to some extent when dead. If you've room to experiment give it a try.

Davidia involucrata   Dove Tree; Pocket Handkerchief Tree   7·5 × 4·5 m (25 × 15 ft)

You'll need patience if you want to grow this tree, for it can take 20 years to flower. But what a sight when it does! The shapely head of branches is furnished with bright green lime-shaped leaves and drips with white handkerchief-like bracts that surround the flowers. With luck it will bloom in its tenth year, but be prepared for disappointment. Flowering time is May.

Eucalyptus pauciflora ssp. niphophila   Snow Gum   6 × 4·5 m (20 × 15 ft)

This is the species I'd choose, though there are now many on offer. The bark is a marbled python's skin of grey and pale orange, and the leaves are long, grey-green and sickle shaped. The tree often leans appealingly and, like other eucalypts, it may be damaged in very severe winters, but regeneration from the base of the trunk is common. Growth is rapid with all species, and young specimens should be planted from pots—older ones are difficult to establish. If the snow gum fails with you due to severe winters, try *E. gunnii* which is tougher.

Ginkgo biloba   Maidenhair Tree
7·5 × 3 m (25 × 10 ft) larger with age

The maidenhair captivates all who set eyes on it. The fan-shaped leaves are rich green, turning to yellow before they fall in autumn, and the tree is of a convenient upright shape. It's the oldest tree in existence—dating back 200 million years.

Gleditsia triacanthos 'Sunburst'
Honey Locust   4·5 × 2·4 m (15 × 8 ft)

Pretty as a picture from spring to autumn on account of its finely cut foliage of bright yellow that turns to fizzing lime green as it ages. Along with *Robinia pseudoacacia* 'Frisia' it is one of the best yellow-leaved trees. Of the two it is the tougher and has smaller leaflets. The leaves turn butter yellow before they fall in autumn.

Ilex × altaclarensis 'Golden King'   Variegated Holly   4·5 × 2·4 m (15 × 8 ft)

This is, I think, about the best variegated holly—its leaves, though not exceptionally spiny, are margined and splashed with bright butter yellow. Remember that holly bushes are male or female and only the females carry berries. To add to the confusion 'Golden King' is a female and produces plenty of scarlet fruits in winter. It can be kept much smaller than its ultimate size by Christmas pruning. Other hollies are described in the shrubs section.

Laburnum × watereri 'Vossii'
Voss's Laburnum   4·5 × 3 m (15 × 10 ft)

In early June there is no finer sight than this tree, laden with its pendulous flowers of bright yellow. The green leaves that follow are a bit dull but at least this variety produces few of the poisonous seeds for which laburnums have become feared. Superb trained over archways and pergolas.

Larix decidua   European Larch
6 × 3 m (20 × 10 ft) and more

Where you've a bit of room to spare don't forget the larch. It's a pretty conifer that has soft, fresh green needles in spring and summer. In autumn they turn bright yellow before falling. Neat cones decorate the stems. Larch is a fast grower, but lovely when planted in groups—set the trees 3 m (10 ft) apart and plant them young.

Malus floribunda   Japanese Crab Apple
4·5 × 6 m (15 × 20 ft)

A wide-spreading tree that's magnificent in spring when its white flowers open from rich pink buds. For the rest of the year it's rather dull, so plant it where it can act as a backdrop for other plants when out of flower. In bloom it is absolutely smothered with blossom.

Malus 'John Downie'   Cherry Apple   4·5 × 3 m (15 × 10 ft)

A crab apple with reasonable white flowers and positively superb red and yellow fruits later in the season. They make delicious crab apple jelly if you can bear to rob the tree.

Metasequoia glyptostroboides
Dawn Redwood   9 × 2·4 m (30 × 8 ft) and more

A rotten latin name for a lovely deciduous conifer. The dawn redwood was thought to be extinct until rediscovered in China in 1941, and now it graces many gardens worldwide. It makes a column of feathery bright green leaves that turn rich coppery shades before falling in autumn. The trunk and stems have russet peeling bark. Few gardens should be without it. Plant young specimens for quick establishment.

Morus nigra   Black Mulberry
3 × 4·5 m (10 × 15 ft) and more with age
Rather 'in' at the moment, the black mulberry makes a rounded, spreading tree with serrated heart-shaped leaves and a gnarled trunk. The red to black fruits are produced on trees over 20 years old and are only fit to eat when really ripe—at which time they fall from the tree. Can be propagated from branches about 1·5 m (5 ft) long, which are relieved of some of their smaller shoots and pushed into the ground for one-third of their length.

Nyssa sylvatica   Tupelo   9 × 3 m (30 × 10 ft) and more with age
For sheltered gardens where there is space to spare, the tupelo is worth planting simply for its autumn colour. The oval leaves are glossy and turn scarlet, orange and crimson in autumn—you'll see no brighter tree at that time.

Ostrya carpinifolia   Hop Hornbeam   4·5 × 3 m (15 × 10 ft)
Here's an oddity. A shapely, upright-growing tree with green hornbeam-like leaves among which hang hop-like fruits in summer. Planted behind lower-growing shrubs it makes a fascinating backdrop. Not spectacular but intriguing nevertheless.

Parrotia persica   Persian Ironwood   4·5 × 6 m (15 × 20 ft)
Here's a tree with more than one attribute. For a start the bark is marbled with grey and peels like a plane tree. In winter, tiny red spidery flowers (like those of the witch hazel, *Hamamelis*, to which it is related) bedeck the branches, and the leaves that follow start to turn reddish in summer, colouring brilliant orange, yellow and scarlet by autumn. A good backdrop to shrubs and border plants.

Picea breweriana   Brewer's Weeping Spruce
6 × 2·4 m (20 × 8 ft) and more with age
A beautiful and statuesque conifer for the patient gardener. It makes a conical tree with graceful weeping branches but should be planted young and not expected to look at its best until almost 20 years old. If it's quick results you're after, ignore it, but if you want something to enjoy during your retirement and you've a bit of space to spare, give it a try.

Picea omorika   Serbian Spruce
9 × 3 m (30 × 10 ft) and more

Better for the impatient gardener, for it's faster growing than *P. breweriana*. The branches droop but are not so pendulous as those of the previous species. The overall colour is a greyish-green and the conical shape makes this one of the most handsome conifers of all.

Picea pungens 'Koster'   Koster's Blue Spruce
6 × 1·8 m (20 × 6 ft)
A conical conifer of blue grey that will add a lift to green plantings. Excellent with a carpet of heathers surrounding it to make a bright winter garden.

Populus × candicans 'Aurora'   Variegated Balm of Gilead Poplar   9 × 2·4 m (30 × 8 ft)
A real stunner where a variegated tree of stature is needed. It is the young foliage that's variegated—splashed with creamy white and tinged with pink—a great sight from a distance or close to. In small gardens it can be pruned hard each winter to encourage the production of plenty of variegated shoots the following spring.

Prunus serrula   Tibetan Cherry
4·5 × 3 m (15 × 10 ft)
Plenty of small white flowers are produced in spring, but the reason why this tree is so popular is that it has shining coppery bark that glows in the sun. Plant it where hands can caress and polish its stems and peel off the older bark. Left untouched the trunk and branches may become dull and moss-covered unless plenty of bright sunshine strikes them.

Prunus serrulata   Sato Cherry; Japanese Cherry
There are dozens of flowering cherries so I've picked just a few of the very best. They are undoubtedly only of value in spring when they bloom, but they flower with such generosity that they cannot be ignored.
'Amanogawa', 4·5 m × 60 cm (15 × 2 ft), upright with pale pink double flowers in April and May.
'Shimidsu', 4·5 × 6 m (15 × 20 ft), spreading, double white flowers in May.
'Shirofugen', 7·5 × 7·5 m (25 × 25 ft), spreading, pale pink to white double flowers in May.
'Tai Haku', Great White Cherry, 6 × 6 m (20 × 20 ft), double white flowers in April. My first choice.
'Ukon', 6 × 9 m (20 × 30 ft), spreading, greenish-white double blossoms in April and May.
In most varieties the foliage unfurls with or after the flowers and is tinged bronze. Most develop good autumn colour.

Prunus × subhirtella 'Autumnalis'
Winter Cherry   4·5 × 3 m (15 × 10 ft)
A fine back-of-the-border tree where during its dull summer season it can act as a backdrop. When the summer border flowers fade, the bare branches of the tree erupt with pink buds that burst into white flowers. There's something to look at from October to April in most years.

Pseudolarix amabilis Golden Larch 6 × 2·4 m (20 × 8 ft)
This lovely, large-leafed larch should be more widely planted. The deciduous leaves are fresh green in spring and summer, turning bright yellow before they fall in autumn. Give it a sheltered spot in full sun where its change of colour can be admired. Youngsters may be damaged by severe frosts.

Pyrus salicifolia 'Pendula'
Willow-leafed Pear 4·5 × 2·4 m (15 × 8 ft)
A good tree for a restricted space, but of muted rather than spectacular shades. The branches arch downwards and are clothed in narrow leaves of silvery grey, studded with small white flowers in spring. I find its habit rather depressing but feel obliged to include it because of its popularity. Cheer it up by planting coloured-leafed shrubs nearby!

Robinia pseudoacacia 'Frisia' False Acacia 6 × 3 m (20 × 10 ft)
A favourite of mine, this tree is a stunning spectacle from June to September when its ferny leaves of brilliant acid yellow stand out against summer skies of blue. Even when the sun's in they will brighten your garden. Compared with *Gleditsia triacanthos* 'Sunburst', this tree is more yellow and, I think, more graceful due to its tissue-thin leaves which flutter gently in every passing breeze, but it has brittle wood and can suffer in colder counties.

Salix × sepulcralis 'Chrysocoma' Golden Weeping Willow 9 × 9 m (30 × 30 ft) and more
This is *not* a tree for small gardens, in spite of the fact that it's often planted there. It is a fast-growing spreader that will rob you of light and shift your foundations if planted too close to your house. Only where there's a vast expanse of lawn (and preferably a lake, or at the very least moist soil) should it be planted. Then it can be allowed to make the magnificent specimen it deserves to be, with its living cascade of yellow stems, thickly decked with narrow green leaves in summer. Cuttings root so readily that they can even be taken when broomhandle sized and stuck into the ground to grow.

Salix babylonica var. **pekinesis** 'Tortuosa'
Dragon's Claw Willow 9 × 3 m (30 × 10 ft)
Better where space is restricted, this willow has an upright habit and stems that are twisted like corkscrews, which accounts for the other common name of Corkscrew Willow. In summer and winter its contorted stems are visible, and the leaves are a fresh green. Raved about by flower arrangers.

Sophora japonica Pagoda Tree
6 × 4·4 m (20 × 15 ft)
Rarely planted but often admired, the pagoda tree has pinnate leaves like the rowan tree and long clusters of creamy white flowers in late summer— when it reaches a reasonable age. It's a tree of grace that relishes a warm, sunny spot.

Sorbus aucuparia 'Beissneri' Rowan, Mountain Ash 6 × 3 m (20 × 10 ft)
This tree deserves a bright future in gardens for it offers orange-pink bark (especially stunning after rain or when a lawn sprinkler has played on it), reddish young stems and bright yellow autumn colour on its ferny foliage. Its habit of growth is attractive too—upright and broadly columnar—and it fits into the smallest gardens. A good choice where there's room for only one tree.

Sorbus 'Joseph Rock' 6 × 3 m (20 × 10 ft)
A stunning rowan of upright habit and with the usual ferny leaves. These take on fiery tints in autumn and are complemented by the generous crop of bright yellow fruits which persist when the leaves are shed. Birds hardly seem to touch them—a great advantage in gardens where fruits are gobbled as fast as they appear.

Stewartia pseudocamellia 4·5 × 2·4 m (15 × 8 ft)
A relative of the camellia, stuartia makes a handsome tree with flaking bark, mottled purplish brown and buff and orange. White, yellow-centred flowers stud the branches in summer, and the leaves (oddly glossy on the undersides and dull above) turn brilliant shades of crimson and yellow in autumn. Plenty of attributes for a modest-sized tree. Sadly it won't put up with chalky soil and it prefers a shady situation to one in full sun.

Taxus baccata Yew 6 × 6 m (20 × 20 ft)
An oppressive tree to plant where space is limited, the dull green yew is best grown as a backdrop in large shrubberies. But the variety 'Fastigiata Aurea' or 'Fastigiata Aureomarginata' is the yellow-variegated form of the Irish yew which makes an upright evergreen composed of towering minarets of growth. It cheers up any plot—especially in winter—and grows 3 m × 60 cm (10 × 2 ft).

Thuja plicata 'Zebrina' Western Red Cedar
9 × 2·4 m (30 × 8 ft) and more
As an alternative to the variegated forms of the Lawson cypress, try this conifer. It makes an upright column of evergreen foliage banded with bright yellow. It's a picture in winter.

Trachycarpus fortunei Chusan Palm
4·5 × 1·8 m (15 × 6 ft)
If you're feeling a little frivolous, try planting a palm tree! This one is surprisingly hardy in many parts of the country and makes a thick stem clad in 'coconut matting' and topped with a cluster of fan-shaped fronds. It will be some time before it reaches its maximum height.

Table 1

Choosing The Right Tree

	Height (m)	Spread (m)	Spring interest	Summer interest	Autumn interest	Winter interest	Flowers of note	Fruits of note	Foliage of note	Bark/stems of note	Autumn colour	Evergreen	Weeping	Upright	Spreading	Yellow-leaved	Grey-leaved	Variegated-leaved	For clay soil	For chalky soil	For dry soil	For cold sites	For seaside gardens
Acer griseum	6·0	4·5	●	●	●	●				●	●			●					●	●		●	
Acer japonicum 'Vitifolium'	4·5	4·5		●	●				●		●				●				●	●			
Acer negundo 'Variegatum'	6·0	4·5	●						●						●			●	●	●	●	●	●
Acer pseudoplatanus 'Brilliantissimum'	6·0	4·5	●	●					●						●			●	●	●	●		
Alnus glutinosa 'Aurea'	4·5	3·0	●	●					●					●		●			●	●			
Arbutus unedo	4·5	4·5	●	●	●	●	●	●		●		●		●					●	●			●
Betula ermanii	6·0	4·5	●	●	●	●				●				●					●	●			
Betula utilis var. jacquemontii	6·0	4·5	●	●	●	●				●	●			●					●	●			
Betula papyrifera	10·5	4·5	●	●	●	●				●	●			●					●	●		●	
Betula pendula 'Laciniata'	10·5	4·5	●	●	●	●				●			●						●	●		●	●
Cercis siliquastrum	4·5	4·5	●	●	●		●	●		●					●				●	●			
Chamaecyparis lawsoniana varieties	9·0	3·0	●	●	●	●						●		●		●	●	●	●	●		●	
Crataegus laevigata 'Paul's Scarlet'	4·5	2·4	●			●									●				●	●	●	●	
Cunninghamia lanceolata	9·0	3·0	●	●	●	●			●		●	●		●					●	●			
Davidia involucrata	7·5	4·5	●	●			●							●					●				
Eucalyptus pauciflora ssp. niphophila	6·0	4·5	●	●	●	●			●	●		●		●			●		●	●			●
Ginkgo biloba	7·5	3·0		●	●				●		●			●					●	●	●		
Gleditsia triacanthos 'Sunburst'	4·5	2·4		●	●				●					●		●			●	●	●		
Ilex × altaclarensis 'Golden King'	4·5	2·4	●	●	●	●		●				●		●				●	●	●	●	●	●
Laburnum × watereri 'Vossii'	4·5	3·0	●			●								●					●	●	●		
Larix decidua	6·0	3·0	●	●	●				●		●			●					●	●	●		
Malus floribunda	4·5	6·0	●			●									●				●	●			
Malus 'John Downie'	4·5	3·0		●	●	●	●	●						●					●	●			
Metasequoia glyptostroboides	9·0	2·4	●	●	●				●	●	●			●					●	●	●		
Morus nigra	3·0	4·5	●					●							●				●				
Nyssa sylvatica	9·0	3·0		●							●			●					●				
Ostrya carpinifolia	4·5	3·0	●					●						●					●				
Parrotia persica	4·5	6·0	●	●	●	●	●			●	●				●				●				
Picea breweriana	6·0	2·4	●	●	●	●			●			●	●						●	●		●	
Picea omorika	9·0	3·0	●	●	●	●			●					●					●	●		●	
Picea pungens 'Koster'	6·0	1·8	●	●	●	●			●			●		●			●		●	●		●	
Populus × candicans 'Aurora'	9·0	2·4		●					●					●				●	●	●	●	●	
Prunus serrula	4·5	3·0	●	●	●	●	●			●				●					●	●			
Prunus serrulata varieties	Various		●		●		●				●				●				●	●			
Prunus × subhirtella 'Autumnalis'	4·5	3·0	●			●	●							●					●	●			
Pseudolarix amabilis	6·0	2·4	●	●	●				●		●			●					●				
Pyrus salicifolia 'Pendula'	4·5	2·4	●	●		●			●				●				●		●	●			
Robinia pseudoacacia 'Frisia'	6·0	3·0		●	●				●		●			●		●			●	●	●		
Salix × sepulcralis 'Chrysocoma'	9·0	9·0	●	●	●		●		●				●						●	●		●	
Salix babylonica var. pekinensis 'Tortuosa'	9·0	3·0	●	●	●					●				●					●	●			
Sophora japonica	6·0	4·5		●			●								●				●	●			
Sorbus aucuparia 'Beissneri'	6·0	3·0	●	●	●	●				●				●					●	●		●	●
Sorbus 'Joseph Rock'	6·0	3·0		●	●	●		●						●					●	●		●	●
Stewartia pseudocamellia	4·5	2·4	●	●	●	●			●	●				●					●				
Taxus baccata 'Fastigiata Aurea'	3·0	0·6	●	●	●	●			●		●		●		●			●	●	●	●	●	
Thuja plicata 'Zebrina'	9·0	2·4	●	●	●				●		●			●				●	●	●	●	●	
Trachycarpus fortunei	4·5	1·8	●	●	●	●			●		●			●					●			●	●

4 Shrubs

Rightly described as the backbone of any garden, shrubs are indispensable. You don't have to pack your plot with gigantic bushes—there's a great diversity of shrub material from the positively dwarf to the gargantuan. The secret is to find the right shrub for your particular purpose. The lists on pp. 55–60 will enable you to do just that, but let me offer a few basic guidelines.

First, it's most important that you use your shrubs to give form to your garden. Consider the shape and style of any shrub, its ultimate height and overall effect. Evergreens are valuable because they lend form to the garden all the year round, but plant too many of them and you'll be bored by an unchanging vista. The secret is to mix them up with deciduous kinds that lose their leaves. Do this and you'll retain form without sacrificing the freshness that spring brings to the garden.

Remember that most flowering shrubs have a brief season of glory—a month is good going when it comes to length of time in bloom. Position these shrubs where they will make a bright pageant in their season of glory, but also where they can act as a plain backdrop to flowers that bloom later—make them work for a living. A shrub that offers more than one attractive feature—bark, stems, leaves, flowers or fruits—is often a better bet than one which puts all its floral eggs in one basket.

A word of warning about coloured foliage—don't overdo it. Green is the colour that should predominate in any garden. Go overboard on the purples and creamy yellows and you'll create a psychedelic nightmare. Choose just a handful of bright-leaved shrubs to show off against the plainer kinds and the effect will be more spectacular.

In really small gardens you can avoid trees and select large or medium-sized specimen shrubs to act as your eye-catchers and focal points. I've recommended suitable choices in the lists at the end of this chapter. Use all your shrubs with their contours in mind. Try to create an undulating landscape, positioning the shrubs so that your eye is taken gradually up or down, not quickly up and down every five seconds as if you were looking at a castellated battlement. This sounds like pretentious clap-trap, but it makes for a more restful scene if the lines are gradual; then, when you aim to create an eye-catching contrast of form—such as an upright yew among a carpet of lower-growing junipers—you'll achieve the effect you want.

The art of clipping shrubs into fanciful shapes—topiary—has rather gone out of fashion today, but it's a useful pursuit if you can't afford to buy statuary for the garden. The secret of making topiary look good is to choose the right plants, and to put them in the right place. You'll have to be patient to succeed, but with things like box, yew, *Lonicera nitida* and even the humble privet, you can make assorted ornaments that will cheer up assorted corners of your garden. Even a simple pyramid of foliage is stunning in a well-chosen spot.

To give shelter and privacy, shrubs are vital. They are also good helpmates in keeping down weeds. I've listed suitable ground-cover shrubs at the end of the chapter. There's nothing magical in this idea, and in the early stages of establishment you'll have to do just as much weeding as in any other part of the garden. But when such shrubs are close-planted they will eventually form a thicket that beats the weeds, hides the bare soil and saves you work.

More than any other plants, shrubs will enable you to carve out a garden that is three-dimensional. However small your patch, try to turn it into a place that's welcoming, yet a little mysterious. There should always be some part of the plot that's not quite visible, so that you're tempted to explore its hidden depths. With a bit of imagination you can make hidden crannies on a plot no bigger than ten feet square—I know it's possible because I've done it!

FINDING THE SHRUBS

As well as being able to locate a good nursery, you should also be able to locate a good plant when you're there. Container-grown shrubs can be bought and planted at any time of year and they are the stock-in-trade of the garden centre. Look for a plant that is relatively young and in the peak of health. Don't go for an old and gnarled specimen even though it is larger and therefore more tempting than a youngster. It will probably have a spiralled mass of roots inside the pot and will resent disturbance. Its roots will also be reluctant to leave the safety of the rootball for the soil outside and the plant may sit and sulk rather than grow away.

That's not to say you should buy a plant that's only just been put into its container. No; it should be established and container *grown*, but not decrepit.

Choose a shapely plant that is not one-sided. It should be furnished with branches down to soil level (unless it is meant to be grown on a bare stem) and if it is a columnar grower it should have a strong central shoot or 'leader'. The compost in the pot should not be dry, neither should there be a gap between compost and pot—a sure sign of previous drying out. Avoid pest- or disease-infected plants and those with brown-edged leaves.

As with trees, deciduous shrubs are sold for dispatch between November and March—the dormant season when they can safely be lifted from the nursery rows and transported with little soil around their roots. If the shrub you order is to be delivered 'bare root' in winter, enquire if it is possible to select the plant you want, otherwise you'll have to rely on the reputation of the nurseryman. In general it is possible to transplant quite large bare-root shrubs, provided the nurseryman has occasionally 'undercut' them to encourage the formation of a fairly compact root ball. This involves simply slicing into the soil along the rows of plants to sever any far-roaming roots. The job results in the formation of more fibrous roots—always easier to deal with at planting time than those long roots that are almost as thick as broomhandles.

PLANTING

The planting of shrubs is identical to the planting of trees except that a stake will seldom be necessary to prevent wind rock. See p. 24 for details.

The spacing of shrubs gives rise to much argument. Some folk suggest that they are planted at their final spacing (to allow room for the indicated spread); others suggest closer planting and a thinning out of the scheme later on. I'd rather see the plants spaced out to allow for ultimate growth, and the gaps between the shrubs filled with short-term annuals or border plants that can easily be transplanted when the space they occupy is needed.

In particularly exposed places shrubs can be protected from winter winds by surrounding them with a 'tube' of sacking held in position by four stout canes or stakes, or by cutting the bottom off a plastic sack and slipping this over the canes (Fig. 12). Watering and mulching are just as important for shrubs as for trees.

TRANSPLANTING

Unless you are exceptionally clear-thinking and full of foresight when it comes to planting, you will occasionally make mistakes. The trouble is that you won't realize it straight away—only after two or three years when the scheme has matured will a plant scream out to be moved. Don't worry; you can still shift it with little danger to its constitution.

Spring and autumn are the best times to transplant, though you can also do the job in winter if you don't

Fig. 12 A plastic fertilizer sack, slit top and bottom and held in the shape of a tube by four canes, makes an effective windbreak around a newly planted shrub.

mind working in cold weather. Evergreens will prefer to be moved in April or May when the sap is starting to rise—it's the deciduous kinds that can tolerate a winter upheaval.

Start off by taking your spade to the plant and cutting round it about 30 or 45 cm (12 or 18 in) away from the stem to sever out-growing roots. If the plant is very large it's a good idea to do this part of the operation some months in advance of the transplanting date. The plant can then recover from the shock while it still has a few roots pushing down underneath the rootball, and it will form a more fibrous network of roots above these which can sustain it after transplanting.

When the sides of the rootball have been cut, push your spade underneath the plant to sever the anchor-roots. Now swing the plant carefully to one side and tuck a sheet of sacking or polythene underneath it. If you roll up the sheet to just half its size and push the rolled edge underneath the plant it is then a simple job to swing the plant back in the other direction and unroll the sheet so that the plant sits in its centre. Wrap the sheet around the plant as quickly and as tightly as possible, tie it or knot it, then soak it (if it's made of sacking) with a couple of buckets of water.

The plant can stand in a sheltered spot in its wrapping for several weeks if necessary, but for best results it should be planted in its new hole without delay, just as for a 'balled' bare-root plant. Stand it in the prepared hole, unwrap the sacking, swing the plant from side to side so that the wrapping can be removed, and then replace the soil—watering the plant in well if necessary.

Anti-desiccant sprays can be used on conifers and evergreens before and after transplanting. These are proprietary solutions that can be sprayed on to foliage to prevent excessive water loss.

PRUNING

I think most gardeners hate pruning—probably because they're not quite sure what to do or when to do it. Calm yourself by remembering that the pruning of shrubs is usually necessary for three basic reasons: to remove dead or diseased wood; to keep a plant shapely and within bounds; and to encourage flowering. Some shrubs need hardly any pruning—they don't grow fast, are naturally shapely, seldom suffer from die-back and flower happily without being cut back; others quickly become a thicket of flowerless stems where pests and diseases proliferate.

I've given specific instructions on pruning each shrub I've mentioned so I won't confuse you by rambling on generally here, except about pruning techniques. Never use anything but a sharp pair of secateurs for pruning, and take a pair of loppers (or long-arm pruners) to any stems thicker than your finger. Make all cuts directly above a leaf or bud—don't leave even a cm ($\frac{1}{2}$ in) snag or 'finger' of stem behind, it will only die back and may allow disease to enter. Cuts larger than 2·5 cm (1 in) in diameter can, if you wish, be painted with a proprietary wound sealant to prevent attack by fungus diseases. It's not the end of world if you don't do this because most wounds will heal naturally.

Whatever else you do, don't tackle all your garden shrubs with the shears as soon as they get out of hand—you'll turn them all into flowerless lollipops of greenery. When you buy a shrub, make sure you know how big it will grow and what pruning it needs, then you can plant with confidence knowing that you'll get the best out of it without being concerned that it will turn your garden into a jungle.

If you've taken over a garden that's already overgrown with shrubs, renovate them by thinning out the stems (Fig. 13). Cut out all old and gnarled branches at ground level, leaving the young ones evenly spaced so that they can breathe and grow. If all the branches are old, cut out two-thirds of them and leave the remainder. With any luck (and a bit of feeding) the plants will soon produce healthy young wood at ground level and then the remainder of the elderly stuff can be cut out. This kind of pruning can be done in summer or autumn and winter. Dead or diseased wood on any shrub, or suckers from rootstocks (see p. 79), should be removed the instant they are noticed.

Fig. 13 Different shrubs demand different pruning techniques but, as a general rule, most are best thinned out rather than chopped back. The complete removal of a few of the oldest branches will make for increased vigour, disease resistance and a handsome appearance. Chopping back may only encourage the formation of a flowerless thicket.

Finally, don't fall into the trap of thinking that because nature doesn't prune her shrubs you needn't. Take a look at a few shrubs in the wild and see how overgrown and full of dead wood they are. They make superb bird nesting sites in a wild part of the garden but they're not much to look at close-to. If you can't bear pruning, there's only one thing to do and that's to select those shrubs that need no cutting back at all. They are clearly marked in the A–Z section.

FEEDING

Don't forget that shrubs are just as hungry as other garden plants. Two or three handfuls of blood, bone and fishmeal scattered around each shrub in April will work wonders, especially if it's followed by a mulch of well-rotted garden compost or manure, or pulverized bark. The soil should be moist when you lay the mulch, and the mulch itself should be moist. That way the soil will be protected from excess drying out and weeds will be suppressed. Mulching saves an awful lot of hard labour.

PROPAGATION

It's always great fun to propagate plants. The healthy youngsters can either be planted in the garden or used as swaps, and though not all your cuttings may root, those that do will make all the fuss and bother worth while. These are the simplest ways to propagate shrubs, and all the plants mentioned in the A–Z section can be increased by at least one of these methods: seeds, softwood cuttings, semi-ripe or half-ripe cuttings, leaf bud cuttings, hardwood cuttings, root cuttings, layering and division. Full details of all these methods are given in Chapter 20.

A–Z OF GARDEN SHRUBS

I make no apologies for the shrub section being so long! The choice is wide and there are so many good garden plants among them that they must be done justice. It's a biased selection; they are all plants that I think deserve a space in your garden, but where the season of interest is limited, or the plant has drawbacks, I've said so.

Make sure that any shrub will put up with the soil and situation you have to offer—I've indicated its preferences and its tolerances, and there are lists of plants for particular situations, soils and characteristics at the end of the chapter. The expected height and spread of each shrub is indicated with the height first and the spread second. Use it as a rough guide to work out whether or not you've room for the plant. Its precise measurements will vary from place to place and soil to soil.

Abelia × **grandiflora**   90 cm × 1·8 m (3 × 6 ft)
A spreading shrub with small, glossy, oval evergreen leaves and masses of pale pink flowers from summer to autumn. It's the length and timing of the flowering season that makes this a valuable shrub, rather than the spectacle of the individual blooms—they are quite small. Use it near the front of borders or to provide a muted background for more striking plants.

Likes a warm spot and well-drained soil. May be cut back by frost in hard winters—try it at the foot of a warm wall. *Tolerates* heavy clay soils and chalk. *Prune* after flowering, removing older stems that have carried blooms. *Propagate* by cuttings of firm shoot tips in summer.

Acer shirasawanum 'Aureum'   Japanese Maple
1·8 × 1·8 m (6 × 6 ft)
A real stunner that's ideal to use as a tree in a tiny garden. The fan-shaped leaves are a glorious acid yellow when they unfold in spring and they retain much of their brilliance until they fall in autumn.

Likes a spot sheltered from winds and a soil that never becomes dust dry. Avoid frost pockets—the new foliage is sensitive. *Tolerates* clay soil and very occasionally chalky soil—worth a try if you're desperate and can improve the ground with organic matter. *Prune* at your peril. Remove only dead wood and any inconveniently placed branches in autumn. *Propagate* with difficulty. Try layering a low-growing branch in spring; sow seeds outdoors as soon as they are ripe; bud on to seedling stocks in early spring if you are really keen.

Acer palmatum varieties   Japanese Maple   Up to 3 × 4·5 m (10 × 15 ft)
Any gardener with an eye for form admires these supremely elegant plants. There are many varieties of which these are some of the best: f. *atropurpureum*, with leaves that are burgundy-purple; 'Dissectum Atropurpureum', the same but very finely cut like lace; var. *dissectum*, with feathery green leaves; 'Senkaki' has stems of rosy pink and pale green leaves that turn orange-yellow in autumn; 'Oskazuki' is one of the best for autumn tints—the lobed green leaves are burnished rich, warm crimson. All make shapely bushes or small trees that are ideal where space is restricted. They'll even grow in tubs.

Like a sheltered spot where cold winds and early frosts will not damage their leaves. They don't like dry soils. *Tolerate* clay soil and occasionally chalky soil provided the latter is enriched, but they fail in shallow earth over chalk. *Prune and propagate* as for *Acer japonicum* 'Aureum'.

Amelanchier canadensis   Snowy Mespilus
2·4 × 3·6 m (8 × 12 ft)
This is the name under which nurserymen sell their snowy mespilus, but botanists mumble that it's likely to be *A. laevis*. It doesn't matter. Either way you'll obtain a large shrub with oval deciduous leaves that take on dazzling tints of orange, red and yellow before they fall in autumn. Clusters of small white starry flowers are carried in spring so the plant has two seasons of interest, even if it's boring in summer. Position summer bloomers in front of it.

Likes any open spot in reasonable soil. *Tolerates* heavy or moist soil and soils containing chalk. *Prune* out a few old stems each winter. *Propagate* by digging up and replanting suckers in autumn.

Aralia elata   Japanese Angelica Tree   3–6 × 3 m (10–20 × 10 ft)
You'll need plenty of space for this whopper, but it has super architectural form that it's a must where a striking plant is needed. The massive leaves are usually about 90 cm (3 ft) long, but divided into many smaller leaflets. Watch out for the spines! Fluffy flower clusters of creamy green are carried in late summer, and the most striking sight is the variegated form of the plant—*Aralia elata* 'Aureovariegata'—whose leaves are edged with creamy white. Stunning.

Likes an open spot in any ordinary soil and plenty of room to spread. *Tolerates* heavy clay soil and chalk. *Prune* out any unwanted stems and any dead wood in spring. Remove unwanted suckers (which these plants can produce rather too freely). Those from the variegated variety will be green-leafed, for it's grafted on to rootstocks of the true species. *Propagate* by removing suckers from the true species, or (if you've the patience) by grafting shoots of the variegated variety on to rootstocks of the true species in spring.

Arundinaria species   Bamboo   60 cm–3 m × 3 m (2–10 ft × 10 ft)
More folk should grow bamboos. There are midgets for small gardens and others that are so rampant they can only be let loose in relatively wild areas, but all produce a thicket of canes decorated with narrow leaves that may be dazzlingly variegated. These are my own favourites: *A. murielae* (now *Fargesia murielae*), 3 m (10 ft), yellowish-green canes with arching tips clad in green leaves; *A nitida* (now *Fargesia nitida*), 3m (10 ft), purplish canes and arching fronds of green leaves; *A viridistriata* (now *Pleioblastus auricomus*), 1 m (3 ft), devastatingly beautiful with short canes and leaves striped with fresh green and butter yellow. The best one for a

small garden. All three keep their leaves on throughout the year. All are fun to grow in tubs.

Like sheltered spots in soil that is unlikely to dry out. *Tolerate* heavy clay and boggy ground and, surprisingly, relatively dry soil and shady sites under trees. They don't mind chalk and will also put up with coastal exposure, though they certainly grow better without it. *Prune* out a few old and dead canes each spring. Leave in some old wood to support the new and act as a windbreak. *Propagate* by lifting and transplanting portions of the clump in spring or autumn.

Aucuba japonica 'Variegata' Spotted Laurel
2·4 × 2·4 m (8 × 8 ft)

Don't be put off this shrub by the fact that you've seen it in dingy shrubberies where it has become overgrown. As a single specimen in the right spot it has a handful of sterling attributes: it is clothed with glossy yellow-spotted leaves all the year round; it is easy to grow, shapely and produces fat red berries in winter if it's fertilized by a nearby male (which will hopefully be planted in someone else's garden). There are other varieties—some are spotted, some are plain; some are male (producing no berries) and some are female. Plant it where it can be admired from a window in winter.

Likes good soil and gentle (but not overpowering) shade. *Tolerates* clay, chalk, heavy shade and coastal exposure. *Prune* only to remove unwanted branches in spring. *Propagate* by cuttings of firm shoot tips in summer.

Azalea (see Rhododendron)

Berberis darwinii Barberry
1·8 × 1·8 m (6 × 6 ft)

One of the best barberries, good in leaf and flower. The evergreen leaves are dark and glossy—like those of a miniature holly—and the orange flowers (like tiny daffodils in close-up) absolutely smother the stems in spring. Thorny and impenetrable—wear gloves when you prune it! Good for hedges (p. 62).

Likes an open spot in any reasonable soil. *Tolerates* clay, chalk, dry soil, cold gardens, some shade and even coastal exposure, though it will burn in really severe salt-laden winds. *Prune* carefully if you value your arms. Remove a few old stems each winter. *Propagate* by cuttings of firm shoot tips in summer.

Berberis × ottawensis 'Purpurea' 2·4 × 2·4 m (8 × 8 ft)

Also called B. × *ottawensis* 'Superba', this is a nicely vigorous, rather upright shrub whose leaves are a rich maroon-purple. The orange flowers look well against them in early summer, and tiny red berries follow. The leaves are shed in winter. Makes a good hedge. A good contrast to lower-growing grey-leaved plants.

Likes an open spot in any reasonable soil. *Tolerates* clay, chalk, dry soil, cold gardens and just a modicum

of shade. *Prune* out a few old stems each winter, or cut back really hard at that time each year to encourage the production of new plum-purple shoots from lower down. Very thorny, so beware. *Propagate* by cuttings of firm shoot tips in summer.

Berberis × stenophylla 2·4 × 3 m (8 × 10 ft)

A spiny, arching thicket-former with tiny evergreen leaves and masses of scented orange-yellow flowers in spring. A really spectacular sight when in flower and one of the densest dog-proof hedges (p. 00).

Likes most sites and soils. *Tolerates* most sites and soils. *Prune* by cutting out overcrowding stems in winter and by digging up unwanted suckers, which it produces generously. *Propagate* by replanting the suckers, or by taking shoot tip cuttings in summer.

Berberis thunbergii
30 cm–1·2 m × 1·2 m (1–4 ft × 4 ft)

It is the forms of B. *thunbergii* that are most valued for their eye-catching foliage. 'Atropurpurea Nana' is purple-leaved and only 30 or 60 cm (1 or 2 ft) high; 'Aurea' is also low-growing and has acid yellow leaves that turn to dazzling green later in the year; 'Rose Glow' is a real curiosity with young leaves splashed and marbled pink on plum purple. Watch out for a newcomer called 'Baggatelle', which makes foot-high domes (about 30 cm) of dark maroon. All shed their leaves in winter and have unremarkable flowers, but in summer the foliage effect is powerful.

Likes open but sheltered sites and reasonable soil. *Tolerates* clay, chalk and a little shade, but not keen about dry soils in which it will grow rather slowly. *Prune* only to remove dead or unwanted stems in spring. *Propagate* by taking cuttings of firm shoot tips in summer.

Buddleja alternifolia 3 × 3 m or more

A graceful alternative to B. *davidii*, this species has an arching habit and narrow green leaves that are shed in winter. Lilac-pink flower clusters are carried right along the cascading stems in June, making the bush a real picture. Unlike B. *davidii* this species flowers on older wood, so pruning is rather different. It can be grown as a standard tree if trained to produce one fat stem from which the branches are allowed to cascade.

Likes full sun and a well-drained soil. *Tolerates* clay, chalk, dry soil, cold gardens and even a modicum of coastal exposure. *Prune* out the older shoots once the flowers have faded. The stems produced through the rest of the summer will carry next year's crop of flowers. *Propagate* by taking cuttings of shoot tips in summer, or by rooting hardwood cuttings outdoors in autumn.

Buddleja davidii Butterfly Bush 3 × 3 m

Vigorous, eye-catching and easy to grow, the butterfly bush earns its name by acting as a hostelry to all manner of butterflies when its flower spikes open in July and August. The deciduous leaves are dark green on the upper surface and greyish below, and there are many varieties with flower spikes of pink, white, crimson, purple and violet. There are also two varieties with variegated leaves. Plant any of them at the back of a border or in gaps between paving stones on a patio to bring butterflies close to you in summer. Every garden should have one.

Likes full sun and a well-drained soil. *Tolerates* clay, chalk, dry soil, boggy soil, cold gardens and some coastal sites. *Prune* hard back each winter, reducing the sideshoots (and even the main stems) to mere stumps. That way you'll maintain a vigorous and flower-laden bush. *Propagate* by taking cuttings of flowerless shoot tips in summer and by rooting hardwood cuttings outdoors in autumn.

Buxus sempervirens Box
Up to 3 × 3 m (10 × 10 ft) and more
A large shrub of box is crashingly dull, but smaller bushes kept close-clipped are fun, as are dwarf hedges around a kitchen garden (p. 62). *B. sempervirens* 'Suffruticosa' is the miniature that will grow to just 30 or 45 cm (1 or 1½ ft) tall and it can be clipped into tiny domes or cones in formal gardens, as well as being used as an edger. Try also the variegated varieties whose leaves are edged with creamy-white.

Likes an open or shady spot in reasonably moisture-retentive soil. *Tolerates* clay, chalk, dry soil and shade. *Prune* by clipping back in May. Excellent for topiary if you are a fan of vegetative peacocks and chessmen. Never cut back into very old wood. *Propagate* by rooting cuttings of shoot tips in summer, or by dividing the dwarf kind in spring.

Calluna, see Heathers

Camellia × williamsii   2·4 × 2·4 m (8 × 8 ft)
I reckon that this is the best of the camellias—evergreen spring-flowering shrubs with blooms as big as roses—for it sheds its flowers when they fade, rather than letting them turn brown on the plant as is the case with *C. japonica* (p. 69). The best variety is 'Donation', a double-flowered confection of pink.

Likes a peaty, moisture-retentive, lime-free soil and a spot in dappled shade. Avoid frost pockets or the blooms will be damaged as they unfurl. *Tolerates* bright sun provided that the soil does not become dust dry. Will tolerate occasional dryness at the expense of making growth. *Prune* only when absolutely essential, removing old or badly placed stems in spring. *Propagate* by inserting cuttings of firm young shoots in summer, or by layering suitably low-slung branches. Leaf-bud cuttings can also be taken.

Caryopteris × clandonensis   Blue Spiraea
90 cm × 1·5 m (3 × 5 ft)
Any shrub of modest size that extends the season of

interest in a garden must be worth planting. So it is with the Blue Spiraea. The deciduous leaves are grey and roughly toothed, and from their axils spring fluffy clusters of blue flowers in late summer and early autumn. Butterflies love it. Superb with other grey-foliage plants and at the front of beds and borders.

Likes full sun and a well-drained soil. *Tolerates* dry soil, chalky soil and coastal exposure. *Prune* back all the shoots quite hard each spring to encourage the production of healthy young growth. *Propagate* by taking cuttings of shoot tips in summer.

Ceanothus, Chaenomeles, see under *Climbers and Wall Plants*, Chapter 6.

Chamaecyparis species   Cypress
30 cm–6 m × 30 cm–2·4 m (1–20 ft × 1–8 ft)
There are dozens of different species and varieties of cypress with varying habits, from the squat to the columnar, and varying colours, from golden yellow to blue-grey. I've room to mention just a few favourites, but there are one or two recommended in Chapter 3, too. *C. lawsoniana* 'Minima Aurea' makes a yellow-tinged pyramid 60 cm (2 ft) high; *C. lawsoniana* 'Gimbornii' is a 60 cm (2 ft) high dome of grey green, eventually; *C. pisifera* 'Boulevard' grows into a 1·2 m (4 ft) high cone of steel grey, and *C. pisifera* 'Filifera Aurea', for all its long name, is a squat spreader with leaves like strands of gold. They'll all provide you with year-round enjoyment.

Like an open site in a well-drained soil enriched with peat. *Tolerate* clay soils, chalky soils, dry soils and cold gardens. *Prune* only when necessary to cut out damaged or dead branches. 'Boulevard' can be lightly clipped each spring to encourage new growth and prevent browning. *Propagate* by taking heel cuttings in summer.

Choisya ternata   Mexican Orange Blossom
1·5 × 2·4 m (5 × 8 ft)
If you want a shrub that really pays ground rent, this is a good one to choose. The fingered evergreen leaves are glossy and aromatic when crushed, and the flowers are certainly a lot like orange blossom. They are white, deliciously scented and carried in large clusters, first in late spring and then again late in summer. It's a shapely plant that's easy to grow in most situations. The variety 'Sundance' has young leaves that are acid yellow; 'Aztec Pearl' has finely-cut leaves and pink-tinged white flowers.

Likes a sunny and sheltered spot in well-drained soil. *Tolerates* clay, chalk, shade and a certain amount of coastal exposure. *Prune* out only dead or damaged branches in spring, plus any straggly shoots that make the bush unshapely. One or two old stems can be removed to rejuvenate ageing bushes. *Propagate* by taking cuttings of shoot tips in summer.

Cistus species and varieties   Sun Rose
30 cm–1·8 m × 90 cm–2·4 m (1–6 ft × 3–8 ft)
These lovely sun-worshipping shrubs produce some of the best flowers of early summer—large round blooms seemingly made of crumpled tissue paper and centred with a boss of yellow stamens. Each flower is short lived, but so many are carried that the bush performs well for several weeks. Often the rough, evergreen foliage is rather tacky to the touch. My favourite three are: *C.* × *purpureus*, 90 cm × 1·5 m (3 × 5 ft), rich pink, each petal blotched at the base with maroon; *C.* 'Silver Pink', 60 cm × 1·2 m (2 × 4 ft), soft pink; and *C.* × *cyprius*, to 1·8 × 2·4 m (6 × 8 ft), white flowers blotched at the base of each petal with maroon. Good near patios.

Like full sun and shelter. *Tolerate* dry soils, chalky soils and coastal exposure. *Prune* out frost-damaged growth in spring. *Propagate* by taking shoot tip cuttings in summer.

Convolvulus cneorum   60 cm × 1·2 m (2 × 4 ft)
Deservedly high-ranking among silver-leaved shrubs, this plant has none of the characteristics of its pernicious relative the bindweed. It makes a sprawling bush with silver-haired spatula-shaped leaves, and the shoots are tipped with white, pink-backed trumpet flowers in summer. A gleaming 'evergrey' treasure.

Likes a warm, sunny, sheltered spot (preferably at the base of a south- or west-facing wall) and well-drained soil. *Tolerates* dry or chalky soil. *Prune* out only stems damaged during winter. It is likely to be severely damaged, or even killed outright, by severe winters. *Propagate* by layering suitable stems in summer, or by rooting cuttings of firm shoot tips in summer.

Cornus alba   Dogwood
90 cm–1·8 m × 1·8 m (3–6 × 6 ft)
Easily kept low, this shrub is available in three different varieties: 'Elegantissima' has cream-variegated leaves; 'Spaethii' has leaves freely splashed with butter yellow, and 'Sibirica' has bright red stems to cheer you through the winter when the leaves have fallen.

Likes an open site and any ordinary soil. *Tolerates* boggy soil, clay, dry soil and chalky soil as well as cold and exposed situations. It also puts up with some shade, though the stems colour up best in full sun. *Prune* by cutting back all stems really hard in early spring. This keeps the shrub low and produces plenty of new growth for foliage and stem colour. Cut back to ground level if you like. *Propagate* by layering suitable stems (earth up around them to induce root formation); by taking cuttings of firm shoot tips in summer, or by inserting hardwood cuttings outdoors in autumn.

Cornus kousa   3 × 2·4 m (10 × 8 ft)
A real spectacle in June when the horizontal branches

are decorated with flowers—each one surrounded by four white, pointed bracts. They nestle like doves among the green leaves. Superb autumn colour provides another good reason for growing the plant. The variety *chinensis* is rather larger altogether and supposedly freer flowering. I'd have either.

Likes a deep, lime-free soil and a situation in dappled shade. *Tolerates* quite heavy shade but hates shallow chalky soils. *Prune* out only dead stems as soon as they are seen. *Propagate* by taking cuttings of firm shoot tips in summer, or by seeds sown in pots in a frame in spring.

Corylus avellana 'Contorta'   Corkscrew Hazel
3 × 3 m (10 × 10 ft)
The best time to look at this weird and wonderful shrub is late winter and early spring when the bare corkscrew branches are dripping with sulphur-yellow catkins. Its other common name of Harry Lauder's walking stick says all. In summer when the leaves appear you'd rather forget about the plant—they are puckered and turned under at the edges as if being attacked by a hidden pest. Plant the shrub where summer flowers will mask its embarrassment at that time of year, but make sure you get a good view in winter.

Likes an open spot in well-drained soil. *Tolerates* clay, dry or chalky soils, and even those that are really damp. It also puts up with shade. *Prune* only to remove overcrowding or dead stems in winter. *Propagate* by hardwood cuttings in autumn.

Corylus maxima 'Purpurea'
Purple-leafed Filbert   3 × 3 m (10 × 10 ft)
It doesn't do to plant too many purple-leaved shrubs in the garden—the effect becomes rather oppressive—but this shrub must be one of the best. It sends up vigorous stems that are clothed in summer with coarse, bold leaves of deep plum purple. Probably the largest-leaved purple foliage plant you'll find.

Likes a spot in the open or dappled shade in ordinary soil. *Tolerates* clay, chalk, dry soils, cold gardens and quite heavy shade. *Prune* to remove a few older stems each winter to reduce the density of the thicket. *Propagate* by layering or by removing and transplanting rooted suckers.

Cotinus coggygria   Smoke Tree
1·8 × 2·4 m (6 × 8 ft)
This shrub was designed by a sensitive architect: the leaves are almost perfectly round and rather thin and the buff flowers are nothing more than a cloud of fluff when they open in midsummer. By autumn they've turned smoke grey. The bush is shapely, too, and wider than it is tall. Two superb purple-leaved varieties are available: 'Notcutt's Variety' and 'Royal Purple'. Both look terrific when planted near coppery roses such as 'Buff Beauty'. The true variety offers

vivid autumn tints, the purple-leaved kinds not quite so bright a spectacle, but they certainly make up for it in summer.

Likes well-drained soil and an open spot. *Tolerates* clay soil, chalky soil and cold gardens. *Prune* only to remove one or two old stems and dead wood in late winter. *Propagate* by cuttings of firm shoot tips in summer.

Cotoneaster species and varieties   30 cm–3 × 3 m (1–10 × 10 ft)
This varied group of plants offers something for almost every situation. Briefly the ones that you'll find most useful are: *C. dammeri*, an evergreen ground-hugger with white flowers followed by scarlet berries; *C. conspicuus* 'Decorus', 1·8 × 1·8 m (6 × 6 ft), whose arching stems are clad in evergreen leaves and studded with bird-proof berries in autumn; and *C.* 'Cornubia', 3 × 3 m (10 × 10 ft), which is semi-evergreen and laden with hefty clusters of red berries on its cascading stems—not so bird proof. *C. horizontalis* is another good ground coverer, but it is dealt with under *Climbers and Wall Plants* (Chapter 6). All of the cotoneasters are among the best berry bearers in any garden.

Like well-drained soil and positions in the open. *Tolerate* any soil and any situation. *Prune* only to remove unwanted or overcrowded growths in spring. *Propagate* by rooting cuttings of firm shoot tips in summer.

Cytisus species and varieties   Broom
15 cm–3 m × 90 cm–3 m (6 in–10 ft × 3–10 ft)
They don't look much in winter, but the Brooms are a treat in spring and early summer when their wiry stems—upright or cascading—are plastered with bright pea flowers. There are many hybrids with flowers of crimson, orange, yellow and creamy white, some of them showing two distinct shades in the same bloom. I'd go for *C × beanii*, 30 × 90 cm (1 × 3 ft), bright yellow and cascading; *C. × kewensis*, 30 cm × 1·2 m (1–4 ft), creamy yellow flowers and rather more upright; and for brighter flowers I'd choose taller hybrids like 'Windlesham Ruby', 1·5 × 1·5 m (5 × 5 ft), bronze-red, and whatever else the nurseryman offered. Few of them will disappoint you, but in general all are short lived. Renew them every five to ten years depending on their health.

Like a sunny spot in lime-free soil. *Tolerate* clay soil, dry soil, and some chalky soils, though not those that are really shallow and poor. Also put up with coastal exposure. *Prune* out most of the flowered shoots when the blooms have faded. Failure to do this will produce an overcrowded bush with plenty of dead wood and little vigour. Try to avoid cutting back into really old wood. *Propagate* by taking heel cuttings in late summer.

Daphne species and varieties   30–90 × 30–90 cm (1–3 × 1–3 ft)
Valuable little shrubs that flower in winter and spring with blooms that are deliciously scented. The mezereon, *D. mezereum*, 90 cm × 1·2 m (3 × 4 ft), with its pink or white flower cockades on bare stems in winter, is undoubtedly the most popular species, but there are others offering a greater season of interest. Try *D. odora* 'Aureomarginata', 1·2 × 1·5 m (4 × 5 ft), with its evergreen leaves margined with cream and its clusters of pale pink perfumed blossoms in spring. *D. × burkwoodii*, 90 cm × 1·2 m (3 × 4 ft), is good too. A semi-evergreen, it carries pale pink flowers in May and June—extending your daphne season. No perfumed plot would be complete without them.

Like to be planted when young in well-drained organically enriched soil that never dries out completely. Enjoy good light. *Tolerate* chalky soil, in the case of *D. mezereum*—the others don't like it much. *Prune* out only dead shoots, nothing else. *Propagate* by taking cuttings of firm shoot tips in summer.

Deutzia × magnifica   1·8 × 1·8 m (6 × 6 ft)
If you're planting a June border, don't forget the deutzias. This one, like most, grows upright before arching its stems to show off the double rosettes of white flowers against the green summer foliage. The flowering season is brief but glorious and you'd be well advised to use the shrub where it can act as a green backdrop for brighter blooms in late summer. There are other species and varieties of similar build with flowers of pink or white.

Likes a sunny spot in any well-drained soil. *Tolerates* clay, dry or chalky soil and cold, exposed gardens. *Prune* out some of the older shoots completely every year as soon as the flowers fade. *Propagate* by taking cuttings of firm shoot tips in summer or by rooting hardwood cuttings in autumn.

Elaeagnus pungens 'Maculata'   Oleaster
2·4 × 3 m (8 × 10 ft)
Showstopping in winter when the sun catches its leaves, this is a variegated evergreen that should be on the top of your list. Each oval leaf is margined with dark green and centred with a splash of bright yellow. Handsome all the year round but comes into its own in the dreary months. A must for any 'winter garden'. The variety *E. × ebbingei* 'Gilt Edge' has yellow rims to its green leaves.

Likes any good soil and an open position sheltered from biting winds. *Tolerates* clay, chalk, dry soil, cold gardens and coastal exposure. *Prune* out any shoots that revert to plain green, and remove or shorten unwanted stems in spring. *Propagate* by taking cuttings of firm young shoots in late summer and early autumn.

Embothrium coccineum var. **lanceolatum**
'Norquinco' Chilean Fire Bush 6 × 3 m (20 × 10 ft)
A gambler's treasure. A stunning tree-like shrub with

semi-evergreen leaves and, in early summer, masses of fiery orange-red flowers that are long and thin and held in dense clusters along the stems. The variety *lanceolatum* is also good, but 'Norquinco' is breathtaking and can be seen thriving at Harlow Car Gardens in Yorkshire.

Likes best a spot in woodland where organic, lime-free soil and dappled shade are found. *Tolerates* moist ground and cold gardens so long as some shelter can be provided from damaging winds. *Prune* out only dead wood in winter. *Propagate* by sowing seeds in a propagator in spring; cuttings of firm shoot tips (or root cuttings) can be taken in summer.

Erica, see Heathers

Escallonia 'Donard Star'   1·8 × 1·8 m (6 × 6 ft)
I choose this variety as being representative of a group of plants that should be valued by more gardeners. They are of pleasing habit, bushy and upright or rather arching; most are clothed all the year round in shiny evergreen leaves, and all are generously decorated from summer to autumn with small but profuse flowers of white, pink or deep rose. 'Donard Star' has deep pink blooms.

Like any reasonably well-drained soil and a position in full sun. *Tolerate* clay, chalky soil, dry soil and coastal exposure. *Prune* out completely large portions of flowered growth once the blooms have faded. Sideshoots can also be shortened after flowering. After severe winters, badly damaged growth can be cut out in spring when new shoots can be seen growing away. *Propagate* by taking cuttings of firm young shoots in summer.

Eucryphia × nymansensis   'Nymansay'
6 × 3 m (20 × 10 ft)
One of my 'Desert Island Shrubs'. The upright branches on this tall bush or tree are clothed all the year round in dark evergreen leaves. In late summer a feast of white flowers erupts all over them, each pristine blossom being centred with a tuft of fluffy stamens. The timing is as welcome as the spectacle itself—a sort of farewell to summer. Just the plant for the back of a wide border. There's a handsome eucryphia planted outside the back door of Beatrix Potter's old home—Hill Top Farm at Sawrey in the Lake District—proving that some species (such as *E. glutinosa*) are tougher than many folk would have you believe.

Likes a moist, preferably lime-free soil that is never likely to dry out. Dappled shade is enjoyed too, but not heavy murk. *Tolerates* chalky soil better than most eucryphias and fairly cold gardens provided that shelter can be given from biting winds. *Prune* not at all, except to remove dead or damaged stems. *Propagate* by layering suitable stems, or by taking cuttings of firm shoot tips in early autumn.

Euonymus europaeus   Spindle Tree
3 × 3 m (10 × 10 ft)
Doubly valuable in autumn, our native spindle tree colours its foliage well with tints of orange and crimson, and carries bunches of four-lobed fruits that are rich crimson-pink, splitting to reveal orange seeds. 'Red Cascade' is a particularly good form.

Likes any reasonable soil and a spot in full sun. *Tolerates* clay, dry soil, chalky soil and cold gardens. Will put up with shade but you won't get such good autumn colour. *Prune* only to remove old and overcrowding stems and dead wood. *Propagate* by hardwood cuttings or layering.

Euonymus fortunei   'Emerald 'n' Gold'
30 × 90 cm (1–3 ft)
A bright little carpeter with evergreen leaves that are blotched with butter-yellow and green. They take on pink tinges during cold winter weather, and the shrub will even scale walls if planted against them. There are other varieties of different habits and variegations, such as the green and white 'Emerald Gaiety'.

Likes ordinary soil and an open site. *Tolerates* most soils and situations. *Prune* not at all, except to restrict its spread. *Propagate* by cuttings of shoot tips in autumn or by layering.

Fatsia japonica   False Castor Oil Palm
1·8 × 1·8 m (6 × 6 ft)
Most folk think of this as a house plant, but it's as tough as old boots in the garden. True, it might be killed back to the stump by really severe winter weather once every five years, but it always seems to sprout again in spring, and in most years it will remain evergreen—those big, glossy, hand-shaped leaves forming a handsome mound of greenery. Starry white flowerheads are often carried in autumn. A plant has grown happily in my parents' garden in the Yorkshire Dales for over thirty years, and it's also an excellent choice for town gardens

Likes good, moisture-retentive soil and full sun. *Tolerates* gentle shade, cold gardens, clay or chalky soil and coastal exposure. *Prune* it not at all. *Propagate* from shoot tip cuttings taken in summer, or by root cuttings.

Forsythia × intermedia 'Lynwood'
Golden Bells   2·4 × 2·4 m (8 × 8 ft)
All right, so it might be in everybody's garden, but that's only because nothing else can touch it when it comes to brilliant spring colour! This, I think, is the best forsythia to grow as a shrub (see also Chapter 6). It makes an upright bush of stature whose bare khaki stems cannot be seen in spring for the profusion of stemless yellow flowers. The large green leaves emerge to hide the fading blooms and provide pleasant verdure for the rest of the year when other plants are doing their stuff. Site it so that you can admire it from a window on dull winter days.

Likes good, well-drained soil and a sunny spot. *Tolerates* clay and chalk and cold, exposed gardens, but don't plant it in shade or it won't flower at all well. *Prune* it immediately after flowering taking out completely those stems that have carried flowers. The shoots that form during the summer will carry next year's blooms. *Propagate* by layering, by hardwood cuttings in autumn and by shoot tip cuttings in summer.

Fuchsia magellanica varieties
1·8 × 1·8 m (6 × 6 ft)

The hardy fuchsias are a delight in summer and on into autumn, when their ballerina flowers drip from the arching, blushing branches. The blooms of this species have a petticoat of purple held below carmine sepals—a vibrant combination of colour to be found in few plants. The foliage of *F. magellanica* 'Versicolor' is a confection of green, pink and cream, and 'Variegata' is similar but without the pink. There are numerous hybrid hardy fuchsias (not to be confused with the more tender greenhouse kinds) but among the very best are 'Mrs Popple'—again with the carmine and purple combination and terribly generous with her flowers; and 'Mrs W. P. Wood', whose little blooms of blush pink dangle like icicles from shapely bushes. A subtle treat. In some years, or in cold gardens, the plants might be killed to ground level by winter frosts; but in milder areas they'll lose their leaves in winter and very little else.

Like sunny spots in good, well-drained soil. *Tolerate* clay, chalk and coastal exposure. *Prune* back to ground level in February in cold gardens or severe winters. Where the stems have survived the winter, remove a few of the older ones in February and shorten all sideshoots to three buds. Earthing up with organic matter in autumn gives welcome frost protection to the roots and crown. *Propagate* from shoot tip cuttings in summer.

Genista species Broom   15 cm–4·5 m × 60 cm–3 m
(6 in–15 ft × 2–10 ft)

There are four genistas I think you ought to know about, and all of them are different. The giant of the race is *G. aetnensis*, the Mount Etna broom, which virtually makes a tree up to 4·5 × 3 m (15 × 10 ft) with wispy, semi-weeping stems. In summer it is studded with yellow pea flowers. A smasher for planting near a patio where it will cast the gentlest shade. Stake it well in its youth. *G. lydia*, 45 × 90 cm (1½ × 3 ft), is a cascading charmer for a bank or rock garden where its wiry stems drip with bright yellow blooms in spring. *G. hispanica*, 30 × 90 cm (1 × 3 ft), is the spitting image of a miniature gorse (which explains why it's called the Spanish gorse). Its barbarous stems are interlaced with yellow pea flowers in late spring. And finally *G. sagittalis*, 15 cm × 1·2 m (6 in × 4 ft), a carpeting curiosity with flattened, winged stems and the usual yellow flowers in early summer. Scrambling

across rocks or paving it's a real eye-catcher.

Like sun and well-drained soil. *Tolerate* clay, dry soil and some chalky soils—though not the poorest and shallowest. Happy in coastal exposure. *Prune* out most of the flowering shoots when the blooms have faded. Avoid cutting back into old wood. *G. aetnensis* can be trained to grow upwards in its youth, and as it matures no pruning (other than the removal of dead wood) is necessary. *Propagate* by sowing seeds in gentle heat in spring or by rooting heel cuttings in late summer.

Hamamelis mollis   Witch Hazel
3 × 4·5 m (10 × 15 ft)

A delight to the senses—both olfactory and visual—when the shuttlecock of bare branches is colonized by fragrant yellow spider flowers in winter. In the true species the blooms are bright yellow, radiating from a central bronze-red core, while in the variety × *intermedia* 'Pallida' they are a soft sulphur yellow, making them even more remarkable against a leaden sky. Some varieties, like 'Ruby Glow', have red flowers—a pleasant variation but not so noticeable in dreary weather. The large, hazel-like leaves unfurl in spring and take on rich autumn tints before they fall.

Likes good soil that's lime-free and not prone to drought. *Tolerates* clay soil and cold gardens. *Prune* not at all, except to remove dead wood. *Propagate* by layering suitable stems in spring or summer.

Heathers   Heath, Heather and Ling
15–45 cm × 90 cm (6 in–1½ ft × 3 ft)

I've cheated on the naming and grouped *Erica* (Heath), *Calluna* (Heather) and *Daboecia* (St Dabeoc's Heath) together to make life easier. They can be had in flower in most months of the year, many of them have brilliant foliage that takes on vibrant tints of yellow, orange and mahogany red in winter, and all are superb ground covers. Some species of *Erica* even tolerate chalky soil, the other two will not. I'll draw your attention to two really tall heaths that should be more widely planted: *E. lusitanica*, 3 × 3 m (10 × 10 ft), with wispy green leaves and tiers of tiny white flowers; and *E. arborea*, the Tree Heath, which is similar but even larger. Both bloom in spring and both need a warm, sheltered spot. They are particularly happy in warm coastal districts.

Like acid, peaty soil that never dries out and an open site. *Tolerate* chalky soil (if you choose varieties of *E. carnea*, *E. × darleyensis*, *E. erigena* and *E. terminalis*), clay soil and dry soil. The dwarf species are happy in cold gardens. *Prune* after flowering—lightly clipping over the foliate with shears. *Propagate* by taking short stem cuttings in summer or by removing rooted layers.

Hebe species and varieties   Shrubby
Veronica   30 cm–1·5 m × 2·4 m (1–5 × 8 ft)

Rather tender shrubs with opposite and decussate

(criss-cross) leaves and bottle-brush sprays of flowers in summer or autumn. They are evergreen and some species and varieties have coloured foliage—purplish on the undersides or glaucous grey all over. I'll recommend but three, for I've space for no more: *H. pinguifolia* 'Pagei', 30 × 60 cm (1–2 ft), makes hummocks of short grey leaves studded with white flowers in summer; *H.* × 'Autumn Glory', 60 cm × 1·2 m (2 × 4 ft), is a valuable late summer and autumn bloomer with purple spikes and glossy green leaves; and *H.* 'Great Orme', 75 cm × 1·2 m (2½ × 4 ft), although not as hardy as some, has slender spikes of such a lovely shade of pink that it's worth the risk. The so-called 'whipcord' hebes are curios worth a try. Their leaves are strands of bronze- or golden-green growth, almost like a conifer, and they are hardier than the larger-leaved species. The most popular whipcord is *H. cupressoides*.

Like warm, sheltered spots in well-drained soil. *Tolerate* dry soil, chalky soil and sometimes heavy clay too. They don't mind coastal exposure. *Prune* out frost-damaged stems in spring when new shoots can be seen breaking from lower down. Cut back aged specimens into old wood in spring or summer—they will soon sprout up again. Remove one or two old stems each May and shorten the other growths by half. If you're lazy simply clip over the bushes lightly with shears in spring. Very dwarf species need not be pruned annually. *Propagate* by taking cuttings of shoot tips in summer.

Hedera helix varieties   Ivy
15 cm–1·5 m × 1·8 m (6 in–5 ft × 6 ft) or more
Although ivy is primarily thought of as a climber, it is invaluable as a weed-suppressing carpeter, particularly in shade and under trees. The varieties of *H. helix* are tremendously varied in appearance, having lobed evergreen leaves that may be dull and dark or shiny and vibrantly coloured in shades of cream, white, yellow and green. The best climbers are mentioned on p. 71, but here I would draw your attention to *H. helix* 'Arborescens', an adult form of the common ivy which has unlobed leaves and woody stems making a bush 1·4 × 3 m (5 × 10 ft) in which birds love to nest. It's the form of ivy that often appears atop trees and wall when the younger stems have done the climbing. *H. hibernica* is unsurpassable as ground cover under trees, making a foot-thick carpet (about 30 cm) of glossy green that is impenetrable to weeds. This, too, has an adult form which is taller and more shrubby. *H. helix* 'Erecta', 45 × 90 cm (1½ × 3 ft), makes a neat, upright bush with leaves piled on top of each other in jumbled tiers. It makes a fine feature at the front of a border.

Like most sites and soils—variegated varieties prefer good light to shade. *Tolerate* most sites and soils. *Prune* most kinds by clipping over with shears in May. The arborescent (shrubby) kinds need no pruning. *Propagate* by taking cuttings of shoot tips in summer—adventitious roots may already be present. Layers can be lifted and transplanted in spring.

Helianthemum, see Rock Gardening, p. 135.

Hibiscus syriacus   2·4 × 1·8 m (8 × 6 ft)
No plant will tax your patience more than a hardy hibiscus. Just when you're about to give it up for dead in June, its grey stems will burst into life with fresh green shoots. The mallow flowers will appear among the green leaves in late summer and autumn before the foliage falls and this lazy plant goes to sleep again. All varieties make upright bushes; 'Woodbridge' has rich rose pink blooms, 'Hamabo' is white, and 'Blue Bird' a wishy-washy lavender—all are blotched with crimson at the base of the petals. At least the plants do make quite an effort when they're in bloom!

Like a warm, sunny, sheltered spot in rich, well-drained soil. Best in the south of England. *Tolerate* clay, dry or chalky soils and warm coastal gardens. *Prune* only to remove dead or damaged shoots in summer. *Propagate* by taking shoot tip cuttings in summer or autumn and rooting them in a propagator. Sometimes they take an age to root. Suitable stems can be layered.

Hoheria, see Climbers and Wall Plants, p. 71.

Hydrangea macrophylla varieties
1·5 × 3 m (5 × 10 ft)
There are two kinds of 'common hydrangea', the fat, mop-headed or 'Hortensia' varieties with their cob-loaf-like flowers of white, pink or blue, and the lace-caps with their flattened heads of tiny flowers surrounded by sterile florets with larger petals. The colour range is the same. All are deciduous and bloom in late summer and early autumn. Your local nurseryman will have his own favourite varieties. Enjoyed by front doors, especially in the southern counties, but excellent too in wide borders where they look good with ornamental grasses and other foliage plants.

Like sunny spots, sheltered from strong winds, and a rich soil that is unlikely to dry out. *Tolerate* clay and chalk and very moist soils. Happy by the coast. Blue varieties colour best in acid soils—they usually turn pink in chalky soil. Water them with proprietary hydrangea colorant to help restore their cerulean qualities, or settle for a rosy glow. *Prune* out weak and very old shoots completely in spring before growth starts. At the same time cut off the faded flowerheads above the topmost pair of fat buds. Single fat buds at the stem tips should not be removed for they are certain to flower. *Propagate* by taking cuttings of firm shoot tips in summer.

Hydrangea paniculata   1·5 × 1·8 m (5 × 6 ft)
Here the white or pink-tinged flowers are more pyramidal in outline than those of the previous species, though they are carried at the same time—in

late summer and autumn. The variety 'Grandiflora' has the largest blooms and is rightly in demand. Plant it where you can get a good look at it during the flowering season.

Likes sunny spots and a good soil that's not likely to suffer from drought. *Tolerates* cold gardens more than the previous species. Also happy in clay and chalk. *Prune* the shoots really hard back to within 2·5 cm (1 in) of the main stem or ground level in late winter—this species flowers on shoots made during the current season, and if not pruned it gets taller and out of hand. *Propagate* by taking cuttings of firm shoot tips in summer.

Hypericum species and varieties
St John's Wort   30 cm–1·5 m × 1·8 m
(1–5 ft × 6 ft) or more
Sneers abound when hypericum is mentioned in high horticultural circles, but this is a deserving race of plants whose only failing is a desire to please (and an occasional attack of rust disease). *H. calycinum*, 30 cm × several metres (1 ft × several yards), is the Rose of Sharon, a rampant spreader that's a boon to the gardener who wants a bright weed smotherer in dry soil under trees. It's semi-evergreen and carries plenty of yellow, shaving-brush-centred flowers in summer and autumn. *H.* 'Hidcote' is one of the best taller varieties at ·5 × 1·8 m (5 × 6 ft). The yellow flowers are similar to the Rose of Sharon but not so well endowed with bristles.

Like reasonably good soil and good light. *Tolerate* shade, clay, chalk and dry soils and coastal exposure. *Prune H. calycinum* by clipping it back to within about 5 cm (a couple of inches) of ground level in spring, just before growth begins. Cut out completely any old and weak stems to be found on *H.* 'Hidcote' at the same time. *Propagate* by lifting and transplanting rooted portions of the plants in autumn or spring. Cuttings may be taken from the shoot tips of *H.* 'Hidcote' in summer.

Ilex aquifolium   Holly
6 × 3 m (20 × 10 ft) at least
As well as making excellent trees and hedges, hollies are very useful evergreen border plants, providing a background of glossy green or green and yellow. Male and female flowers are carried on separate plants and only the females will carry berries (provided there is a male in the vicinity to pollinate their flowers). Varieties of *I. × altaclarensis* are as good as those of the common holly, though their leaves are usually larger and less spiny. There are dozens of different variegations described in detail in nurserymen's catalogues—check the sex as well as the colouring.

Likes good, well-drained soil not prone to drought. *Tolerates* almost any soil and situation in sun or shade. *Prune* only to remove Christmas holly, or clip after fruiting to produce a formal shape. Regular pruning is unnecessary. *Propagate* by rooting shoot-tip cuttings in a propagator in summer/autumn.

Jasminum, see *Climbers and Wall Plants*, p. 71.

Juniperus species and varieties
Juniper, Savin
Fuzzy-foliaged conifers of upright or spreading habit, the junipers can be used either as elegant and deep ground cover or as columnar eye-catchers in flat border plantings. Forms of *J. horizontalis* and *J. sabina* (savin) are among the best spreaders, sending out rocket-like growths over or above the ground. They grow to between 30 cm and 1·5 m (1 and 5 ft) high and to between 1·2 and 3 m (4 and 10 ft) across. *J. communis* provides plenty of upright forms—the favourite being the tiny *J. communis* 'Compressa'—a bollard just 45 cm (1½ ft) high and 15 cm (6 in) across. The spreading forms are superb at covering manhole covers—even if they do make inspection a prickly job!

Like soil enriched with peat. *Tolerate* any soil and situation except severe drought. *Prune* only to remove dead wood. *Propagate* by heel cuttings of young shoot tips in summer.

Kerria japonica 'Pleniflora'
Jew's Mallow   1·8 × 1·8 m (6 × 6 ft)
Nobody would recommend kerria as a specimen front-of-the-border plant, its season is so short; but it is good at the back! Its wiry green canes are bare of leaves in winter and dotted with inch-wide (about 30 cm) double chrysanthemum flowers of bright yellow in spring before the foliage unfurls. Soon it becomes an arching shuttlecock of green, but hardly a year goes by without its flowers drawing comments from gardeners unfamiliar with the spectacle. There is a single-flowered variety but it's not so good as the double.

Likes good soil and a sunny spot. *Tolerates* clay and chalky soil, some shade and cold, exposed gardens. *Prune* out plenty of older stems completely as soon as the flowers fade. *Propagate* by division or layering. Cuttings of firm shoot tips can be rooted in a propagator in summer.

Laurus nobilis   Sweet Bay, Victor's Laurel
Up to 15 × 4·5 m (50 × 15 ft)
Plant your own sweet bay and never buy another packet of bay leaves! Choose a young plant, though, for older ones are prohibitively expensive. It's an evergreen, with leathery oval leaves that are aromatic and fruity-flavoured when used in cooking. It can be left to grow unchecked, or clipped quite formally into a pyramid or lollipop—whatever takes your fancy. Only after many years and no clipping or pruning will it reach the given height.

Likes a warm, sheltered spot and a good soil that's not likely to dry out in summer. Drought or biting winds will burn the foliage. *Tolerates* sun or light shade, clay or chalky soil and coastal exposure. *Prune* in spring or summer when necessary. *Propagate* by taking cuttings of shoot tips in summer.

Lavandula species and varieties
Lavender   60 cm × 1·2 m (2 × 4 ft)
Brushing past a bank of lavender on a warm summer's day is a treat to the senses. Nothing else has that sweet and fruity aroma. Whichever variety you choose the plant will have downy grey foliage (though one or two are nearer grey-green) and spikes of purple-blue flowers on slender stems in summer. There are pink- and white-flowered forms but both are remarkable for their insipidity. I'd go for 'Hidcote' as first choice (not 'Hidcote Giant', which has longer flower stems that fall over), and then, perhaps, Miss Jekyll's 'Munstead'. The foliage is just as fragrant as the flowers, and the plants make unsurpassable edging to beds, borders and paths.

Like reasonably well-drained soil that is not heavily acid, and a spot in full sun. *Tolerate* dry soil and chalky soil. *Prune* by clipping over the plants once the flowers have faded. *Propagate* by taking cuttings of shoot tips in summer.

Lavatera 'Rosea'   Tree Mallow
2·4 × 2·4 m (8 × 8 ft)
A smashing shrub for a warm garden, I've never known any plant to be more generous with its flowers; they deck the downy grey stems from July to November—large pink mallow blooms that look a treat with the lobed, grey-green leaves. The shrub grows vigorously in any season so give it plenty of space to spread its branches. Lovely against a south-facing wall of mellow brick.

Likes a warm, sheltered spot in full sun and a poor, well-drained soil. *Tolerates* dry or chalky soil and coastal exposure. *Prune* hard back each spring, to ground level or to shoots breaking from mature stems. *Propagate* from shoot tip cuttings rooted in a propagator in late summer. Plant a young specimen and be prepared to replace it after a few years—it may flower itself to death or, in the very cold parts of the country, be killed by severe winters.

Leycesteria formosa   Himalayan Honeysuckle
2·4 × 2·4 m (8 × 8 ft)
Here's a good plant for the impatient gardener. Each spring it sends up a number of bright green bamboo stems that arch at the tips. In July, August and September white flowers drip from the leaf-laden stems in long tassels, but you can hardly see them for the deep maroon bracts that overlap them. Black berries follow. Good for adding beefiness to a border.

Likes a rich soil in sun. *Tolerates* chalky soil, clay soil, shade and coastal exposure. *Prune* everything to ground level in spring (in which case you'll have to make sure the plant is mulched annually with manure at the same time), or prune out older, flowered stems in spring, leaving just the healthy young ones. *Propagate* by dividing clumps in spring and by digging up and transplanting self-sown seedlings (of which there will be plenty).

Lippia, see *Climbers and Wall Plants*, p. 71.
Lonicera, see *Climbers and Wall Plants*, p. 72.
Magnolia species and varieties
2·4–6 m × 2·4–6 m (8–20 ft × 8–20 ft)
'Ooh' and 'aah' shrubs. There are two species that are regularly planted; of these the commoner and, I think, the more beautiful, and perhaps the most beautiful magnolia of all, is M. × *soulangeana*. It makes a wide-spreading bush with upturned branches. Examine a plant in winter and you'll see silky hairy buds just waiting to do their stuff in spring. Come April and May, with any luck, they'll erupt into white eggs and then burst into the typical waxy magnolia flowers. As they fade, the large green leaves will emerge to hide them. There are pure white varieties such as 'Alba Superba', but my heart belongs to 'Rustica Rubra' with its basal flushing of rosy purple. The other magnolia of renown is M. *stellata*, smaller at 2·4 or 3 m (8 or 10 ft) round, and bedecked with starry white flowers earlier in spring. The trouble is that it is frequently burned by frost. M. × *loebneri* 'Merrill' is slightly later in bloom and also tolerates my chalky soil. Give all magnolias room to spread.

Like a sunny, sheltered spot in a good soil that's not chalky. *Tolerate* a little shade, clay or moist soil and chalky soil provided the topsoil is deep and suitably enriched. *Prune* only to remove dead wood. *Propagate* by layering in spring.

Mahonia species and varieties
90 cm–2·4 m × 1·8 m (3–8 ft × 6 ft)
Architectural evergreen shrubs that add shape and form to the garden, as well as colour and perfume from their flowers. M. *japonica* is my first choice. Its large leaves composed of holly-like leaflets are held out at right angles to the stem, the top of which is decorated with long yellow flower tassels in winter. It is superbly scented. The most popular mahonia with landscape architects is M. × *media* 'Charity'—similar to M. *japonica* but rather more angular and a little taller at around 2·4 m (8 ft). For the improvement in architectural standing you'll have to sacrifice the scent. Everyman's mahonia is M. *aquifolium*, the Oregon grape—so called because of the black spherical fruits that follow the bunches of yellow spring flowers. It makes a yard-high thicket of growht (about 90 cm) on the poorest soil, and its leaves are burnished maroon in winter. Use the first two as specimen plants—especially in town gardens—and the last as deep ground cover.

Like any well-drained soil and a spot in dappled shade. *Tolerate* clay and chalky soil and heavy shade. *Prune* only to remove dead wood or unwanted stems in winter or spring. *Propagate* carefully—these shrubs have spiny leaves. Take shoot tip cuttings in summer, or layer suitable stems in spring. M. *aquifolium* can sometimes be divided in spring.

Myrtus communis Myrtle
2·4 × 2·4 m (8 × 8 ft)
Sweet of scent in leaf and flower, the myrtle is an old English garden plant that seems to have been unjustly neglected of late. The leaves are dark, glossy, evergreen and quite narrow but thickly carried on the stems of a dense bush. The flowers are white with a tuft of stamens in the centre—there's no daintier sight in the garden than myrtle bush in flower. Plant one at the end of a border to act as a fragrant full stop.

Likes a warm and sheltered spot in well-drained soil (it's not a shrub for a cold, exposed garden). *Tolerates* dry soil, chalky soil and coastal exposure in the warmer counties. *Prune* only lightly in spring to shorten unwanted stems; otherwise leave it alone. *Propagate* by taking shoot tip cuttings in summer.

Olearia species Daisy Bush
1·2–3 m × 1·8–3 m (4–10 ft × 6–10 ft)
Underrated shrubs with evergreen leaves and white daisy flowers. Great for adding form to a garden. The commonest is *O. × haastii* with oval dark green leaves that are grey and downy beneath. Billowing heads of white daisies smother the plant in summer. It's the hardiest and the easiest of the bunch and grows to about 1·5 m (5 ft) high and 2·4 m (8 ft) wide. *O. × macrodonta* is the biggest of my chosen three at up to 4·5 m (15 ft) high and across—even a little more if it's really happy. Here the green leaves (downy beneath) are holly shaped so that even when the summer flower display is over the bush is good to look at. *O. × scilloniensis* is 1·8 m × 1·8 m (6 × 6 ft), oval-leaved and a superb sight in flower with its long clusters of daisies. It's the tenderest of the three but perhaps the most spectacular in bloom.

Like warm, sheltered spots in sun and a well-drained soil. *Tolerate* coastal exposure, clay, dry or chalky soils. Prune out unwanted shoots in spring—the bushes will usually produce shoots from quite old wood (but try to avoid leaving a cluster of stumps—thin the stems rather than chopping them all back). Leave unpruned if you like, but after a few years you might possess an overgrown bush. *Propagate* by taking shoot tip cuttings in summer.

Osmanthus delavayi 1·8 × 2·4 m
(6 × 8 ft) or taller
Three paces after you've passed this shrub in spring you'll catch the most delectable scent—it travels at least that far on the air. It's a handsome bush with tiny evergreen leaves that are dark and glossy. The neat clusters of white tubular flowers nod from the stems to provide you with that spring treat when there's not much else to delight your nose. Best planted by a path to arrest your progress.

Likes a sunny spot in well-drained soil. *Tolerates* clay, chalky and dry soils and sheltered coastal gardens. *Prune* out overgrown stems after flowering. Can train as a wall shrub. *Propagate* by shoot tip cuttings in summer, or from hardwood cuttings in autumn.

Paeonia species and varieties
Tree Peony 1·5 × 1·5 m (5 × 5 ft)
Even when they've finished flowering these are handsome plants with a statuesque quality. They make long woody stems atop which their finely cut leaves radiate in a sort of Japanese style (in spite of the fact that they are from China!). *P. lutea* var. *ludlowii* has sharp-toothed leaves of quality and yellow cup-shaped flowers in late spring. It looks good when planted in association with spiky-leaved irises and round-leaved bergenias. The varieties of *P. suffruticosa* are certainly the most spectacular when in bloom. Their flowers are the size of dinner plates and may be single or double in shades of pink, yellow, crimson, lavender and white. My own favourite has single white flowers blotched at the base of each petal with deep maroon. There is always a central crown of stamens on the single varieties.

Like a sheltered, sunny spot which is not liable to be frosted in spring. Organically enriched but well-drained soil. *Tolerate* chalky soil. *Prune* out dead stems and one or two old stems after flowering. *Propagate* by sowing seeds in spring, by rooting shoot tip cuttings in summer or by layering suitable stems.

Pernettya (now **Gaultheria**) **mucronata**
60 cm × 1·2 m (2 × 4 ft)
Knee-high thickets of tiny, pointed evergreen leaves don't sound very interesting, but smother them in purple, pink, red or white berries in autumn and you'll have a sight worth seeing. The get plenty of fruits you'll need several plants to ensure adequate pollination (some have predominantly male flowers, others female). There are named varieties offering berries of certain colours. Good under trees.

Likes peaty, lime-free soil and a spot in dappled shade. Don't let the earth dry out in summer. *Tolerates* clay and moist soils and cold, exposed gardens in light or heavy shade. *Prune* hardly at all. It's sufficient to cut out unwanted stems at ground level in spring. *Propagate* by division in spring or by shoot tip cuttings in summer.

Philadelphus species and varieties
Mock Orange, Syringa (which is really the botanical name for lilac)
1·8–3 m × 1·8–3 m (6–10 ft × 6–10 ft)
Indispensable shrubs for the flower border where they'll produce arching wands of headily scented white blossoms in early summer (if you choose the right varieties). My number one favourite is 'Beauclerk'—the most powerfully perfumed of the lot. Its single flowers are flushed at the base of each petal with purple. 'Virginal' is the one to choose if you prefer double, pure white flowers. Both make good-sized bushes of considerable thickness. *P. coronarius*

'Aureus' produces creamy white flowers, but it's the acid-yellow foliage that makes it desirable. It retains its vibrancy until well into summer and looks superb in planting of golden-leaved shrubs, or where it can be placed against a contrasting purple-leaved plant.

Like sunny spots in ordinary soil. *Tolerate* clay, dry and chalky soils and cold, exposed gardens. *Prune* out all flowered stems as soon as the blooms have faded. *Propagate* by taking shoot tip cuttings in summer or by rooting hardwood cuttings in autumn. *P. coronarius* 'Aureus' produces self-sown seedlings which are as brightly coloured as the parent.

Phlomis fruticosa Jerusalem Sage
90 cm × 1·5 m (3 × 5 ft)

Patio gardeners can plant this shrub with confidence—it will not take up too much room and it will enjoy the sun and warmth. The evergreen grey-green leaves are densely felted, and from the shoot tips arise tiered flowers of yellow in summer. The blooms are carried in whorls around the stem—each flower a little hooded masterpiece.

Likes a warm, sunny spot in well-drained soil. *Tolerates* dry or chalky soil and coastal planting. *Prune* back the shoots in spring to buds that are opening lower down on the stem. *Propagate* by cuttings of firm shoot tips in summer. Replace old plants every five years or so.

Photinia × fraseri 'Red Robin' 3 × 2·4 m (10 × 8 ft)

Don't gnash your teeth if you're on chalky soil and can't grow pieris—grow photinia instead. It's an evergreen shrub of considerable vigour and its leaves are long yet broad. In spring the young shoots are bright red—not quite so luminous as pieris but not a bad compromise! White flowerheads appear in early summer—they're not much to write home about but they do extend the season of interest.

Likes an open sunny spot that's not subject to spring frosts. Any ordinary soil. *Tolerates* dry or chalky soil and clay. *Prune* out a few old stems and shorten new ones to keep the bush shapely as soon as flowering is finished. Left unpruned the bushes can fall open. *Propagate* by cuttings of firm shoot tips in summer.

Phygelius, see Climbers and Wall Plants, p. 72.

Pieris formosa var. forrestii
Lily-of-the-Valley Bush
3 × 3 m (10 × 10 ft)

For reasons that are obvious even to the casual observer this shrub is almost always grown in gardens in its variety 'Wakehurst'. The young shoots that emerge over the dark evergreen leaves in spring are a rich and vibrant red. As they age, the bright shoots turn pink, white and then dark green. Long chains of white lily-of-the-valley flowers are carried at the same time. You can't deny that this shrub does its

best to please. *P.* 'Forest Flame' is equally brilliant in leaf, but if flowers are your aim go for the heavily laden *P. japonica* 'Purity'.

Like a peaty, leafy, lime-free soil and a sheltered spot in dappled shade. *Tolerate* little else. *Prune* only to remove unsightly or damaged stems. *Propagate* by layering or by taking cuttings of firm shoot tips in summer.

Pittosporum tenuifolium
4·5 × 3 m (15 × 10 ft)

Evergreens have a not altogether undeserved reputation for being dingy and oppressive, but this shrub dispels such maudlin thoughts. It has black stems, but there the sombre colouring ends, for the leaves are light green, glossy and wavy at the edges so that they constantly reflect the light. The variety 'Silver Queen' has brighter leaves still—edged with silvery white—but the crown for brilliance must go to 'Garnettii' (of hybrid origin), which has white variegation and pink flushing in winter. Purple-leaved varieties are also available. Super background shrubs that take on an important role in winter.

Like sunny spots in well-drained soil. *Tolerate* coastal exposure (for which they are famous), clay, chalk and dry soil. *Prune* out dead wood, or shorten unwanted stems in spring. Otherwise leave untouched. *Propagate* by cuttings of firm young shoot tips in summer.

Potentilla fruticosa varieties Cinquefoil
60 cm–1·2 m × 1·2–1·8 m (2–4 ft × 4–6 ft)

Dumpy bushes, naked in winter but thickly clothed in fingered, silky-haired leaves in summer, when they also produce their rounded flowers of yellow, white, orange, and now red. There are dozens of different varieties, and among the best are: 'Elizabeth', primrose yellow; 'Jackman's Variety', bright yellow; 'Sunset', orange, fading to yellow; 'Abbotswood', white. The two newcomers, over which much fuss was made originally, are 'Red Ace', with vermilion-scarlet flowers; and 'Royal Flush', nearer to rose red. Both are excellent in the right situation but, to use the words of the breeders, they 'fade in conditions of extreme heat, drought and wet'. As the British climate is almost always at some extreme or another the plants are a gamble. All varieties are well suited to being grown in small gardens and they tumble attractively over path edges and down banks.

Like sunny spots in most well-drained soils. *Tolerate* dry, chalky or clay soil, cold, exposed and coastal gardens. *Prune* out a few older stems each spring and shorten long youngsters at the same time. *Propagate* by shoot tip cuttings in summer or by hardwood cuttings in autumn.

Prunus species and varieties Cherry, Cherry Laurel, Almond, Peach, Plum. Various heights.

I've mentioned the flowering cherries as valued as trees on p. 33, and the Cherry Laurel as a hedger on p. 62; here I want to mention three species of *Prunus* that are valuable shrubs. The first is *P. laurocerasus* 'Otto Luyken', a sort of dwarf laurel 1·2 m (4 ft) high and as much across with glossy evergreen leaves and white candles of flowers in spring. Smart and shapely ground cover. *P. tenella* 'Fire Hill' stopped me in my tracks the first time I saw it. It is a bare-branched shrub in winter, but in spring its stems are plastered with starry pink flowers mixed with the bright green of the emerging leaves. It's a sprawling but erect-stemmed shrub 60 cm–1·2 m (2–4 ft) high and more across, and often known as the Dwarf Russian Almond. If you want a spring stunner, look no further. *P. triloba* is another early bloomer, though not quite so reliable. In a warm, sheltered garden it will smother its stems with double rosettes of pink blossom. It makes an upright bush to 3 m (10 ft) or more and as much across, but pruning will keep it smaller. Florists sell it by the bucketful as a cut flower.

Like most soils and situations, but the flowering types need good light and *P. triloba* grows best in warm, sheltered gardens. *Tolerate* most sites and soils but don't relish coastal exposure. *Prune* 'Otto Luyken' of any unwanted branches in spring or summer. 'Fire Hill' can be relieved of a few old stems after flowering and any young ones can be shortened. *P. triloba* should be relieved of shoots that have flowered immediately the blooms fade—new stems sent up during the summer will carry next year's flowers. *Propagate* by layering suitable stems. 'Otto Luyken' can be propagated from shoot tip cuttings in summer.

Pyracantha, see *Climbers and Wall Plants*, p. 73.

Rhododendron species and hybrids
(Include Azalea)   Various heights
I can't hope to do justice to the hundreds of different species of rhododendron and the thousands of different varieties, so I'll give you no more than a brief outline of the main types and their cultivation—that way at least you'll be able to keep the plant you selected at the nursery alive and well. Azaleas, by the way, are rhododendrons. The name is usually given to smaller-flowered rhododendrons and those that are deciduous. Apart from the countless species of rhododendron, the bulk of those that find their way into gardens are the evergreen 'hardy hybrids'; hefty plants of strong constitution. But there are compact varieties too, and you should check with the nurseryman how high any plant will grow before you stagger home with it. Some of the 'azaleas' have delicious fragrances—especially the deciduous types—and many have flowers of almost luminous intensity. If your garden is really small, don't neglect the hybrids derived from *R. yakushimanum*, a dim-

inutive plant that takes years to make a dome 90 cm (3 ft) high and as much across. Its hybrids are expensive but very choice.

Like a peaty, leafy, lime-free soil that's not likely to dry out in summer. Dappled shade is preferred to heavy gloom or full sun. Annual spring mulching is appreciated as are occasional waterings with iron sequestrene in the early years. Compact varieties can be grown in tubs provided they are never allowed to dry out. *Tolerate* clay soils and those that stay moist all the year round. *Prune* only to remove dead or badly placed stems in spring. *Propagate* by layering in spring and summer, or by taking cuttings of shoot tips in summer and early autumn and rooting these in a propagator.

Rhus typhina   Stag's Horn Sumach
3 × 3 m (10 × 10 ft)
Don't be conned into planting this shrub unless you've a bit of room to spare—it will eventually make a huge dome of growth smothered in ash-tree shaped leaves that are softly hairy. In autumn the foliage turns vivid shades of orange, yellow and red before falling to reveal the felted, antler-like stems. The autumn fruits are knobs of pink velour. The variety 'Dissecta' has more finely cut leaves than the true species and is deservedly popular, for with careful pruning it can be fitted into a small plot. A handsome architectural feature in the right place.

Likes ordinary soil and full sun. *Tolerates* chalk, clay and dry soil. *Prune* away lower branches in the early stages of growth if a clean stem is required. If space is short and you feel you must grow the plant, choose 'Laciniata' and prune back the sideshoots to three buds every March. In this way the plant can be kept down to about 1 m (3 or 4 ft). *Propagate* by the removal of rooted suckers (which should be torn up anyway to prevent the formation of a thicket). Root cuttings can also be taken.

Ribes sanguineum   Flowering Currant
2·4 × 1·8 m (8 × 6 ft)
We used to have a flowering currant outside the back door when I was knee high to the proverbial grasshopper and since then I've always had a soft spot for it. In winter it's bare, but in spring, along with forsythia, its blooms start to open—dripping from the branches like blobs of raspberry jam until they open into rich crimson-pink tassels. The sycamore-shaped leaves follow and have a thick aroma all their own—I love it; some folk hate it! 'Pulborough Scarlet' and 'King Edward VII' are the best deep pink varieties, and I've recently discovered the delights of a healthy pure white variety called 'Tydeman's White'. Lovers of golden foliage will appreciate the less vigorous 'Brocklebankii' with its luminous yellow leaves and pink flowers—a strident, if unsubtle, contrast. It brightens large pots and tubs on a patio.

Likes ordinary, well-drained soil and a sunny spot.

Tolerates clay, chalky and dry soil, cold and coastal gardens and a modicum of shade, though flowering will not be so spectacular. 'Brocklebankii' prefers gentle shade. *Prune* immediately after flowering, removing completely older stems that have bloomed. Can also be clipped formally and makes a good hedge. Clip after flowering. *Propagate* by cuttings of firm shoot tips in summer, or by hardwood cuttings in autumn.

Romneya coulteri   Tree Poppy
1·2 × 90 cm (4 × 3 ft)

Do have a go with the tree poppy, even though it is a bit tender. It has the most sumptuous finely cut foliage of grey—not hairy but rather waxy—and its stems are topped in late summer and autumn with fragrant white poppy flowers—each one tissue-paper thin and centred with a doughnut of yellow stamens. In severe winters it may well be killed back to ground level, but it will still recover to flower the following year.

Likes a warm, sunny, sheltered spot, preferably at the foot of a west- or south-facing wall. The soil should be well drained and not too rich. *Tolerates* dry or chalky soil and a coastal situation. *Prune* back to the nearest sprouting buds in spring. *Propagate* by root cuttings inserted in boxes of sandy soil and placed in a frame in winter.

Rosmarinus officinalis   Rosemary
1·5 × 1·5 m (5 × 5 ft)

Rosemary must be at the front of a border—there you can brush past it and savour the savoury aroma of its narrow, dark, evergreen leaves as well as being able to pick it with ease for the roast lamb on Sunday. It is rather an upright plant, even though its stems often run along the ground before they start to ascend, and is especially vertical in the variety sold as 'Miss Jessop's Upright'. In spring it carries masses of pale blue hooded flowers on its towering stems.

Likes a sunny, sheltered spot in well-drained soil. *Tolerates* dry soil, chalky soil, coastal exposure and colder weather than many folk would have you believe. *Prune* out dead stems in spring (severe winters may lead to die-back but seldom to death, provided the soil is well drained). Straggly stems can be shortened in spring or summer. Replace old, worn out plants with youngsters. *Propagate* by taking shoot tip cuttings in summer.

Ruta graveolens   'Jackman's Blue'   Rue
45 × 60 cm (1½ × 2 ft)

Tidy, grey and acrid—it doesn't sound like much of a recommendation, but this really is a fine little shrub. The foliage is as finely cut as filigree, a really blue grey, and topped with greenish yellow flowers in summer. It is virtually evergreen. There is also a variegated variety whose leaves are mottled green and cream. A super patio plant that's supposed to keep away flies—don't brush against it or the aroma will keep you away too, and may cause a painful rash.

Likes a chalky soil and a spot in full sun. *Tolerates* dry, non-chalky soils. *Prune* hard back in spring (to within a few centimetres or inches of ground level) to encourage fresh, new growth. *Propagate* by taking shoot tip cuttings in summer, or by inserting harder shoots outdoors in autumn.

Salix species   Willow
60 cm–1·2 m × 60 cm–1·2 m (2–4 ft × 2–4 ft)

There are a number of low-growing willows, and some that are pruned to keep them short. The two I want to recommend are both naturally diminutive: *S. hastata* 'Wehrhahnii', 1·2 × 1·2 m (4 × 4 ft), has plum-purple stems that are gilded with the most beautiful catkins in spring before the leaves emerge. Pussy willow appears first—silver grey and silky—then the yellow pollen lights up the whole plant. The foliage is plain green. *S. lanata*, 60 × 60 cm (2 × 2 ft), has pussy willow, but here it is the grey-felted leaves that are the main attraction. Both plants have rather upright stems and are suited to being planted in restricted spaces.

Like moist soil and a sunny spot. *Tolerate* clay, boggy and chalky soil and a modicum of shade. Happy in cold gardens. *Prune* these two hardly at all. The removal of dead or badly placed stems in spring is all that is necessary. One or two old stems can be removed each year. *Propagate* by hardwood cuttings in autumn.

Sambucus species and varieties   Elder
4·5 × 4·5 m (15 × 15 ft)

I'm a real fan of these beefy shrubs—they grow fast and furiously in most situations and are available in such variety of form that there's something to please every gardener. *S. nigra*, the common elder, has a superbly elegant variety 'Laciniata' in which the leaves are finely cut to give a lacy look; 'Aurea' is yellowish in spring, becoming greener later; 'Guincho Purple' is a dusky plum purple; and 'Albovariegata' is green edged with creamy white. All have the vigour you would expect of an elder, but they respond well to hard pruning so don't worry if your patch is small. *S. racemosa*, the red-berried elder, is rather less vigorous and most often seen in its variety 'Plumosa Aurea' with deeply slashed leaves of acid yellow. It's as vibrant as any garden shrub, but I can't say in all honesty that the combination of luminous yellow leaves and bright red berries in autumn is a colour scheme of impeccable taste. Still, it is bright and the fruits don't set every year.

Like any ordinary or moist soil that's not likely to dry out in summer and a spot in sun or dappled shade. *Tolerate* clay, chalky soil, boggy soil and heavy shade, though this is not to be recommended for the bright-leaved varieties. Cold, exposed and coastal situations are also tolerated. *Prune* shoots hard back in late winter if growing in a confined space, otherwise allow the plant to grow freely, removing only badly placed and weak shoots. *Propagate* from shoot tip cuttings in summer or hardwood cuttings in autumn.

Santolina species   Lavender Cotton
60 cm × 1·5 m (2 × 5 ft)

Endearing little shrubs with wispy foliage that's grey, feathery and highly aromatic—really fruity. They are evergrey and the shoots are topped in summer with yellow button-like flowers, if you let them run up high enough. I suggest you don't, for although the blooms are pretty in themselves, they weigh down the plant and pull it open, spoiling its shape. Sorry to be a spoilsport. Two varieties are commonly grown: *S. chamaecyparissus* is the more compact and wiry-stemmed of the two, and *S. neapolitana* is softer and a little more fluffy. Both make delightful dwarf edging when clipped, or, if you insist on having those flowers, you can grow them next to a wide path so that they can tumble their blooms over the flagstones.

Like sun and well-drained soil. *Tolerate* dry or chalky soils and coastal exposure. *Prune* by clipping or snipping just before the flowers swell and open. *Propagate* from shoot tip cuttings in summer.

Sarcococca confusa   Christmas Box
90 cm × 1·8 m (3 × 6 ft)

This spreading evergreen is just like *Osmanthus* in one respect—its flowers have a perfume that will arrest you several paces after you've passed it by. The leaves are small, glossy and thickly packed on the stems, and the fluffy white flowers open in very early spring, filling you with optimism. A smashing plant for a border or bed beneath a window where its fragrance can drift up into the room.

Likes chalky soil and a spot in sun. *Tolerates* shade, clay and dry soil. *Prune* only to remove dead wood in spring. *Propagate* by removing and rooting firm shoot tips in summer.

Skimmia species and varieties
90 cm × 1·5 m (3 × 5 ft)

Council shrubberies are packed with skimmias, though usually the boring kinds that have few fruits and just a load of soot-laden evergreen foliage. The plain species, *S. japonica*, can be crashingly dull, but varieties such as 'Veitchii'—a female with large red fruits in winter—and 'Rubella'—a male with white flowers that are rosy pink in bud—will brighten any garden. Male and female flowers are carried on separate plants in the case of all varieties of *S. japonica*, but *S.* ssp. *reevesiana* has the advantage of being both compact and hermaphrodite, which makes life easier. White flowers open in May and red fruits cheer up the plant in winter. A good choice for a bed or border that needs perking up in winter.

Like ordinary well-drained soil in sun or light shade. *Tolerate* dry, chalky or clay soil, cold gardens and coastal exposure. *S. reevesiana* isn't keen on chalky soil; the others don't mind. *Prune* only when

the plants become straggly. Then a few stems can be shortened in spring to encourage branching from lower down. *Propagate* by taking cuttings of firm shoot tips in summer.

Spiraea species and varieties
Various heights

Lots of spiraeas are grown in gardens and a few of them are a bit dull—blooming for a brief spell in spring or summer and then packing up for the rest of the year. The two I'm going to recommend do that too, but at least their display is spectacular. *S.* 'Arguta', 2·4 × 2·4 m (8 × 8 ft), is the bridal wreath, beloved of anyone with an ounce of sentiment or an eye for a graceful plant. Even if it doesn't flower for long at least it's a picture when it does—the arching branches are thickly dotted with tiny white flowers like miniature apple blossoms in spring. The small green leaves follow. *S. japonica* 'Anthony Waterer' is altogether smaller at 60 × 60 cm (2 × 2ft) and blooms in summer, producing flat-topped heads of rosy pink flowers. Another variety, 'Goldflame', has spring foliage that's bright yellow tinged with orange. At least one of them should grace your garden.

Like ordinary soil that's not prone to dry out in summer, and a position in sun or dappled shade. *Tolerate* any soil and situation, though a few don't like chalk much. *Prune S.* 'Arguta' by removing a few old stems completely after flowering. Cut *S. japonica* down to within a few inches of soil level in spring. *Propagate S. japonica* by division in autumn or spring; *S.* 'Arguta' can be propagated from cuttings of firm shoot tips in summer

Symphoricarpos species and varieties
Snowberry, Coral Berry   1·2–1·8 m × 1·2–2·4 m (4–6 ft × 4–8 ft)

You'll not find a thicker-growing shrub than this; in any of its species and varieties it makes a dense, suckering bush ideal for bird cover and food, thanks to a plentiful supply of autumn berries. These follow the tiny white summer flowers. All the different kinds are deciduous, and all have plain but attractive leaves that are oval, fresh green and quite thin. The largest and commonest species is the snowberry, *S. albus* var. *laevigatus* (often listed as *S. rivularis*). The fruits are almost as big as marbles and pure white. *S. orbiculatus*, the coral berry, is a small-fruited species with pink berries and it has been hybridized with snowberry to produce the Doorenbos Hybrids. These are without doubt the best garden plants of the lot, making rather small shrubs with large berries that may be white, pale or dark pink. 'Magic Berry' is rose pink; 'Mother of Pearl', pink and white; and 'White Hedge' is pure white. All make good hedges and brighten up autumn borders. Those outside my study window are aflutter with nectar-drinking moths on summer nights.

Like ordinary soil that's not liable to dry out in

summer, and a spot in sun. *Tolerate* clay, chalk, dry soil, moist soil, cold exposed and coastal gardens and heavy shade. *Prune* to remove a few older stems each winter if you can get into the bush. Most folk give it up as a bad job—the bushes become so thick that pruning is impossible. Lazy gardeners rejoice! *Propagate* by lifting and transplanting suckers in autumn or spring, or by hardwood cuttings in autumn.

Syringa species and varieties   Lilac
3·6 × 3 m (12 × 10 ft)

Brief but glorious—that's the lilac season. But what a show it is! In late spring the varieties of the common lilac, *S. vulgaris*, fill the air with pastel shades and sweet scents. Even though the season is short it's worth squeezing in one plant at the back of a border—out of flower it can act as a verdant backcloth to other blooms. The true species has pale, thinly furnished blooms, so avoid being palmed off with a plant of dubious origin. Settle instead for one of these: 'Madame Lemoine', double white; 'Charles Joly', double, deep crimson-purple; 'Massena', single, deep purple; 'Maud Notcutt', single white; 'Primrose', single, pale yellow; 'Esther Staley', single, warm pink. There are other good named varieties too. *S. × josiflexa* 'Bellicent' is an altogether more graceful plant than the common lilac, with flower trusses that consist of smaller florets. But it makes a superb shrub, blooming in late spring with the other lilacs, and arching its long, rose-pink flower spikes from the foliage. It's delectably scented and deserves a much greater popularity.

Like ordinary well-drained soil and sun. *Tolerate* chalky soils with pleasure; also clay. Usually happy in cold gardens. *Prune* only occasionally, removing one or two older stems in winter. *Propagate* by layering in spring, or by rooting cuttings of firm shoot tips in summer. Suckers can be dug up from plants on their own roots and transplanted. However, some nurserymen graft on to common lilac rootstock (in the old days privet was used) and any suckers that appear will be inferior. Remove and discard them.

Tamarix ramosissima   Tamarisk
3 × 3 m (10 × 10 ft)

Every September we spend a week in a house right on the Sussex coast; the garden gate opens on to the beach. It's a balmy time of year—the calm before the autumn storm—and the glorious tamarisks that surround and shelter the garden are at their best. The heather-like grey-green leaves set off a treat the feathery spikes of pink flowers. The whole, massive bush is so ethereal that it looks as if it would blow away in the first sea breeze, but in reality it's as tough as old boots. The Sussex plant is the common tamarisk, *T. gallica* (see Chapter 5), but perhaps a better choice for gardens is *T. ramosissima* (also called *T. pentandra*), which is a little brighter and a fraction more shapely. It flowers at the same time as the common tamarisk and both are deciduous.

Like sun and well-drained soil. *Tolerate* clay, dry and chalky soil, cold gardens and coastal exposure. *Prune* shoots hard back in spring. Failure to do this may result in a straggly bush. *Propagate* by hardwood cuttings in autumn.

Viburnum species and varieties
Various heights

Here's a real jewel box of plants: some are deciduous and some are evergreen; some have superb autumn colour; some produce fat flowerheads and others brilliant fruits. Here's the pick of the crop:

V. farreri (or *V. fragrans*) 2·4 × 2·4 m (8 × 8 ft), is a deciduous species whose bare, upright stems erupt with little pinkish-white flower clusters in winter. Catch its fragrance in a burst of watery sunshine and it will keep you going until spring. The leaves open after the flowers—bronze at first, changing to dull green.

V. × bodnantense, in its forms 'Dawn', pink, and 'Deben', pink in bud, white in flower, beats *V. farreri* by opening a month earlier—in October. It's a rather stiffer, more upright plant and its flowers are not quite so resistant to frost as those of *V. farreri*.

V. carlesii, 1·5 × 1·5 m (5 × 5 ft), follows in spring, producing large, flat-topped clusters of gloriously fragrant pink and white flowers over the coarse green leaves. These will sometimes take on rich tints in autumn. 'Aurora' is its best variety—a real stunner.

V. plicatum tomentosum in its forms 'Mariesii' or 'Lanarth' is a heck of a mouthful to quote to your nurseryman, but it will bring you a handsome, horizontally branched plant, naked in winter but furnished with deeply veined leaves in summer. Flat-headed flower clusters like those of a cream lace-cap hydrangea are arranged in rows along the shelf-like stems in late spring. A real treat that eventually makes a shrub 2·4 × 3·6 m (8 × 12 ft).

V. opulus 'Sterile' is the snowball tree—so called because of its spherical heads of ivory-white flowers that are carried on the stems in early summer. It is deciduous, a splendid sight in flower, and a host to blackfly, so give it an occasional spray.

V. tinus is that dingy-foliaged evergreen, but looks quite a treat in its pink-budded form 'Eve Price'. It grows about 1·2 × 1·8 m (4 × 6 ft) or more and blooms in winter and spring, so it's well worth bunging in a border even though its foliage is black as night.

Like sun or dappled shade and a soil that is well drained yet never likely to dry out in summer. *Tolerate* clay, chalk (provided it's not shallow and dry), moist soil, (*V. tinus* doesn't mind dry soil), cold gardens and shady spots. *Prune* out a few old stems in later winter and remove dead wood as soon as it is seen. *V. tinus* withstands hard pruning or clipping in summer. *Propagate* by layering, or by shoot tip cuttings taken in summer.

Vinca species and varieties   Periwinkle
15 cm × 1·8 m (6 in × 6 ft)
The greater periwinkle (*V. major*) and the lesser periwinkle (*V. minor*) are cheap and cheerful ground coverers that will seldom give you much trouble. They send their long, trailing shoots out over the soil to help smother weeds (eventually) and they brighten early summer with round, five-petalled flowers of blue, white or mauve. The difference in them lies in the size of their leaves. The best periwinkle of all is *V. major* 'Variegata', a vigorous beast with superb evergreen leaves that are fresh green splashed with creamy yellow. It makes a thick rug of growth.

Like ordinary soil in sun or shade. *Tolerate* chalk, clay, dry soil, cold gardens and heavy shade. *Prune* only to prevent unwanted spread. *Propagate* by lifting and transplanting rooted portions—the plant's stems root as they creep.

Weigela   Bush Honeysuckle, Diervilla
1·8 × 1·8 m (6 × 6 ft)
It's impossible for me to think about weigela without thinking about philadelphus—they are both the first spectacular shrubs of late spring and early summer. Philadelphus definitely has the edge when it comes to spectacle and perfume, but a well-grown, arching weigela is a welcome addition to any garden during its brief season of bloom. The bare winter stems erupt with leaves in spring, and then in June the bell-shaped flowers of white, pink or crimson appear in close array. Varieties such as 'Bristol Ruby', deep pink, and 'Candida', white, are popular, but don't neglect the two varieties of *W. florida* that will cheer you up for the rest of the summer, too, with their leaves of plum-purple, in the case of 'Foliis Purpureis', and creamy-edged in the case of 'Variegata'. Both harmonize delightfully with the pink flowers.

Like ordinary well-drained soil and a place in the sun. *Tolerate* clay or chalky soils, a modicum of shade and even coastal or inland exposure. *Prune* after flowering, removing older, flowered stems. *Propagate* by hardwood cuttings in autumn or by firm shoot tip cuttings in summer.

Yucca filamentosa   Adam's Needle   90 × 90 cm
Stately plants with upright rosettes of spiky leaves; a must if you're creating a tropical effect. They grow slowly and will eventually produce flower spikes from the top of the rosetts—one spike on each plant. The blooms are beautiful, creamy white and carried thickly up the 5 ft stalk (about 1·5 m) in summer. Lovely in pots and tubs on patios, provided you don't walk into them! Be patient; your plant won't flower until it's a few years old.

Likes ordinary well-drained soil and sun. *Tolerates* dry and chalky soil and coastal exposure. These blighters are tougher than you'd think. *Prune* only to remove faded flower spikes. *Propagate* by root cuttings or division—pot up or transplant suckers.

FIND THE RIGHT SHRUB

These lists should help you in the search for a shrub to suit a certain part of your garden, a particular type of soil or situation, or to provide a certain effect at a chosen time of year.

If you want a plant to put up with dry shade, for instance, check that it is listed under both these categories. Consult the A–Z section for further details.

SHRUBS FOR SHADE (**d** = dappled shade only)
Arundinaria
Aucuba
Berberis
Buxus
Camellia
Choisya **d**
Cornus kousa **d**
Corylus
Cotoneaster
Embothrium **d**
Euonymus fortunei
Fatsia
Hedera
Hypericum
Ilex
Juniperus
Kerria **d**
Laurus
Leycesteria **d**
Mahonia
Pernettya (syn. Gaultheria)
Pieris
Prunus laurocerasus 'Otto Luyken'
Rhododendron
Salix
Sambucus
Sarcococca
Skimmia
Symphoricarpos
Viburnum
Vinca
Weigela **d**

SHRUBS FOR DRY SOIL
Remember that the plants must not be allowed to dry out in their first year of establishment.
Arundinaria
Berberis
Buddleja
Buxus
Caryopteris
Chamaecyparis
Cistus
Convolvulus
Cornus alba varieties

Corylus
Cotoneaster
Cytisus
Deutzia
Elaeagnus
Escallonia
Euonymus
Genista
Heather
Hebe
Hedera
Hibiscus
Hypericum
Lavatera
Mahonia aquifolium
Myrtus
Olearia
Osmanthus
Philadelphus
Phlomis
Photinia
Pittosporum
Potentilla
Prunus
Rhus
Ribes
Romneya
Rosmarinus
Ruta
Santolina
Sarcococca
Skimmia
Spiraea
Symphoricarpos
Tamarix
Viburnum tinus
Vinca
Yucca

SHRUBS FOR CHALKY SOIL

Those described as being 'sometimes' suitable will often fail over really shallow chalk soils that are poverty stricken. They are worth chancing if you're desperate.

Abelia
Amelanchier
Aralia
Arundinaria
Aucuba
Berberis
Buddleja
Buxus
Caryopteris
Chamaecyparis
Choisya
Cistus
Convolvulus
Cornus alba varieties

Corylus
Cotinus
Cotoneaster
Cytisus (sometimes)
Daphne mezereum
Deutzia
Elaeagnus
Escallonia
Eucryphia (sometimes)
Euonymus
Fatsia
Forsythia
Fuchsia
Genista (sometimes)
Heathers (some species)
Hebe
Hedera
Hibiscus
Hydrangea
Hypericum
Ilex
Juniperus
Kerria
Laurus
Lavandula
Lavatera
Leycesteria
Magnolia (sometimes
    and some species)
Mahonia
Myrtus
Olearia
Osmanthus
Paeonia
Philadelphus
Phlomis
Photinia
Pittosporum
Potentilla
Prunus
Rhus
Ribes
Romneya
Rosmarinus
Ruta
Salix
Sambucus
Santolina
Sarcococca
Skimmia japonica
Spiraea (some)
Symphoricarpos
Syringa
Tamarix
Viburnum (sometimes)
Vinca
Weigela
Yucca

SHRUBS FOR CLAY SOILS

Abelia
Acer
Amelanchier
Aralia
Arundinaria
Aucuba
Berberis
Buddleja
Buxus
Chamaecyparis
Choisya
Cornus alba varieties
Corylus
Cotinus
Cotoneaster
Cytisus
Deutzia
Elaeagnus
Escallonia
Euonymus
Fatsia
Forsythia
Fuchsia
Genista
Hamamelis
Heathers
Hebe
Hedera
Hibiscus
Hydrangea
Hypericum
Ilex
Juniperus
Kerria
Laurus
Lavandula
Leycesteria
Magnolia
Mahonia
Olearia
Osmanthus
Pernettya
Philadelphus
Photinia
Pittosporum
Potentilla
Prunus
Rhododendron
Rhus
Ribes
Salix
Sambucus
Sarcococca
Skimmia
Spiraea
Symphoricarpos
Syringa

Tamarix
Viburnum
Vinca
Weigela

SHRUBS FOR COASTAL GARDENS

Arundinaria
Aucuba
Berberis
Buddleja
Caryopteris
Choisya
Cistus
Cotoneaster
Cytisus
Elaeagnus
Escallonia
Euonymus fortunei
Fatsia
Fuchsia
Genista
Hebe
Hedera
Hibiscus
Hydrangea
Hypericum
Ilex
Juniperus
Laurus
Lavandula
Lavatera
Leycesteria
Myrtus
Olearia
Osmanthus
Phlomis
Pittosporum
Potentilla
Ribes
Romneya
Rosmarinus
Sambucus
Santolina
Skimmia
Spiraea
Symphoricarpos
Tamarix
Weigela
Yucca

SHRUBS FOR COLD AND EXPOSED GARDENS

Berberis
Buddleja
Chamaecyparis
Cornus alba varieties
Corylus
Cotinus

Cotoneaster
Deutzia
Elaeagnus
Euonymus
Fatsia
Forsythia
Hamamelis
Heathers (some)
Hedera
Ilex
Juniperus
Kerria
Mahonia aquifolium
Pernettya (syn. Gaultheria)
Philadelphus
Potentilla
Prunus
Ribes
Rosmarinus
Salix
Sambucus
Skimmia
Spiraea
Symphoricarpos
Syringa
Tamarix
Viburnum
Vinca
Weigela

SHRUBS FOR GROUND COVER

The measurement given after each plant is the recommended planting distance when the shrub is used in quantity as ground cover.

Cistus 60 cm (2 ft)
Convolvulus 45 cm (1½ ft)
Cotoneaster dammeri 45 cm (1½ ft)
Cytisus (some) 45 cm (1½ ft)
Euonymus fortunei 45 cm (1½ ft)
Fuchsia 60 cm (2 ft)
Genista (some) 45 cm (1½ ft)
Heathers 30 cm (1 ft)
Hebe 45 cm (1½ ft)
Hedera 30 cm (1 ft)
Hypericum 45 cm (1½ ft)
Juniperus 90 cm (3 ft)
Lavandula 45 cm (1½ ft)
Mahonia aquifolium 60 cm (2 ft)
Pernettya (syn. Gaultheria) 45 cm (1½ ft)
Phlomis 45 cm (1½ ft)
Potentilla 60 cm (2 ft)
Prunus laurocerasus 'Otto Luyken' 60 cm (2 ft)
Rhododendron (dependent upon type) 60 cm to 1·5 m (2 to 5 ft)
Ruta 30 cm (1 ft)
Salix 60 cm (2 ft)
Santolina 45 cm (1½ ft)
Sarcococca 45 cm (1½ ft)

Skimmia 60 cm (2 ft)
Symphoricarpos 60 cm (2 ft)
Viburnum tinus 60 cm (2 ft)
Vinca 45 cm (1½ ft)

SHRUBS SUITABLE FOR PLANTING AS SINGLE FEATURES

Where there is no room for a small tree, these shrubs can be relied on to act as focal points.

Acer japonicum 'Aureum'
Acer palmatum varieties
Aralia
Buddleja alternifolia
Camellia
Chamaecyparis
Cornus kousa
Cotinus coggygria varieties
Cotoneaster conspicuus 'Decorus'
Elaeagnus pungens 'Maculata'
Embothrium
Eucryphia
Fatsia
Genista aetnensis
Hamamelis
Hibiscus
Ilex
Juniperus
Laurus
Lavatera
Leycesteria
Magnolia
Mahonia × media 'Charity'
Paeonia
Pieris
Pittosporum
Prunus triloba
Rhododendron
Rhus
Sambucus
Syringa
Tamarix
Viburnum (some)
Yucca

SHRUBS FOR WINTER COLOUR AND INTEREST

Acer palmatum 'Senkaki' (syn. 'Sango-kaku')
Arundinaria
Aucuba
Chamaecyparis
Cornus alba varieties
Corylus avellana 'Contorta'
Cotoneaster
Daphne mezereum
Elaeagnus pungens 'Maculata'
Euonymus
Hamamelis

Heathers
Hebe (some)
Hedera
Ilex
Juniperus
Mahonia
Pernettya
Ruta
Salix
Skimmia
Symphoricarpos
Viburnum × *bodnantense* varieties
Viburnum farreri
Viburnum tinus
Vinca major 'Variegata'
Yucca

SHRUBS WITH COLOURFUL BERRIES

Aucuba
Berberis
Cotoneaster
Euonymus europaeus
Ilex
Leycesteria (black)
Mahonia aquifolium (black)
Pernettya (syn. Gaultheria)
Sambucus (black)
Skimmia
Symphoricarpos

SHRUBS WITH EVERGREEN LEAVES

Abelia
Arundinaria
Aucuba
Berberis darwinii
Berberis × *stenophylla*
Buxus
Camellia
Chamaecyparis
Choisya
Cistus
Convolvulus
Cotoneaster (some)
Daphne (some)
Elaeagnus
Escallonia
Eucryphia
Euonymus fortunei
Fatsia
Heathers
Hebe
Hedera
Hypericum
Ilex
Juniperus
Laurus

Lavandula
Mahonia
Myrtus
Olearia
Osmanthus
Pernettya (syn. Gaultheria)
Phlomis
Photinia
Pieris
Pittosporum
Prunus laurocerasus 'Otto Luyken'
Rhododendron
Rosmarinus
Ruta
Santolina
Sarcococca
Skimmia
Viburnum tinus
Vinca
Yucca

SHRUBS FOR AUTUMN FOLIAGE COLOUR

Acer palmatum varieties
Amelanchier
Berberis (some)
Cornus kousa
Cotinus
Euonymus
Hamamelis
Heathers (some)
Mahonia
Rhus
Viburnum (some)

SHRUBS WITH ATTRACTIVE BARK OR STEMS

Acer palmatum 'Senkaki' (syn. 'Sango-kaku') (orange-red)
Cornus alba 'Sibirica' (deep red)
Corylus avellana 'Contorta' (corkscrew stems)
Deutzia (brown and peeling)
Kerria (green)
Leycesteria (green)
Pittosporum (young stems black)
Salix (purplish-brown or bronze)

SHRUBS WITH GREY FOLIAGE

Caryopteris
Chamaecyparis pisifera 'Boulevard'
Convolvulus
Hebe pinguifolia 'Pagei'
Juniperus (some)
Lavandula
Lavatera
Phlomis
Potentilla (some)
Romneya
Ruta
Santolina

SHRUBS WITH VARIEGATED FOLIAGE

Aralia elata 'Aureovariegata'
Aucuba japonica 'Variegata'
Berberis thunbergii 'Rose Glow'
Buxus sempervirens 'Elegantissima'
Cornus alba 'Elegantissima'
Cornus alba 'Spaethii'
Elaeagnus pungens 'Maculata'
Euonymus fortunei 'Emerald 'n' Gold'
Fuchsia magellanica 'Versicolor'
Hedera helix varieties
Ilex × altaclarensis varieties
Ilex aquifolium varieties
Ruta graveolens 'Variegata'
Sambucus nigra 'Variegata'
Vinca major 'Variegata'
Weigela florida 'Variegata'

SHRUBS WITH YELLOW FOLIAGE

Acer japonicum 'Aureum'
Arundinaria viridistriata (syn. *Pleioblastus auricoma*)
Berberis thunbergii 'Aurea'
Chamaecyparis lawsoniana varieties
Heathers (some)
Philadelphus coronarius 'Aureus'
Ribes sanguineum 'Brocklebankii'
Sambucus nigra 'Aurea'
Sambucus racemosa 'Plumosa Aurea'
Spiraea japonica 'Gold Flame'

SHRUBS WITH PURPLE OR RED FOLIAGE

Acer palmatum f. *atropurpureum*
Acer palmatum 'Dissectum Atropurpureum'

Berberis × ottawensis 'Purpurea'
Berberis thunbergii 'Atropurpurea'
Corylus maxima 'Purpurea'
Cotinus coggygria 'Notcutt's Variety' & 'Royal Purple'
Photinia × fraseri 'Red Robin' (young leaves)
Pieris formosa forrestii 'Wakehurst' and 'Forest Flame' (young leaves)
Sambucus nigra 'Purpurea'
Weigela florida 'Foliis Purpureis'

SHRUBS WITH SCENTED FLOWERS

There's much argument over which flowers in the garden are scented and which are not. I firmly believe that fragrance is in the nose of the inhaler—some scents seem overpowering to one nose and feeble to another. The few plants listed here should delight all olfactory glands. Any that are not listed can come as a gentle surprise to you!

Buddleja
Choisya
Daphne
Hamamelis
Lavandula
Mahonia
Myrtus
Osmanthus
Philadelphus
Rhododendron (some)
Sambucus
Sarcococca
Skimmia
Syringa
Viburnum (some)

5 Hedges

In the quest for privacy (and perhaps to keep the dog in too) you'll be tempted to plant a hedge, but before you do, make sure you know what you're letting yourself in for. The effect will be pleasing if you choose the right plant, but there are snags too.

On a very small plot a tall hedge can cut out light, so avoid planting a vigorous grower if your garden is very narrow. A deciduous hedge (one that loses its leaves in autumn) will let in just a bit more light in winter to brighten shady sites. The roots of any hedge will rob nutrients from adjacent flower borders—privet is a real brute in this respect and in my last garden I made vertical slits with a spade in the soil alongside the hedge and inserted old roofing slates to keep back the roots. In these circumstances additional feeding of the border plants helps them to win the battle.

The most labour-intensive job of all is clipping—most hedges need at least two cuts a year, and one or two (such as privet) will sometimes need three if you're a real stickler for neatness—I'm not!

But in spite of all that, hedges are still planted and still appreciated. You can soon tire of looking at a close-boarded fence, and so many of them pop up on housing estates nowadays that the whole place takes on the appearance of a cattle market packed with pens. Fencing is pricey too.

A hedge will cut down wind, screen you from eyesores and the eyes of your neighbours, cut down noise and act as a lush green backdrop to other garden plants. It's also a haven for many forms of wildlife, from stick insects and moths to birds and mammals. With country hedgerows disappearing at the rate of hundreds of miles a year, planting a hedge will help to conserve a vanishing habitat. Wood-boring beetles are the only form of wildlife supported by a fence.

Don't think of a hedge as always being formally clipped. Some shrubs planted as hedges will grow best if lightly trimmed to shape rather than clipped flat, and many of them offer bright flowers and cheerful berries in addition to the usual leaves. One of these hedges is a far better bet in a small garden than the ubiquitous privet—the magpie of the plant world. Table 2 (p. 62) offers suggestions for hedges that are colourful in leaf, flower and fruit. If your hedge has to act as a barrier to livestock (domestic or farm) go for a thorny one that will make a dense thicket. The table offers recommendations here too.

HEDGE PLANTING

Just like trees, hedges are usually in one place for a very long time. They say you can calculate the age of a hedge in the countryside by the number of different species of tree or shrub that are present—each one counts as a hundred years, so if you see a hedge with five different shrubs in it then it's 500 years old. A well-prepared planting site right at the start will give the hedge that kick in the pants it needs to establish itself with a view to outlasting you.

Time of planting is as for trees and shrubs—November to March for bare-root plants; September or April and May for bare-root or balled evergreens; and any time of year for container-grown plants (provided the soil is not dust-dry, frozen or muddy). Just as with other shrubs and trees, the roots of hedging plants should never be allowed to dry out. Heel them in (see p. 24) if they arrive before you are ready to plant.

One of the quickest and most successful ways to plant a hedge is to prepare a strip of ground along the line the hedge is to take. With bamboo canes and string, mark out a 60 cm (2 ft) wide strip of the required length. Dig it, working in two handfuls of bonemeal to each running 30 cm (1 yd) and any organic matter you can lay your spade on. There's great satisfaction to be obtained from digging such a long, narrow strip because you can motor on at a rate of knots. When the strip is dug you can let it settle for a few days. Alternatively you can dig a trench along the line and return the soil at planting time, but don't let too much time elapse or the trench will become a muddy ditch.

Having decided on the type of hedge you want you'll have to locate the plants, and here one thing is vital—they should be young. Don't waste your money on tall plants just because they'll look good immediately after planting. Smaller plants will settle in much more quickly and even overtake taller ones after only a year or two. What's more they'll make a thick barrier right down to ground level, and that's the most important requirement of any hedge. They'll be cheaper too. So settle for plants about 1 ft high, and buy enough to plant at the distance recommended in the table on p. 62. Most hedges are created by planting a single row of plants, but if you want to make an exceptionally dense thicket plant two staggered rows 38 cm (15 in) apart.

Table 2

Hedge Plants

	Planting distance (m)	Years taken to grow to 1·5 m	Formal clipped	Informal pruned	Prune with shears/trimmers	Prune with secateurs	Prune May	Prune August	Prune after flowering	Prune after fruiting	Evergreen	Deciduous
Aucuba japonica (Spotted laurel)	0·6	5	●	●	●	●		●			●	
Berberis darwinii (Barberry)	0·45	6	●	●	●		●		●		●	
Berberis × stenophylla (Barberry)	0·45	5	●	●	●		●		●		●	
Buxus sempervirens (Box)	0·3	8	●		●		●	●			●	
Buxus sempervirens 'Suffruticosa' (Dwarf box)	0·23	0·3 m max.	●		●		●	●			●	
Carpinus betulus (Hornbeam)	0·3	6	●		●			●				●
Chamaecyparis lawsoniana varieties (Lawson cypress)	0·6	5	●		●			●			●	
Corylus maxima 'Atropurpurea' (Purple-leafed hazel)	0·6	4	●	●	●	●		●				●
Cotoneaster simonsii	0·45	5	●	●	●	●				●	●	
Crataegus monogyna (Hawthorn, Quick)	0·3	7	●		●		●	●				●
× Cupressocyparis leylandii (Leyland cypress)	0·75	3	●		●			●			●	
Escallonia rubra var. macrantha	0·45	4	●	●	●	●			●		●	
Euonymus japonicus	0·45	6	●		●			●			●	
Fagus sylvatica (Beech)	0·3	5	●		●			●				●
Forsythia × intermedia 'Spectabilis' (Golden bells)	0·45	4	●	●	●	●			●			●
Fuchsia magellanica	0·3	5		●		●	●					●
Ilex aquifolium varieties (Holly)	0·45	8	●		●	●				●	●	
Lavandula varieties (Lavender)	0·3	0·6 m max.		●		●		●	●		●	
Ligustrum ovalifolium (Privet)	0·3	4	●		●		●	●			●	
Lonicera nitida	0·3	5	●		●		●	●			●	
Metasequoia glyptostroboides (Dawn redwood)	0·6	5	●		●			●				●
Olearia × haastii (New Zealand daisy bush)	0·3	7		●		●			●		●	
Pittosporum tenuifolium	0·45	5		●		●	●				●	
Potentilla fruticosa	0·45	0·9 m max.		●		●	●					●
Prunus × cistena (Purple-leaf sand cherry)	0·3	5		●		●			●			●
Prunus laurocerasus (Cherry laurel)	0·6	3	●	●	●	●		●			●	
Pyracantha rogersiana (Firethorn)	0·45	4		●		●				●	●	
Rhododendron ponticum (Common rhododendron)	0·6	5	●	●	●	●			●		●	
Rosa eglanteria (Sweet briar)	0·45	3		●		●				●		●
Rosa rugosa (Ramanas rose)	0·45	5		●		●				●		●
Rosmarinus officinalis (Rosemary)	0·45	1·2 m max.		●		●	●				●	
Tamarix gallica (Common tamarisk)	0·3	4		●		●	●					●
Taxus baccata (Yew)	0·6	8	●		●			●			●	
Thuja plicata varieties (Western red cedar)	0·6	5	●		●			●			●	
Ulex europaeus (Gorse)	0·45	6		●		●	●		●		●	
Viburnum tinus (Laurustinus)	0·45	5	●	●	●	●	●				●	

Rig up a garden line along the strip to be planted and take out a hole for every plant (unless you're using the trench method). Trim broken roots from bare-root plants and spread out the remainder in the hole (Fig. 14). Return the soil, firming it into place with your feet, so that the old soil mark on the stem of the plant is just below the new soil level. Water container-grown plants an hour before planting. At planting time, remove the container and tease out any in-growing roots. Don't disturb the rest of the rootball. Plant so that the top of the rootball is just below the surface of the soil. Don't stint on the firming—really put the boot in. If you leave the soil light and fluffy the roots might dry out, or on heavy soils the trench will act like a sump for the surrounding drainage water, drowning the roots.

Good flowers	Good foliage	Good fruits	Thorny	Good by seaside	Good on chalk	Good on clay	Good on cold and windy sites	Good on dry soil	Details
	●	●			●	●			Shiny green leaves sometimes spotted yellow. Victorian effect.
●	●		●		●	●	●	●	Dark green thicket plastered with orange flowers in April/May.
●	●		●		●	●	●	●	Another thicket-former; quite dog-proof. Orange flowers April/May.
	●				●	●		●	Dense barrier of round, dark green leaves. Good variegated variety.
	●				●	●		●	Neat miniature for edging formal beds. Superb around kitchen garden.
	●				●	●	●		A pleasant alternative to beech. Good, plain green leaves.
	●				●	●		●	Varieties like 'Green Hedger' are particularly good. Good yellow forms.
	●				●	●	●	●	Bold leaves of dark plum-purple. Don't overdo it.
●	●	●		●	●	●	●	●	Boring green leaves but super white flowers and orange berries.
●	●	●	●	●	●	●	●	●	Thick and dog-proof. Flowering and fruiting restricted by pruning.
	●			●	●	●	●	●	Don't use this unless you've room to spare. Quick and dense.
●	●			●	●	●		●	A marvellous hedge with shiny leaves and pink flowers in summer.
	●			●	●	●	●	●	Shiny green leaves, splashed with yellow in variety 'Aureopictus'.
	●				●	●	●		Common but lovely. Bright green leaves in spring; russet in autumn.
●	●				●	●	●		A bit overdone but unsurpassed for spring brightness of yellow blooms.
●	●				●	●			Graceful and colourful with cerise and purple flowers in summer.
	●	●	●	●	●	●	●	●	Avoid the dark green types which can be oppressive.
●	●			●	●			●	Superbly aromatic dwarf hedge for paths and borders. 'Hidcote' is best.
	●				●	●		●	Overplanted and greedy. Plant the golden form if you have to.
	●			●	●	●	●	●	A bit dull but reliable. Tiny, glossy, oval, evergreen leaves.
	●				●	●		●	Unusual. Feathery foliage of fresh green. Super autumn colour.
●	●			●	●	●		●	Leaves dark green above, grey beneath. White daisy flowers.
	●			●	●	●		●	Shiny, wavy-edged leaves. An attractive evergreen.
●	●			●	●	●	●	●	A tumbling charmer with yellow, orange, white or red summer flowers.
●	●				●	●	●	●	Purple leaves and white spring flowers. Best kept to around 90 cm (3 ft).
●	●	●			●	●	●	●	Victorian favourite. Shiny and green and good in the right place.
●	●	●	●	●	●	●	●	●	Dark evergreen leaves; thorny stems; cream flowers summer, orange berries winter.
●	●					●	●		Dingy of leaf but bright of flower in spring. Good in shade.
●	●	●	●	●	●	●			Deliciously aromatic leaves and pink flowers followed by hips.
●	●	●	●	●	●	●			Fresh green leaves, mauve flowers, bright hips. Thorny as hell.
●	●			●	●	●		●	Aromatic leaves—use prunings in cooking. Blue flowers in spring.
●	●			●	●	●	●	●	Wispy leaved and beautiful. Fluffy pink flowers in summer. Try it.
	●				●	●	●		Dark green or gold variegated. Poisonous to cattle. Dense.
	●				●	●			Aromatic feathery foliage, shinier than Lawson cypress.
●	●			●	●	●	●	●	Bright yellow flowers smother impossibly thorny stems in spring.
●	●			●	●	●	●	●	Boring evergreen leaves brightened with white flowers in winter to spring.

Water the plants in if the soil is at all dry, and in spring spread a 5 cm (2 in) mulch of leafmould, pulverized bark, well-rotted compost or manure over the soil—if you've any to spare. If not, keep a close watch on the soil and turn on a sprinkler to soak the earth whenever it looks dry. Drought will put paid to all your good work.

Autumn-planted hedges will need to be re-firmed into contact with the soil after frosts have lifted them—failure to boot them back in may result in death due to the roots drying out.

HEDGE CARE

Immediately after planting, most hedging shrubs should be pruned to produce really dense growth at ground level. Forget to do this and you'll have a

Fig. 14 Hedge planting (*a*) Dig a 60 cm (2 ft) wide trench along the line to be occupied by the hedge and fork some compost or manure into the base. (*b*) Trim back any thick or damaged roots on bare-root plants and keep them in a bucket of water until you're ready to plant. (*c*) Stand each plant where it is to be planted and feed back the soil, firming it with your foot. The old soil mark on the stem should match the new soil level.

gappy hedge later on. Really vigorous growers such as privet, hawthorn, blackthorn, snowberry, tamarisk and *Lonicera nitida* should be cut back to within 15 cm (6 in) of ground level. Hornbeam, beech, hazel and flowering currant should have all their shoots cut back by one third of their length. Yew, laurel, holly, gorse, osmanthus, laurustinus and all conifers should have their sideshoots shortened a little but their leading or topmost shoots should be left intact.

All other plants are best relieved just of long and straggling shoots which should be cut back to a bud or leaf near the base of the offending stem.

Subsequent clippings may have to be carried out twice a year—May and August are the best times. The traditional pruning tool for hedges is a pair of garden shears which will make a neat job on most shrubs. If you can't rely on your eye when clipping, stretch a taut length of twine between two stakes to mark the cutting line (Fig. 15). Aim to create a hedge that is a little narrower in cross section at the top than it is at the bottom. That way it will cast less shade and will be less likely to suffer snow damage. Don't be

frightened of clipping hard in the early years—it will encourage the hedge to thicken up. The top surface of the hedge should also be trimmed back a little each time, even though it has not yet reached the required height. If you don't do this the hedge will be even more likely to suffer from snow damage—its stems giving way under the lightest powdering.

Electric trimmers really do make life easier by clipping at a fast rate, but take care—one false move and you'll have made a hole in your hedge! Wear the cable of the trimmer over your shoulder to keep it out of the way of the blade, or, better still, invest in one of the special harnesses that can be worn to hold the cable out of the way. Both shears and trimmers should be oiled after use and rubbed down with emery paper to free them of dried sap which glues the blades together.

Shears or electric trimmers are essential for clipping formal hedges with straight outlines, but informal hedges such as tamarisk, fuchsia, olearia, escallonia, cotoneaster and large-leaved plants such as laurel and aucuba are best pruned with secateurs—

unwanted stems being snipped out above a bud or leaf. Where such hedges are very long then shears or trimmers can be used but some sacrificing of form will have to be faced. Flowering hedges are always best pruned immediately after their blooms have faded—unwanted wood can be removed and the plants will still have time to produce stems which will carry next year's flowers. Berry-bearing hedges should be clipped after the fruits have fallen.

If you really hate hedge clipping then try one of the new hedge growth retardants. These come in liquid form and are diluted in water and sprayed on to the hedge a few weeks after the spring clipping. No further pruning is then needed until the same time the following year. There are restrictions on the types of hedge that can be treated with these chemicals, so check the information on the label before you buy. It is also difficult to use them effectively where the hedge abuts a flower border—only on paths and drives or lawn perimeters will they be really useful.

Hedge clippings are difficult to dispose of. They won't really compost because they're too woody, and they produce foul smoke if burned. There are two ways of getting round this: either ferry them to the local tip in your car (or have a gentle word with your dustman to see if he's amenable to shifting bagfuls of clippings) or dry them out in a corner of the garden and then burn them. I'm not a great fan of garden fires, but if the material is crisp and dry it burns without too much smoke and will not make you unpopular with your neighbours.

Try to keep your hedge bottoms clean—pull out any weeds that grow there and any waste paper that has lodged among the branches.

RENOVATION

If you take on a battered old hedge that's riddled with holes you'll want to know what to do with it. Some hedges, such as laurel, privet and yew, will regenerate (produce new shoots) when cut back really hard into old wood. Others, such as box and most conifers, won't. Once the inner parts of conifer branches have gone crisp and brown there's little you can do to perk

Fig. 15 If you don't trust your eye when it comes to clipping the top of a hedge, fasten a taut line between two posts and cut to this.

them up. It's far easier to dig out the plants and replant with something else after enriching the soil—provided you're not averse to hard labour.

All hedges can be propagated exactly as for other shrubs (see p. 38), but there's a trick of growing privet in particular which any miser should know of. Get hold of some clippings from the hedge—shoots that are firm and woody and about 30–45 cm (1–1½ ft) long are ideal—and strip off the lower leaves. Push the shoots into the soil for one third of their length along the line the hedge is to take. Stick one shoot in every 15 cm (6 in). Unless you're really out of luck (or you let the soil dry out) you'll soon have a privet hedge where once you pushed in your prunings.

But privet should be one of your last choices; look for something a little different that's going to offer you more than a green fence. Steer clear, too, of Leyland cypress (× *Cupressocyparis leylandii*) unless you've bags of room to spare. Where there's room for it to grow it looks a treat, but in tiny gardens it soon outstays its welcome and fills the plot with gloom.

6 Climbers and wall plants

Houses without climbers always look naked to me. I think too many home owners worry about the effect of roots on their foundations and tendrils on their mortar, but if the right plants are chosen and trained properly the only worry will be an extra spider or two in your bedroom.

Trees and some vigorous shrubs can certainly move foundations, but all the plants I've recommended here can safely be planted right up to your walls. Only on badly mortared walls (which should be repointed anyway) and on pebbledash will clinging climbers ever do any damage. If your house is pebbledashed, rig up a support system that will take the weight of the plant so that the rendering does not peel off in one large sheet.

Mind you, don't think that walls and fences are the only place for climbing plants. They can also be used to cover screens that hide the compost heap, to smother an unsightly garden shed, and to scramble through old and decrepit fruit trees that you can't bring yourself to chop down.

Arches and pergolas (a series of linked arches) are still found in gardens, but it's time the arbour made a comeback. This ancient nook appeared in every garden at one time—a corner where carefree and colourful climbers made their way over an open-roofed structure under which lovers billed and cooed. If you've a sun-dappled corner of the garden that needs brightening up, try making a three-sided enclosure of white-painted trellis fastened to stout posts (Fig. 16). Several rails across the top will make a 'roof' over which fragrant honeysuckle, colourful clematis or mysterious wisteria can drip in summer.

Smaller gardens can sport climbers on rustic pole tripods (Fig. 17) among border plants, or in pots and tubs which can be equipped with stout cane tripods of their own or placed against walls fitted with horizontal wires or trellis. And remember that many flimsy climbers like clematis can simply be grown alongside other garden shrubs and allowed to scramble through them (Fig. 18). It's not a system for tidy-minded gardeners, but it's one for greedy gardeners who can prolong the season of interest of a shrub when its own blooms have faded.

Take into account the habit of any climber or wall plant before deciding where you will grow it. Some of the plants recommended here are twiners, others have sticky pads or aerial roots that need a flat surface to hold on to; yet more simply scramble and ramble over a support system, and some won't climb at all— they just enjoy the sheltered atmosphere a wall provides.

SITE AND SOIL

There are climbers for walls of all aspects—sunny and shady—and I've given specific recommendations in the A–Z section. What all the plants have in common is a desire for good growing conditions when they are first planted. Your kindness to them in their youth will nearly always be repaid by good growth later in life.

The soil against a house wall is almost always bone dry because it's in what's known as a 'rain shadow' area. Dig it well before you plant and enrich it with plenty of leafmould, pulverized bark or, better still, well-rotted manure or garden compost. A dusting of blood, bone and fishmeal will also give encouragement to the roots.

If climbers are to be grown in tubs, give them a good compost—such as John Innes No. 3 potting compost—over a drainage layer of pebbles. Make sure there are plenty of holes in the base of the tub to allow drainage, and make the container as large as possible if you want the plant to be in residence for some time. It's a good idea to remove some of the old compost each spring and replace it with fresh—take off the top 8 cm (3 in).

PLANTING

Plant your climbers from pots and you can put them in at any time of year but they'll grow away best if introduced to their new site in spring when the soil is still a little moist. Bare-root climbers can be planted in autumn, but if the plant is the slightest bit tender, wait until spring.

General planting instructions are as for trees and shrubs, but set the plants about 30 cm (1 ft) away from the tree, shrub, wall, trellis or arch that is to act as the support system. That way the roots have a little more room to explore.

Plant when the soil is moist and water in the plant if necessary. Lay a 5 cm (2 in) thick mulch of organic matter immediately planting is completed to keep in moisture and keep down weeds.

Fig. 16 The arbour has slipped out of fashion and it's high time it made a comeback. Build a three-sided trellis screen around a patio or a corner of the lawn. Roses, clematis, honeysuckle and other fragrant climbers can be trained over the structure to create a secluded, scented haven.

SUPPORTING

On walls and fences self-clinging climbers such as ivy will need no help at all (though you can paint the surface with manure-water if they refuse to cling at first). Other plants will need to be provided with either horizontal wires held at 30 cm (1 ft) intervals, or with trellis. I prefer the wire system. It's cheaper and longer-lasting than trellis. Drill and plug the wall, then insert galvanized screw eyes which will support horizontal strands of plastic-covered wire (Fig. 19a). If your house wall is painted and will have to be re-painted in future, trellis supports will be better. Fasten the trellis to a batten frame which can be hinged against the wall at the base and held with butterfly catches at the top (Fig. 19b). When painting is necessary the entire framework can be carefully swung away from the wall—most climbers are more flexible than you might think.

TRAINING AND PRUNING

All plants will need to be trained against the support system and their stems spaced out and tied in. I find that wire twist-ties (similar to the kind sold for sealing freezer bags) are the most convenient things to use.

Fig. 17 Climber-covered tripods (*a*) will give instant height to flat borders. Rustic arches (*b*) can brighten gateways, and series of linked arches becomes a pergola

(*c*) and makes a flower-covered walkway that will lead feet and eyes to other parts of the garden.

Pinch out the shoot tips of young plants to encourage a branching habit and good wall coverage.

Detailed instructions on pruning are given in the A–Z section, but remember to use a sharp pair of secateurs or loppers and to cut back without fail to a healthy bud or just above a leaf.

AFTERCARE

Don't, whatever you do, let the soil around the plant dry out during its first year of establishment. Soak it with a hosepipe when necessary and keep the mulch in place. Apply a fresh mulch each spring.

A good feed of a general fertilizer each April will work wonders—use tomato fertilizer to coax any

Fig. 18 Before you chop down a gnarled and delapidated tree, consider training a rampant climber through it to brighten its boring boughs.

flowering climber to bloom more freely (it contains lots of potash which is necessary for flower and fruit formation).

A–Z OF CLIMBERS AND WALL PLANTS

Here you'll find some real beauties, valued in leaf, fruit and flower. Don't stick solely to the common stuff, experiment a little with something unusual. All these plants will give value for money, but I've done my best to point out the drawbacks where they exist.

Abutilon vitifolium   3–9 m (10–30 ft)
A little tender it might be, but this abutilon is a treasure worth risking. The leaves are maple shaped and covered in soft down, and the mallow flowers are a delicate shade of lilac, darker in the variety 'Veronica Tennant', white in 'Album'. All three bloom in early summer and lose their leaves in winter.
Aspect South or west. *Likes* sun and shelter and a rich, well-drained (but not dry) soil. *Tolerates* clay, dry and chalky soils and coastal exposure. Sometimes short lived. *Prune* out dead stems in spring and remove faded flowerheads. *Propagate* by sowing seeds in heat during January, or by rooting cuttings of stem tips in a propagator in summer.

Actinidia kolomikta   1·8–2·4 m (6–8 ft)
and occasionally up to 6 m (20 ft)
This climber needs patience. In the right spot, and when it's settled in, it will turn the tips of its green, heart-shaped leaves bright pink and white. Quite a spectacle. The flowers are insignificant and the leaves deciduous.
Aspect South or west. *Likes* a sheltered, sunny spot and well-drained soil. *Tolerates* clay and dry soils; enriched chalky soils. *Prune* out unwanted growths in summer. Shorten sideshoots to two or three buds in winter and remove a few older stems, replacing them with young ones which should be tied in. *Propagate*

Fig. 19 (*a*) Stout horizontal wires fastened to the surface of a wall by metal vine eyes make a cheap, sturdy and unobtrusive support system for climbing plants. (*b*) On surfaces that have to be painted, climbers can be trained against a trellis framework that can be swung away from the wall on hinges.

by rooting shoot tip cuttings in a propagator in summer, or by layering suitable shoots, also in summer.

Camellia japonica varieties   3 m (10 ft)
I've talked about *C. × williamsii* (which I think is a better plant for general garden cultivation) on p. 41, but the varieties of *C. japonica* are worth growing on sunny walls (though not those which face east or the early morning sun might damage frosted buds). Their glossy evergreen leaves show off well the waxy double or single flowers of red, white, pink or magenta which appear in spring. Rely on your nurseryman to suggest suitable varieties from his stock.

Aspect North, south or west. *Likes* well-drained, lime-free soil enriched with peat and leafmould. Apply diluted iron sequestrene in spring if the leaves are a bit yellow. *Tolerates* clay soil and sheltered coastal gardens. *Prune* out only unwanted or badly placed shoots in spring. Shorten spindly shoots of older plants by half at the same time. *Propagate* by taking leaf bud or shoot tip cuttings in summer and rooting them in a propagator.

Carpenteria californica   Californian
Mock Orange   1·8–2·4 m (6–8 ft)
Not a climber, but a tender shrub deserving a sheltered spot. The leaves are oval and evergreen and the large, papery white flowers are centred with a boss of yellow stamens. One of the scented pleasures of midsummer.

Aspect South or west. *Likes* light, well-drained soil, shelter and full sun. *Tolerates* dry or chalky soil and sheltered coastal gardens. *Prune* out one or two older branches and any dead shoots in spring. *Propagate* by shoot tip cuttings rooted in a propagator in summer. Seeds can be sown under glass in spring.

Ceanothus   Californian Lilac
2·4–3 m (8–10 ft)

The upright habit of the ceanothuses makes them a good choice for walls. *C.* 'Delight' is a spring flowerer, and *C.* 'Autumnal Blue' adds colour to the latter part of the year. Both have rough, tiny ever-green leaves and soft blue powderpuff flowers.

Aspect South or west. *Likes* sunny, sheltered spots and a well-drained soil. *Tolerates* dry or chalky soil and sheltered coastal gardens. *Prune* the flowering shoots back by half their length when the blooms have faded. Cut out dead stems in spring. *Propagate* by rooting shoot tip cuttings in a propagator in summer.

Chaenomeles   Japonica, Japanese Quince,
Cydonia   1·2–3 m (4–10 ft)
Indispensable spring flowers. Varieties of both *C. speciosa* (the earliest to flower, often starting in winter), and *C. × superba* are showy. All are de-ciduous and have appleblossom-shaped flowers of red, white or pink. Among the best varieties of *C. speciosa* are: 'Brilliant', scarlet; 'Moerloosii', pink and white; and 'Nivalis', white. *C. × superba* is especially good (and popular) in its variety 'Knap Hill Scarlet'. Most produce aromatic fruits that make sumptuous jelly.

Aspect North, south, east or west. *Likes* a sunny site if possible, and well-drained soil. *Tolerates* dry, clay or chalky soil. *Prune* by shortening the sideshoots back to two or three buds after flowering. *Propagate* by layering in spring or by rooting firm shoot tips in a propagator in summer.

Clematis   The Queen of Climbers,
Virgin's Bower   3 m (10 ft) plus
No garden should be without its complement of clematis, scrambling up walls, through trees and shrubs and over arches and pergolas. There are dozens of different varieties, most of them deciduous, which produce their wide-faced single or double flowers at various times during spring and summer. Here's my pick of the large-flowered hybrids (for the

final group number see under Pruning):
'Barbara Dibley'—magenta; May, June and Sept. 2
'Barbara Jackman'—lavender, striped magenta; May, June and September. 2
'Comtesse de Bouchard'—rose pink; June–Aug. 3
'Elsa Spath'—lavender blue; May, June and Sept. 2
'Ernest Markham'—magenta; June to September. 3
'Etoile Rose'—deep pink, quartered bells with paler edges; June to September. 3
'Hagley Hybrid—shell pink; June to September. 3
C. 'Jackmanii Superba'—violet purple; July to September. 3
'Lasurstern'—lavender blue with wavy edges; May, June and September. 2
'Marie Boisselot'—pale pink to white; May to October. 2
'Nelly Moser'—pale pink striped magenta; May, June, August and September. 2
'Vyvyan Pennell'—bluish mauve; double in May and June, single in September. 2

For covering buildings, C. montana is a rampant white-flowered species, most frequently planted in its pink form var. rubens. Both are gloriously scented (1). C. tangutica offers the best value of any clematis. It produces masses of bright yellow lantern flowers in summer and these are followed by fluffy spherical seedheads which persist through the winter. Grow it through a shrub or over a shed (3).
C. macropetala produces nodding double blooms of lavender blue and white in May and June. It looks delightful in tubs and large pots (1).

Aspect North, south, east or west. *Like* their roots in cool, moist soil. Place flagstones or gravel over the soil surrounding them. Most prefer their heads in the sun. *Tolerate* clay or chalky soil; sheltered coastal gardens. *Prune* the plants according to the group they are in: Group 1: Prune only when they are becoming overgrown. Remove shoots that have carried flowers and any dead growth as soon as the blooms fade. Group 2: Remove dead or damaged stems in March and cut back all the rest to a pair strong buds. Group 3: Cut all stems back to a healthy pair of buds 3 ft above ground level in March. Remove completely any damaged stems.
Propagate by layering firm stems in summer, or by taking internodal cuttings and rooting these in a propagator in summer.

Note: Clematis wilt may result in rapid collapse of the entire plant. Cut out any affected stems and spray the plant with a copper fungicide. The plant should soon re-grow (even if it has to be cut back to ground level). Give all varieties time to settle in before expecting masses of flower. Three years may have to elapse before they really feel at home.

Cotoneaster horizontalis   Fishbone
Cotoneaster   1·8–2·4 m (6–8 ft)
Planted against a wall this cotoneaster sidles up against it to quite a height, spreading out its fans of symmetrical branches. It decorates them with tiny green leaves in summer and red berries in autumn and winter.

Aspect North, south, east or west. *Likes* ordinary well-drained soil. *Tolerates* dry, chalky or clay soil and coastal exposure. *Prune* out only unwanted or overcrowding stems in spring. *Propagate* by rooting cuttings of firm shoot tips in a propagator in summer.

Cytisus battandieri   Moroccan Broom
3–3·6 m (10–12 ft)
Take a sniff at the bright yellow cockade-like blooms of this open-growing broom and you'll detect the aroma of freshly cut pineapple. Early summer is the time of flowering, and the blooms are carried at the tips of stems that are clad in silky-haired deciduous leaves. Bees love it.

Aspect South or west. *Likes* full sun and a sheltered spot in well-drained soil. *Tolerates* dry, clay or chalky soil and sheltered coastal gardens. *Prune* out one or two of the oldest stems each winter, and any that grow straight out from the wall. *Propagate* by sowing seeds in spring, or by taking cuttings of firm shoot tips in summer and rooting them in a propagator.

Eccremocarpus scaber   Chilean Glory
Flower   3 m (10 ft)
Easy to grow and especially lovely when rambling through other shrubs. The green foliage is ferny and the tubular flowers are burning orange, decorating the plant from summer to autumn.

Aspect South or west. *Likes* sun and shelter and light, well-drained soil. *Tolerates* dry or chalky soil; coastal exposure. *Prune* out dead wood in spring. The plant will be killed back to soil level in severe winters. *Propagate* from seeds sown in heat during spring.

Fremontodendron californicum
Fremontia   3 m (10 ft)
A tender evergreen for gambling gardeners. The lobed leaves are a dreary dull green but the starry yellow flowers that appear in summer will make up for the foliar deficiency. Very classy.

Aspect South or west. *Likes* full sun and shelter and a well-drained soil. *Tolerates* dry or chalky soil and sheltered coastal gardens. *Prune* only to remove badly placed or dead branches in spring. Severe winters may see it off. *Propagate* by seeds sown in heat in spring, or by cuttings of firm shoot tips rooted in a propagator in summer.

Garrya elliptica   Silk Tassel Bush
3·6 m (12 ft)
Funereal in leaf but fabulous in flower, the Silk Tassel Bush produces living icicles of bloom in winter. The grey-green catkins can be 15 cm (6 in) or more long and show up well against the deep evergreen foliage. A superb plant to floodlight.

Aspect North, south, east or west. *Likes* a sheltered spot in a well-drained soil. *Tolerates* dry, clay or chalky soil and coastal exposure. It may suffer in severe winters. *Prune* out only dead or out-growing, unwanted branches in spring. *Propagate* by layering low-hanging stems in autumn; by taking cuttings of firm shoot tips in summer and rooting them in a propagator.

Hedera Ivy 6 m (20 ft) plus

Valuable evergreens with leaves that may be finely cut, crimped or splashed with cream and yellow. They cling by means of tenacious aerial roots—avoid planting them against pebbledash which they may pull off. The small-leaved ivies are varieties of *H. helix* and among the best for walls are:

'Buttercup'—young leaves bright yellow.
'Chicago'—green leaves burnished purple.
'Glacier'—green leaves edged with white.
'Gold Heart'—dark green leaves with a central yellow splash.
'Parsley Crested'–green leaves with wavy edges.
'Sagittifolia'—dark green fingered leaves.

The lengthy-named *H. colchica* 'Dentata Variegata' is a larger-leaved variety with foliage attractively splashed and marbled with bright creamy yellow. All lend colour and form to the garden, especially in winter.

Aspect North, south, east or west. *Likes* almost any soil and situation. *Prune* mature plants by clipping them back with a pair of shears in spring every other year. *Propagate* by rooting shoot tip cuttings in a propagator or outdoors in summer. Low-hanging shoots can be layered at any time of year.

Hoheria lyallii 3 m (10 ft) plus

Not half so widely grown as it should be, this shrub is just a little tender and so benefits from being sheltered by a wall. The oval green leaves are deciduous but make a fine backdrop for the thick array of scented white flowers in summer. Try it in the open in sheltered gardens.

Aspect South or west. *Likes* sun and a well-drained soil. *Tolerates* dry or chalky soil and coastal gardens. *Prune* out dead wood and one or two older stems each spring. *Propagate* by sowing seeds in gentle heat in spring, by layering in summer, or by rooting cuttings of firm shoot tips in a propagator in summer.

Humulus lupulus 'Aureus'
Golden-leafed Hop 4·5 m (15 ft)

This deciduous twiner is a stunning sight in spring and summer when its acid-yellow vine-shaped leaves decorate the questing stems. Good for brightening up dingy corners, and superb with green-flowered euphorbias.

Aspect South, east or west. *Likes* rich, well-drained soil and sun. *Tolerates* enriched clay, dry or chalky soil. *Prune* away all dead growth in spring—it usually dies back to ground level in winter. *Propagate* by division or seed in spring.

Hydrangea petiolaris Climbing Hydrangea
Up to 15 m (50 ft)

If you like the bushy hydrangeas, then you must have a go with the climbing type. The leaves are similar but the stems are rather more tortuous and equipped with aerial roots that enable them to cling to walls. Large white flowerheads open in June.

Aspect North, south, east or west. *Likes* rich and well-drained soil. *Tolerates* well-enriched dry, chalky or clay soils; coastal exposure. *Prune* out only unwanted or dead stems in spring. *Propagate* by taking cuttings of firm shoot tips and rooting them in a propagator in summer.

Jasminum nudiflorum Winter Jasmine
3·6 m (12 ft)

You'll see it squirting through fences in cottage gardens all over the country, and billowing from walls where it makes a thick mattress of stems. The bright yellow blossoms are especially welcome, for they push out well in advance of the leaves any time from November to March.

Aspect North, south, east or west. *Likes* almost any soil and situation. *Prune* out flowered shoots immediately after blooming; that way you'll prevent the build-up of that thick mattress of flowerless wood. *Propagate* by layering or by rooting hardwood cuttings in the open ground in autumn.

Lathyrus latifolius Everlasting Pea
2·4 m (8 ft)

Here's something that makes a change from the annual sweet pea—it's a perennial version that will last for years. The foliage is typically pea-like, and the winged flowers are pink or white. Sadly it lacks the powerful fragrance of its annual relations.

Aspect South, west or east. *Likes* rich, well-drained soil and sun. *Tolerates* clay or chalky soil. *Prune* to ground level each autumn. *Propagate* by division or seeds in spring.

Lippia citriodora (syn. Aloysia triphylla)
Lemon Verbena, Aloysia 1·2 m (4 ft)

Never much to look at, this is a shrub valued for its strong citrus scent—crush the leaves and you'll get the full impact. It doesn't climb but certainly appreciates the shelter a wall can give. The leaves are deciduous (and useful for making pot-pourri) and the pale lilac flower spikes are pleasing, though hardly spectacular, in summer.

Aspect South or west. *Likes* sun and shelter and a light, well-drained soil. *Tolerates* dry or chalky soil and coastal situations. *Prune* back dead stems to suitable buds in spring. Hard winters will kill the bush to ground level but it usually sprouts from below the surface. A winter mulch of dry bracken or straw will help to preserve it. *Propagate* by rooting cuttings of firm shoot tips in a propagator in summer.

Lonicera   Honeysuckle, Woodbine
6–9 m (20–30 ft)
The common honeysuckle (and there is none better) is *L. periclymenum*, sold in two varieties: Early Dutch ('Belgica') and Late Dutch ('Serotina'). The first carries its pale yellow, pink-flushed flowers in May, June, and again in September, and the second blooms continuously from July to September. Both are deciduous. If you want an evergreen, try *L. sempervirens* with orange and yellow trumpet flowers. Sadly it lacks the fragrance of its leaf-losing relations. *L. japonica* 'Aureoreticulata' is a good honeysuckle for foliage—its semi-evergreen leaves are oval, fresh green and netted with yellow veins. All these honeysuckles will scramble and twine over anything put in their way.

Aspect L. periclymenum likes a south- or west-facing position; the other two will tolerate any aspect. *Like* rich, well-drained soil and shelter. *Tolerate* enriched clay, dry or chalky soil. *Prune* out older, flowered growths of *L. periclymenum* and *L. sempervirens* immediately after flowering. Clip back *L. japonica* 'Aureoreticulata' each spring. *Propagate* by layering or by taking cuttings of firm shoot tips and rooting them in a propagator in summer.

Magnolia grandiflora   Bull Bay,
Laurel Magnolia   12 m (40 ft)
Now here's a stately wall plant. The leaves, as the second common name suggests, are evergreen and rather like those of laurel except that they often have the additional attraction of russeting on the undersides. You'll have to wait a good many years for the waxy cup-shaped flowers of creamy white to appear, but the plant is still good to look at even when out of flower. The variety 'Exmouth' will bloom earlier in its life than the true species and flowers during summer and autumn. The blooms are scented (if any are within sniffing distance). For large walls only.

Aspect South or west. *Likes* rich, well-drained soil and a sheltered spot. *Tolerates* enriched clay, dry or chalky soils. *Prune* out only dead or badly placed branches in spring, otherwise leave it alone. *Propagate* by spring layering.

Parthenocissus   Virginia Creeper,
Boston Ivy   12 m (40 ft) plus
The true Virginia creeper is *P. quinquefolia* with much divided green leaves that turn brilliant crimson before falling in autumn. *P. tricuspidata*, Boston ivy, is perhaps the better plant for most walls for it clings more efficiently, needing no support at all. The true Virginia creeper needs a few horizontal wires to give its scrambling stems a bit of a hand. Boston ivy has another advantage too—its maple-shaped leaves are glossy and even better equipped to show off their fiery autumn tints. Keep both plants away from pebbledash.

Aspect North, south, east or west. *Likes* well-drained soil and a bit of sun for the best autumn colour. *Tolerates* clay, dry or chalky soil. *Prune* in winter clipping back any stems that are growing away from the wall and shortening any that are venturing where they are not wanted. *Propagate* by layering in summer, or by rooting cuttings of firm shoot tips in a propagator in summer.

Passiflora caerulea   Passion Flower
6 m (20 ft) plus
In spite of its exotic appearance, the passion flower does well in many sheltered British gardens. It is a rampant climber, equipped with tendrils to speed it on its way. The hand-shaped leaves are evergreen and the white, blue-centred flowers are produced in summer, followed by orange, egg-shaped fruits if the weather is kind. They are edible but pippy. The 'Passion' referred to is Christ's passion, not some aphrodisiac property of the fruit. The five petals and five sepals represent the Apostles (minus Judas and either Doubting Thomas or Peter), the blue frill of filaments represents the crown of thorns, the five anthers the wounds, three stigmas the nails, the hand-shaped leaves are the hands of His persecutors and the tendrils the whip with which He was scourged.

Aspect South or west. *Likes* sun, shelter and a well-drained soil. *Tolerates* dry or chalky soil and sheltered coastal gardens. *Prune* in spring cutting back any long, trailing growths to within 10 cm (4 in) of the main stems. *Propagate* by cuttings of shoot tips which can be rooted in a propagator in summer.

Phygelius capensis   Cape Figwort
1·2–1·8 m (4–6 ft)
A pretty-flowered shrub that enjoys the protection of a warm and sunny wall. The leaves are unremarkable, but the flowers that appear in branched heads at the stem tips during summer are a jolly sight, little tubular red jobs like tiny trumpets. Tied in, the stems will grow to around 1·8 m (6 ft). Severe winters will kill them back to soil level.

Aspect South or west. *Likes* sun, shelter and well-drained soil. *Tolerates* dry or chalky soil and coastal exposure. *Prune* back to ground level or to breaking buds each spring. *Propagate* by removing suckers in spring, by sowing seeds in warmth in spring, or by rooting shoot tip cuttings in a propagator in summer.

Polygonum baldschuanicum (now **Fallopia baldschuanicum**)   Russian Vine, Mile-a-Minute
6 m (20 ft) plus
The fastest climber of all, but one I could only recommend to the desperate gardner. It produces a rampant thicket of twining stems and a fluffy mass of creamy-white flowers in summer and autumn. The arrowhead shaped leaves are deciduous, leaving you to look at a matress of brown stems in winter. But if you want a rapid grower—it puts on a good 4·5 m (15 ft) each year—you can give it a go; for a couple of months in summer it does look quite charming

Aspect North, south, east or west. *Likes* almost any site and soil. *Prune* by clipping back any unwanted stems in early spring. *Propagate* by rooting hardwood cuttings outdoors in autumn, or by rooting cuttings of firm shoot tips in a propagator in summer.

Pyracantha   Firethorn   4·5 m (15 ft)

Here's a plant that gives good value for money. The dark leaves are evergreen; creamy white flowers are produced in summer and are followed in autumn and winter by a heavy crop of berries: red in *P. atalantioides*, orange in *P. coccinea* 'Lalandei', and yellow in *P. rogersiana* f. *flava*. The birds love the berries, but then if you enjoy their company what does it matter? Yellow berries are the last to be taken.

Aspect North, south, east or west. *Like* ordinary well-drained soil. *Tolerate* dry, clay or chalky soil and coastal exposure. *Prune* out only those stems that outgrow their allotted space. Prune after flowering but watch those thorns. *Propagate* by rooting cuttings of firm shoot tips in a propagator in summer.

Ribes speciosum   Fuchsia-flowered Gooseberry   2·4 m (8 ft)

Tiny red tubular flowers, each with a central tuft of stamens, decorate the gooseberry-like stems of this wall shrub in spring, making it look as if it were hung with rosy icicles. The green lobed leaves fall in winter, but the spring show makes cultivation well worth while.

Aspect South or west. *Likes* sun and shelter and well-drained soil. *Tolerates* dry or chalky soil. *Prune* out any dead and one or two older stems each winter. Shorten to two or three buds any shoots that grow out from the wall in summer. (Be careful; the stems are thorny.) *Propagate* by hardwood cuttings in autumn or by inserting cuttings of firm shoot tips in a propagator in summer.

Solanum crispum   Chilean Potato-tree 7–8 m (25 ft)

A pretty scrambler with purple and yellow tomato flowers any time between June and September. It looks delightful when allowed to wander through *Abutilon vitifolium*. The best variety is 'Glasnevin'—hardier and even longer flowering than the true species. The foliage is deciduous and certainly nothing to write home about but that doesn't matter if the plant is trained through another.

Aspect South or west. *Likes* sun, shelter and a light, well-drained soil. *Tolerates* dry or chalky soil and sheltered coastal gardens. *Prune* in spring, shortening all sideshoots to three or four buds. Cut out dead or unwanted stems at the same time. Such precise pruning is not necessary where the plant is grown through a shrub or tree. *Propagate* by rooting cuttings of firm shoot tips in a propagator in summer.

Tropaeolum speciosum   Scotch Flame Flower 3 m (10 ft) plus

At Hidcote Manor in Gloucestershire, England, and Powys Castle in Wales you'll find dreary yew hedges brought alive by this nasturtium relative that loves to scramble through them. The fresh green hand-shaped leaves are almost as attractive as the tubular scarlet flowers; both are at their best in summer and autumn. The plant dies down completely in winter.

Aspect North walls and the shady side of shrubs. *Likes* the cooler northern counties and a moist soil enriched with leafmould and peat. *Tolerates* coastal gardens. *Prune* by cutting away all dead growth in winter. *Propagate* by division or sow seeds in a frame in spring.

Vitis   Vine   6 m (20 ft) plus

If you want a grape you can eat on a plant that's ornamental, go for *V. vinifera* 'Brandt' (or, more correctly, *V.* 'Brant'). The leaves burnish well in autumn, and the black grapes are delicious at the end of a good summer. For bold foliage colour you'll not do better than the gross *V. coignetiae* which has massive vine leaves coated in a light down. They turn vivid shades of orange and crimson before they fall to the ground in autumn.

Aspect South or west. *Like* sun and a rich soil. *Tolerate* enriched clay or chalky soil. *Prune* by shortening the sideshoots to 8 cm (3 in) in winter. Can be left unpruned if growing rampantly over arbours and through trees. *Propagate* by layering in spring or autumn or by rooting cuttings of firm shoot tips in a propagator in summer.

Wisteria sinensis   Chinese Wisteria 15 m (50 ft)

This plant brings back fond memories for me; it enveloped our first house, dangling its scented lilac-purple flower trails outside our windows so that the air was permanently scented during May. The deciduous leaves are pinnate (like those of an ash tree) and make a handsome fresh green covering for a house wall in summer even when no flowers are showing. There's a second, lighter flush of bloom later in the summer. Give it a go over tall tree stumps, arches and pergolas and be patient—it may take a few years to settle in. Correct pruning (and an occasional feed of tomato fertilizer) can force young plants to flower more easily. If your plant still refuses to bloom after about five years, dig it up and replace it with a wisteria that's known to have been grafted from a free-flowering parent. Some forms are just shy of flowering and a real waste of time. Good ones are stupendous.

Aspect South or west. *Likes* sun, shelter and a well-drained soil. *Tolerates* dry and chalky soil. *Prune* first in July—shortening all unwanted shoots to about 15 cm (6 in). Prune again in January, shortening all sideshoots to four buds. *Propagate* by layering in spring or summer. Cuttings of firm shoot tips can be rooted in a propagator in summer.

FIND THE RIGHT CLIMBER

If you're looking for a plant that will grow on a wall of a particular aspect, or through an old tree, the following lists should give you some ideas. Plants suitable for different soils are also indicated, as are those with pronounced scents: climbers are especially welcome when they perfume the rooms around which they grow.

PLANTS FOR NORTH-FACING WALLS
Camellia
Chaenomeles
Clematis
Cotoneaster
Garrya
Hedera
Hydrangea
Jasminum
Lonicera (some)
Parthenocissus
Polygonum
Pyracantha
Tropaeolum

PLANTS FOR SOUTH- OR WEST-FACING WALLS
Abutilon
Actinidia
Camellia
Carpenteria
Ceanothus
Chaenomeles
Clematis
Cotoneaster
Cytisus
Eccremocarpus
Fremontodendron
Garrya
Hedera
Hoheria
Humulus
Hydrangea
Jasminum
Lathyrus
Lippia (syn. Aloysia)
Lonicera
Magnolia
Parthenocissus
Passiflora
Phygelius
Polygonum (syn. Fallopia)
Pyracantha
Ribes
Solanum
Vitis
Wisteria

PLANTS FOR EAST-FACING WALLS
Chaenomeles
Clematis
Cotoneaster
Garrya
Hedera
Humulus
Hydrangea
Jasminum
Lathyrus
Lonicera (some)
Parthenocissus
Polygonum (syn. Fallopia)
Pyracantha

PLANTS FOR DRY SOILS
Abutilon
Actinidia
Carpenteria
Ceanothus
Chaenomeles
Cotoneaster
Cytisus
Eccremocarpus
Fremontodendron
Garrya
Hedera
Hoheria
Humulus
Hydrangea
Jasminum
Lippia (syn. Aloysia)
Lonicera
Magnolia
Parthenocissus
Passiflora
Phygelius
Polygonum (syn. Fallopia)
Pyracantha
Ribes
Solanum
Wisteria

PLANTS FOR CHALKY SOILS
Abutilon
Actinidia
Carpenteria
Ceanothus
Chaenomeles
Clematis
Cotoneaster
Cytisus
Eccremocarpus
Fremontodendron
Garrya
Hedera
Hoheria

Humulus
Hydrangea
Jasminum
Lathyrus
Lippia (syn. Aloysia)
Lonicera
Magnolia
Parthenocissus
Passiflora
Phygelius
Polygonum (syn. Fallopia)
Pyracantha
Ribes
Solanum
Vitis
Wisteria

PLANTS FOR CLAY SOILS
Abutilon
Actinidia
Camellia
Chaenomeles
Clematis
Cotoneaster
Cytisus
Garrya
Hedera
Humulus
Hydrangea
Jasminum
Lathyrus
Lonicera
Magnolia
Parthenocissus
Polygonum (syn. Fallopia)
Pyracantha
Vitis

PLANTS FOR COASTAL GARDENS
Abutilon
Camellia
Carpenteria
Ceanothus
Clematis
Cotoneaster
Cytisus
Eccremocarpus
Fremontodendron
Garrya
Hedera
Hoheria
Hydrangea

Jasminum
Lippia (syn. Aloysia)
Passiflora
Phygelius
Polygonum (syn. Fallopia)
Pyracantha
Solanum
Tropaeolum

CLIMBERS TO GROW THROUGH TREES AND SHRUBS
Clematis
Eccremocarpus
Humulus
Lathyrus
Parthenocissus
Passiflora
Polygonum (syn. Fallopia)
Solanum
Tropaeolum
Vitis
Wisteria

PLANTS WITH SCENTED FLOWERS
Carpenteria
Clematis (some)
Cytisus
Hoheria
Lonicera
Magnolia
Wisteria

PLANTS WITH EVERGREEN LEAVES
Camellia
Carpenteria
Ceanothus
Fremontodendron
Garrya
Hedera
Lonicera (some)
Magnolia
Passiflora
Pyracantha

PLANTS FOR WINTER INTEREST
Chaenomeles
Cotoneaster
Garrya
Hedera
Jasminum
Pyracantha

7 Roses

A friend of mine swears that roses grow in spite of their owners. Perhaps that's why most gardeners hold roses dear to their hearts, but they also have romantic connections, delectable scents, glorious colours and one hundred and one uses.

Before you can even begin to choose a rose for your garden you really ought to know the different types that are available. Rose classification can legitimately be called a thorny problem; there are many different groups of plants and a new classification system has just been adopted. For me and the average gardener life can be a little simpler, so here's my offering which I hope is reasonably clear and capable of ensuring that you come away from the nursery or garden centre with the right plant:

Hybrid tea roses (Fig. 20*a*) The buffs now call these 'large-flowered roses'. The blooms are fat and fully double and are usually carried in small numbers at the tip of each stem. They will bloom from early summer until the frosts—and sometimes beyond—and the flowers tend to come in flushes. The type to grow for winning prizes.

Floribunda roses (Fig. 20*b*) Now correctly known as 'cluster-flowered roses', here are the bushes with much-branched flower clusters at the stem tips and usually rather smaller blooms. But don't make the mistake of thinking that all floribundas are single—some of them have decidedly double flowers. The difference is in the size and quantity of flowers. They flower almost continuously through the summer but are usually slightly less vigorous than the hybrid teas. They are easily the best choice for bedding.

Standard roses (Fig. 21) These are simply hybrid tea or floribunda roses (and very occasionally shrub roses) grown on a single, tall stem. They are used as specimen roses to add height to low plantings and should be individually supported by a $2 \cdot 5 \times 2 \cdot 5$ cm (1×1 in) stake which finishes just below the head of branches. Two proprietary ties should hold stem to stake. To my eye they look too artificial, but they do make rose-sniffing an easier pastime for elderly gardeners who have trouble bending down!

Miniature or **'patio' roses** Don't think that these are house plants. They might come in pots but they will turn into spindly, fly-ridden thickets if you grow them indoors for any length of time. Planted out at the edges of beds and borders, on patios and in tubs and windowboxes they will perform well, making wiry little shrubs that are peppered with flowers right through the summer. They usually grow between 15 and 45 cm (6 and 18 in) high. The secret of growing miniatures well in containers is to keep the compost gently moist at all times and to give the plants plenty of light.

Climbing roses These are roses with long and questing stems which can be trained around arches, over pergolas and up walls. There are several different groups of climbing roses, the most useful of these being the 'repeat-flowering climbers' which will bloom right through the summer, unlike most rambler roses and many other climbers. The so-called 'climbing sports' were all derived from hybrid tea or floribunda roses which, for some reason best known to themselves, suddenly sent up a climbing shoot from an otherwise stocky bush. Eagle-eyed gardeners over the years have spotted these shoots and propagated from them and we now have plenty of climbing sports, all of which can be easily spotted because they are simply referred to as 'Climbing Ena Harkness' or 'Climbing Iceberg'. Sadly, climbing sports do not flower as freely as the bushes from which they were propagated. They usually have one large flush of flowers in early summer. I'll talk about pruning later, but the important thing about the climbing sports is that they should not be pruned too hard, otherwise they might lose their climbing ten-

Fig. 20 Hybrid tea, or large-flowered roses (*left*) are full centred and carried in small numbers on each stem; floribundas (*right*) or cluster-flowered roses, carry more blooms.

Fig. 21 Standard roses will give welcome height to flat floral displays. They are simply hybrid tea or floribunda varieties budded on to a tall stem.

dency. Climbers in general tend to have stiffer stems than ramblers.

Rambling roses Like the climbers these are useful where they can be planted against tall supports but preferably not against walls where the lack of air circulation can encourage mildew. They are especially good when planted at the base of old fruit trees and allowed to scramble through the branches above, giving them what appears to be a new lease of life. The stems of ramblers are sometimes more supple than those of climbers, but, as explained above, the flush of flowers is usually confined to a grand burst in early summer, and the blooms are usually relatively small.

Shrub roses Here are to be found roses old and roses new; roses of history and wild species. The term 'shrub roses' is a sensible one, for these plants should be grown as shrubs and not as rose bushes. They vary tremendously in shape and size and have minimal pruning requirements, and as a general rule they are dead easy to grow. Many of them have disease-resistant foliage, attractive fruits or 'hips' (don't be conned by the pernickety into calling them heps), flowers that are fully double or moon-faced and single, and the deepest, most complex scents imaginable. Modern roses have not lost the scent for which nostalgic gardeners yearn; many of them are as highly

fragrant as a cheap tin of talcum powder. What they lack is the thick, sweet aroma which only the old roses seem to possess. The disadvantages of shrub roses are two-fold. First, many of them have just one flush of bloom—in early summer. Second, many of them are large and look out of place in small gardens. But there are plenty of exceptions to both these rules; there are repeat-flowering, and continuous-flowering shrub roses, and some that grow no more than 1 m (3 ft) high and as much across. You may have guessed from my enthusiasm that I rather like these roses.

USING ROSES

I've covered some of the many uses of roses in the foregoing explanation of the groups, but just to make sure that you know where they can be used here are some suggestions:

In windowboxes and tubs—miniatures.

As hedges—shrub roses, especially the rugosas and hybrid musks and some gallicas such as 'Rosa Mundi'. (I apologize for the inclusion of more complicated names, but the shrub roses are a mixed and motley band.)

Through trees—climbers and ramblers.

Up walls, screens, arches and pergolas—climbers and ramblers.

In beds—hybrid teas and especially floribundas. Always most effective when planted in large numbers of a single variety.

In borders—hybrid teas, floribundas and shrub roses used as shrubs.

As ground cover—low-growing and miniature varieties. They are compact and spreading in habit, and sometimes root where they touch the ground. The best bloom throughout summer into autumn. Look for the County Series, such as 'Avon' (pearl white), 'Kent' (white) or 'Hampshire' (scarlet).

WHERE TO PLANT

There are a few roses that can tolerate shade, but in general they like an open, sunny spot that's sheltered from wind at a distance. You'll often be told to avoid planting roses in frost pockets—those dips in the land that collect cold air. But something's got to be grown there and quite honestly roses are more reliable in such situations than most plants.

The other common myth is that roses need heavy soil to do really well. In reality they'll thrive on any soil if you perk it up a bit before planting. You can double dig the site if you really feel better for such exercise, but single digging is all that's necessary on most reasonable soils. Good drainage is essential, as it is for most plants, and work in as much organic matter as you can spare—compost, manure, or even crumbly leafmould plus a little fertilizer. The plants will be there for a heck of a long time so you might as well make them feel at home right away. I've seen thirty-year-old roses blooming as happily as youngsters in a good soil that's been well prepared and looked after.

Avoid, if you can, planting new roses on ground that's previously been occupied by old roses. The soil might be rather tired and in need of a change of crop.

If there's an ideal pH for roses (see p. 13) then it's in the region of 6·0 to 6·5—where most plants are happy. They'll still grow, though, on chalky earth, but plenty of organic matter will be appreciated.

BUYING THE ROSES

You can buy and plant container-grown roses at any time of year, and the great advantage is that in summer you can see the bush in flower and check it for scent. 'Bare-root roses', like bare-root shrubs, are planted in the dormant season—from November to March. Specialist rose growers despatch most of their plants in this state, and they are undoubtedly the best source of supply if you want unusual varieties and first-class bushes. Pre-packed roses sold in supermarkets and chain stores are not usually available in very wide variety, and they are seldom top quality bushes, but I've had some splendid plants that started life in this way. When it comes to price, the pre-packed roses are cheapest, followed by the bare-root plants. Container-grown roses are slightly more expensive—you'll have to pay for the privilege of planting at any time of year.

If you can see what you're buying, go for a shapely bush with at least three stems. If you can't you'll have to rely on the reputation of the grower. If you buy pre-packed roses, make sure they are fresh in and not starting to sprout in the bag.

HOW TO PLANT

The planting technique is exactly the same as that adopted for trees and shrubs (see p. 24). Climbers and ramblers that are to be planted against walls, pillars or old trees should be given the same kind of support system and treatment as any other climber (see pp. 67–68). Plant hybrid tea and floribunda roses 60 cm (2 ft) apart when they are massed together in beds. Allow shrub roses sufficient room for their indicated spread.

ROSE PRUNING

The pruning of roses need not be the confusing job that it's made out to be. Approach your bush with the courage of your convictions, a sharp pair of secateurs and a clear idea of what you're setting out to achieve. The different kinds of roses are pruned as follows:

Hybrid teas Immediately after planting bare-root hybrid tea roses, shorten all stems to 8 or 10 cm (3 or 4 in). It seems cruel but it will force them into producing a healthy framework of new stems (Fig. 22). Make clean cuts just above an outward-facing bud (all you'll see at this stage are little red dots). Container-grown roses planted during spring and summer are treated as mature plants by their first

winter and are pruned between January and March as follows: first remove all dead wood, then any weak, diseased or crossing stems. Leave a cup-shaped framework of well-spaced branches. Cut all these stems back to just below knee height, preferably just above an outward-facing bud. Remove one or two old branches from ageing plants every year so that a relatively young framework is built up. If you can't find an outward-facing bud don't worry; find one that points anywhere other than right into the centre of the bush. The cardinal rule with all rose pruning is that cuts must be made cleanly and just above a bud; torn cuts will allow in disease, and long snags will simply die back.

Floribundas Prune at the same time as hybrid tea roses, but not quite so low. Prune newly planted bare-root bushes back to 15 cm (6 in) and established bushes to just above knee height. Otherwise the technique is exactly the same.

Standard roses Depending on whether the variety is a hybrid tea or a floribunda, prune the head of branches exactly as for bush roses (taking a guess at what is knee height).

Miniatures and ground cover Other than the removal of dead or weak stems, or shortening over-long stems in March, they need little or no pruning.

Shrub roses It's possible to make a real mess of shrub roses by pruning them, so I leave them entirely alone, apart from trimming away dead shoot tips in spring. Occasionally, old stems can be cut out completely, and it's a good idea to remember that total removal of a branch is always likely to produce a more shapely plant than if a branch is cut back by half or a third of its length. There are occasional exceptions to this rule, but not many. 'Rosa Mundi', for instance, can be grown as a small hedge and trimmed back by one third in spring to keep it neat. On most other varieties you can be much more circumspect.

Climbing roses There are several distinct groups of climbers, as I've said, and they all need slightly

Fig. 22 To prune a bush rose: cut out any dead stems, then any that are diseased, weak or crossing the centre. Reduce the well-spaced framework that remains to knee height or just below.

different pruning if you want to be really precise. However, it's possible to prune them all in the same way and get away with it, provided you're not too heavy handed. Simply cut off any dead shoot tips in March, and shorten any sideshoots that have previously carried flowers; cut them back to about 10 cm (4 in). One or two very ancient stems can be removed each year, but only when they are exhausted and flowering poorly. If in doubt, don't cut it out!

Rambling roses Most ramblers are pruned immediately after flowering, when a few very old and gnarled stems are cut out completely at ground level and new ones trained in to replace them. If not many new ones have appeared, simply cut back lateral shoots that have flowered to within 10 cm (4 in) of the main stem. Hefty ramblers such as 'Kiftsgate' need not be pruned so drastically (in fact you'll have a job to get at them if they're running through a tree). Trim out visible dead wood.

WATERING

Fortunately roses are deep rooted and, once established, are capable of resisting mild spells of drought more than most shrubs. Soak the earth around them thoroughly during the first spring and summer after planting whenever it shows signs of drying out. Turn on a sprinkler if you can, but if this is not possible, give each plant a couple of gallons of water from a can. In succeeding years the plants will only need soaking when drought threatens. It does pay off and can prevent the flowering season from coming to an abrupt end.

FEEDING

Like all plants that are generous with their blooms, roses like you to be generous with the fertilizer. Give them a good helping of general fertilizer such as blood, bone and fishmeal in April, scattering it on to the soil at the rate of two handfuls around each bush. In June a specially prepared rose fertilizer based on the Tonks formula will help to give them a boost. One handful to each bush will be sufficient. Hoe both helpings into the top few inches of soil. The general fertilizer supplies all the major nutrients, but the Tonks contains extra magnesium and potash which keeps the bushes healthy and free flowering.

MULCHING

Just as with other shrubs, a mulch laid around your roses will keep in moisture, keep down weeds and generally boost plant health. Pulverised bark or garden compost can be used but well-rotted manure is certainly most enjoyed.

DEADHEADING

Unless the flowerheads eventually produce decorative hips, snip them off to save the plant's energy and keep up appearances. Cutting the blooms of

Fig. 23 Suckers are shoots that emerge from the rootstock of the rose—the briar. Remove them as soon as you see them by tearing them from their point of origin.

hybrid teas actually encourages them to form a second flush of flowers. If you don't cut the blooms for indoor decoration, a bit of light summer pruning won't go amiss—shorten the stems a little when the first flowers have faded.

SUCKER REMOVAL

Most roses are budded by the nurseryman on to a rootstock or briar because they can be grown to a saleable size more quickly in this way. Any shoots that emerge from the rootstock will be different in character and appearance from those that arise from the stems above ground. They can usually be differentiated from legitimate shoots by their paler colouring, lack of bronzing and, sometimes, by the presence of more leaflets (though this does not always hold good). Remove suckers as soon as they are seen or they will swamp the bush. Scrape away the soil at the base of the plants until the junction of sucker and rootstock can be seen. Tear away the sucker so that no part of it is left behind (Fig. 23).

RENOVATING

Old bushes that have been allowed to grow unchecked can get into a sorry state. Ancient hybrid teas and floribundas can be renovated, if you fancy a challenge, simply by cutting out a portion of old and gnarled wood each year until sufficient new stems have been produced to take over completely. Shorten them gradually each year, until they can be pruned to around the regulation knee height. You'll have to be a bit patient but the results should be worthwhile.

WEEDING

Mulching is the best answer and hoeing the second best—but be careful not to damage the stems or suckers might arise. If you're really idle you can resort to a rosebed weedkiller that can be watered on to freshly cleaned soil with the object of keeping it weed free for an entire season. The trouble is that regular application of the stuff can result in sour soil and damage to the rose stems at ground level. It also stops you growing anything underneath your roses—plants which would, themselves, help to suppress weeds.

UNDERPLANTING

I don't much enjoy looking at bare soil—especially when it can be used to grow more plants. Some rose experts seem to like their rose beds bare of anything except roses, but there's no reason why other low-growing plants should not make a pleasant carpet below them. You can choose all manner of things but

the following are especially good either as edgers or as carpeters:

Alchemilla, Dianthus, Geranium, Pulmonaria, Heuchera, Aubrieta, Arabis, Viola, Lavender (edging) Primula (auriculas and polyanthus), Stachys, Ajuga, Lamium, Nepeta, spring-flowering bulbs.

PESTS AND DISEASES

Roses have their own peculiar band of pests and diseases and some of these occur with such regularity each season that routine spraying is worthwhile. I'm thinking of mildew, blackspot and greenfly (aphids). Other problems that may strike are rust, leaf-rolling sawfly, leaf-cutter bee, pincushion gall, capsid bug, caterpillars, froghopper (cuckoo spit), and die-back. All are covered in Chapter 21 on pests and diseases. There are more, but these are the most commonly

Table 3: Roses

	Height	Spread	Flowers
SHRUB ROSES			
Alchemist	3 m (10 ft)	2·5 m (8 ft)	Warm orangey yellow; confused double centre
Ballerina	1·25 m (4 ft)	1·25 m (4 ft)	Pink with a white eye; masses of small, single blooms
Blanc Double de Coubert	2 m (6 ft)	1·5 m (5 ft)	Pure white; semi-double
Buff Beauty	2 m (6 ft)	2 m (6 ft)	Buff-orange; semi-double
Canary Bird	2 m (6 ft)	2 m (6 ft)	Bright yellow, small, single flowers
Cardinal de Richelieu	1·25 m (4 ft)	1 m (3 ft)	Mauve purple, fading dusky purple; double
Chapeau de Napoleon (Cristata)	1·5 m (5 ft)	1·25 m (4 ft)	Rich rose pink; double; mossy buds
Complicata	2·5 m (8 ft)	2·5 m (8 ft)	Rich rose pink, white eye; single
Cornelia	1·5 m (5 ft)	2 m (6 ft)	Apricot pink; fully double
Fantin-Latour	2 m (6 ft)	1·5 m (5 ft)	Pale pink; flattened double
Fru Dagmar Hastrup	1·25 m (4 ft)	1·5 m (5 ft)	Pale pink; single; large red hips
Fruhlingsgold	2·5 m (8 ft)	2 m (6 ft)	Bright primrose yellow; semi-double
Fruhlingsmorgen	2 m (6 ft)	1·5 m (5 ft)	Rich pink with primrose yellow eye; single
Golden Chersonese	2 m (6 ft)	1·5 m (5 ft)	Bright yellow; single
Königin von Dänemark	1·5 m (5 ft)	1·25 m (4 ft)	Pale pink; double, quartered blooms
Lady Penzance	2 m (6 ft)	2 m (6 ft)	Bright rose pink, tuft of yellow stamens; single; good hips
Maiden's Blush	1·5 m (5 ft)	1·5 m (5 ft)	Blush pink; double, quartered blooms
Marguerite Hilling	2·25 m (7 ft)	2·25 m (7 ft)	Warm pink; semi-double
Max Graf	60 cm (2 ft)	2 m (6 ft)	Rich pink, tuft of yellow stamens; single
Mme. Hardy	1·5 m (5 ft)	1·5 m (5 ft)	Pure white, green button-eye centre; double
Mme. Pierre Oger	1·25 m (4 ft)	1·25 m (4 ft)	Shell pink; double and cupshaped
Nevada	2·25 m (7 ft)	2·25 m (7 ft)	Creamy white; semi-double
Pink Grootendorst	1·25 m (4 ft)	1 m (3 ft)	Rich pink, small flowers in clusters; double and frilly
Reine des Violettes	2 m (6 ft)	2 m (6 ft)	Violet purple; double, quartered, button-eyed
Rosa gallica 'Versicolor' (Rosa Mundi)	1·25 m (4 ft)	1·25 m (4 ft)	Cerise-pink, striped white; semi-double
Rosa moyesii 'Geranium'	2·5 m (8 ft)	2·5 m (8 ft)	Bright red; single; scarlet, flask-shaped hips
Rosa rubrifolia (Rosa glauca)	2·25 m (7 ft)	2·25 m (7 ft)	Rich pink, white eye, yellow anthers; small, single; good hips
Roseraie de l'Hay	2 m (6 ft)	1·5 m (5 ft)	Rich magenta; fully double
Scabrosa	1·25 m (4 ft)	1·25 m (4 ft)	Mauve pink, yellow stamens; single; good hips
Stanwell Perpetual	1·5 m (5 ft)	1·5 m (5 ft)	Blush pink; double

occurring disasters.

Routine spraying with one product that controls the big three—mildew, blackspot and aphids—is now possible. Start in April, as growth commences, and repeat at the recommended intervals. Watch for early infestations of aphids which, if left untreated, will cause horrible distortions of leaves and flowers.

PROPAGATION

Although the nurseryman propagates his roses by budding, it's much easier for the home gardener to increase his stock by taking hardwood cuttings in September or October. The plants may take a little while to come into flower (some of my shrub roses have taken five years) but there is no problem with suckers and the technique is cheap and easy. All you need is patience. Full details can be found on p. 219.

It is also easy to propagate climbers and ramblers by layering (see pp. 220–221).

A–Z OF ROSES (Table 3)

Out of the thousands of roses available, these are the ones I'd take with me to a desert island. Other gardeners will have different favourites, but in my roses I look for vigour and shapeliness of the bush, good flower colour for as long a season as possible, and a sigh-provoking scent. Roses which have leathery, disease-resisting foliage should be chosen whenever possible. Now and again one or two of these attributes have to be sacrificed if a plant is stunning in other ways. I make no apologies for the fact that the shrub rose list is longer than the others—I love them best.

Flowering Time	Foliage	Distance apart for Hedging	Suitable for Shade	Suitable for Ground Cover	Scent	Disease Resistance
Repeat	Rich green				★★★	★★★
Repeat	Glossy green	60 cm (2 ft)			★	★★
Repeat	Rough, rich green	60 cm (2 ft)	▲		★★★	★★★
Repeat	Purplish green	1 m (3 ft)			★★	★★
Late spring	Light green; ferny	1 m (3 ft)	▲		★	★★★
Early summer	Dull green				★★★	★★
Midsummer	Mid green				★★	★★
Early to midsummer	Mid green	1 m (3 ft)	▲		★	★★★
Repeat	Deep bronze green	1 m (3 ft)			★★★	★★★
Early summer	Dull green	1·25 m (4 ft)			★★	★★
Repeat	Rough, bright green	1 m (3 ft)	▲	▲	★★	★★★
Early summer	Light green	1 m (3 ft)	▲		★★	★★★
Early & late summer	Dull green	1 m (3 ft)	▲		★★	★★★
Late spring	Mid green; ferny				★★	★★★
Early summer	Pale green	60 cm (2 ft)	▲		★★★	★★★
Early summer	Apple scented	1 m (3 ft)	▲		★★★	★★★
Early summer	Grey-green	1 m (3 ft)	▲		★★★	★★★
Early & late summer	Mid-green	1 m (3 ft)			★	★★★
Midsummer	Mid-green		▲	▲	★★	★★★
Midsummer	Mid-green				★★★	★★★
Repeat	Pale green				★★	★
Early & late summer	Mid-green	1 m (3 ft)			★	★★
Repeat	Rough, rich green	60 cm (2 ft)	▲			★★★
Repeat	Grey-green	1 m (3 ft)	▲		★★★	★★★
Midsummer	Light green	60 cm (2 ft)				★
Early summer	Mid-green					★★★
Midsummer	Blue grey, purple tinged	1 m (3 ft)	▲			★★★
Repeat	Rough, rich green	1 m (3 ft)	▲		★★	★★★
Repeat	Rough, rich green	1 m (3 ft)			★★	★★★
Repeat	Grey-green		▲		★★	★★★

Table 3: Roses—*continued*

	Height	Flowers	Foliage	Scent	Disease Resistance
HYBRID TEAS					
Alec's Red	1 m (3 ft)	Deep, rich red	Glossy green	★★★	★★★
Ena Harkness	75 cm (2½ ft)	Dark, velvety crimson; necks sadly weak	Mid-green	★★	★★
Fragrant Cloud	1 m (3 ft)	Geranium red is the best description	Deep glossy green	★★★	★★
Grandpa Dickson	1 m (3 ft)	Light yellow and massively full	Deep glossy green	★	★★★
Just Joey	75 cm (2½ ft)	Coppery orange, veined red	Deep green	★	★★★
Mischief	1 m (3 ft)	Warm salmon pink	Mid-green	★	★★
Pascali	1 m (3 ft)	The best white hybrid tea	Glossy green	★	★★
Peace	1·5 m (5 ft)	Massive pale yellow blooms edged pink	Deep glossy green	★	★★★
Piccadilly	75 cm (2½ ft)	Carmine red above; yellow beneath	Glossy purplish green	★	★★★
Precious Platinum	1 m (3 ft)	Brilliant, rich red	Glossy green	★	★★★
Rose Gaujard	1 m (3 ft)	Rich pink above; white beneath	Deep glossy green	★	★★★
Silver Jubilee	75 cm (2½ ft)	A mixture of pinks	Glossy green	★	★★★
Wendy Cussons	1 m (3 ft)	Rich cerise pink; very vibrant	Deep glossy green	★★★	★★★
Whisky Mac	75 cm (2½ ft)	Rich, coppery orange	Purplish green and glossy	★★★	★★
FLORIBUNDAS					
Allgold	60 cm (2 ft)	Bright yellow; double	Glossy green	★	★★★
City of Belfast	60 cm (2 ft)	Bright scarlet; double	Glossy green	★	★★★
Evelyn Fison	75 cm (2½ ft)	Bright scarlet; double	Deep glossy green	★	★★
Eye Paint	1·25 cm (4 ft)	Masses of small red flowers with white eyes; single	Glossy green		★★
Iceberg	1·25 cm (4 ft)	Plenty of pure white flowers; double	Glossy green		★★
Lilli Marlene	75 cm (2½ ft)	Deep red, attractive petal formation; double	Glossy purplish green	★	★★
Margaret Merril	1 m (3 ft)	White with a touch of blush; double	Deep glossy green	★★★	★★★
Pink Parfait	1 m (3 ft)	Rich pink mixture; double	Glossy green		★★★
Queen Elizabeth	2 m (6 ft)	Light pink; fully double; good hedger	Deep glossy green	★	★★★
Southampton	1 m (3 ft)	Coppery orange; double	Deep glossy green	★	★★★
Sue Lawley	75 cm (2½ ft)	Yellow stamens, white eye, rich pink edged white; semi-double	Deep glossy green	★	★★★
Trumpeter	60 cm (2 ft)	Vibrant scarlet; double	Deep glossy green		★★★
Yesterday	1 m (3 ft)	Rich lilac pink and white; semi-double	Glossy green	★★	★★★
MINIATURES					
Angela Rippon	30 cm (1 ft)	Salmon pink; double	Rich green	★	★★★
Baby Faurax	30 cm (1 ft)	Purplish pink; semi-double	Glossy green	★★	★★★
Darling Flame	30 cm (1 ft)	Vivid orange and yellow; double	Glossy green	★	★★★
Josephine Wheatcroft	38 cm (15 in)	Mid-yellow; double	Glossy green		★★★
Magic Carrousel	38 cm (15 in)	White, deeply flushed pink at the edges; double	Glossy green	★	★★★
New Penny	23 cm (9 in)	Rich pink rosette flowers; double	Glossy green		★★★
Snow Carpet	15 cm (6 in)	White, semi-double blooms; a spreader that makes good ground cover	Deep glossy green	★	★★★

Table 3: Roses—*continued*

	Height	Flowers	Flowering Time	Suitable for north walls	Scent	Disease Resistance
CLIMBERS						
Aloha	2·5 m (8 ft)	Rich rose pink; double	Repeat		★	★★★
Bantry Bay	2·5 m (8 ft)	Soft pink; semi-double	Repeat		★	★★★
Compassion	2·5 m (8 ft)	Pink flushed apricot; double	Repeat		★★★	★★★
Climbing Crimson Glory	3 m (10 ft)	Deep red; double	Repeat		★★★	★
Climbing Iceberg	3 m (10 ft)	Pure white; double	Repeat			★★
Danse du Feu	2·5 m (8 ft)	Fiery scarlet; double	Repeat			★★★
Gloire de Dijon	4 m (12 ft)	Buff to pale orange; old-fashioned button-eyed, double blooms	Repeat		★★★	★★
Golden Showers	2·5 m (8 ft)	Bright yellow; double	Repeat		★	★★★
Handel	3 m (10 ft)	White, boldly edged deep pink; double	Repeat		★	★★★
Mermaid	9 m (30 ft)	Yellow with amber stamens; single	Repeat	★	★	★★★
Mme. Grégoire Staechelin	5 m (15 ft)	Rich pink wavy-edged petals; double	E. summer	★	★★★	★★★
Pink Perpetué	2·5 m (8 ft)	Rose pink; double	Repeat		★	★★
Schoolgirl	3 m (10 ft)	Apricot; double	Repeat		★★	★★★
Zéphirine Drouhin	3 m (10 ft)	Cerise pink; semi-double; thornless	Repeat		★★★	★★
RAMBLERS						
Albéric Barbier	5 m (15 ft)	Creamy yellow; double, confused centres	Midsummer		★★	★★★
Albertine	5 m (15 ft)	Pale pink tinged salmon; double	E. Summer		★★★	★★
Félicité et Perpetué	6 m (20 ft)	Globular, creamy white; double	Midsummer		★	★★★
New Dawn	4 m (12 ft)	Pale, blush pink; double	Repeat		★★	★★★
Kiftsgate	9 m (30 ft)	Masses of small, creamy white flowers; single; through trees or as ground cover	Midsummer		★	★★★
GROUND COVER						
Blenheim	1 m (3 ft)	Palest blush, double	Repeat		★★	★★★
Kent	50 cm (20 in)	Creamy white; double	Repeat		★	★★★
Pink Bells	75 cm (30 in)	Clear pink; fully double	Midsummer		★	★★★
Red Meidiland	75 cm (30 in)	Deep red, white eyed, single	Repeat		★	★★★
Suma	60 cm (24 in)	Deep pink; fully double	Repeat		★	★★★

8 Border plants

Shrubs might be the backbone of the garden, but border plants certainly help to flesh out the skeleton. Those that are covered in this chapter are the plants which the gardener calls hardy perennials. 'Hardy' means that they can stay outdoors all the year round, usually putting up with the worst that the British weather can offer; 'perennial' means that they will last indefinitely. True enough there are a few perennials that are short-lived, lasting maybe two or three years, but most of them will outlive you if you treat them well.

Hardy herbaceous perennials form the bulk of the A–Z section, and these are the tough, long-lived plants that die down to soil level each autumn, keeping alive through the winter by means of roots and resting buds at soil level. They might not have the year-round appeal of shrubs, but this gives them a different advantage—they provide seasonal change in the garden so that it's fresh whatever the time of year.

The obvious place for your border plants is a flower bed or border. The traditional herbaceous border has bitten the dust in all but the most stately of gardens, and it's been replaced by the mixed border, where shrubs, bulbs, bedding and border plants keep each other company in a longer-lasting display. The old herbaceous border started its season of glory in late May or June and was spent by September.

There's an awful lot of fuss made about island beds nowadays. These are simply flower beds of regular or informal shape, around which you can walk. Planted up wisely they show off border plants to perfection. The trouble is that there's seldom room for island beds in very small gardens, unless you want to turn your plot into something resembling a traffic round-about. Where space is short, sweeping borders made as wide as possible are the best bet. You'll get plenty of plants into them and they'll be easy to work.

Think carefully before you plant. Consider all the known characteristics of the plant and compare them with the characteristics of its neighbours. Bear in mind its season of flowering, its ultimate height and spread and its foliage form as well as flower colour.

It's a good idea to plant shrubs first and to fill in among them with border plants. The latter are easy to dig up and move when the space they occupy is needed by some expanding shrub. Not only will they tolerate disturbance, but they'll thrive on it. The tattiest border plants are those that are left alone, apart from peonies, agapanthus and one or two others that like to stay in one place for years.

Plan your border for a long display of colour, or for a burst of glory during one particular season. That revered gardener of the Victorian and Edwardian era, Gertrude Jekyll, had borders for every month of the year. Most small gardens would have a job to fit in all twelve, but it's no bad idea to set aside a patch outside a window which can act as a winter border; or another corner that billows with flowers in June.

If you can't or won't do this, make sure that as one plant fades from its season of glory there is another one nearby to take over and delight the eye. And remember that vivid colour isn't everything. A bright, bold bloomer set in front of some handsome or muted foliage shows up far better than half-a-dozen assorted flowers vying for attention.

The popularity of Sissinghurst Castle in Kent, and its 'white garden' in particular, has encouraged more gardeners to plant borders with a single-colour theme. Yellow, red, blue, grey or white schemes are great fun to create, but do make sure that other parts of the garden act as an antidote to these monochrome amusements or they'll bore the pants off you.

Some border plants are stately enough to lend themselves to being planted as individual specimens, others spread into a dense rug or canopy that will smother the weeds and ground once they are well established. Such ground cover planting is useful but it needs efficient maintenance in the early stages. For a start the ground must be dug free of perennial weeds before planting. Watering will have to be attended to and emerging weeds must be removed by hand or hoe until the plants are large enough to do the smothering. Remember, too, that herbaceous ground-cover plants will disappear in winter.

Gravel and cobble beds are great fun, very labour saving and will show off foliage plants to great effect. All you need to do is cultivate the ground, plant your chosen specimens or arrangements, pat the soil level with the back of a fork and then lay 5 cm (2 in) of washed pea shingle or a single layer of large pebbles or cobbles on top (Fig. 24). This will keep down weeds and will always look smart; against a patio a gravel bed looks delightful. When you want to change or add to the planting, scrape away the gravel or lift off the cobbles; do your planting and then replace the stony mulch.

Fig. 24 Foliage plants look especially good when growing in gravel or cobble beds. Plant up the bed, firm the soil and spread a single layer of cobbles or 5 cm (2 in) of washed pea shingle over the surface. Mix the two if you like; the effect is always smart.

THE RIGHT SPOT

You probably won't have much choice when it comes to selecting a site for your bed or border. It's always recommended that hardy perennials are given a spot in full sun and a well-drained soil, but as the lists at the end of the A–Z section show, there are plants for shade as well as sun, and some for heavy clay or chalk. If you can't pick the ideal site, at least pick the plants that are ideal for your particular situation. Versatile as they are, few plants will thrive in really heavy shade cast by trees whose roots riddle the ground, or in very windy places. Only a handful will enjoy growing in really boggy soil. Do your best to improve the earth, whatever its composition.

Making the best of your soil

Just because a plant is said to tolerate dry soil, it doesn't mean that if, on one baking hot summer day, you dig a hole in the dust and plant it it will survive. Every plant needs a chance to establish itself before it can settle down and cope with inhospitable conditions.

Whether you garden on clay, chalk, sand or dust, cultivate the soil well and work in as much well-rotted garden compost, manure, spent hops, mushroom compost, pulverized bark or leafmould as you can afford—a bucketful to each square yard of ground will do nicely. The last two contain few nutrients, so a dusting of general fertilizer can be scattered over them before they are dug in.

Digging or forking is essential—it will enable you to remove thick-rooted weeds as well as letting in air and incorporating the organic enrichment. Living soil full of muck, bacteria and worms produces better plants than sterile, tired earth. Soil can be dug at any time of year, but heavy clay will be easier to work in late summer or early autumn when it's gently moist rather than sodden or baked hard. Leave it in large lumps through the winter and the frost will have broken it down into a more crumbly soil by spring. Sandy soil can be dug in spring—it needs no frost to shatter it and it will only be compacted by winter rains and snow if dug earlier.

You might have heard of the 'no-dig' technique. It sounds appealing. If you decide to make a border without digging or forking the soil you'll first have to kill off the weeds with one or two applications of a total weedkiller such as 'Tumbleweed' (glyphosate). Then an 8 cm (3 in) thick mulch of organic matter will have to be laid on the soil and the border plants planted through this into pockets of enriched earth below. It involves a lot of organic matter and I feel rather sorry for any plant that has to push its roots down into poor, compacted earth before it can think of enjoying life. It's digging for me.

PLANNING

I've never been one for planning gardens on bits of graph paper, but I suppose it does help to sketch out some idea of the scheme when you're planting up a bed or border—then you can juggle the plants around in the cosy comfort of your fireside until you have the effect you want. I've already mentioned the things you should bear in mind when deciding what plant goes where—height, spread, colour, shape, season of flowering—but remember, too, that the most impact is created by large patches of one particular plant. To this end, stately herbaceous borders possess 'drifts' of three, five, or seven plants (odd numbers always seem to be the order of the day) of one particular species. In tiny gardens, or where the collecting bug has bitten, single plants can be used, but the effect will be more like a patchwork quilt. In cottage gardens there's nothing wrong with that.

If you really can't be bothered to plan the scheme you can go to the garden centre and buy what's pretty. Bring the plants home and juggle with them on the soil around your existing border plants; but you'll still have to consider their height, spread and flowering season if you want good results. The garden centre might offer plants in flower, but seldom will it give you the choice that a specialist nursery offers. The larger, specialist firms do a healthy mail order trade, and can be relied on to supply good, healthy plants. They will even replace plants that appear to be dead or damaged on arrival if they are informed immediately. Plan your border and buy the bulk of your plants from a specialist—the garden centre can be used for infillers. If you don't like that idea, then go along to the garden centre for a look round before planning your border to include only the stock they offer.

One final word on planning—consider carefully the shape of the bed or border. It should be as large as your plot will allow and arranged so that its shape can be appreciated. All curves should be gradual—that way they are easy on the eye and on the mower. Lay a hosepipe on the ground to mark out the shape (run hot water through it first if it's a cold day). Take out a strip of turf or a little 'V'-shaped drill to mark the line and then remove the hosepipe before digging. In general tall plants should be set at the back of the border (or the centre of a bed) and shorter ones at the front, but bring a few of the giants forward a little to vary the contours and to create hidden pockets. Even a border should hold a few surprises.

PLANTING

Almost all border plants sold in garden centres will be container grown—this means that they have been growing for some time in the pot in which they are sold. The advantage with this system is that the plants can be planted in your garden at any time of year provided the soil is not frozen, muddy or bone dry. Plants bought from a specialist nursery by mail order, and plants obtained from friends, are usually lifted from the ground in October or November. If your soil is well drained or on the light side this is by far the best planting season, for the plants will have time to sink their roots into the soil and become well established before growing away vigorously next spring. If your soil is heavy, avoid autumn planting. It's better

to wait and get the plants in during spring when drainage is improving, rather than have them sit in a cold quagmire through their first winter.

The planting method for both lifted and container-grown plants is the same. Scatter a handful of blood, bone and fishmeal over each square yard of soil and hoe it in. Make sure the plant's root system, or the compost in the container, is moist, and dig a hole with a trowel that will take all the roots, allowing an 8 cm (3 in) gap all round. Remove the pot if the plant is container grown and sit the rootball in the hole. Any large and obviously ingrowing roots can be gently teased out, but the rest should be left undisturbed. Spread out all the roots of plants that have been lifted from open ground. Replace and firm back the soil with your feet so that the old soil mark on the stem or crown of the plant is level with the new surface. Water the plant in thoroughly if necessary, and don't let the soil around it dry out during the first spring and summer. Plant at a spacing which will allow the plant to grow to its full spread before meeting its neighbour, or plant a little closer and thin out later if you want to achieve the full effect more quickly—it will cost you money, though.

LOOKING AFTER YOUR PLANTS

Don't neglect them once you've bunged them in. Remove any weeds that might compete and water thoroughly with a lawn sprinkler in dry weather (unless the plants are tall or leafy and will be weighed down by water droplets—in this case support a hosepipe fitted with a sprinkler head on the handle of a garden fork and let it play on the surrounding soil.

A sprinkling of blood, bone and fishmeal can be scattered on the soil around the plants in April and again in June if you're feeling generous and can get in to do the job. Hoe it into the surface.

Tall plants such as delphiniums will need individual cane supports for their stems—push a bamboo in by each spike as soon as it's 90 cm (3 ft) tall and gently tie the stem to it as it extends (Fig. 25). Bushier plants can be held up either by proprietary wire plant supports such as Link stakes, or by pushing among them twiggy branches pruned from trees and shrubs in winter. Don't make a forest—just a thin plantation.

There's an excellent method of supporting border plants to be seen at Crathes Castle in Scotland—stout 2·25 cm (1 in) square dahlia stakes run around the border and black nylon netting with a 10 cm (4 in) wide mesh is stretched between the posts right across the border (Fig. 26) at a height of about 45 cm (1½ ft). When the foliage grows through the netting the strands disappear but the plants are well supported. Whatever kind of staking you use, make sure it's in position before the plants need it. You'll never get them to stand up properly once they've fainted. I've indicated in the A–Z section which plants need your support and which can stand on their own feet.

Renovation

Apart from those plants that are indicated as being best left undisturbed, all border plants can be kept in good condition by regular division of the clumps. With age the central portion usually dies out, and every three or four years such clumps should be lifted and divided into pieces as big as your fist before being replanted in freshly enriched soil (Fig. 27). The dead central portions of each clump should be thrown away. Overgrown borders that are inherited when you move house can be completely renovated in this way in autumn or spring.

In winter, when the top growth of herbaceous perennials dies down, go over the border and chop off the stems at ground level. Leave 5 cm (2 in) high stumps and you'll stab your fingers when you come to do the job next year. One or two tender plants can be left with a little stem or foliage in place to give them a bit of frost protection, but most need no such coddling. When the stems have been chopped off a light forking over will tidy the soil for winter.

Fig. 25 Tall bamboo canes should be pushed among delphiniums while they are quite small so that the flower spike can be tied in as it extends.

Fig. 26 A nifty support system used at Crathes Castle in Scotland. Wooden stakes support wide-mesh black plastic netting through which the plants grow.

Fig. 27 Divide old clumps of border plants by digging them up and chopping them into smaller lumps with a spade. Discard the dead central portion and replant the youngsters.

Removing faded flowerheads from border plants can be a bit of a bore, but it will often encourage a second flush of bloom later in the season—it saves the plants the job of producing unwanted seeds. If the seedheads are needed for decoration or propagation, leave them be.

If you can afford the time and money needed, then do lay a mulch of compost or pulverized bark over the soil in March each year—or even every other year if funds are short. It really does keep the soil in good condition (as well as suppressing weeds and holding in moisture) and the plants will enjoy the benefits it provides, especially on sandy soils. After four years of trying to cope with a dry sandy soil I resorted to spring mulching with pulverized bark while the soil was moist. The plants that summer grew as they had never grown before.

PROPAGATION

Details of propagation are included in Chapter 20, but I've indicated how each plant in the A–Z section can be increased. Div. = division; Cutt. = stem cuttings; Root = root cuttings; Seed = seed, and

Graft. = grafting. They are given in the order of popularity with which they are used on each plant.

A–Z OF BORDER PLANTS

Here I've included not only the floriferous border plants that make the brightest summer show, but also a few ferns, bamboos and grasses too. These provide a welcome change or a suitable backdrop for the more blatant bloomers. The word 'Stake' appears below any plant that needs a bit of support.

Acanthus   Bear's Breech
1·5 m × 90 cm (5 × 3 ft)
Superbly architectural. *A. mollis* has bold, arching, glossy green leaves that are deeply lobed. Those of *A. spinosus* are more finely cut. Prickly flower spikes of white and rosy purple appear in late summer.
Likes ordinary, well-drained soil and full sun. *Tolerates* gentle shade; dry, chalky and clay soils.   *Div. Root. Seed.*

Achillea   Yarrow   60 cm–1·5 × 45 cm
(2–5 × 1½ ft)
Statuesque plants with flat heads of yellow flowers carried on feathery-leaved stems in summer. 'Gold Plate' is rich yellow, 1·5 m (5 ft) tall; 'Moonshine' is sulphur yellow, 60 cm (2 ft) tall, and 'Coronation Gold' is mid-yellow, 90 cm (3 ft) tall. The last two have greyish leaves. *A. ptarmica* 'The Pearl' has tiny double white rosette flowers on 60 cm (2 ft) stems.
Like well-drained soil and full sun. *Tolerate* dry, chalky and clay soils; coastal gardens.
Stake.   Div.

Aconitum   Monkshood, Wolfsbane
1·2–2·1 m × 60 cm (4–7 × 2 ft)
Towering plants with spires of hooded flowers— blue, pink, yellow or white in late summer. *A. napellus* is the common blue Monkshood. The entire plant is very poisonous, as are all aconitums—avoid it where children are at large.
Likes moisture-retentive soil and full sun. *Tolerates* chalk, clay and shady spots.   *Div. Seed.*

Agapanthus   Blue African Lily
60 × 60 cm (2 × 2 ft)
The 'Headbourne Hybrids' are among the best and hardiest, producing rounded white or blue heads of 'lily' flowers on stiff stalks amid glossy strap-shaped leaves in midsummer.
Like well-drained soil and a sunny, sheltered spot. *Tolerate* dry or chalky soil; coastal exposure. *Div. Seed.*

Ajuga   Bugle   15 × 90 cm (6 in × 3 ft)
Colourful carpeters making dense ground cover. Blue flower spires are carried in spring over leaves that may be deep purple, in the variety 'Purpurea'; cerise, cream and pale green, 'Burgundy Glow'; cream and

green, 'Variegata'; or purple with orange marbling, 'Multicolor'.
Like moisture-retentive soil and gentle shade. *Tolerate* clay, chalk, heavy shade, sun (but not dry soil).   *Div.*

Alcea   Hollyhock   2·4 m × 90 cm
(8 × 3 ft) and more
Tall spires of red, pink, yellow or white mallow flowers open in summer over clumps of lobed leaves. *A. rosea* has single and double varieties. Best renewed from seed every couple of years to keep rust disease at bay (those orange spots underneath the leaves).
Likes a sunny spot in well-drained soil. *Tolerates* clay soil.   *Stake.   Seed. Div.*

Alchemilla   Lady's Mantle
45 × 60 cm (1½ × 2 ft)
Scalloped green leaves covered in silky hairs hold water droplets like mercury. Fluffy lime-green flower-heads appear in summer. *A. mollis* is the commonest species and the loveliest. It seeds itself freely unless faded flowerheads are snipped off.
Likes gentle shade and a moisture-retentive soil. *Tolerates* sun, dry soil, chalk and clay.   *Div. Seed.*

Alstroemeria   Peruvian Lily
60 cm–1·2 m × 45 cm (2–4)1½ ft)
Spectacular lily flowers are carried in large clusters atop narrow-leafed stems. The blooms are orange, marked with brown lines in *A. aurea*, or salmon and pink in the beefier, more expensive, *A. ligtu* hybrids which are trickier to grow. Plant them young and don't disturb. They flower in summer.
Like a warm and sunny spot in well-drained soil. *Tolerate* a fraction of shade; dry or chalky soil; coastal exposure.   *Stake.   Div. Seed.*

Anaphalis   Pearly Everlasting
30 × 45 cm (1 × 1½ ft)
Neat stems clad in long, grey-haired leaves are topped with clusters of white, bead-like everlasting flowers in summer. The best species is *A. triplinervis*. Essential in any white garden or grey-foliage scheme.
Likes full sun and a soil not likely to dry out. *Tolerates* clay and chalky soils; gentle shade.   *Div.*

Anchusa   90 × 60 cm (3 × 2 ft)
True gentian-blue flowers are carried over hairy leaves in early summer. *A. azurea* (syn. *A. italica*) offers excellent value in the varieties 'Loddon Roya-list' and 'Little John'—the latter grows to just 45 cm.
Like well-drained soil and full sun. *Tolerate* clay and chalky soil.   *Stake.   Div. Root.*

Anemone   Windflower   1·5 m × 90 cm (5 × 3 ft)
It is the varieties of *A. × hybrida* that are most valued in borders for their late summer and early autumn display of wide-faced flowers on tall branching stalks. 'Honorine Jobert' is white, and 'Queen Char-lotte' is pink. There are others. All have a central

crown of gold stamens and are good value when most plants are past it.

Like a well-drained but moisture-retentive soil in full sun. *Tolerate* clay and chalky soil; some shade and coastal exposure.   *Div. Root.*

Aquilegia   Columbine   75 × 45 cm (2½ × 1½ ft)
Bright border plants for early summer when their branched heads of bonnet-shaped flowers open above finely cut grey-green leaves. The blooms may be white, blue, pink, yellow and red. There are many hybrids. Most last only a few years but set plenty of seed and can be divided.

Like ordinary well-drained soil in a sunny spot. *Tolerate* clay and chalky soils and gentle shade. *Seed Div.*

Artemisia   Lad's Love   60 × 90 cm (2 × 3 ft)
The true lad's love, southernwood, or old man is *A. abrotanum*. It makes a fruity-aromatic, feathery thicket of grey-green leaves. There are many other species, of which one of the best is *A. absinthium* 'Lambrook Silver' with exceptionally finely cut silver foliage. Grow any you can lay your trowel on. All are valued for their foliage.

Like warm and sunny spots in well-drained soil. *Tolerate* dry and chalky soil; coastal exposure. *Cutt. Div.*

Arum   Cuckoo Pint; Lords and Ladies
30 × 30 cm (1 × 1 ft)
Our native cuckoo pint, *A. maculatum*, pops up all over my chalky garden, but *A. italicum* 'Marmoratum' is a better choice for most plots. The arrowhead leaves are veined with cream and, as in the native species, fat clubs of orange berries follow the spring arum flowers in late summer and autumn.

Likes a shady spot in moisture-retentive soil. *Tolerates* chalk, clay and full sun (but not drought. *Div.*

Aruncus   Goat's Beard   2·1 × 1·2 m (7 × 4 ft)
Like a massive astilbe, *A. dioicus* (syn. *A. sylvester*) has ferny dark green leaves, over which tower feathery plumes of creamy white flowers in summer. Give it room to show off.

Likes dappled shade and a moisture-retentive soil. *Tolerates* sun, quite heavy shade; clay soil. Div. Seed.

Asplenium   Hart's Tongue Fern
30 × 45 cm (1 × 1½ ft)
The crested forms of *A. scolopendrium* with their wavy-edged strops of lime-green leaves are grand front-of-the-border foliage plants. Protect them from spring frosts, which may burn the newly emerging leaves. Chop off old leaves in March.

Likes moisture-retentive soil. *Tolerates* sun or shade; clay, chalk and some dry soils.   *Div.*

Aster   Michaelmas Daisy
30 cm–1·5 m × 60 cm (1–5 × 2 ft+)
Unsurpassable for late summer and autumn colour, most of the asters are super garden plants. The neat *A. amellus* is the shortest at 30 cm (1 ft), and has varieties with purple, crimson, pink, violet and white flowers—as have most of the other species. There are dozens of different michaelmas daisies in assorted shades and sizes, but *A.* × *frikartii* 'Mönch' is an aster to cherish. It has lavender-blue flowers from summer to autumn and lasts longer than any other aster I know.

Like full sun and good soil. *Tolerate* clay and chalky soils.   *Stake.*   *Div.* (every 3 years)

Astilbe   Spiraea   60 cm–1·2 m × 60–90 cm (2–4 × 2–3 ft)
All the varieties of *A.* × *arendsii* have ferny leaves and feathery plumes of white, pink, mauve or crimson flowers in summer. Most grow to between 60 cm and 1·2 m high, but 'Sprite' is a charming pink-flowered variety at just 23 cm (9 in). All are good streamside plants. The young foliage is often bronzed.

Like moisture-retentive soil and sun. *Tolerate* shade; some chalky soils and clay soil.   *Div.*

Astrantia   Hattie's Pincushion;
Masterwort   60 × 60 cm (2 × 2 ft)
Sterling plants making domes of fingered leaves from which spurt stems of starry flowers from early to midsummer. *A. major* is the best white; its variety 'Rubra' has rich crimson flowers, and 'Sunningdale Variegated' has leaves that are splashed cream early in the season. *A. maxima* has pink flowers but a weaker constitution.

Like moisture-retentive soil in sun or light shade. *Tolerate* quite heavy shade; chalky, clay and some dry soils (where plenty of organic matter has been worked in).   *Div. Seed.*

Ballota   60 × 60 cm (2 × 2 ft)
A straggly but endearing shrublet, *B. pseudodictamnus* has rounded leaves about 2·5 cm (1 in) across. Both they and the stems are thickly covered in white wool. The tiny mauve flowers are carried in compact clusters below the leaves but are hardly visible.

Likes sun and a well-drained soil. *Tolerates* dry or chalky soil.   *Cutt.*

Bergenia   Elephant's Ears, Megasea
30 × 60 cm (1 × 2 ft)
Glossy leaves like table tennis bats—and in some species just as big—and pink flower clusters on fat stalks in spring make this a cherished ground cover plant. The most popular species is *B. cordifolia*, and its variety 'Purpurea' is one of the best bergenias for autumn colour, turning reddish purple. Evergreen.

Likes sun and well-drained soil. A superb path edger. *Tolerates* shade; clay, chalky or dry soil; coastal exposure.   *Div.*

Blechnum 15×90 cm$+$ (6 in $\times 3$ ft$+$)
The tiny evergreen fern, *B. penna-marina*, is neat and jolly ground cover at the front of a shady border where its upright fronds make a thick, dark rug.

Likes gentle shade and a peaty, leafy, acid soil. *Tolerates* full sun if kept moist at the roots.   *Div.*

Brunnera 45×60 cm ($1\frac{1}{2} \times 2$ ft)
A forget-me-not-flowered woodlander with heart-shaped green leaves. *B. macrophylla* blooms in spring and is available in three variegated varieties; 'Dawson's White', roughly bordered with creamy white; 'Hadspen Cream', with deeper cream variegation; 'Langtrees' whose margins are spotted with silvery-grey blobs. The last two are the best.

Like a shady spot in organic, moisture-retentive soil. *Tolerate* dry soils (in the case of the true species and the variety 'Langtrees').   *Div. Seed.*

Calamintha   Calamint 30×30 cm (1×1 ft)
Underrated edgers with aromatic leaves and small, hooded flowers carried in summer and autumn. *C. nepeta* has pale blue flowers; *C. grandiflora* has pink flowers. Good ground coverers.

Like sunny spots in well-drained soil. *Tolerate* dry or chalky soil and shade.   *Div. Seed.*

Campanula   Bellflower   Various
I'd grow any campanula that came my way, but space allows me to mention just three that I think are the best. *C. persicifolia*, 90×30 cm (3×1 ft), I've discovered in both my gardens. From evergreen clumps it produces tall stalks of pale blue or white bells. *C. latifolia* 'Alba' is a queen among campanulas for shade, producing deep-toothed white bells up its $1 \cdot 2$ m (4 ft) stems in clumps 60 cm (2 ft) wide. *C. glomerata*, 45×60 cm ($1\frac{1}{2} \times 2$ ft), has densely packed heads of violet-blue, upturned bells. All these species bloom in early to midsummer.

Like sun and any well-drained but moisture-retentive soil. *Tolerate* dry soils (*C. persicifolia*), chalky soils (all), and shade (*C. latifolia*). *Stake.*   *Div. Seed.*

Carex   Sedge 30×30 cm (1×1 ft)
Fountains of bright yellow leaves spurt up from the soil where *C. morrowii* 'Variegata' is planted. It's an ever-yellow plant to cheer you the year round.

Likes moist soil and full sun. *Tolerates* clay, chalky soil (provided it's not dry) and a little shade.   *Div.*

Catananche   Cupid's Dart 60×45 cm ($2 \times 1\frac{1}{2}$ ft)
Pale blue dandelion flowers on wiry stems are produced by *C. caerulea* in summer from a clump of narrow leaves. Plant it between beefier foliage plants. It can be short lived.

Likes sun and a well-drained soil. *Tolerates* dry or chalky soil; coastal exposure.   *Stake.*
Seed. Root.

Centaurea   Cornflower
Knapweed $45–90 \times 90$ cm ($1\frac{1}{2}–3 \times 3$ ft)
Most gardens boast the spring- and summer-flowering *C. montana* with its spiky blue cornflowers and narrow grey-green leaves. More should give a home to the impressive *C. macrocephala*, 90×90 cm (3×3 ft), which has large leaves and hefty thistle heads of yellow. They dry well.

Like sun and well-drained soil. *Tolerate* dry, chalky or clay soil; coastal exposure.   *Stake.*
Div. Seed.

Centranthus   Valerian 90×60 cm (3×2 ft)
The red valerian, *C. ruber*, is a summer beauty beloved of butterflies and gardeners. It makes an upright plant with deep pink flowerheads and there is also a white variety. Both will grow well in crevices between paving and walling.

Like sun and a well-drained soil. *Tolerate* dry or chalky soils and coastal exposure.   *Cutt. Seed.*

Ceratostigma   Hardy Plumbago
90×90 cm (3×3 ft)
A rounded bush clad in coarse leaves and topped with bright blue flowers in late summer and autumn. *C. willmottianum* is not totally hardy and may be killed to ground level in winter.

Likes warm, sunny spots in well-drained soil. *Tolerates* chalky soil.   *Cutt. Seed.*

Chrysanthemum   Shasta Daisy
90×90 cm (3×3 ft)
The white, thick-centred shasta daisy is *C. maximum* (now *Leuchanthemum* × *superbum*), also known by the name of one of its varieties 'Esther Read'. One of the best white flowers of summer and a vigorous clump former.

Likes full sun and a well-drained soil. *Tolerates* clay or chalky soil and coastal exposure. *Stake. Div.*

Cimicifuga   Bugbane $1 \cdot 5$ m $\times 90$ cm (5×3 ft)
Tricky plants with ferny foliage and arching sprays of white flowers in late summer and early autumn. *C. racemosa* is the easiest to find and flowers earliest of all.

Likes shade and a rich, moist soil. *Tolerates* organically enriched chalk and clay soils.   *Div. Seed.*

Convallaria   Lily-of-the-valley
23×90 cm$+$ (9 in $\times 3$ ft$+$)
A spreader with upright, pointed, oval leaves and arching flower stalks that carry tiny white bells in spring. Headily scented. *C. majalis* is the true species, and it has several varieties including the pink-flowered var. *rosea* and the larger-flowered 'Fortin's Giant'. All spread greedily.

Likes dappled shade and well-drained soil. *Tolerates* full sun or heavy shade; dry or chalky soil.   *Div.*

Coreopsis Tickseed
60 × 60 cm (2 × 2 ft)
The finely cut bright green foliage of *C. verticillata* sits like tangled wire netting below the orange-yellow daisy flowers that open from midsummer to early autumn. It's a showy but graceful plant for the front of a border.
Likes full sun and well-drained soil. *Tolerates* clay or chalky soil. *Div.*

Cortaderia Pampass Grass
2·4 × 2·4 m (8 × 8 ft)
It is the varieties of *C. selloana* that are most popular, producing tall plumes of creamy white flowers in early autumn once the plant is a few years old and well suited. Chop off dead foliage in spring.
Likes a sunny spot in light, well-drained soil. *Tolerates* some clay or chalky soils. *Div.*

Corydalis Fumitory
23 × 45 cm (9 in × 1½ ft)
The finely cut green leaves of *C. lutea* make a fine foil for the spires of pale yellow flowers that nod over them from spring to autumn. An extremely invasive charmer. Good between paving stones.
Likes dappled shade and well-drained soil. *Tolerates* full sun; dry soil and chalk. *Seed.*

Crambe 1·8 × 1·2 m (6 × 4 ft)
The massive *C. cordifolia* produces hefty dark green leaves over which splay the billowing flower stems in early summer. The blooms are tiny and white, combining to form a dense cloud. For big borders only.
Likes a sunny patch of well-drained soil. *Tolerates* chalky and dry soils; coastal exposure (though strong winds may buckle its stems). *Div. Root.*

Crocosmia Montbretia
60 cm–1·2 m × 60 cm (2–4 ft × 2 ft)
A popular late summer flower with grassy green leaves carried in dense, upright tufts. The blooms are held on arching stems and may be orange, as in the common *C. × crocosmiiflora*, or brilliant scarlet as in the superb 'Lucifer'. This showy hybrid starts to flower in June and carries on until late summer. It is almost 60 cm (2 ft) taller than the previous species at around 1·2 m (4 ft) and is a hybrid between *Crocosmia aurea* and *C. pottsii*.
Like sun and a well-drained soil. *Tolerate* dappled shade; dry, chalky and clay soils; coastal exposure. *Div.*

Curtonus Aunt Eliza
1·2 m × 30 cm (4 × 1 ft)
Rather like a giant Montbretia, *C. paniculatus* used to be called *Antholyza paniculata*, which explains its common name. Botanists now call it *Crocosmia paniculata*. The orange-red blooms appear in late summer. The leaves are broader and taller than those of *Crocosmia* with marked pleating.
Likes sun and a well-drained soil. *Tolerates* dappled shade; dry, chalky and clay soils. *Div.*

Cynara Cardoon 1·8 m × 90 cm (6 × 3 ft)
Stunning, arching leaves of grey are boldly cut, making *C. cardunculus* an exceptionally attractive foliage plant. Artichoke flowerheads appear on tall stems in summer. Cheap to grow from seed.
Likes sun and well-drained soil in a sheltered spot. *Tolerates* dry or chalky soil. *Seed. Div. Root.*

Delphinium Larkspur
1·8 m × 90 cm (6 × 3 ft)
The hybrids of *D. elatum* have become firm towering features in many gardens and always seem to be bracketed with lupins. The flower spikes rise from clumps of serrated leaves in summer, and have dozens of blooms ranging in colour from rich blue through paler shades to pinks, mauves and primrose yellow as well as white. The red delphinium, no doubt, will be with us shortly.
Like sun and a rich, well-drained soil. *Tolerate* chalky and clay soils. *Stake. Div. Seed.*

Dianthus Carnation, Pink
15–30 × 30–60 cm (6–12 in × 1–2 ft)
There are many named varieties of pink and border carnations and all make superb edgers for beds, borders and paths. Their spiky foliage is usually neat and grey, they bloom freely in summer, and they possess the most exquisite scents. Varieties are available with crimson, pink, mauve, pale yellow and white flowers, single or double. Some are bicoloured.
Like sun and well-drained chalky soil. *Tolerate* other well-drained soils if lime is added; coastal exposure. *Cutt. Seed.*

Dicentra Bleeding Heart, Lady in the Bath
45 × 60 cm (1½ × 2 ft)
The true bleeding heart is *D. spectabilis*, which has finely cut green leaves and arching stems of pink and white locket flowers in late spring. *D. formosa* is a smaller version with leaves like carrot foliage and more slender flowers. Several hybrids are offered, among the best of which are 'Stuart Boothman', with filigree grey leaves and pink flowers in spring and summer, and 'Langtrees' (grey leaved but not so finely cut) with white flowers tinged pink. 'Bacchanal' has dusky crimson flowers. The smaller versions grow to around 23 × 45 cm (9 in × 1½ ft).
Like gentle shade and moisture-retentive soil. *Tolerate* sun and chalky soil (provided the roots do not dry out) and clay. *Div.*

Dictamnus Dittany
75 × 60 cm (2½ × 2 ft)
Both *D. albus* (syn. *D. fraxinella albus*), with white flowers, and its variety *purpureus*, with rich pink flowers, are superb border plants. The leaves are

fingered and the flowers rather starry in appearance. They open in early summer and later form seedpods which give off a volatile oil. Hold a lighted match underneath them and you'll hopefully see a minute explosion! The plant is citrus scented.

Likes full sun and a well-drained soil. *Tolerates* dry and chalky soils. *Div. Root. Seed.*

Dierama   Fairy Wand Flower; Angel's Fishing Rod   1·2 m × 90 cm (4 × 3 ft)
From a clump of grassy evergreen leaves the flower stems erupt in summer, carrying rich pink bell flowers on arching fusewire-thin stalks. Very graceful and always a conversation piece. The smaller *D. draeomontanum*, 30 × 30 cm (1 × 1 ft), is similar but even more graceful and a good front-of-the-border plant. Plant in spring.

Likes full sun and a well-drained but moisture-retentive soil. *Tolerates* dry soil and chalk; coastal exposure. Be patient—it may die down after planting but will re-emerge. *Div. Seed.*

Digitalis   Foxglove   60 × 30 cm (2 × 1 ft)
A pale yellow foxglove of modest height, *D. grandiflora* is a reliable perennial where most other foxgloves are biennial (p. 116). The flower spikes shoot from downy, evergreen leaf rosettes in summer.

Likes organically enriched soil in dappled shade. *Tolerates* sun, quite heavy shade; dry, chalky or clay soil. *Seed. Div.*

Doronicum   Leopard's Bane
45 × 45 cm (1½ × 1½ ft)
These bright yellow spring daisies are always welcome heralds of a new season and the variety 'Miss Mason' is one of the best. Doubles like 'Spring Beauty' ('Frühlingspracht') are dazzling but look too much like a summer pot marigold at this time of year. The rounded leaves are a good, fresh green.

Likes sun and well-drained soil. *Tolerates* gentle shade; clay and chalky soil. *Div.*

Dryopteris   Male Fern
90 × 90 cm (3 × 3 ft)
The arching green fronds of *D. filix-mas* add an ethereal look to any border. Plant this fern where you can appreciate its form and where the mid-green of its fronds can set off other plants. Good by paths.

Likes shade and well-drained soil. *Tolerates* sun; dry, clay and chalky soils. *Div.*

Echinacea   Purple Coneflower
1·2 m × 60 cm (4 × 2 ft)
Rich pink daisies are not plentiful in the garden but *E. purpurea* makes up for the deficiency by producing a good show over its green foliage in summer. 'Robert Bloom' is an exceptionally good variety of a dusky rose colour; it's long-flowering too.

Likes sun and a rich, well-drained soil. *Tolerates* chalk and well-worked clay. *Stake.* *Div. Root.*

Echinops   Globe Thistle
1·2 m × 60 cm (4 × 2 ft)
A real whopper of a border plant with finely cut dark green leaves (grey underneath) and spherical flower-heads of steely blue in late summer. *E. ritro* is the most popular species, but *E.* 'Taplow Blue' is taking over from it and is even more vigorous at around 1·5 or 2 m (5 or 6 ft).

Likes full sun and a good, well-drained soil. *Tolerates* dry, chalk and clay soils; coastal exposure. *Stake.* *Div. Root.*

Epilobium   Rose Bay Willowherb
1·2 m × 30 cm (4 × 1 ft)
When the Emperor of Japan came to Kew Gardens in 1971 he was offered any plant he wanted—and took away a packet of Rose Bay willowherb seeds. You might not want to plant this invasive, if beautiful, weed, but its white variety *E. angustifolium* f. *album* is a green-and-white-flowered treasure that's not so rampant. It flowers in late summer. Super in white borders.

Likes well-drained soil and sun or dappled shade. *Tolerates* clay and chalky soils. *Div. Seed.*

Epimedium   Bishop's Hat; Barrenwort
30 × 30 cm (1 × 1 ft)
Whichever species you choose you'll inherit a fine ground-cover plant with mitre-shaped leaves that are often burnished with crimson when they unfurl in spring. The tiny, short-lived flowers may be red, yellow or white and they open in spring. The stems and stalks are stiff and wiry, an altogether admirable race of plants valued for foliage contrasts.

Like some shade and a moisture-retentive soil. *Tolerate* sun provided not dry at the roots; chalk and clay. Slow in dry soils. *Div.*

Eremurus   Foxtail Lily
1·5–2·4 m × 60 cm (5–8 × 2 ft)
You'll find no showier border plants than the hybrids of eremurus that are now freely available. In early summer they send up rocket-like stems, packed for most of their length with starry flowers of white, pink, yellow or orange. The strappy leaves die down in summer so the plants should be clearly marked. Mulch in winter.

Like sun and well-drained soil; a sheltered spot. *Tolerate* nothing but excellent drainage; chalky soil. *Div. Seed.*

Erigeron   Fleabane
45–60 × 60 cm (1½–2 × 2 ft)
Pretty daisies with petals of pink, mauve, violet or white, surrounding a central disc of yellow. They flower for a good two months in early to midsummer. Take your pick from the varieties listed in nurserymen's catalogues.

Like sun and well-drained soil. *Tolerate* clay, dry or chalky soil and coastal exposure. *Div.*

Metal screw eyes hold horizontal plastic-covered wire against the wall to allow the climbers to be tied in.

Everyone's idea of the perfect cottage garden, with roses around the door.

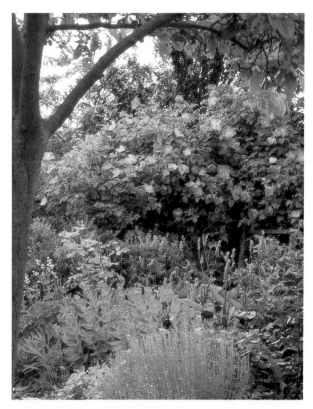

For the larger garden scrambling shrub roses provide summer blossoms and autumn fruits.

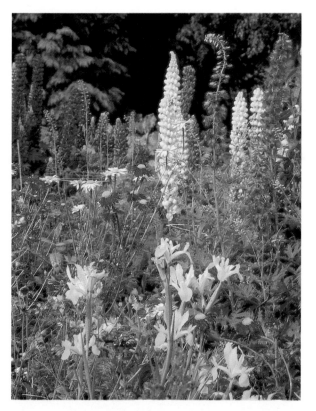

The luxuriance of high summer; here are traditional lupins, iris, pyrethrums.

Right: A pale blue bridge crosses a shallow pool in our garden. Variegated iris and knotwood decorate its banks and purple-and yellow-leaved Japanese Maples provide an Oriental flavour.

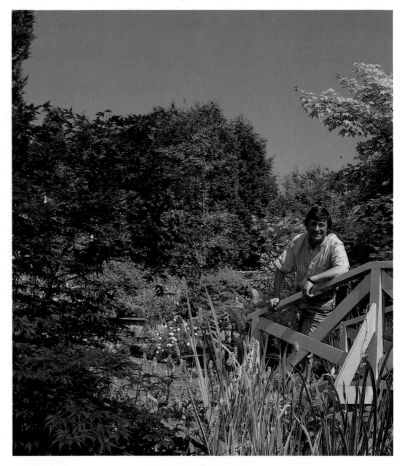

Below left: The marble-sized berries of *Gaulteria mucronata* (prickly heath) which first appear in autumn, and last until the end of winter.

Below right: A mass of gold only 10 cm (4 in) from the ground: *Eranthis hyemalis* (winter aconite).

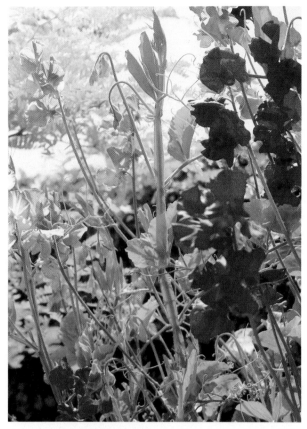

Try to make flower and foliage contrasts; here's *Gleditsia triacanthos* 'Sunburst' with sweet peas.

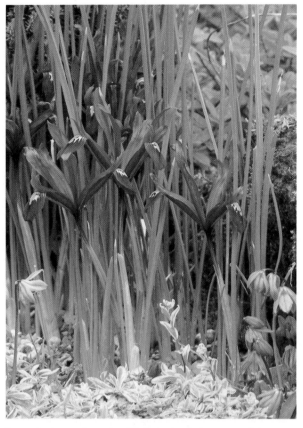

Dwarf winter-flowering bulbs take little space. *Iris reticulata* here grows with *Scilla sibirica*.

1. Rock gardens Use local rocks to make a natural-looking outcrop – easier on sloping ground. Ram the soil firmly around the rocks so there are no air pockets.

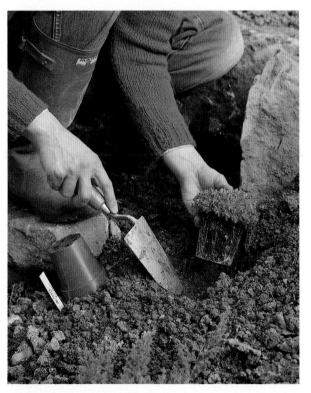

2. Water a container-grown alpine, knock it from its pot and plant without disturbing the rootball. Water in and topdress with gravel.

3. Here's the rock bank in our garden immediately after it had been planted. The gravel topdressing ensures good surface drainage.

4. One year later the scheme is becoming well established and there is still room for a few more plants – simply scrape away the gravel, plant the newcomer and push the gravel back.

5. Ten years later the same bank is now totally covered with plants and ready for renovation!

Eryngium Sea Holly
60 cm–1·2 m × 30–60 cm (2–4 × 1–2 ft)
No garden should be without sea hollies. From rosettes or clumps of leaves the branched stems erupt in summer carrying aloft spiky steel-blue flowers—a central knob of tiny florets is surrounded by a ruff of spiny bracts. The flowers are many and miniature on species such as *E. planum*, or large and spectacular in the fuzzy-collared *E. alpinum* or the more open-bloomed *E.* × *oliverianum*. Sneak the plants between other border inhabitants who will hold them up. They look silly staked. The plant known as 'Miss Willmott's Ghost' is *E. giganteum*, a glorious silver-leaved sea holly of modest size 45 × 30 cm (1½ × 1 ft) but it is biennial. Grow it in spite of this minor drawback.

Like well-drained soil and full sun. *Tolerate* dry or chalky soil and coastal exposure. Some can put up with clay.   *Div. Seed.*

Euphorbia Spurge Various
Classy plants with leaves arranged in spirals up the fleshy stems. The tallest and most stately is *E. characias*, 1·5 m × 90 cm (5 × 3 ft), most popular in its variety *wulfenii*. The flowerheads are the yellowish green so common in euphorbias. None is more luminous than those of *E. polychroma* (syn. *E. epithymoides*) 45 × 45 cm (1½ × 1½ ft), which makes a neat, rounded dome of acidic yellow heads. *E. amygdaloides* var. *robbiae* 60 × 60 cm (2 × 2 ft) makes a dense, evergreen, weed-suppressing blanket of attractive growth. All these flower in spring and look terrific planted in front of the golden-leafed hop or near yellow-leafed shrubs. The stunning *E. griffithii* 'Fireglow' blooms in early summer, plastering its stems with rounded heads of brick-red blooms.

Like sun and a good, well-drained soil. *Tolerate* shade; dry or chalky soil; coastal exposure.   *Div. Seed.*

Festuca Fescue Grass
23 × 30 cm (9 in × 1 ft)
Big, blue-grey shaving brushes sprouting from the ground—that's the best description I can offer of *F. glauca*, the blue fescue. It's a neat foliage plant to squeeze into any bed or border and looks good among cobbles or gravel. It's evergreen but can be chopped to ground level in spring when tatty; it will soon sprout again.

Likes sun and well-drained soil. *Tolerates* dry or chalky soil; coastal exposure.   *Div.*

Gaillardia Blanket Flower
75 × 45 cm (2½ × 1½ ft)
Bright-petalled double daisies of red, orange or yellow that are at their best in summer. There are many varieties, but 'Mandarin' is one of the best; orange-red petals radiate from a central boss of mahogany brown.

Likes light, well-drained soil and sun. *Tolerates* dry or chalky soil.   *Stake.   Div. Root.*

Galega Goat's Rue
1·2 m × 90 cm (4 × 3 ft)
Goat's rue should be much more popular. It makes a thicket of vetch-like stems and leaves, decorated in summer with clusters of white, pink, lilac or pale blue pea flowers. *G. officinalis* is the species from which the varieties are derived.

Likes sun and well-drained soil. *Tolerates* chalk, dry and clay and soils.   *Stake.   Div.*

Gentiana Gentian   60 × 60 cm (2 × 2 ft)
The willow gentian, *G. asclepiadea* looks a treat in late summer and early autumn when its arching stems produce pairs of blue trumpet flowers among the topmost leaves. The leaves are willow-shaped, which accounts for the common name. One of late summer's most cheering sights.

Likes rich, leafy soil and gentle shade. *Tolerates* sun (but not drought); chalky soil.   *Seed.*

Geranium Cranesbill Various
Vital plants in my garden where they make billowing flower-spotted ground cover from spring to autumn. Grow any of them—they're all worth a try. Among the best are: *G. macrorrhizum*, 30 × 60 cm (1 × 2 ft), aromatic, pink or white; *G.* 'Claridge Druce', 45 × 90 cm (1½ × 3 ft), pink; *G. phaeum*, 60 × 30 cm (2 × 1 ft), the mourning widow, dusky purple; *G. pratense* 'Plenum Violaceum', 60 × 60 cm (2 × 2 ft), double blooms of violet and mauve; *G. psilostemon* (syn. *G. armenum*), up to 1·8 × 1·8 m (6 × 6 ft) usually less, magenta centred with deep purple.

Like sun and well-drained soil. *Tolerate* shade; dry, chalky or clay soil; coastal exposure. *Stake G. psilostemon.*   *Div.*

Geum Avens   30–60 × 45 cm (1–2 ft × 1½ ft)
Most hybrid geums have double flowers of red, yellow, orange or pink, held like rosettes at the tips of sturdy stems. 'Mrs Bradshaw' is a good, solid red, and 'Lady Stratheden' a double yellow. *G. rivale* 'Leonard's Variety' is altogether more classy with its orange-pink bells that nod on 30 cm (1 ft) stems. All bloom from early to midsummer.

Like full sun and good, well-drained soil. *Tolerate* gentle shade; chalky or clay soil.   *Div.*

Glyceria   60 cm × 1·5 m (2 × 5 ft)
A clump of upright grassy leaves with blades that are boldly striped in white and green makes *G. maxima* 'Variegata' (syn. *G. aquatica* 'Variegata') a must. It's a stunner and grows itself in any reasonable spot. Give it room—it's invasive.

Likes moisture-retentive soil and sun. *Tolerates* gentle shade; chalky or clay soil. Slow in dry soil.   *Div.*

97

Gunnera   Prickly Rhubarb
$2\cdot4 \times 2\cdot4$ m (8×8 ft)
For massive gardens only. *G. manicata* makes gargantuan parasols of leaves, dull green above, lighter green below, with prickly stalks. Best by a lake if you happen to have one. Mulch with bracken in winter to protect the tender crowns.
   Likes rich, leafy, moisture-retentive soil; sun. *Tolerates* gentle shade.   *Div.*

Gypsophila   Baby's Breath
30 cm–$1\cdot2$ m $\times$ 60 cm–$1\cdot2$ m (1–4 ft $\times$ 2–4 ft)
Billowing clouds of tiny blooms float over this plant in summer. *G. paniculata*, $1\cdot2 \times 1\cdot2$ m (4×4 ft), is white and single; 'Bristol Fairy', 90×90 cm (3×3 ft), is a double white; and 'Rosy Veil' a double pink. Can be short lived.
   Like a warm, sunny spot in well-drained, chalky soil. *Tolerate* other well-drained soils; coastal exposure.   *Seed. Graft.* (varieties)

Helenium   Sneezeweed
60–90×60 cm (2–3 $\times$ 2 ft)
Summer and autumn daisies of yellow, orange and mahogany red. There are many varieties, all of which have a prominent central boss of yellow or brown. 'Butterpat', yellow; 'Wyndley', orange brown; and 'Moerheim Beauty', mahogany, are particularly good.
   Like good, well-drained soil and sun. *Tolerate* clay or chalky soil.   *Stake. Div.*

Helleborus   Christmas Rose;
Hellebore 30–60×30 cm (1–2 $\times$ 1 ft)
By flowering in winter and spring this group of plants really earns its keep. *H. niger*, the Christmas Rose, usually carries its waxy white saucers in January or February (unless cloche covered). *H. orientalis* is the undoubted aristrocrat with its many-flowered 30 cm (1 ft) stalks, of creamy white, purple or purple-spotted blooms that precede the leaves. *H. corsicus* is evergreen with spiny-edged fingered leaves, and in its second year each stem is topped with a cluster of pale green flowers. Grow any hellebores that come your way. Most require a little patience until they settle in.
   Like gentle shade and well-drained but moisture-retentive soil. *Tolerate* sun; chalky or well-cultivated clay soils.   *Seed. Div.*

Hemerocallis   Day Lily
60–90×60 cm (2–3 $\times$ 2 ft)
Grassy, fresh green leaves make a perfect background to the branched heads of lily flowers carried over them in summer. There are dozens of varieties with short-lived (but regularly produced) blooms of yellow, orange, white, pink or mahogany red. A good contrast for broader-leaved plants.
   Like sun and well-drained but moisture-retentive soil. *Tolerate* gentle shade; chalky or clay soils. *Div.*

Heuchera   Coral Bells; Alum Root
30–60×45 cm (1–2 $\times$ $1\frac{1}{2}$ ft)
Valued as pretty ground cover, the heucheras produce a thick pile of flowering-currant-shaped leaves over which are carried upright stems decorated with little bells of pink or red. The named varieties have now upstaged the true species. They bloom in early summer and some have leaves marbled bronze. 'Pewter Moon' is especially good in leaf.
   Like rich, well-drained but moisture-retentive soil. *Tolerate* sun or shade; chalky or clay soils; coastal exposure.   *Div.*

Hosta   Plantain Lily; Funkia
30–60×60 cm (1–2 $\times$ 2 ft)
Bold foliage plants of great merit. The leaves are always juicy and squeaky, and tall stems of bell-shaped lily flowers tower over them in summer. The blooms are usually white or pale lilac in colour, but it is the leaves that are the main attraction. They die down in autumn but emerge afresh each spring. *H. sieboldiana* 'Elegans' has whopping blue-grey leaves that are rounded and ribbed; *H. fortunei* 'Albopicta' is striped and blotched with butter yellow on green in spring, fading to green later; *H. crispula* has narrower leaves, twisted at the edges and margined with creamy white. Of the many good newcomers 'Frances Williams' is strikingly bold. It has the size and colour of *H. sieboldiana* 'Elegans' but with a pale yellow margin.
   Like gentle shade and a rich, moisture-retentive soil. *Tolerate* sun (but not dryness); chalky or well-worked clay soil.   *Div. Seed.*

Incarvillea 45×30 cm ($1\frac{1}{2} \times 1$ ft)
The rich pink trumpets of *I. delavayi* blow a colourful fanfare from the tops of sturdy stalks in early summer. The much-divided leaves are deep bronzy green. Spectacular in sheltered gardens.
   Likes sun and a well-drained soil. *Tolerates* dry or chalky soil. *Div. Seed.*

Iris   Flag   Various
Sword-like or grassy leaves and bright, often bearded flowers combine to make the irises indispensable garden plants. The German bearded irises—in tremendous variety of colour—make that brilliant June display of bloom, but their glaucous leaves are still useful later in the season for foliage contrasts. Prolong the iris season by growing *I. unguicularis* (syn. *I. stylosa*) in really dry soil at the foot of a sunny wall. Its grassy leaves remain all the year round, but from November to February it can produce pale violet blue flowers to brighten your winter. Starve it and don't disturb it. *I. pallida* in either its white-variegated or yellow-variegated leafed forms is a superb foliage plant, and *I. foetidissima* is the species that has those fat seed pods that burst to reveal orange seeds in autumn.

Like well-drained soil, especially if it's chalky; full sun. *Tolerate* gentle shade (in the case of *I. pallida* and *I. foetidissima*); dry or clay soils; coastal exposure. *Div. Seed.*

Kirengeshoma   90 × 60 cm (3 × 2 ft)
Not half so widely grown as it should be. Rich green paired leaves show off a treat the upside-down shuttlecock flowers of pale yellow which dangle from branched, purple-flushed stems in late summer and early autumn. *K. palmata* is its full name.

Likes a rich, moisture-retentive and lime-free soil in dappled shade. Keep it sheltered from strong winds. *Tolerates* full sun if it's not dry at the roots.   *Div. Seed.*

Kniphofia   Red Hot Poker
45 cm–1·8 m × 45 cm–1·2 m (1½–6 ft × 1½–4 ft)
Striking plants with sceptre-like flower stems that appear from early summer to autumn depending on the species or variety. The leaves are grassy and make a massive clump. Most varieties have red and yellow flowers, but there are now some with pale yellow or green flowers, and a good race of miniatures that can be easily fitted into the small garden. *K. uvaria*, 1·5 m × 90 cm (5 × 3 ft), is the common autumn-flowering poker, but try 'Little Maid', 60 × 30 cm (2 × 1 ft), with its pale yellow flowers; 'Green Jade', 1·2 m × 60 cm (4 × 2 ft), with cool green blooms, and 'Strawberries and Cream', 45 × 30 cm (1½ × 1 ft), pale yellow and rich pink, all raised by that observant lady Beth Chatto.

Like full sun and well-drained soil. *Tolerate* dry, chalky or well-worked clay soil; coastal exposure.   *Div.*

Lamium   Deadnettle
30 cm × 1·2 m (1 × 4 ft)
As a ground-cover plant at the front of a border *L. maculatum* has little competition. Choose a variety such as 'Chequers' with white-striped leaves and rich mauve hooded spring flowers, or 'Beacon Silver' whose leaves are almost entirely silver green. *L. galeobdolon* (syn. *Galeobdolon luteum, Lamiastrum galeobdolon*) is a firework plant—light the blue touch-paper and stand back. In its variety 'Florentinum' it has trailing stems clad in green, grey-spotted leaves and produces yellow flowers in early summer. Once established it's unstoppable and thrives where little else will grow. All are evergreen.

Like any well-drained soil and sun. *Tolerate* heavy shade; dry, chalky or clay soil.   *Div. Cutt.*

Lathyrus   45 × 45 cm (1½ × 1½ ft)
This is a neglected plant which should soon make a come-back. Over a mound of finely cut leaves it produces plenty of pinkish purple pea flowers in spring. *L. vernus* has several varieties, among which is 'Spring Delight' with paler pink flowers. Give it a try.

Likes sun and well-drained soil. *Tolerates* dry or

chalky soil; coastal exposure.   *Div.*

Liatris   Kansas Gayfeather
60 × 30 cm (2 × 1 ft)
It is *L. spicata* that appears in most catalogues and in most gardens. It has shiny, narrow leaves that make a bold tuft of growth, and in summer it sends up pokers of fluffy pink flowers. Butterflies love them. 'Kobbold' is a good purplish-pink variety, and 'Alba' is white.

Likes sunny spots in well-drained soil. *Tolerates* dry or chalky soil.   *Div.*

Linaria   Toad Flax
90 × 30 cm (3 × 1 ft)
The spires of *L. purpurea* pop up all over my garden and will do so for ever—the plant seeds itself freely. The stiff stems sport spirals of narrow grey leaves and are topped with spikes of tiny purple snapdragon flowers, pink in the variety 'Canon Went', which seems just as prolific and come true from seed. Good in paving stone crevices and walls and flowering freely from early to late summer.

Likes sun and well-drained soil. *Tolerates* dry and chalky soil; coastal exposure.   *Seed. Div.*

Linum   Flax   45 × 45 cm (1½ × 1½ ft)
If you want a good sky blue flower, look no further than *L. narbonnense*. Its bell-shaped blooms decorate the wiry stems for several weeks in summer. It can be rather short lived.

Likes sun and a well-drained soil in a sheltered spot. *Tolerates* dry and chalky soils.   *Seed. Cutt.*

Liriope   30 × 30 cm (1 × 1 ft)
I'm never quite sure whether I like the appearance of *L. muscari*, but it's so useful that it's worth a mention. It makes a clump of darkest green, grassy leaves that arches into a small fountain, and in autumn stiff stalks appear carrying pale purple blobs of flowers. It's useful because it can put up with dense, dry shade under trees.

Likes sun or shade and good, well-drained soil. *Tolerates* well-worked clay or chalky soil.   *Div.*

Lobelia   Cardinal Flower
90 × 30 cm (3 × 1 ft)
As distinct from the bedding lobelia, *L. cardinalis* produces tall stems thickly set with scarlet flowers in summer. *L. fulgens* is similar but redder in leaf.

Like sun and rich soil that is unlikely to dry out. *Tolerate* dappled shade and well-worked, enriched, chalky soil.   *Stake. Div. Seed.*

Lupinus   Lupin
1·2–1·8 m × 60 cm (4–6 × 2 ft)
George Russell, an assiduous Yorkshireman, raised many different varieties of tall-spired lupin with towers of close-packed pea flowers in shades of blue, pink, red, yellow, mauve, purple and white. They were all grown on allotments and he wouldn't take a

penny for them from any nurserymen; instead he distributed them free of charge. We still have many of his excellent varieties, at their best in June. The blooms look well over the fingered green leaves that hold water drops in their centre like globules of mercury.

Like good, well-drained soil and full sun. *Tolerate* well-worked clay soils and, reluctantly, organically enriched chalky soils. On shallow chalk they sulk. *Cutt. Seed. Div.*

Lychnis   Maltese Cross
90 × 30 cm (3 × 1 ft)
There are two species of lychnis which have particularly striking flowers in summer. *L. coronaria* makes upright branching stems covered all over with white down; the leaves are felted too. Atop the stems are magenta flowers in early summer. *L. chalcedonica* has plain green leaves and stems topped with clusters of zingy scarlet flowers—there is no truer red in the garden. Place them carefully to avoid clashes.

Like sun and a well-drained soil. *Tolerate* dry, chalky or clay soils and coastal exposure, though they appreciate shelter from strong winds. *Stake. Div. Seed.*

Lysimachia   Loosestrife, Creeping Jenny
Various
The yellow loosestrife, *L. punctata*, makes a clump 60 × 60 cm (2 × 2ft) and sends up stems of starry yellow flowers in summer. Creeping Jenny (*L. nummularia*) is a sprawling plant with tiny rounded leaves the size of a new penny. Little yellow cup-shaped flowers appear in the leaf axils in early summer. The variety 'Aurea' has leaves of an eye-catching acid yellow. All are rampant.

Like moisture-retentive soil in dappled shade. *Tolerate* chalk and clay; sun but not drought. *Stake L. punctata.*   *Div.*

Macleaya   Plume Poppy
2·4 m × 90 cm (8 × 3 ft)
The dusky green, lobed leaves of *M. microcarpa* (syn. *Bocconia cordata*) are grey beneath and flash brightly when disturbed by wind. The plumes of orange-pink flowers appear in summer and are·most attractive in the variety 'Coral Plume'. A hefty plant that needs room to spread itself. It suckers freely.

Likes well-drained soil in a sunny, sheltered spot. *Tolerates* dry or chalky soil. *Stake.*   *Div. Root.*

Malva   Mallow   1·2 × 1·5 m (4 × 5 ft)
The easiest mallow to get hold of is *M. alcea* var. *fastigiata*, which produces upright stems decorated with round, pink flowers in summer. *M.* 'Primley Blue' deserves to be better known, for it makes a spreading, vigorous plant that never ceases to carry myriads of soft blue flowers from early summer to autumn. Give it room to spread. Rust disease can

sometimes attack and it can be short-lived.

Like sun and well-drained soil. *Tolerate* chalk and well-worked clay.   *Cutt.*

Matteuccia   Ostrich Plume Fern
60 × 60 cm (2 × 2 ft)
Shuttlecocks of bright green fronds unfurl in spring, making *M. struthiopteris* (syn. *Struthiopteris germanica*) one of the most striking ferns, if one of the most unpronounceable. Superb in small colonies.

Likes dappled shade and leafy, moisture-retentive soil. *Tolerates* well-enriched chalk or clay; sun and heavy shade.   *Div.*

Meconopsis   Himalayan Blue Poppy;
Welsh Poppy   Various
The Welsh poppy, *M. cambrica*, 30 × 30 cm (1 × 1 ft), is the easiest to please; seeding itself around so freely that it amounts to a weed in my garden. But its bright yellow poppy flowers are a treat in late spring. The coveted blue poppy, *M. betonicifolia* (syn. *M. baileyi*), 1·2 m × 30 cm (4 × 1 ft), is the showstopper of the bunch, producing branched heads of almost luminous blue flowers in early summer. But beware; there are wishy-washy varieties, and the plant's performance varies from garden to garden—as does its length of life.

Likes dappled shade and a rich, lime-free soil. Best in the cooler northern counties. *Tolerates* full sun if happy at the roots.   *Div. Seed.*

Milium   Bowles' Golden Grass
60 × 60 cm (2 × 2 ft)
A superb yellow-foliage plant, *M. effusum* 'Aureum' was spotted by that Enfield plantsman E. A. Bowles, which accounts for its common name. It makes dainty, arching clumps of acid yellow leaves which produce airy flower stems in summer. It seeds about freely.

Likes gentle shade and a well-drained soil. *Tolerates* dry or chalky soil and full sun.   *Seed. Div.*

Mimulus   Monkey Flower
30–90 × 60 cm (1–3 × 2 ft)
There are lots of different monkey flowers with fleshy green leaves and trumpet flowers of red, yellow or orange, often contrastingly spotted. They bloom in summer and especially enjoy being planted by ponds and streams.

Like sun and moisture-retentive soil. *Tolerate* dappled shade, chalk and clay; coastal exposure. *Stake taller varieties.*   *Cutt. Div. Seed.*

Monarda   Bee Balm; Bergamot; Oswego Tea
60 × 60 cm (2 × 2 ft)
Crush the leaves of monarda and you'll smell Earl Grey Tea! The aromatic foliage is just one of the attractions; the main benefit is the summer display of hooded flowers carried in tiers around the stems. *M. didyma* 'Cambridge Scarlet' is the best variety with

rosy-crimson flowers; 'Croftway Pink' is a good paler pink, and 'Prairie Night' a violet purple. The last two make less impact than the first.

Like sun and well-drained but moisture-retentive soil. *Tolerate* chalky or clay soils. *Div.*

Morina 90 × 30 cm (3 × 1 ft)

The leaves of *M. longifolia* are just like those of a glossy thistle—don't uproot the plant by mistake when it's young. Later the leaves are longer and more handsome—then you'll have no difficulty in distinguishing them. The flower spikes of hooded white blooms appear above the leaf rosettes in summer. They turn to deep rose pink as they age. A plant deserving greater popularity, and one of my all-time favourites.

Likes sun and well-drained soil in a sheltered spot. *Tolerates* chalk and well-worked clay soil; coastal exposure. *Div. Seed.*

Nepeta Catmint 45 × 60 cm (1½ × 2 ft)

Our cat loves this plant so much that she chews it off at ground level every time it tries to emerge. *N.* × *faassenii* (syn. *N. mussinii*) is the one you want. Its aromatic leaves are dusky grey and it has long stems of lavender-blue flowers in summer. 'Six Hills Giant' is the most robust variety.

Likes sun and well-drained soil. *Tolerates* dry or chalky soil. *Div. Cutt.*

Oenothera Evening Primrose
23–45 × 60 cm (9 in–1½ ft × 2 ft)

The bright yellow cup-shaped flowers of *O. macrocarpa* are held on 23 cm (9 in) stems right through summer, making this grand for the front of a border where a long-lasting display is wanted. Taller varieties like 'Fireworks' (Fyrewerkeri') 45 × 45 cm (1½ × 1½ ft), with masses of yellow flowers and orange buds are even more showy.

Like full sun and well-drained soil. *Tolerate* ry and chalky soils; coastal exposure. *Div. Seed.*

Paeonia Peony
60–90 × 90 cm (2–3 × 3 ft)

Fleeting but fabulous flowers of spring, the Chinese peonies make a stupendous show before any summer flowers have time to compete. There are dozens of varieties with double or single blooms of white, pink, crimson and magenta, and single kinds with crested centres. Pick where you like from nurserymen's pictures. Try also *P. mlokosewitschii* (you'll have to point at the name if you can't say it). It makes a glorious show of golden goblets centred with yellow stamens and a red 'eye' in May. Plant peonies and leave them—they don't like disturbance.

Like full sun and a rich, well-drained soil, especially if it's chalky. *Tolerate* dry or clay soils, provided the latter is well worked. *Div.*

Papaver Poppy 90 × 90 cm (3 × 3 ft)

The varieties of *P. orientale*, the oriental poppy, are flowers of June. It's a relatively brief display but one which can truthfully be described as dazzling. The massive bowl-shaped blooms of orange, salmon, pink, scarlet or white are centred with a crown of black stamens and may be contrastingly blotched or picotee edged. Others have frilly-edged petals. 'Marcus Perry' is a good orange; 'Mrs Perry' a warm salmon pink; and 'Picotee' is white-edged with orange; 'Black and White' is just as its name.

Like sun and well-drained soil, especially if it's chalky. *Tolerate* dry soil. *Stake. Div. Root.*

Penstemon 60 × 45 cm (2 × 1½ ft)

Many penstemons are rather tender, but there are now a good few hybrids that can be gambled with as hardy plants in the milder counties. All carry their foxglove-like flowers on elegant spikes and bloom generously from mid- to late summer. 'Garnet' ('Andenken an Friedrich Hahn') is rosy red; 'Sour Grapes' is lilac purple; and Firebird' ('Schoenholzeri') is scarlet. There are other varieties with pink and salmon flowers.

Like a warm, sunny, sheltered spot in well-drained soil. *Tolerate* dry or chalky soil and warm coastal gardens. *Cutt.*

Phlox 1·2 m × 60 cm (4 × 2 ft)

Essential ingredients of a summer border, the varieties of *P. paniculata* are lovely plants with fat, rounded heads of flower—each bloom often being marked with a darker central eye. They'll flower from mid- to late summer, in shades of pink, crimson, lavender blue, mauve, violet-purple and white. Take your pick from the glowing descriptions in nurserymen's catalogues. If your plants develop puckered, twisted leaves and swollen stems they've fallen prey to eelworm. Dig them up and take root cuttings (all else will be affected) and replant in uninfected ground.

Like sun and well-drained soil. *Tolerate* dry, chalky or clay soil but only if all three are enriched with organic matter and well worked. *Stake. Root. Div.*

Phormium New Zealand Flax
60–90 × 60–90 cm (2–3 × 2–3 ft)

Certainly among the most spectacular foliage plants in the border, the phormiums send up great sword-leafed fountains of tough foliage that may be rich bronze or striped with green, cream, orange and red. There's a new vogue for these plants which are hardy (if they are forms of *P. cookianum*) or on the borderline of hardiness (in the case of *P. tenax* varieties). There are now plenty of named varieties of varying heights. Use them for evergreen foliage contrasts.

Like sun and a warm, sheltered spot in well-drained soil. *Tolerate* well-worked clay or chalky soil;

coastal exposure in the milder counties. *P. tenax* varieties are only reliably hardy in southern counties. *Div.*

Physalis   Chinese Lantern Flower
60 × 60 cm (2 × 2 ft)

No flower arranger will want to be without this plant in the garden. In autumn the stems of *P. alkekengi* var. *franchetii* are hung with Chinese paper lanterns of bright orange. They keep their colour when dried. An easy-to-grow treasure.

Likes sun and a well-drained soil. *Tolerates* dappled shade; dry, chalky or clay soil. *Stake. Div.*

Physostegia   Obedient Plant
75 × 60 cm (2½ × 2 ft)

Here's a curiosity; the obedient plant produces densely packed flower spikes in late summer, and each of the tiny tubular blooms can be nudged on its stalk to any position you want—hence the common name. *P. virginiana* has two good varieties: 'Vivid', which is rich mauve-pink, compact at around 45 × 45 cm (1½ × 1½ ft) and particularly late, flowering in early autumn; and 'Summer Snow', a white form.

Like sun and a good, well-drained soil that's not likely to dry out. *Tolerate* clay and chalky soils; coastal gardens. *Div.*

Platycodon   Balloon Flower
30–45 cm × 45 cm (1–1½ × 1½ ft)

The inflated buds of platycodon are pushed up over the greyish leaves where they open out into beautiful campanula flowers in mid- to late summer. *P. grandiflorus* has several varieties, of which var. *mariesii* is a good sky blue, and 'Snowflake' a dainty white. Good front-of-the-border plants which are fun to 'pop'.

Like sun and a rich, well-drained but not dry soil. *Tolerate* clay and chalky soils. *Div. Seed. Cutt.*

Polemonium   Jacob's Ladder
60–75 × 75 cm (2–2½ × 2 ft)

Attractive flowering and foliage plants with pinnate leaves carried thickly on upright stems that are topped with lavender-blue flower clusters in early summer. *P. caeruleum* is the commonest species; its white form is lovely. 'Pink Beauty' is mauve pink. Can be short lived if neglected.

Like sun and a rich, moisture-retentive soil. *Tolerate* shade; chalky and clay soil. *Stake. Div.* (regularly)

Polygonatum   Solomon's Seal
60 × 60–90 cm (2 × 2–3 ft)

I'm lucky enough to have this plant growing wild in my garden and it looks a treat in late spring when its arching stems drip with tiny ivory bells. The bold leaves sprout from the stems like wings. An invaluable foliage plant for use with other bold beauties like hostas and sword-leafed irises. The British native is *P. multiflorum. P.* × *hybridum* is beefier.

Likes shade and a leafy, moisture-retentive soil.

Tolerates chalk and well-worked, enriched clay. *Div.*

Polygonum   (now **Persicaria**) Knotweed Various

Make a point of exploring the polygonum tribe—it offers such a varied and valuable collection of plants. *P. bistorta* 'Superbum', 75 × 90 cm (2½ × 3 ft), is a spring beauty with green, dock-like leaves over which tower pink pokers. It continues to throw up a few blooms right through summer. *P. campanulatum*, 90 × 90 cm (3 × 3 ft), is a more frothy treasure with dusky green leaves and branched flowerheads of miniature blush-pink bells from summer to autumn. *P. milettii*, 45 × 60 cm (1½ × 2 ft), is the brightest polygonum I know, with deep rose-red flower spikes carried over lush green leaves in summer. And finally a giant—*P. cuspidatum* 'Spectabile', 1·8 × 2·4 m (6 × 8 ft) and more. Don't let this blighter loose unless you have plenty of room to spare. Where it can be entertained it will certainly entertain you in summer with its vigorous hollow stems that arch at the tips to show off the leaves. These are variegated green and creamy yellow with a tinge of pink—like some revolting foreign cheese. I can never make up my mind whether the plant is lurid or spectacular, but it always attracts gasps from onlookers.

Like sun and good, moisture-retentive soil. *Tolerate* dappled shade and clay or chalky soils; sheltered coastal gardens. *Stake (some). Div.*

Potentilla   Cinquefoil
45 × 60 cm (1½ × 2 ft)

There are lots of hybrid herbaceous potentillas that can be used to bring brightness to beds and borders in summer. They offer double or single flowers in shades of red, yellow, orange and salmon carried on floppy stems over fingered, downy leaves. 'William Rollison' is a favourite double red, and 'Yellow Queen' a double yellow. The doubles last longer than the singles.

Like sun and a well-drained soil. *Tolerate* dry or chalky soil and coastal exposure. *Stake. Div.*

Primula   Polyanthus Various

The polyanthus is the pride of spring in most folk's gardens, making neat mounds of primrose leaves that are iced with red, orange, yellow, blue or white flowers over many spring weeks. The plants grow to maybe 23 × 30 cm (9 in × 1 ft) but repay annual division after flowering. Try also the choice 'Garryarde' varieties of primrose with their dusky pastel flowers and bronze-burnished leaves. The candelabra primulas come in all sorts of colours, carrying their blooms in tiers up stems that may be anything from 30 to 90 cm (1 to 3 ft) tall. *P. japonica*, *P. pulverulenta*, *P. chungensis* and *P. bulleyana* are good examples, and *P. sikkimensis* has nodding clusters of sulphur–yellow bells. The others may be yellow, red, pink, orange, crimson, magenta or white. At Harlow Car Gardens near Harrogate they look better than anywhere else.

Late spring and early summer is their season of glory.

Like sun or dappled shade and a leafy, peaty, moisture-retentive soil. *Tolerate* clay soil and chalky soil (though the candelabra types prefer acid ground and sometimes fail on chalk). *Seed. Div.*

Pulmonaria Lungwort, Soldiers and Sailors 30×90 cm (1×3 ft)
The lungwort is one of the earliest and most reliable flowers of spring. Its nodding clusters of pink and blue flowers unfurl in March and look a treat with hellebores. As they fade the bold, oval leaves, splashed with silver-grey, push up to take their place. *P. saccharata* is the type best in leaf, but for flowers (without the foliage spotting) try *P. rubra*, which has glorious, large, rich pink blooms especially early in the season. 'Munstead Blue' is a lungwort with especially good blue flowers.

Like gentle shade and a moisture-retentive soil. *Tolerate* clay and chalky soils; full sun but not drought. *Div.*

Rheum Rhubarb 2.4×1.5 m (8×5 ft)
The bold maroon leaves of *R. palmatum* 'Atrosanguineum' (syn. 'Atropurpureum') take some spectators aback in spring when they unfurl from huge scarlet buds of rather rude appearance. But soon the deeply cut rhubarb leaves assume stately proportions, eventually being accompanied by a towering rose-red flower spike in summer. By then the upper surfaces of the leaves are dull green, but the ruddiness remains beneath.

Likes dappled shade and a rich, moisture-retentive soil that's not likely to dry out. *Tolerates* full sun (but not drought), clay and chalky soil. *Div.*

Rodgersia Rodger's Bronze Leaf
90×90 cm (3×3 ft)
Imagine some bronze horse-chestnut leaves stuck on 60 cm (2 ft) stalks and pushed into the soil and you have some idea what rodgersia looks like, except that it is rather more graceful than my crude description implies. *R. pinnata* 'Superba' is perhaps the best form, and it carries frothy plumes of pink flowers over its leaves in summer.

Likes dappled shade and a rich, moisture-retentive soil. *Tolerates* well-worked and enriched clay or chalky soils; full sun but not dry soil. *Div.*

Rudbeckia Coneflower, Black-eyed Susan
75×60 cm ($2\frac{1}{2} \times 2$ ft)
More bright summer daisies with vivid yellow flowers centred with a prominent brown boss. 'Goldsturm' is the most popular variety and blooms from mid- to late summer. 'Goldquelle' starts and finishes rather later if you want to prolong your daisy days.

Like sun and a well-drained soil. *Tolerate* clay or chalky soils. *Stake. Div.*

Salvia Sage Various
The ornamental sages are a varied bunch, among the best of which are *S. nemorosa* 'Lubecca' (syn. *S. superba* 'Lubeca'), 60×60 cm (2×2 ft), with slender spikes of violet blue in summer; and a lovely grey-foliaged plant, *S. argentea*, which produces a rosette of large, rumpled leaves covered in silky white wool. When the flower spike appears the leaves become a greyish green, so try to chop off the stalk as soon as you see it emerging. Older leaves can be cut off too. Best treated as a biennial on heavy soils—longer-lived on lighter earth.

Like full sun and a well-drained soil. *Tolerate* dry and chalky soils; coastal exposure. *Stake tall varieties. Seed. Div.*

Saponaria Soapwort; Bouncing Bet
75 cm $\times 1.2$ m ($2\frac{1}{2} \times 4$ ft)
Buy a plant by the name of *S. officinalis* 'Rosea Plena' and you'll own a glorious late-summer bloomer that produces masses of double pale pink campion flowers over a thicket of mid-green leaves. It starts in midsummer and doesn't finish until autumn. A treat with blue-grey foliage like that of *Hosta sieboldiana*. Not for tidy gardeners.

Likes sun and well-drained soil. *Tolerates* dappled shade; chalk and clay soils. *Stake Div.*

Scabiosa Scabious 60×60 cm (2×2 ft)
Pale blue scabious always brings back memories of my grandfather, who grew the plant as a cut flower on his allotment. 'Clive Greaves' is the best variety of *S. caucasica*, and it produces masses of sky-blue-petalled flowers with their complicated white and lilac-pink centres in summer. The green leaves stay low and are finely cut. Lovely among silver-foliaged plants.

Likes sun and well-drained, especially chalky, soil. *Tolerates* well-worked clay; coastal exposure. *Stake. Div.*

Sedum (now **Hylotelephium**) Ice Plant; Stonecrop 30×45 cm ($1 \times 1\frac{1}{2}$ ft)
Grow a patch of *S. spectabile* at the foot of a buddleja and you'll have a combination of plants that butterflies find irresistible. The grey-green succulent leaves start to push up in spring, making the plant a fine foliage subject. In late summer and autumn the flat flowerheads of dusky pink open to attract your eyes and the insects (though butterflies are said to be less fond of the variety 'Autumn Joy' than they are of the true species). From the human point of view 'Brilliant' is another good form with flowers of a warmer and rather deeper shade of pink.

Like full sun and a well-drained soil. *Tolerate* dry or chalky soils and well-worked clay; coastal exposure. *Div. Cutt.*

Sidalcea 90×90 cm (3×3 ft)
Like elegant miniature hollyhocks the sidalceas are bright clump formers for summer borders. They produce towering stems of mallow flowers at their

best in the glorious pink of 'Rose Queen' or the rather shorter 'Loveliness'. There is also a smaller-flowered white species, *S. candida*. The rich pinks are derived from *S. malviflora*.

Like full sun and a well-drained but moisture-retentive soil (they resent dryness at the roots). *Tolerate* chalk and well-worked clay. *Stake taller varieties.* *Div.*

Smilacina False Spikenard
90 × 60 cm (3 × 2 ft)
Take the stems and leaves of Solomon's seal and the creamy white flower plumes of an astilbe; fasten the two together and you've got smilacina. It's a superbly attractive plant at its best in spring. It is deliciously and overpoweringly scented.

Likes shade and leafy, well-drained lime-free soil. *Tolerates* well-worked clay. *Div.*

Solidago Golden Rod
60 cm–1·8 m × 60 cm–1·8 m (2–6 × 2–6 ft)
Railway embankments countrywide are decorated with the sceptre-like stems of Golden Rod in late summer and autumn, so happy is it to colonize any ground. Don't let the tall and dead-bottomed stems of sooty yellow flowers put you off growing the better varieties which are brighter and less rampant. 'Goldenmosa' has an elegance and bright colouring that few others can rival. At 75 × 60 cm (2½ × 2 ft) it fits into any garden.

Likes sun and well-drained soil. *Tolerates* dry, chalky and clay soil. *Div.*

Stachys Betony; Lamb's Ears
45 × 60 cm (1½ × 2 ft)
There are two good species here. The first is *S. macrantha* 'Superba', which has toothed green leaves and dense heads of mauve-purple hooded flowers in summer. It makes deep ground cover and is smart without being prissy. *S. byzantina* (syn. *S. lanata*, *S. olympica*) is the white and woolly lamb's ears, tongues or lugs (depending on your part of the country). It makes a rag-rug of leaves over which tower spikes of tiny mauve flowers interspersed with leafy bracts. Beth Chatto offers a variety known as 'Cotton Boll', whose flower cluster are orbs of white velvet dotted up the stem. These summer blooms are a treat and sadly lacking in the dreary 'Silver Carpet', often recommended as ground cover. It gets mildew and dies out in places and so needs frequent lifting and dividing.

Like full sun and a well-drained soil. *Tolerate* shade (*S. macrantha* only), dry and chalky soils; coastal exposure. *Div.*

Stipa Feather Grass 1·8 × 1·2 m (6 × 4 ft)
A massive, elegant, oat-like grass with arching tufts of narrow green leaves over which hover the bronze flowerheads in summer. *S. gigantea* is a bold, yet graceful grass that glints in the sun. The heads turn strawy as they age. Don't be without it if you can spare the space it requires.

Likes full sun and a well-drained soil. *Tolerates* dry and chalky soil. *Div.*

Thalictrum Meadow Rue
90 cm–1·5 m × 60 cm (3–5 × 2 ft)
Feathery mounds of columbine foliage—finely cut and grey-green—are topped in summer with airy sprays of fluffy flowers. The blooms are lilac-pink in *T. delavayi* (syn. *T. dipterocarpum*) and even more fluffy in 'Hewitt's Double'. Pays ground rent amply on account of both foliage and flowers.

Likes sun and well-drained but moisture-retentive soil. *Tolerates* dappled shade; well-worked clay and chalky soils. *Stake.* *Div. Seed.*

Tradescantia Spiderwort; Flower of a Day
60 × 60 cm (2 × 2 ft)
The varieties of *T. virginiana* (now more correctly known as *T. Andersonia* Group) are lush border plants with succulent stems and long, fresh-green leaves. In summer and on into autumn the stems are topped with three-petalled flowers of purplish blue—at least that's the colour of the type most frequently seen in gardens. Go to a nurseryman and you can choose from 'Osprey', white; 'Purewell Giant', magenta; and 'J. C. Weguelin', pale blue; as well as that good dark blue 'Isis'.

Like sun and well-drained soil. *Tolerate* dappled shade; well-worked clay and enriched chalky soils (they fail on poor, shallow chalk); coastal exposure. *Stake.* *Div.*

Trollius Globe Flower
60–90 × 60 cm (2–3 × 2 ft)
That bright yellow spherical flower of spring, *T. europaeus*, is a good streamside plant where its flowers are shown off well against a mound of rich green buttercup leaves, but the king of the race is *T. chinensis*, a bright orange spring and summer bloomer with flowers that are composed of an outer cup and an inner tuft of spiky petals. There is no brighter orange in the garden.

Like sun and moisture-retentive soil. *Tolerate* dappled shade; well-worked clay and chalky soil but never drought. *Div.*

Tropaeolum Scotch Flame Flower
Climbing/trailing
Over the gloomy countenance of evergreen hedges the Scotch flame flower, *T. speciosum*, will blaze a trail of bright red tubular flowers in summer and autumn, accompanied by its neat, fingered leaves of fresh green. Once suited it will scramble to 3 m (10 ft) or more. *T. polyphyllum* is a different kettle of fish. It spreads its stems sideways over the soil for 90 cm (3 ft) or more. They are thickly plastered with blue-grey leaves and, in early summer, with pale orange blooms—a brave combination of colours. *T. spec-*

iosum likes the cool, damp northern counties better than those in the south, but it will often romp away if planted on the north side of hedges or trees. Plant the tubers on their sides 10 cm (4 in) deep and mark them well. It likes a peaty, moisture-retentive soil. *T. polyphyllum likes* deep, well-drained soil and a sunny spot. Plant its tubers 30 cm (1 ft) deep. Both plants die down after flowering.   *Div.*

Verbascum Mullein 45 cm–1·8 m × 30–90 cm
Many mulleins are biennial and die after flowering, but a few will stay with you for years. Two in particular: 'Golden Bush', 60 × 60 cm (2 × 2 ft), with spires of yellow flowers in summer, and *V. chaixii*, 90 × 60 cm (3 × 2 ft), whose yellow blooms are spotted in the centre with purple, are good garden plants. Varieties like 'Gainsborough' are not reliably perennial but can be increased by root cuttings annually.
Like sunny spots in well-drained soil. *Tolerate* dry and chalky soil and well-worked clay.
Seed. Div. Root.

Veronica Various
If you're seeking upright spires of blue summer flowers, you can safely plump for veronicas. *V. spicata*, 60 × 60 cm (2 × 2 ft), offers them, and provides additional shades in its varieties 'Barcarolle', rose pink, and 'Red Fox', deep rose. 'Icicle' will give you white spikes.
Like sun and a well-drained soil. *Tolerate* dry, clay or chalky soils; coastal exposure.   *Stake taller varieties.*   *Div.*

Viola Violet; Pansy 30 × 90 cm (1 × 3 ft)
Charming plants, violas can grow in the tiniest, dimmest corner. I'll pick just two. *V. cornuta*, the horned violet, makes sprawling clumps of green leaves alive with pale lavender or white flowers in summer. Clip over the plants in late July and they'll bloom again in autumn. *V. labradorica* 'Purpurea' (now *V. riviniana* Purpurea Group) is much neater at around 10 cm (4 in) and makes carpets of maroon leaves, studded with lavender-purple flowers in spring.
Like dappled shade and a well-drained but moisture-retentive soil. *Tolerate* heavy shade or sun; chalky or well-worked clay soil.   *Div. Seed. Cutt.*

Zantedeschia Arum Lily 90 × 60 cm (3 × 2 ft)
Bold, lustrous, juicy green arrowheads of leaves and white vase-shaped flowers centred with a yellow club-like spadix are the hallmarks of *Z. aethiopica*. It will bloom annually in summer in sheltered gardens. Its variety 'Crowborough' is apparently more tolerant of dry soils. Both need the winter protection of dry straw or bracken until well established.
Likes sun or gentle shade and a moisture-retentive, preferably boggy soil. *Tolerates* ordinary well-drained soil but not drought; coastal exposure. *Div. Root. Seed.*

FIND THE RIGHT BORDER PLANT

If you're looking for a border plant to fill a particular spot these lists should give you some ideas. But remember that even those plants which are tolerant of inhospitable conditions should be given every help in the first year of establishment.

PLANTS FOR DRY SOIL
Acanthus
Achillea
Agapanthus
Alchemilla
Alstroemeria
Artemisia
Asplenium
Astrantia
Ballota
Bergenia
Brunnera (some)
Calamintha
Campanula (some)
Catananche
Centaurea
Centranthus
Convallaria
Corydalis
Crambe
Crocosmia
Curtonus
Cynara
Dictamnus
Dierama
Digitalis
Dryopteris
Echinops
Erigeron
Eryngium
Euphorbia
Festuca
Gaillardia
Galega
Geranium
Incarvillea
Iris
Kniphofia
Lamium
Lathyrus
Liatris
Linaria
Linum
Lychnis
Macleaya
Milium
Nepeta
Oenothera
Paeonia
Papaver

Penstemon
Phlox
Physalis
Potentilla
Salvia
Sedum
Solidago
Stachys
Stipa
Verbascum
Veronica

PLANTS FOR CLAY SOIL

Acanthus
Achillea
Aconitum
Ajuga
Alchemilla
Althaea
Anaphalis
Anchusa
Anemone
Aquilegia
Arum
Aruncus
Asplenium
Aster
Astilbe
Astrantia
Bergenia
Carex
Centaurea
Chrysanthemum
Cimicifuga
Coreopsis
Cortaderia (sometimes)
Crocosmia
Curtonus
Delphinium
Dicentra
Digitalis
Doronicum
Dryopteris
Echinacea
Echinops
Epilobium
Epimedium
Erigeron
Eryngium (some)
Galega
Geranium
Geum
Glyceria
Helenium
Helleborus
Hemerocallis
Heuchera
Hosta

Iris
Kniphofia
Lamium
Liriope
Lupinus
Lychnis
Lysimachia
Malva
Matteuccia
Mimulus
Monarda
Morina
Paeonia
Phlox
Phormium
Physalis
Physostegia
Platycodon
Polemonium
Polygonatum
Polygonum (syn. Persicaria)
Primula
Pulmonaria
Rheum
Rodgersia
Rudbeckia
Saponaria
Scabiosa
Sedum
Sidalcea
Smilacina
Solidago
Thalictrum
Tradescantia
Trollius
Verbascum
Veronica
Viola

PLANTS FOR CHALKY SOIL

Acanthus
Achillea
Aconitum
Agapanthus
Ajuga
Alchemilla
Alstroemeria
Anaphalis
Anchusa
Anemone
Aquilegia
Artemisia
Arum
Asplenium
Aster
Astilbe (sometimes)
Astrantia
Ballota

Bergenia
Calamintha
Campanula
Carex
Catananche
Centaurea
Centranthus
Ceratostigma
Chrysanthemum
Cimicifuga
Convallaria
Coreopsis
Cortaderia (sometimes)
Corydalis
Crambe
Crocosmia
Curtonus
Cynara
Delphinium
Dianthus
Dicentra
Dictamnus
Dierama
Digitalis
Doronicum
Dryopteris
Echinacea
Echinops
Epilobium
Epimedium
Eremurus
Erigeron
Eryngium
Euphorbia
Festuca
Gaillardia
Galega
Gentiana
Geranium
Geum
Glyceria
Gypsophila
Helenium
Helleborus
Hemerocallis
Heuchera
Hosta
Incarvillea
Iris
Kniphofia
Lamium
Lathyrus
Liatris
Linaria
Linum
Liriope
Lobelia
Lupinus (sometimes)

Lychnis
Lysimachia
Macleaya
Malva
Matteuccia
Milium
Mimulus
Monarda
Morina
Nepeta
Oenothera
Paeonia
Papaver
Penstemon
Phlox
Phormium
Physalis
Physostegia
Platycodon
Polemonium
Polygonatum
Polygonum (syn. Persicaria)
Potentilla
Primula (sometimes)
Pulmonaria
Rheum
Rodgersia
Rudbeckia
Salvia
Saponaria
Scabiosa
Sedum
Sidalcea
Solidago
Stachys
Stipa
Thalictrum
Tradescantia
Trollius
Verbascum
Veronica
Viola

PLANTS FOR COASTAL GARDENS

It is always worth experimenting with plants not on this list to see if they can cope with your particular coastal situation—no two maritime gardens seem to grow the same plants.

Achillea
Agapanthus
Alstroemeria
Anemone
Artemisia
Bergenia
Catananche
Centaurea
Centranthus

Chrysanthemum
Crambe
Crocosmia
Dianthus
Dierama
Echinops
Erigeron
Eryngium
Euphorbia
Festuca
Geranium
Gypsophila
Heuchera
Iris
Kniphofia
Lathyrus
Linaria
Lychnis
Morina
Oenothera
Penstemon
Phormium
Physostegia
Polygonum (syn. Persicaria)
Potentilla
Salvia
Scabiosa
Sedum
Tradescantia
Veronica
Zantedeschia

PLANTS FOR SHADE
The A–Z section gives a more precise indication of the type of shade the plants can cope with—gentle, dappled or otherwise.

Acanthus
Aconitum
Ajuga
Alchemilla
Anaphalis
Anchusa
Anemone
Aquilegia
Arum
Aruncus
Asplenium
Astilbe
Astrantia
Bergenia
Blechnum
Brunnera
Calamintha
Campanula (some)
Carex
Cimicifuga
Convallaria
Corydalis

Crocosmia
Curtonus
Dicentra
Digitalis
Doronicum
Epilobium
Epimedium
Euphorbia
Gentiana
Geranium
Geum
Glyceria
Gunnera
Helleborus
Hemerocallis
Heuchera
Hosta
Iris (some)
Kirengeshoma
Lamium
Liriope
Lobelia
Lysimachia
Matteuccia
Meconopsis
Milium
Mimulus
Physalis
Polemonium
Polygonatum
Polygonum (syn. Persicaria)
Primula
Pulmonaria
Rheum
Rodgersia
Saponaria
Smilacina
Stachys
Thalictrum
Tradescantia
Trollius
Viola
Zantedeschia

PLANTS FOR GROUND COVER
The measurement given after each plant is the recommended planting distance when large numbers are used for ground cover.

Acanthus 90 cm (3 ft)
Ajuga 23 cm (9 in)
Alchemilla 30 cm (1 ft)
Aruncus 60 cm (2 ft)
Astilbe 45 cm (1½ ft)
Astrantia 45 cm (1½ ft)
Bergenia 45 cm (1½ ft)
Blechnum 30 cm (1 ft)
Brunnera 30 cm (1 ft)
Calamintha 30 cm (1 ft)

Convallaria 23 cm (9 in)
Corydalis 23 cm (9 in)
Crocosmia 30 cm (1 ft)
Curtonus 45 cm (1½ ft)
Doronicum 45 cm (1½ ft)
Epimedium 30 cm (1 ft)
Euphorbia 60 cm (2 ft)
Geranium 45 cm (1½ ft)
Glyceria 60 cm (2 ft)
Hemerocallis 60 cm (2 ft)
Heuchera 30 cm (1 ft)
Hosta 60 cm (2 ft)
Kniphofia (some) 60 cm (2 ft)
Lamium 45 cm (1½ ft)
Liriope 30 cm (1 ft)
Lysimachia 30 cm (1 ft)
Nepeta 60 cm (2 ft)
Polygonum (syn. Persicaria) 60 cm (2 ft)
Primula 23 cm (9 in)
Pulmonaria 45 cm (1½ ft)
Saponaria 30 cm (1 ft)
Stachys 30 cm (1 ft)
Tradescantia 45 cm (1½ ft)
Viola 23 cm (9 in)

PLANTS WITH ATTRACTIVE FOLIAGE
Acanthus
Achillea
Ajuga
Alchemilla
Aquilegia
Artemisia
Arum
Asplenium
Astilbe
Ballota
Bergenia
Blechnum
Carex
Cimicifuga
Convallaria
Coreopsis
Corydalis
Crocosmia
Curtonus
Cynara
Dianthus
Dryopteris
Echinops
Epimedium
Euphorbia
Festuca
Galega
Glyceria
Gunnera
Helleborus (some)
Hemerocallis
Heuchera

Hosta
Iris
Kniphofia (some)
Lamium
Lathyrus
Linaria
Liriope
Lysimachia (some)
Macleaya
Matteuccia
Milium
Morina
Nepeta
Phormium
Polemonium
Polygonatum
Polygonum (syn. Persicaria) (some)
Pulmonaria (some)
Rheum
Rodgersia
Salvia (some)
Sedum
Smilacina
Stachys
Thalictrum

SPECIMEN PLANTS
These are plants which strike me as having such good form and appearance that they are worth planting as eye-catchers in a bed or border, or as single specimens on patios or in gravel and cobble beds. Not all of them are huge; some are small and capable of being fitted into the tiniest back yard.
Acanthus
Aruncus
Carex
Cortaderia
Cynara
Dierama
Dryopteris
Euphorbia
Festuca
Glyceria
Gunnera
Hemerocallis
Hosta
Iris
Kniphofia
Macleaya
Matteuccia
Phormium
Polygonatum
Polygonum (syn. Persicaria)
Rheum
Rodgersia
Sedum
Smilacina
Stipa

9 Annuals, biennials and bedding plants

Take some blue lobelia and some white alyssum and plant them alternately along the edge of a flowerbed. Plant behind them a dense array of orange french marigolds, and behind these a forest of scarlet salvias, perhaps with a fuchsia or white-leaved *Senecio cineraria* to act as a dot plant. And there you have it: the typical bedding out scheme. Nothing in the garden will be brighter, and nothing will be less inspiring.

Persuading gardeners to be adventurous with their bedding out might have been the eighth labour of Hercules, so difficult is it to accomplish. Now I'm not sneering at lobelia, alyssum, French marigolds and salvias (even though I have to try really hard to like the last two), I'm sneering at the way they are used. People who'd never dream of painting a room of their house in contrasting shades of red, orange, blue and white, will do it to a border in the garden. But it's much more fun to think of a different colour scheme for your bedding every year and to avoid planting in serried ranks as though your bedders were advancing troops clad in their ceremonial colours. Plan each bed or border with a particular colour theme—it will have tremendous impact. If you insist on a rainbow border, then plan one on paper so that the colours are displayed gradually as you round a corner or progress along the bed—that way the spectacle can be fun, rather than a reason for taking out the Polaroids.

But before all dedicated bedders flip over a few pages I'll cool down and sing the praises of a grand bunch of plants. Annuals, biennials and bedding plants are invaluable in any garden for their cheapness, cheerfulness and speedy growth. They are nearly all raised from seeds (which will fill you with a deep sense of achievement, should all go well), they are valuable gap fillers (especially in new gardens when the more permanent shrubby occupants have not yet filled their allotted space), and they offer a surprising variety of form, texture and colour (provided you splash out a little on the unusual kinds). Almost all of them adore full sun and a well-drained soil; they won't thrive in shade unless indicated as being shade tolerant in the lists on pp. 113–116.

The names given to the different groups of 'bedding plants' (a term that embraces any temporary garden occupant) can be confusing, but basically this is what they mean:

HARDY ANNUALS

For a start, annuals are those plants that complete their life cycle (from seed to flowering and setting new seed) within the space of a year. If you want a quick mnemonic think of *Beano* and *Dandy* Annuals—both last for just a year. Hardy annuals are the bold little blighters that can be sown outdoors in April to bloom *in situ* later on in the summer. Some of them are even so tough that they can be sown outdoors in September to struggle through the winter and flower quite early the following summer. Doesn't this make them biennials? No; they are still flowering within twelve months of being sown.

HALF-HARDY ANNUALS

These are more lily-livered. They need to be sown in pots in a greenhouse or porch, or on a windowsill where they can be coaxed into action with a little warmth. As soon as they emerge they need 'pricking out' (that strange phrase that brings a smirk to the novices' cheeks) into seed trays and growing on before being 'hardened off' (gradually accustomed to outdoor temperatures). These are the plants that are bought by the boxful from garden centres and greengrocers countrywide in early summer. Only when all danger of frost is past can they be planted out. Tender annuals fall into much the same category, though often these are grown in a greenhouse all their brief lives. If you simply cannot provide these plants with the protection they need to germinate don't worry. Some of them can be sown outdoors in late May as for hardy annuals. They'll flower later but are nonetheless welcome for that.

BIENNIALS

Gardeners are not known for their perversity, but it's a fact that most of the plants they grow as biennials are truly perennials; take the wallflower for instance—it will make a small shrub if grown on for several years but it won't be so plastered with flower as it was in its youth. True biennials complete their life cycle within the space of two years. They are sown during one year and grown on to flower and set seed the next. Here we are not talking so much about calendar years as about years consisting of a period of twelve months. Most biennials are sown in May to bloom the following May and June before they seed themselves and die off—probably during the summer. The whole episode probably takes about fourteen months, but this varies from plant to plant. Your average annual will cram its life into 6–8 months.

OTHER BEDDERS
Gardeners love exceptions, and there are a host of superb bedding plants that are really tender perennials—pelargoniums (geraniums), greenhouse fuchsias and the like. These must be overwintered in a greenhouse or on a windowsill where the frost can't get at them. Most can be propagated from cuttings each spring or autumn and so youngsters can be used each year, instead of the ancient gnarled parents who have just about exhausted themselves during a summer of over-generous blooming.

RAISING THE PLANTS
The techniques of raising the plants from seed differ slightly according to the plants' hardiness and length of life. These are the methods generally used for each group:

Hardy annuals are sown in prepared patches of soil in beds and borders, usually among the permanent inhabitants, but there's nothing to stop you from having a bed devoted entirely to them. Fork over the earth in March and scatter over it a dusting of blood, bone and fishmeal at the rate of about a handful to the square metre (yard). Don't add too much manure or compost—it turns the plants into Billy Bunters—fat and full of leaf but rather short on flowers.

April (and on through May for later summer

flowers) is a good time to sow, for by then the soil has usually warmed up a little and yet is still moist. Rake over the surface of the soil to break it down a little (don't over-rake or the surface will cake in the first shower of rain) and mark out the shape or 'drift' that is to be occupied by each plant (Fig. 28). Use the rake handle or a trail of sand to show each drift shape.

You can plan your border or bed in advance on a

(b) Mark out the areas to be occupied by each plant— use the rake handle or a trail of sand. Sow the seeds thinly and evenly on the surface.

Fig. 28 (a) Hardy annuals are those flowers that can be sown direct in the garden. Soil that has been previously dug should be raked level to produce tiny furrows.

(c) Lightly rake in the opposite direction and label each 'drift' if you like. Plastic netting will deter birds; and watering in dry weather will aid germination.

sheet of paper if you like, or rely on inspiration when you're out in the garden. Either way, try to place most of the taller plants at the back of the bed and the smaller ones at the front, but vary this arrangement occasionally and bring tall plants forward. They will create bays in the bed and make for a few surprises—the smaller plants crouching behind them will be revealed as you stroll along.

With the soil prepared and the drifts marked out you are ready to sow. First, draw the rake across each drift to leave tiny furrows. Scatter the seeds over the surface and lightly rake in the opposite direction to cover them. That's all they need—apart from labelling. Failures usually occur either as a result of the seeds being buried too deeply, or because they've been allowed to dry out during germination. Keep a watering can or lawn sprinkler handy and really soak the soil before it has a chance to dry out. There's also a slight chance that cats might patronize the area when performing their vital functions. Twiggy pea sticks laid on the ground will discourage them. Remove them after germination.

When the seedlings emerge they'll need thinning out to give the survivors room to grow and flower well. Thin them twice—once to a spacing of 5 cm (2 in), and finally (when they are touching again) to the spacing recommended on the chart. Instead of pulling up the unwanted seedlings, pinch them off at

Fig. 29 Annuals that need supporting can be held up unobtrusively if a few twiggy branches are pushed into the soil around them. Don't overdo it!

soil level. This prevents the roots of the remaining plants from being disturbed. Alternatively dig them up with a trowel and they'll often transplant quite well to fill other gaps.

Most annuals can support themselves. Some can't. Push twiggy pea sticks among the feeble kinds when they are 15 cm (6 in) high; they'll soon grow to mask the supports (Fig. 29).

Half-hardy annuals are sown in pots usually during March in a greenhouse or on a windowsill. Scatter the seeds *thinly* on the surface of moist seed compost that's been firmed down to 1 cm ($\frac{1}{2}$ in) below the pot rim. Dust-fine seeds such as begonias and lobelia need no further covering, but most seeds can be lightly covered with sieved seed compost—stop sieving as soon as the seeds disappear from view. Place a label in the pot and a sheet of glass or polythene, then a piece of newspaper over it. Stand the pots where they can be kept at a temperature of around 18 or 21°C (64 or 70°F). Check them every day and remove glass and paper from each pot as soon as the first seedling breaks the surface. Water by immersing the pot to half its depth in a bowl of water whenever the surface of the compost is just beginning to look dry.

Transfer the seedlings to trays of potting compost with a pencil—carefully lifting them individually and making a hole into which the roots can be lowered. Firm the compost around each seedling and then water them in. Grow them on in gentle heat and good light until early May, when they can be gradually accustomed to the temperatures outdoors (stand them out during the day and bring them under cover at night). By late May (early June in the north) they can stand outdoors at all times, for by then all danger of frost should be past and they can be planted out.

Plant them with a trowel (after giving them a really good soak in their trays) at the distances recommended in the chart. Water them in with a lawn sprinkler left running for a good two hours, and soak them again at any time when the earth around them starts to look dry. Forget to water and you'll have wasted your time—they'll turn crisp and die.

Biennials are usually sown on the vegetable plot. Here they can be trickled thinly into drills (just like turnips or lettuces) and transplanted to a wider spacing of 15 or 23 cm (6 or 9 in) when they are large enough to lift with a trowel. May and June are the months during which to sow, and the first transplanting can be carried out in July—still in rows on the vegetable plot. In September the plants can be dug up and planted at their final spacing in beds and borders. Most biennials are grown for spring bedding schemes but there are exceptions and these are indicated on the chart.

Tender perennials are usually planted out in late May or early June along with the half-hardy annuals and lifted and brought under cover during September before the frosts strike. Their cultivation is covered in Chapter 17, *Greenhouse Gardening*.

A–Z OF ANNUALS, BIENNIALS AND BEDDING PLANTS

The plants are arranged in their respective groups in this at-a-glance guide to cultivation and selection.

HARDY ANNUALS (Table 4)

If gardeners don't do something about it soon, a host of beautiful hardy annuals will disappear from the seed catalogues leaving us with more and more petunias and French marigolds. Included here are some charming flowers that are still to be had for a few pence. Do try to grow some of them before the seedsmen decide to scrap them for lack of demand. I've asterisked the plants that need your patronage and I've also listed them under the names you'll find in the seed catalogues; it's a weird mixture of botanical and common names.

S = Spring; A = Autumn.

HALF-HARDY ANNUALS (Table 5)

These slightly tender plants are available in greater variety than you'd think. Steer yourself away from the commoner types on to those that are less frequently planted. Generally speaking, those varieties described as F$_1$ hybrids are more expensive than all others, but they usually offer superb value for money, producing high quality and uniform plants.

Again the plants are listed under the names which are used in the catalogues of most seedsmen.

BIENNIALS (Table 6)

Do remember that all these plants are sown one year to flower the next. I've asterisked those that are truly perennials and which can, if you like, be left to grow on for another year or so. An asterisk in brackets indicates that some species are perennial, others true biennials. That stalwart of the spring bedding scheme, the polyanthus, is included in the entry devoted to *Primula* in the border plants section (Chapter 8). It is a true perennial and will last for years if divided regularly after flowering.

Table 4: Hardy Annuals

Plant	Height	Sow	Stake	Final Spacing	Details
Acrolinium (*Rhodanthe roseum*)	0·45 m (1½ ft)	S	★	23 cm (9 in)	Dainty pink and white 'everlasting' flowers.
* *Adonis aestivalis* (Pheasant's eye)	0·45 m (1½ ft)	S/A		23 cm (9 in)	Feathery leaves; scarlet, black-eyed flowers.
* *Agrostemma* 'Milas' (Corn cockle)	0·9 m (3 ft)	S/A	★	23 cm (9 in)	Lovely pink blooms pencilled with darker streaks.
Alyssum (Sweet alyssum)	10 cm (4 in)	S/A		15 cm (6 in)	Pink, white or violet scented flowers in dense bunches.
Anchusa 'Blue Angel'	23 cm (9 in)	S		0·3 m (1 ft)	Spreading domes of blue forget-me-not flowers.
* Argemone (Prickly poppy)	0·6 m (2 ft)	S		0·3 m (1 ft)	Prickly, thistle-like foliage and yellow flowers.
* *Asperula azurea setosa* (Annual woodruff)	0·3 m (1 ft)	S		23 cm (9 in)	Pale blue, tubular flowers carried in rounded heads. Tolerates some shade.
Atriplex hortensis 'Rubra' (Orach)	1·2 m (4 ft)	S		0·45 m (1½ ft)	Dock-like flowerheads and leaves of deep maroon.
* Bartonia (Mentzelia)	0·45 m (1½ ft)	S		23 cm (9 in)	Deeply cut leaves and scented, pointed-petalled yellow flowers.
Cabbage, Ornamental	0·3 m (1 ft)	S		0·45 m (1½ ft)	Cabbages with cream, white or pink hearts. Stunning!
* Cacalia (Tassel flower, Emilia)	0·45 m (1½ ft)	S		15 cm (6 in)	Fluffy 'composite' flowerheads of burning orange.
Calendula (Pot marigold)	0·3 m+ (1 ft+)	S/A		23 cm (9 in)	Cream, yellow or orange daisies; double or single.
Calliopsis (Coreopsis)	0·3 m+ (1 ft+)	S/A		23 cm (9 in)	Single yellow flowers with red centres. Very bright.
* *Campanula speculum* 'Violetta' (Venus looking glass, *Legousia*)	0·3 m (1 ft)	S/A		10 cm (4 in)	Violet-blue flowers with white eyes.
Canary creeper (*Tropaeolum peregrinum*)	Climber	S	★		Fingered green leaves and frilly yellow flowers.
Candytuft (Iberis)	0·3 m (1 ft)	S/A		10 cm (4 in)	Rounded flowers of white, pink, lilac or carmine.
Chrysanthemum carinatum	0·6 m (2 ft)	S/A	★	0·3 m (1 ft)	Single daisies banded in orange, yellow, red and white.
Clarkia elegans (*C. unguiculata*)	0·6 m (2 ft)	S/A	★	23 cm (9 in)	Double varieties are best. Rosettes of pink, mauve or crimson blooms.
Convolvulus 'Blue Flash'	15 cm (6 in)	S		15 cm (6 in)	Blue trumpets centred with yellow and white.
Cornflower (*Centaurea cyanus*)	0·9 m (3 ft)	S/A	★	23 cm (9 in)	Blue, white or pink fluffy 'cornflower' heads.
* *Crepis rubra* (Hawksbeard)	0·45 m (1½ ft)	S/A	★	15 cm (6 in)	Dainty pink 'dandelion' flowers. Endearingly dainty.
Dimorphotheca (Star of the Veldt)	23 cm (9 in)	S		15 cm (6 in)	Delightful white, yellow or orange daisies.
* *Dracocephalum moldavica* (Dragon's head)	0·6 m (2 ft)	S	★	15 cm (6 in)	Spires of hooded lavender-blue flowers. Aromatic.
* Echium (Viper's bugloss)	0·3 m (1 ft)	S/A		23 cm (9 in)	Violet-blue cup-shaped flowers among 'fluffy' buds.
Eschscholzia (Californian poppy)	0·3 m (1 ft)	S/A		15 cm (6 in)	Lacy foliage and poppy flowers of red, pink, yellow, orange or white.
* Gilia 'Summer Song'	0·3 m (1 ft)	S/A		15 cm (6 in)	Masses of lilac-blue and white five-petalled flowers.
Godetia (dwarf varieties, *Clarkia*)	0·3 m (1 ft)	S/A		15 cm (6 in)	Wide-faced blooms in shades of pink, red and white.

Plant	Height	Sow	Stake	Final Spacing	Details
Gypsophila elegans	0·45 m (1½ ft)	S/A	★	15 cm (6 in)	Sprays of tiny white or pink flowers.
* Ionopsidium (Violet cress)	8 cm (3 in)	S/A		–	A carpeter with plenty of pale lilac flowers. Enjoys a little shade.
Kochia (Burning bush, *Bassia*)	0·6 m (2 ft)	S		0·45 m (1½ ft)	Fuzzy columns of green turning red in autumn.
Larkspur (Annual delphinium)	0·9 m (3 ft)	S/A	★	23 cm (9 in)	Feathery leaves and spires of blue, pink, violet or white.
Lavatera (Mallow)	0·6 m (2 ft)	S	★	0·3 m (1 ft)	Huge trumpets of pink (Silver Cup) or white (Mont Blanc).
* *Layia elegans* (Tidy tips)	0·3 m (1 ft)	S		15 cm (6 in)	Yellow daisies whose petals are tipped with white.
* Leptosiphon (Stardust)	10 cm (4 in)	S		5 cm (2 in)	Small flowers of orange, red, cream or yellow over needle-like leaves.
* Limnanthes (Poached egg flower)	23 cm (9 in)	S/A		10 cm (4 in)	Feathery green leaves and white, yellow-centred blooms.
* Linaria 'Fairy Bouquet' (Toadflax)	23 cm (9 in)	S/A		10 cm (4 in)	Tiny snapdragon flowers in a bright range of colours.
* *Linum grandiflorum* 'Rubrum' (Scarlet flax)	0·3 m (1 ft)	S		10 cm (4 in)	Single wide-faced flowers of bright red.
* *Lonas inodora*	0·3 m (1 ft)	S		15 cm (6 in)	Clusters of bright yellow powder-puff flowers.
Love-lies-bleeding (*Amaranthus caudatus*)	0·9 m (3 ft)	S		0·6 m (2 ft)	Oval green leaves and drooping velvet tassels of of crimson or green.
* Malope	0·75 m (2½ ft)	S		23 cm (9 in	Single mallow flowers of pink, white or crimson.
Matthiola bicornis (Night-scented stock)	23 cm (9 in)	S		–	Dingy lilac but strongly perfumed at night. Sow mixed with Virginian stocks.
* Mignonette (*Reseda odorata*)	0·3 m (1 ft)	S		10 cm (4 in)	Fluffy rusty-orange flowers; strongly perfumed.
Moluccella (Bells of Ireland)	0·9 m (3 ft)	S		23 cm (9 in)	Spires of white flowers which fall to reveal cockle-shaped calyces.
Nasturtium (*Tropaeolum majus*)	0·3 m (1 ft)	S		0·3 m (1 ft)	Parasol-shaped leaves and red, orange or yellow flowers.
* Nemophila (Baby blue eyes)	15 cm (6 in)	S/A		8 cm (3 in)	Carpeter with sky-blue flowers centred with white.
* Nicandra (Shoo-fly plant)	0·75 m (2½ ft)	S		0·3 m (1 ft)	Pale lavender and white flowers; inflated seed cases.
Nigella (Love-in-a-mist)	0·45 m (1½ ft)	S/A		15 cm (6 in)	Feathery foliage; blue, white or pink flowers followed by spherical seed heads.
Perilla	0·6 m (2 ft)	S		0·3 m (1 ft)	Deeply cut purple foliage—like a dark coleus.
* *Phacelia campanularia*	23 cm (9 in)	S/A		8 cm (3 in)	Pure gentian blue bells—indispensable.
Poppy 'Pink Chiffon'	0·75 m (2½ ft)	S/A	★	23 cm (9 in)	Double pink, peony-like blooms.
Poppy (Shirley types)	0·6 m (2 ft)	S/A	★	15 cm (6 in)	Lovely poppies of pink, yellow, orange and red.
Rhodanthe (*Helipterum manglesii*)	0·3 m (1 ft)	S		15 cm (6 in)	Dainty pink 'everlasting' daisies that dry well.
Rudbeckia (Coneflower)	0·6 m (2 ft)	S		15 cm (6 in)	Orange (Marmalade) or mahogany (Rustic Dwarfs) daisies.
Salvia horminum (Clary)	0·45 m (1½ ft)	S/A		15 cm (6 in)	Tall spires clad in pink, white or blue bracts.
* *Saponaria vaccaria*	0·6 m (2 ft)	S/A	★	15 cm (6 in)	Plenty of dainty pink flowers.
Sunflower (Helianthus)	3·0 m + (10 ft +)	S	★	0·6 m (2 ft)	Massive yellow or orange daisies atop gigantic stalks.
Sweet pea (Lathyrus odoratus)	1·8 m + (6 ft +)	S/A	★	0·3 m (1 ft)	Fragrant pea flowers in assorted colours.
Sweet pea 'Jet Set'	0·9 m (3 ft)	S/A	★	15 cm (6 in)	Lower and easy to support with twiggy branches.
Sweet sultan (*Centaurea imperialis*, *Amberboa moschata*)	0·45 m (1½ ft)	S		23 cm (9 in)	Starry 'cornflower' blooms of purple, yellow, pink and white.
* Viscaria 'Blue Angel'	0·3 m (1 ft)	S		10 cm (4 in)	Five-petalled lavender-blue flowers.
Xeranthemum	0·6 m (2 ft)	S	★	15 cm (6 in)	'Everlasting' daisy flowers of pink, yellow and white.

Table 5: Half-hardy Annuals

Plant	Height	Can sow outdoors	Spacing	Details
Ageratum (Floss flower)	15–23 cm (6–9 in)		15 cm (6 in)	Hairy green leaves topped with fluffy lavender-blue or white pom-pons.
Amaranthus 'Illumination'	0·75 m (2½ ft)		0·45 m (1½ ft)	Brilliant leaves marked red, bronze, yellow and green.
Anagallis 'Coerulea'	15 cm (6 in)	★	15 cm (6 in)	True blue, large pimpernel flowers over green domes of foliage.
Antirrhinum (Snapdragon)	15 cm–0·9 m (6 in–3 ft)		23 cm (9 in)	'Snapdragons' of every hue except blue or green.
Arctotis (African daisy)	0·45 m (1½ ft)		23 cm (9 in)	Vibrant daisies of red, orange, yellow, pink or white.
Asters	0·3–0·45 m (1–1½ ft)	★	23 cm (9 in)	Double or single daisies in a wide range of colours.
Begonia semperflorens	15 cm (6 in)		15 cm (6 in)	Shiny leaves of green or brown; red, pink or white flowers.
Brachyscome (Swan River daisy)	15 cm (6 in)	★	10 cm (4 in)	Finely cut leaves and blue or white daisy flowers.
Calandrinia umbellata (Rock purslane)	15 cm (6 in)		15 cm (6 in)	Neat tufts of foliage topped with crimson-magenta flowers.

Plant	Height	Can sow outdoors	Spacing	Details
Calceolaria 'Sunshine'	23 cm (9 in)		23 cm (9 in)	Bright yellow pouch-like flowers over green leaves.
Carnation 'Chabaud Mixed'	0·45 m (1½ ft)		15 cm (6 in)	'Annual' carnations of mixed colours.
Carnation 'Dwarf Mixed'	0·3 m (1 ft)		23 cm (9 in)	F₁ hybrid mixture; pricy but very showy.
Centaurea gymnocarpa	0·45 m (1½ ft)		0·3 m (1 ft)	Finely cut grey leaves; an exceptional foliage plant.
Cineraria maritima (Dusty miller, *Senecio cineraria*)	0·3 m (1 ft)		0·3 m (1 ft)	Not so finely cut as the above, but more densely felted.
Cleome spinosa (Spider flower)	0·75 m (2½ ft)	★	0·3 m (1 ft)	Fingered green leaves and spidery flowers of pink or white.
Cosmos (Cosmea)	0·6–0·9 m (2–3 ft)		23 cm (9 in)	Finely cut leaves and single 'dahlia' flowers of red, yellow, orange, pink or white.
Dahlia	0·3–1·2 m (1–4 ft)		0·3 m (1 ft)	Fleshy leaves and double or single mixed flowers.
Dahlia 'Redskin'	0·45 m (1½ ft)		0·3 m (1 ft)	Mixed flowers over deep bronze-purple leaves.
Delphinium 'Blue Butterfly'	0·45 m (1½ ft)		0·3 m (1 ft)	Tall spires of rich blue flowers.
Dianthus heddewigii (Pink)	15–30 cm (6–12 in)		15 cm (6 in)	Brilliant annual pinks of red, pink, white and bi-coloured flowers; there are some superb F₁ hybrids; try Queen's Court.
Gaillardia (Blanket flower)	0·3–0·6 m (1–2 ft)		23 cm (9 in)	Double or single daisies of orange, red and yellow.
Gazania	0·3 m (1 ft)		15 cm (6 in)	Single starry daisies often bi-coloured in red, orange and yellow.
Gourd	climber	★	0·3 m (1 ft)	Cucumber-like vine with decorative fruits of orange, yellow and green.
Helichrysum (Strawflower)	0·45 m (1½ ft)	★	15 cm (6 in)	'Everlasting' flowers of orange, yellow, red and white.
Heliotrope (Cherry pie)	0·45 m (1½ ft)		0·3 m (1 ft)	Deep-veined leaves and lilac-purple scented flower clusters.
Impatiens (Busy Lizzie)	23 cm (9 in)		23 cm (9 in)	Fleshy leaves and stems; red, white, orange or magenta flowers.
Ipomoea (Morning glory)	climber		0·3 m (1 ft)	Heart-shaped leaves and trumpets of sky-blue or carmine.
Lobelia	10 cm (4 in)		10 cm (4 in)	Lipped flowers of blue, white or carmine over fresh green leaves.
Marigold, African	0·45–0·60 m (1½–2 ft)		0·3 m (1 ft)	Hefty double flowers of orange or yellow.
Marigold, Afro-French	0·45 m (1½ ft)		23 cm (9 in)	Very floriferous. 'Nell Gwynn' is one of the best.
Marigold, French	10–30 cm (4–12 in)		15–23 cm (6–9 in)	Neat aromatic plants with smaller double blooms of orange and yellow.
Matricaria 'Golden Ball' (Feverfew, *Tanacetum*)	0·3 m (1 ft)		0·3 m (1 ft)	Rounded plants covered in yellow 'button' flowers
Mesembryanthemum (Livingstone daisy)	8 cm (3 in)	★	15 cm (6 in)	Trailer with orange, cerise, pink or yellow daisy flowers.
Mimulus (Monkey flower)	0·3 m (1 ft)	★	15 cm (6 in)	Red, orange or yellow trumpets, often contrastingly spotted. Tolerates a little shade.
Mirabilis (Four o'clock plant)	0·45 m (1½ ft)		0·3 m (1 ft)	Red, yellow or white trumpets open in late afternoon.
Nemesia	23 cm (9 in)		23 cm (9 in)	Large-lipped flowers of red, yellow, orange or white.
Nicotiana (Tobacco plant)	0·3–0·75 m (1–2½ ft)		23 cm (9 in)	Fragrant starry flowers of red, yellow, green or white.
Nolana 'Lavender Gown'	15 cm (6 in)	★	15 cm (6 in)	Pretty mounds covered in trumpets of lavender blue centred with white and yellow.
Penstemon	0·6 m (2 ft)		23 cm (9 in)	Spires smothered in foxglove flowers of mixed colours.
Petunia	23 cm (9 in)		23 cm (9 in)	Huge trumpets in assorted colours; some are striped, others fully double.
Phlox drummondii	15–30 cm (6–12 in)	★	15 cm (6 in)	Dense heads of 'primula' flowers in assorted colours.
Portulaca (Purslane)	15 cm (6 in)	★	15 cm (6 in)	Succulent leaves and double or single 'poppy' flowers in mixed colours.
Pyrethrum 'Golden Moss'	10 cm (4 in)		15 cm (6 in)	Fluffy acid yellow leaves; yellow and white daisies.
Pyrethrum 'Silver Lace'	15 cm (6 in)		15 cm (6 in)	Finely cut grey filigree foliage.
Ricinus (Castor oil palm)	0·9 m (3 ft)		0·9 m (3 ft)	Large hand-shaped leaves of dark green or bronze.
Salpiglossis	0·6 m (2 ft)		23 cm (9 in)	Trumpets of mixed colours contrastingly veined; stunning.
Salvia 'Blaze of Fire'	0·3 m (1 ft)		0·3 m (1 ft)	Green leaves and scarlet flower spikes (only scarlet varieties are any good).
Sanvitalia procumbens	15 cm (6 in)		23 cm (9 in)	Black-eyed, starry yellow daisies on compact plants.
Scabious (Pincushion flower)	0·6 m (2 ft)	★	23 cm (9 in)	Dainty double flowers of pink, crimson, white or lavender.
Statice (Sea lavender)	0·45 m (1½ ft)		23 cm (9 in)	Branched sprays of pink, blue, white or yellow 'everlasting' flowers.
Stocks, Ten-week	0·3 m (1 ft)	★	23 cm (9 in)	Columns of fragrant magenta, purple, yellow, pink or white flowers.
Tagetes	23 cm (9 in)		23 cm (9 in)	Rounded, aromatic domes studded with single orange or yellow flowers.
Tithonia	1·2 m (4 ft)		0·45 m (1½ ft)	Single bright orange 'dahlia' flowers on tall stems.
Ursinia	0·3 m (1 ft)		23 cm (9 in)	Dazzling daisies of orange, yellow or red.
Verbena (Vervain)	23 cm (9 in)		23 cm (9 in)	Clustered flowerheads of red, violet, pink or white.
Zinnia	0·3–0·6 m (1–2 ft)		23 cm (9 in)	Double round-petalled flowers in mixed colours; even green.

Table 6: Biennials

Plant	Height	Sow	Final Spacing	Details
* *Bellis perennis* (Double daisy)	15 cm (6 in)	June	15 cm (6 in)	Neat double daisies with white, pink or crimson 'pom-pons'.
Campanula medium (Canterbury bell)	0·75 m (2½ ft)	June	23 cm (9 in)	Thick spires of pink, white or lavender bellflowers.
(*) Digitalis (Foxglove)	0·9–1·5 m (3–5 ft)	May	0·3 m (1 ft)	Tall spires of pink, mauve, yellow or white bells. Enjoy a little shade.
Dipsacus fullonum (Fuller's teasel)	2·4 m (8 ft)	May	0·6 m (2 ft)	Towering flowerheads with spiny blooms that dry well.
Honesty (Lunaria)	0·6 m (2 ft)	June	23 cm (9 in)	Mauve flowers followed by translucent 'pennies' that dry well. There is a variegated variety that comes true from seed. Tolerate shade.
Myosotis (Forget-me-not)	0·3 m (1 ft)	June	15 cm (6 in)	Sprays of pale blue, pink or white flowers.
* Pansy	15–23 cm (6–9 in)	June	15 cm (6 in)	Wide-faced blooms in assorted colours (truly perennial). Tolerate some shade.
* *Papaver nudicaule* (Iceland poppy)	0·75 m (2½ ft)	May	23 cm (9 in)	Glorious, single, papery blooms of orange, pink, yellow and white. Devastating when massed.
* Penstemon	0·3–0·6 m (1–2 ft)	May	23 cm (9 in)	Spires of foxglove flowers in mixed colours.
* Stock, Brompton	0·45 m (1½ ft)	June	23 cm (9 in)	Columns of mauve, pink, magenta, violet or white flowers.
* Sweet William (*Dianthus barbatus*)	0·45 m (1½ ft)	June	23 cm (9 in)	Clustered heads of crimson, pink or white flowers, often bi-coloured. Make sure you find a sweetly scented mixture.
(*) Verbascum (Mullein)	1·2–1·8 m	May	0·6 m (2 ft)	Tall spires of yellow, orange or white flowers; downy leaves.
* Viola (Pansy)	15–23 cm (6–9 in)	June	15 cm (6 in)	Especially good in the 'Universal' strains which will flower in winter as well as spring and summer. Tolerate a little shade.
* Wallflower (*Cheiranthus cheiri*, *Erysimum cheiri*)	0·3–0·45 m (1–1½ ft)	May	0·3 m (1 ft)	Gloriously scented blooms of red, yellow, pink, orange and mauve. Massed single colours give the best effect.
* Wallflower, Siberian (*Cheiranthus allionii*, *Erysimum × allionii*)	0·3 m (1 ft)	June	0·3 m (1 ft)	Orange-yellow flowers.

10 Garden bulbs

Every bulb is a do-it-yourself kit. Packed inside it are roots, shoots, leaves and flowers—all you have to do is add water and stand well back. Well, almost.

First of all let's clear up the confusion that exists between bulbs, corms, tubers and rhizomes. I've included plants that arise from all four of these 'storage organs' in this section so I suppose it's only fair to tell you how they differ. Basically they are all designed for food storage, rather like a camel's hump—they keep the plant alive during its dormant season (while it's resting and not growing). A bulb is really a condensed shoot or bud (Fig. 30). It has a flat bottom called a base-plate which is really the stem. The fat scales that arise from it are modified leaves, and they shield a central flower bud (with any luck). The roots arise from the base-plate as soon as moisture is placed within their reach.

A corm is a modified stem (Fig. 31). Roots appear from its base and buds and shoots from its tip. The crocus is a typical corm; the daffodil a typical bulb.

A tuber may be a swollen stem (as in the case of the potato, Fig. 32) or a swollen root (as in the case of the dahlia, Fig. 33). The potato shows it's a stem because buds appear all over it; they only appear at the top of a dahlia tuber.

A rhizome is an underground stem which usually grows horizontally just below the surface of the soil, e.g. the large-flowered border irises (Fig. 34).

So now that you know the technical differences between bulbs, corms, tubers and rhizomes you can settle down to fitting all of them into your garden. And remember, bulbs are not simply plants that flower in spring; plan your selection carefully and they'll give you blooms in spring, summer, autumn and winter.

BUYING BULBS

Most folk buy their bulbs from chain stores. There's nothing wrong with this provided the bulbs are fresh in and have not had a chance to dehydrate. However, you'll have a much wider choice of varieties if you order from a specialist catalogue (post your order for spring-flowering bulbs during the summer) or even from a nursery or garden centre. If you're buying

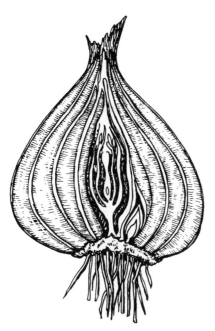

Fig. 30 A bulb is a condensed shoot. The flattened base plate is the stem; the scales are leaves and the flower nestles in the centre. Roots emerge from the base plate.

Fig. 31 A corm is really a condensed stem. This crocus shows that the flesh is solid—a bud sits on top of the 'stem' and roots emerge below it.

Fig. 32 Tubers are effective food storage organs. The potato tuber is a swollen stem—a fact which is proved by the buds which appear all over it.

Fig. 33 Dahlia tubers are root tubers—shoots arise only at the top, so it's vital that a bud or shoot is attached to any parts of the tuber removed for propagation.

bulbs over the counter, check that they are firm and of a good size. Very tiny or dehydrated bulbs may not flower during their first year, and some may even die. One or two types of bulb (such as snowdrops, snowflakes and cyclamen) are best bought 'in the green'—as growing plants. They resent even slight desiccation and will receive less of a check if planted

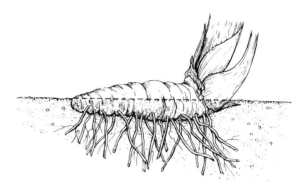

Fig. 34 Flag irises have rhizomes—flattened stems which grow on or just below the surface of the soil. They make propagation easy.

when in leaf. Sadly they are usually more pricey when sold in leaf and it may be worth risking the loss of a few dry bulbs if the prices are markedly cheaper.

WHERE TO PLANT BULBS

The most obvious place to plant them is in the flower border among herbaceous plants and shrubs. This is undoubtedly the best home for them in small gardens, because the bulbs that can remain in the garden undisturbed must always be allowed to make plenty of foliage for at least six weeks after the flowers have faded. It nearly always looks untidy, but is masked to some extent by the growth of border plants and shrubs. If you chop the foliage off instantly after flowering you're stopping the plants from building up their food reserves. Tie it in pigtails with elastic bands and you're still impeding feeding, for the leaves need light to let them manufacture food. No; take a firm hold on your tidy-mindedness and let the bulbs go mad for six weeks, then, in most cases, you can chop off the leaves and neaten your border. Mind you, it's a good idea to mark the site they occupy to prevent accidents with a hoe or fork.

Most bulbs are happy left in the soil (in which case they are said to be 'naturalized'); those that are not, and which need to be dried off and ripened, can be dug up soon as the flowers fade and brought into a dry shed or garage. As soon as their foliage dies off they can be cleaned up and stored in a cool, dry, dark, frostproof place until planting time next year. I've indicated which bulbs need this treatment under the individual headings so you need worry no more about it here.

Bulbs in grass Naturalizing bulbs in grass (planting them in haphazard formations and letting them grow on undisturbed) is an attractive proposition, but one I would not recommend in small gardens. After they've flowered the grass around them must remain uncut (along with their foliage) for six weeks—the untidiness and restriction of movement on the lawn may be something you cannot cope with. Where you have space to let a little of your lawn run riot for a few weeks in spring, nothing looks nicer and more promising of a flower-filled summer to come.

Bulbs in beds Spring-flowering bulbs planted in beds with other temporary occupants such as wallflowers, forget-me-nots, dwarf double daisies and polyanthuses are always lifted after flowering so that the bed can be made ready for its summer occupants. I always find this a rather tiresome exercise and would rather fit these bulbs into pockets in a mixed border where they can be quickly replaced after flowering without having to clear the entire bed.

Bulbs in pots Pot-grown bulbs should be every gardener's joy—they can be fitted into the smallest garden or even on to a windowsill. The time at which the bulbs are potted up will depend on their time of flowering, but don't be conned into thinking that all pot-grown bulbs must be planted in bulb fibre. They'll usually do far better in John Innes No. 1 potting compost, preferably (but not essentially) with a little sharp sand added.

Bulb fibre (a mixture of peat, charcoal and crushed oyster shell) was originally developed for use in containers with no drainage holes—such as the bowls in which most folk plant hyacinths. The charcoal and oyster shell kept the mixture 'sweet' in the face of bad drainage. Today most bulb fibres are nothing more than peat plus a few nutrients—they do nothing to ameliorate the conditions prevalent in a hole-less bowl and seem to have become simply a money-making proposition for enterprising compost merchants. Spurn them in favour of John Innes which will feed your bulbs and keep them in good condition, allowing them to be planted out in the garden after blooming to give pleasure in future years.

When you plant large bulbs in containers, leave their 'noses' just showing through the surface of the compost. Smaller bulbs and corms such as crocuses can be planted just below the surface. There's a neat trick you can try with daffodils and narcissi (daffodil, by the way, is simply the common name for any narcissus with a large trumpet). Spread 5 cm (2 in) of compost in the bottom of the pot, cram in a layer of bulbs, add a little compost and then cram in a second layer before topping up with compost leaving the noses of the top layer showing (Fig. 35). You'll get twice as many flowers from your pot than if you use a single layer of bulbs.

In general, pots with drainage holes are always more satisfactory than bowls without them, unless you take exceptional care not to overwater.

All bulbs appreciate eight weeks of cool temperatures and darkness after potting. You can stand them outdoors and cover them with peat and ashes if you like (it's what the old gardeners used to recommend) but it's far easier to stand them in a cellar or coal shed, or to stand them outdoors and cover them with black polythene. Whatever you do, don't put them in the airing cupboard. Your washing will get dirty and your bulbs won't enjoy the heat. They need cool conditions for the first two months so that they can

Fig. 35 To get as many flowers as possible from one pot, use a double layer of daffodil bulbs, positioning the upper layer so that the shoots below can squeeze past.

establish their root system; only then can they take more heat, and this should be applied very gradually; bring them first into a cool room (if you're flowering them indoors) and then into a warmer one if you must. Most will bloom better and last longer in well-lit but cool rooms.

Bulbs grown in tubs, pots and windowboxes outdoors need none of this coddling; simply treat the bulbs as though they were being planted in the ground, but use John Innes No. 2 potting compost plus a little sharp river sand for extra drainage.

HOW TO PLANT

Outdoors all bulbs are best planted with a trowel. As a general rule they should be covered with soil to twice their depth. That is, if a bulb measures 5 cm (2 in) from tip to toe it should be planted in a hole 15 cm (6 in) deep.

Bulb-planting tools which take out a core of soil are useful for planting large numbers of bulbs in grass (Fig. 36), but they are hell to use effectively on stony soil. If you do use one, take out all your holes first, push your bulbs in and then replace the divots.

I find it easier, when naturalizing bulbs in grass, to lift up a flap of turf and plant the bulbs underneath it with a trowel before turning back and firming the flap (Fig. 37).

Never plant bulbs too shallowly. It's one of the greatest causes of failure. Shallow-planted bulbs will often refuse to flower well because they are short of water and nutrients. Seldom can a bulb be planted too deeply (unless you're lunatic enough to plant a tiny snowdrop 30 cm or 1 ft under).

If you're planting bulbs among spring bedding plants, put the plants in first and the bulbs in

Fig. 36 Except on hard and stony soils a bulb planter is a useful tool. It removes a core of soil so that the bulb can be inserted and the divot replaced.

Fig. 37 Save time when bulb planting in grass by lifting a flap of turf. The bulbs can be planted with a trowel in the soil below and the flap replaced.

afterwards—that way they won't be disturbed by the trowel.

FEEDING
People are as rotten to their bulbs as they are to their lawns—they often forget completely about feeding. You'll have better flowers each year if you treat your bulbs to a square meal of general fertilizer as the flowers fade. A light dusting of blood, bone and fishmeal will do them nicely. Lack of food will often cause 'blindness' (failure to flower), especially in bulbs that grow among grass (which robs them of food anyway), but dry springs can also be responsible for the failure of flower formation. If you can water your spring-flowering bulbs well during a parched April and May you might notice a difference the following year.

PROPAGATION
Almost all bulbs are obliging enough to reproduce themselves by natural multiplication and division without any help from us, but I have included a few tips on encouraging them to increase in Chapter 20.

A–Z OF GARDEN BULBS
These are the bulbs, corms, tubers and rhizomes that are grown in the garden or in tubs and other containers outdoors, although some of them are often brought indoors during their flowering season.

Some bulbous plants are so commonly grown as border plants that I have sneaked them into that chapter. If the plant you seek is not here, check to see if it is included between pp. 84 and 109. Where a specific planting depth is given for a bulb, it refers to the depth of the hole that should be taken out and not to the depth from the tip of the bulb to the surface.

Allium   Ornamental Onion
Most of them don't smell too strongly of onions unless they're bruised so don't be put off. They are a tremendously varied and valuable bunch of plants that can be relied on to bring colour to the garden from spring to autumn, and they vary in stature from the very small to around head height. Many have attractive seedheads. I can mention just a few—the ones I'd grow in preference to all others (some species—none of those mentioned here—can become annoying weeds):

A. cristophii (syn. *A. albopilosum*), 45 cm (18 in) high, football-sized flowerheads composed of glistening, mauve-pink metallic stars; dries strawy brown; summer; loves sun.
A. moly, 30 cm (1 ft), clusters of starry yellow flowers; naturalizes well in sun or light shade; early summer.
A. bulgaricum (syn. *A. siculum dioscoridis*, now called *Nectaroscordum*), 1–1·25m (3–4 ft), towering heads of drooping creamy flowers striped with green and tinted purple; superb seed-heads like pointed Bavarian castles; summer; sun and well-drained soil.
A. oreophilum (syn. *A. ostrowskianum*), 15 cm (6 in), is a mouthful but cheap and easy to find; rosy pink flower clusters in early to mid summer; well-drained soil and sun for preference.
A. giganteum, 2 m (6 ft), has lilac-purple ball-shaped flowerheads on top of its tall stems in early summer; sun or very gentle shade.
A. karataviense, 20 cm (8 in), is remarkable, for its spherical flowerheads of dirty pink nestle between a pair of very broad grey-green leaves in late spring or early summer; sun and good drainage.

Plant in autumn or as soon as bulbs become available; cover all bulbs to twice their depth. Rich soil is appreciated. *Suitable for* naturalizing, rock gardens (dwarf species), shade (as indicated)—most adore sun. *Propagate* by division of bulbs in summer.

Amaryllis belladonna   Belladonna Lily
This is the only true amaryllis and one to treasure. It produces green, strap-shaped leaves and, once it is

happy, a flowerhead carrying several large, pink, white-flushed flowers shaped like gigantic stars. It grows to about 60 cm (2 ft) high and flowers in autumn. There are darker-flowered forms and a good white. Only in a sun-baked border will it thrive and become reliably perennial. In colder counties it may be killed in severe winters and it will not tolerate poorly drained soil. Leave clumps undisturbed for many years for best results. Good against south- and west-facing walls. Feed with blood, bone and fish-meal in late summer and cover with dry straw or bracken in winter.

Plant in summer 15 cm (6 in) deep and 30 cm apart. The leaves die down altogether in summer. *Propagate* by division of established clumps in summer.

Anemone Windflower

Little charmers of small stature but considerable impact. The Mothering Sunday bunches of anemones are generally the 'De Caen' (single) and 'St Brigid' (double) varieties of *A. coronaria* with flowers of red, pink, white, mauve and lavender blue. They grow to around 30 cm (1 ft) high and will bloom in spring (if planted in October); summer (if planted in April), or late summer and autumn (if planted in June). Give them a well-drained soil that has been laced with a little garden compost.

A. blanda, 10 cm (4 in), is my own favourite. It has starry wood-anemone flowers of white, pink, blue or (in the variety 'Radar') rich magenta. This last-named is iniquitously expensive; the others are very cheap. All flower in early spring and will multiply into large colonies if left alone in any decent soil (they can even be planted in grass).

A. nemorosa, 10 cm (4 in), is our native wood anemone with finely cut leaves and white flowers flushed mauve on the outside. It has a double form and a glorious lavender-blue variety called 'Robinsoniana'; both flower in spring and enjoy a peaty, leafy soil.

Plant both these species in autumn, 8 cm (3 in) deep. *Suitable for* naturalizing in sun or gentle shade, or for growing in pots, but keep them cool. Good in rock gardens and under shrubs and trees, but avoid really dry soils. *Propagate* by division of the tubers after flowering.

Camassia Quamash

Variable but always beautiful bulbs with starry flowers in tapering spires. *C. cusickii*, 75 cm (2½ ft) high, is usually pale blue, and *C. quamash* (syn. *C. esculenta*), 45 cm (1½ ft) high, is usually darker blue but both vary considerably in colour depending on source of supply. Both flower in summer and both deserve to be more popular.

Plant in autumn, 15 cm (6 in) deep and as much apart. *Suitable for* naturalizing in beds and borders where they can be left undisturbed. They enjoy full sun and a moisture-retentive soil with a bit of body. They resent drought. *Propagate* by sowing seeds

outdoors in spring (they take three or four years to come to flowering size) or by division in autumn (though increase is slow).

Chionodoxa luciliae (now called **C. forbesii**)
Glory of the Snow

Grows without any fuss at all. It makes 15 cm (6 in) high arching stems of starry blue and white flowers in spring, and produces tufts of glossy green leaves.

Plant in autumn, 8 cm (3 in) deep. *Suitable for* naturalizing in beds and borders, for rock gardens and for planting in pots, tubs and window boxes. They enjoy sun or gentle shade and any reasonable soil. *Propagate* by division after flowering.

Colchicum Meadow Saffron, Naked Ladies, Autumn Crocus

It's a shame about the third inaccurate common name. If ever you want to know whether or not you've got a colchicum or a true autumn-flowering crocus, count the stamens: crocuses have three (and a shorter name); colchicums have six (and a longer name). Some species flower in spring, but the most popular are the autumn bloomers such as *C. autumnale*, 15 cm (6 in), with its dainty crocus-shaped flowers of lilac pink. *C. speciosum*, 23 cm (9 in), is better still and a good deal beefier—absolutely breathtaking in flower. It has various varieties with lighter and darker blooms, and one glorious double called 'Waterlily' which is a warm pink. Some species, such as *C. aggripinum*, have blooms that carry a chequered pattern (the experts refer to them as 'tessellated'), and the species that flower in winter and spring (including a rare yellow one) should be fitted in where there is room. Remember that all have vast leaves like huge leeks which push up *after* the flowers. If the foliage can be masked by shrubs and border plants, so much the better.

Plant in late summer 15 cm (6 in) deep and as much apart; plant spring-flowering kinds in autumn. *Suitable for* naturalizing in beds and borders, under trees and among shrubs. They enjoy a rich, leafy soil, preferably organically mulched, which is not likely to become baked in summer. Bulbs of *C. autumnale* can be stood, quite dry, on a windowsill in late summer where they will flower with no attention whatsoever. Plant them out afterwards. *Propagate* by seeds sown outdoors in summer (allow three to four years for flowering) or by division in summer. Most folk simply buy in more bulbs.

Crocus

I hardly know where to begin with the crocuses, they are such a delightfully varied bunch. I've never been a fan of the fat Dutch hybrids, but I rave over the smaller varieties of such species as *C. chrysanthus*, 5–8 cm (2–3 in), that flower in spring. Try the warm yellow 'E. A. Bowles' and 'Ladykiller' with white petals flushed purple on the undersides. *C. ancy-*

rensis, 8 cm (3 in), is a good orange-yellow that can be had in flower in winter in pots or outdoors, and by far the best naturalizer is *C. tommasinianus*, 8 cm (3 in), whose amethyst-purple buds spear the soil in late winter before opening in the sunshine like floral stars. There are several species that flower in autumn—some in September and some in October and November—and it's time more folk knew about them. *C. speciosus*, 10 cm (4 in), pale mauve; *C. zonatus*, 10 cm (4 in), pale lilac; *C. niveus*, 10 cm (4 in), white with red stigmas; *C. nudiflorus*, 15 cm (6 in), deep violet purple, are all worth planting outdoors or in pots.

Plant or pot up in late summer (for autumn-flowering kinds); in autumn (for spring-flowering kinds). Plant 5 cm (2 in) deep and 8 cm (3 in) apart. *Suitable for* naturalizing in grass or beds and borders, even under trees and shrubs. Good on the rock garden and in bowls, pots, tubs and windowboxes. If you plan to bring the containers indoors when the crocuses are in flower, try to keep them cool at all times. In the garden leave the bulbs undisturbed to multiply on their own. All will tolerate any ordinary, well-drained soil. *Propagate* by seed if you've the patience (it will be two or three years before the progeny flower). Most gardeners buy in new bulbs and leave their existing ones to increase naturally by both division and seed.

Cyclamen   Sowbread

It's not the large, pot-grown cyclamen so popular at Christmas that can be grown outdoors, but the smaller hardy species such as *C. hederifolium* (syn. *C. neapolitanum*). It grows just 8 cm (3 in) or so high, produces its pretty reflexed-petalled flowers of warm pink from summer to autumn, and then a show of marbled heart-shaped leaves.

Plant the tubers while they are growing, for preference, or take a gamble and hope that dry ones (which you can buy from department stores and garden centres) will succeed. Plant the tubers so that they rest *fractionally* below the surface of the soil. *Suitable for* dappled shade under trees and shrubs, and shady pockets on the rock garden. They like a peaty, leafy soil that doesn't dry out. *Propagate* by sowing fresh seeds in pots of compost placed in a garden frame.

Dahlia

The dahlia is a tuber that can grow happily outdoors in summer, but which needs frost protection in winter. There are hundreds of different varieties with flowers in 'pompon', 'cactus' and 'decorative' shapes, in shades of red, orange, yellow, mauve, purple and white. The stems and foliage are juicy and succulent and the plants may grow anything from 45 cm to 1·5 m (1½ to 5 ft) tall.

Plant dormant tubers 15 cm (6 in) deep in late April or early May; young plants in late May or early June.

Stake the plants as they grow. Feed fortnightly in summer and control earwigs (p. 228), which will nibble both flowers and leaves. *Suitable for* beds and borders in full sun. The soil should be rich—work in plenty of compost or manure and a dusting of blood, bone and fishmeal before planting. Water well in dry spells. When the stems are blackened by autumn frosts, lift the plants, cut off the top growth and store the tubers in an airy, cool but frostproof place in trays of dry peat. If you're idle you can risk leaving them in the ground outdoors, in which case mulch the soil above them with a thick layer of compost, manure, straw or bracken. Prepare for total losses in severe winters. *Propagate* by taking cuttings from tubers boxed up in compost, watered and kept warm in a greenhouse during early spring. Alternatively, divide these tubers into sections (each with a shoot) as soon as they start to sprout. Grow on a little in heat and plant out when danger of frost is past.

Eranthis hyemalis   Winter Aconite

These pretty yellow buttercup flowers, each with a green ruff, are welcome heralds of spring, flowering in February just 8 cm (3 in) above the cold, damp soil.

Plant growing plants if you can find them; if you can't, plant dry tubers in autumn and be prepared to wait a few years for the plants to settle in and flower well. Plant 8 cm (3 in) deep and 10 cm (4 in) apart. *Suitable for* naturalizing in rock gardens or in beds and borders under trees and shrubs in sun or dappled shade. Really dry soils will not be appreciated. *Propagate* by division of tubers after flowering.

Erythronium   Dog's Tooth Violet, Trout Lily

Grey-green, liver-spotted leaves and pink or white pagoda-shaped flowers make *E. dens-canis* a popular plant. It grows just 15 cm (6 in) high, but there are taller species such as *E. tuolumnense* at 25 cm (10 in), which has glossy green leaves and yellow flowers. All bloom in spring, and all are well worth growing.

Plant growing plants in spring or (if this is not possible) dormant (but not totally desiccated) corms in late summer. Plant 8 cm (3 in) deep and 10 cm (4 in) apart. *Suitable for* dappled shade under trees and shrubs in a peaty, leafy soil that is never likely to dry out. Happy in shady pockets on the rock garden. A light mulch of leafmould or pulverized bark will be appreciated after flowering. Once established the corms resent disturbance. *Propagate* by division after flowering.

Fritillaria   Crown Imperial, Snakeshead Fritillary

The stately *F. imperialis*, with its 1 m (3 ft) stem, pendant orange or yellow bells and topknot of leafy green bracts, is a startling feature in the May garden and is criticized only for its foxy odour. The daintier *F. meleagris*, 23 cm (9 in), is altogether more coy, with nodding chequered bells of dusky plum purple, pink or creamy white. Its leaves are narrow and grassy, unlike those of the crown imperial which radiate in whorls from the thick stem.

Plant bulbs of *F. imperialis* 15 cm (6 in) deep on their sides; those of *F. meleagris* the right way up, 10 cm (4 in) deep and as much apart. Plant both in autumn. *Suitable for* rich but well-drained soil in full sun for *F. imperialis*; moisture-retentive soil in dappled shade for *F. meleagris*. Both are best left undisturbed after planting—the snakeshead fritillary can even by naturalized in grass. *Propagate* by seeds sown in a garden frame as soon as ripe. A job for the patient gardener—others will by in fresh bulbs.

Galanthus   Snowdrop
The common snowdrop is *G. nivalis*, usually at its best during February when its green and white ballerina flowers dangle from 15 cm (6 in) stems. There are dozens of other species and varieties with quaint markings and broader leaves—some of them possess delightful scents, and some flower earlier, even in autumn if you choose the right species. Many are expensive to buy, but the double form of the common snowdrop is cheap and produces masses of tulle-petticoated flowers at the same time as the true species.

Plant growing plants 'in the green' immediately after flowering if you can. Dry bulbs can be planted in autumn but may not establish so quickly. Plant the bulbs 8 cm (3 in) deep and 5 cm (2 in) apart. *Suitable for* naturalizing in beds and borders under trees and shrubs and in grass. Happy in full sun or dappled shade. Good on rock gardens. *Propagate* by dividing mature clumps after flowering.

Galtonia candicans   Spire Lily
Stately spires of creamy-white bells 1 m (3 ft) tall are the summer trademark of galtonia. The blooms are deliciously fragrant and open in July or August.

Plant in spring 15 cm (6 in) deep and as much apart. *Suitable for* well-nourished and well-drained soil in beds and borders among summer-flowering perennials and shrubs. Full sun is essential. Galtonia can also be grown in pots for room decoration. Plant one bulb (with its nose just showing) in a pot of compost in autumn. Keep it cool and dark for eight weeks and then gradually introduce to light and warmer temperatures. It will flower in spring. *Propagate* by the removal of offsets in autumn.

Gladiolus   Sword Lily
Sword-leafed plants with tapering spikes of wide-faced flowers in shades of red, yellow, orange, pink, mauve and white, as well as a rather lurid green. There are many different forms with strangely shaped flowers such as the 'butterfly' types. They grow to between 30 cm and 1·5 m (1 and 5 ft) high and flower in summer. Most are not winter hardy and

have to be lifted, dried and stored before severe frosts have a chance to kill them, but *G. communis* ssp. *byzantinus*, 60 cm (2 ft), is a magenta-flowered species that can survive outdoors all the year round. It's daintier and flowers earlier—in June.

Plant G. communis ssp. *byzantinus* in autumn 8 cm (3 in) deep and 15 cm (6 in) apart. Plant the hybrid types at intervals between March and May for a succession of flowers. Set the corms 10 cm (4 in) deep and 23 cm (9 in) apart. The hybrids will need staking as soon as the flower spikes appear. Feed fortnightly in summer. *Suitable for* rich and well-drained soil in full sun. Water well in dry spells. Six weeks after flowering lift the hybrid varieties, cut off the foliage 2.5 cm (1 in) above the corm, remove the old corm (which will be a shrivelled button below the new one), and store the new corms in seeds trays kept in a cool, dry, frostproof place during winter. *Propagate* by planting 'cormels' (tiny corms that form around the main one) and allowing them to grow on to flowering size. Plant them in spring.

Hyacinthus   Hyacinth
Unsurpassed for fragrance, the hyacinth is part of the Christmas tradition in many homes. The dense spikes of bloom may be rich rose red, pink, blue, salmon, pale yellow or white. 'L'Innocence', white, 'Jan Bos', rich pink, 'Ostara', blue, and 'City of Haarlem', pale yellow, are probably the most popular varieties. All bloom in winter (in pots) or spring (outdoors) and are around 25 cm (10 in) high.

Plant 'prepared' bulbs in pots or bowls of compost in late August and September for Christmas flowers. Plant one variety to each container to make sure that all the bulbs flower simultaneously—mix your colours and blooming may be staggered and less effective. Keep the pots of bulbs cool and dark for eight weeks, bringing them indoors when the flower spikes can be seen nestling among the leaves. Ordinary bulbs can be planted in bowls at the same time but they will not flower quite so quickly. Plant outdoors during September and October, setting the bulbs 10 cm (4 in) deep and 15 cm (6 in) apart. The bulbs are so expensive nowadays that few folk can afford to grow them outdoors except in tubs and window-boxes. *Suitable for* beds and borders (for the rich); pots, tubs, bowls and windowboxes (for the cost-conscious). Plant pot-grown bulbs in the garden when the flowers fade. If the soil is well nourished and in full sun they should bloom again in succeeding years, but plant them a good 10 cm (4 in) deep. *Propagate* by scooping and scoring (see Chapter 20 on *Propagation*) if you're really mean. Otherwise save up and buy in more bulbs.

Iris
In January, February and March, when most gardeners' hopes are at a low ebb, the varieties of *I. reticulata* burst into flower. Their blooms may be

blue or violet in various intensities, and are almost always attractively etched with yellow and white. They're just 15 cm (6 in) tall, but if you can get your nose down to them you'll detect a sweet scent in the winter sun. *I. histrioides* 'Major' is another 'must'. It's slightly shorter but rather larger flowered and coloured blue and white. The foliage follows the flowers and in all the varieties is grassy and not too untidy. The Dutch, Spanish and English irises are all much taller at around 45 cm (1½ ft) and bloom in late spring or early to midsummer. They are valuable and easy plants which are neglected by too many gardeners. Plant them for a succession of flowers: the Dutch types bloom in May; the Spanish in June, and the English in June and July offering flowers of blue, violet, yellow and white.

Plant in autumn 8 cm (3 in) deep. Space the dwarf types 8 cm (3 in) apart and the taller varieties 15 cm (6 in) apart. *Suitable for* beds and borders in full sun (taller varieties); rock gardens in full sun (dwarf varieties). All appreciate a gritty, well-drained soil. The tall varieties can be lifted and divided every three years in autumn; the others left undisturbed. The dwarfs can also be grown in pots for winter colour indoors. Keep them cool at all times. *Propagate* by division of established clumps in autumn.

Leucojum   Snowflake

There are three snowflakes grown with frequency by discerning plantsmen: the summer snowflake, *L. aestivum*, 45 cm (1½ ft), white, green-tipped bells in late spring and early summer; the spring snowflake, *L. vernum*, 30 cm (1 ft), similar flowers in early spring; and the autumn snowflake, *L. autumnale*, 15 cm (6 in), a dainty miniature with reed-like leaves and papery white or pale pink bells in autumn.

Plant the spring- and summer-flowering species in early autumn; the autumn-flowering species in late summer. Alternatively, plant 'in the green' after flowering as for snowdrops. Plant 10 cm (4 in) deep and as much apart. Both *L. aestivum* and *L. vernum* appreciate a leafy, moisture-retentive soil, while *L. autumnale* likes something grittier and well drained. All are happy in full sun or dappled shade. *Suitable for* beds and borders and (in the case of *L. autumnale*) rock gardens. The bulbs may not flower in their first year. *Propagate* by lifting and dividing mature clumps after flowering.

Lilium   Lily

How can I even begin to tell you about lilies in such a small space? I can't, but I can perhaps persuade you to try them in beds and borders among your herbaceous plants and shrubs, and in pots on a patio or doorstep. They possess starry, bell-shaped, trumpet or turk's cap flowers in a wide colour range, and some fragrances which surpass anything that comes out of a bottle. If you've never grown lilies before, start off with *L. regale*, 1·25 m (4 ft), which has white and pale

yellow trumpets flushed with purple on the outside; and *L.* 'Enchantment', 60 cm (2 ft), whose vibrant orange blooms are dotted with brown. Don't be put off by the daunting mystery that surrounds the lily—some are notoriously difficult, it's true, but others are easy if you give them their simple requirements.

Plant these two species in October or in spring—as soon as the bulbs become available. Plant them 15 cm (6 in) deep and 20 cm (8 in) apart. They need a well-drained soil that is not prone to drought in summer. Winter sogginess will encourage rotting. Alternatively, pot up the bulbs in autumn in gritty compost—one bulb to a 13 cm (5 in) pot or three to a 20 cm (8 in) pot. Cover the bulbs with 8 cm (3 in) compost. Keep cool and dark until growth begins, then gradually introduce to light and warmth. Water carefully at all times—little will be needed until the plants are growing well. Outdoors and in pots the plants may need staking. Plant out the bulbs in the garden after flowering. *Suitable for* beds and borders in well-drained soil and full sun or dappled shade. Many can be grown in pots. If you plan to specialize in lilies, lay your hands on a book that offers comprehensive advice. Some lilies hate chalk; others don't much care for acid ground, yet more are 'stem rooting' and need to be planted quite deeply; others, like the Madonna lily, need shallow planting in late summer. See how confusing it gets? No wonder some gardeners are frightened of lilies! *Propagate* by seed or by the removal and growing on of bulb scales or bulbils (those little bulbs that appear in the leaf axils of some species). Further details are given in Chapter 20 on *Propagation*.

Muscari   Grape Hyacinth

Easy spring-flowering bulbs with spires of blue or white flowers held on stout stalks 15 cm (6 in) long. *M. armeniacum* is the commonest species.

Plant in autumn 8 cm (3 in) deep and 8 cm (3 in) apart. *Suitable for* beds and borders, tubs, window-boxes and pots. Ordinary soil and full sun are appreciated. There is no need to disturb the bulbs once they are planted, but should they become all leaf and no flower in succeeding years, dig them up in June and discard all but the largest bulbs, which can be replanted in freshly fertilized soil. *Propagate* by division after flowering.

Narcissus   Daffodil

'King Alfreds' pop up in gardens countrywide, but there are hundreds, and maybe even thousands more varieties that are equally valuable to stately gardeners and windowbox owners. Catalogues offer a vast choice of form and colour—large- and small-cupped varieties, doubles and singles, and even blooms that are pale green or salmon pink. I'll leave you to pick your favourites from the glossy pages, but will sneak in a recommendation for the useful dwarf varieties such as *N. asturiensis*, *N. bulbocodium* and *N. cycla-*

mineus and some of their hybrids such as 'Little Witch', 23 cm (9 in), yellow, and 'Tête-à-Tête', 15 cm (6 in), yellow, which are marvellous for rock gardens, pots and windowboxes. All bloom during spring. Cottage gardeners should not be without 'Van Sion', the double yellow daffodil; and orchard owners can carpet the ground around their trees with the headily fragrant 'Old Pheasant Eye', which has white petals and a tiny red and yellow centre. Both are just over 30 cm (1 ft) tall.

Plant in September and October—10 cm (4 in) deep in beds and borders; 15 cm (6 in) deep if naturalizing the bulbs in grass. The miniature varieties should be planted 8 cm (3 in) deep. All varieties can be planted 8 cm (3 in) apart. Plant in groups, not lines. Alternatively plant the bulbs in pots (see page 119 for details) in autumn for winter flowering indoors. The varieties 'Soleil D'Or' and 'Paper White' are often potted for Christmas flowering. *Suitable for* beds, borders, rough grass, rock gardens (dwarf varieties), pots, tubs and windowboxes. Pot-grown plants can be planted out in the garden after flowering. All appreciate full sun and a well-drained soil. Feeding with a balanced general fertilizer (such as blood, bone and fishmeal) after flowering will encourage regular blooming. Dry springs may account for 'blindness' (lack of flowers) the following year. *Propagate* by division after flowering.

Nerine bowdenii   Diamond Lily

Find this September-flowering bulb a sheltered patch of well-drained soil in full sun and it will demand little attention. It will gradually make a congested clump of bulbs from which will spring branched heads of rich pink, wavy-petalled flowers at the end of summer, followed by a small forest of glossy green strap-shaped leaves. The flower stems are about 45 cm (1½ ft) high, and the leaves persist through winter, dying down in early summer.

Plant in late summer, positioning the bulbs just below ground level. *Suitable for* light, well-drained, even dry soils in full sun. A spot at the foot of a south-facing wall is ideal and the plants will usually come through the winter unscathed (though they may suffer in the north and in sticky earth). They can also be grown in pots of gritty compost and protected from winter cold and wet in a frame. Withhold water in summer when the leaves die down. Repot in late summer when the bulbs become overcrowded. Those growing in the garden seem to flower best when jammed close together. Protect them from slugs and snails. *Propagate* by division of clumps in late summer.

Ornithogalum umbellatum

Star of Bethlehem

A neat and cheerful little plant with branched heads of white, starry flowers that are green on the undersides. They open on top of 23 cm (9 in) stalks in April

and May and make a pretty edging to a bed or border. They open late morning and close again in the afternoon, but they're nice when they're out!

Plant in autumn, 8 cm (3 in) deep and as much apart. *Suitable for* ordinary soil in sunny beds, borders or containers. *Propagate* by dividing clumps after flowering.

Schizostylis coccinea   Kaffir Lily

Rich pink, starry flowers emerge at the top of slender stems in autumn to make the Kaffir lily a valuable border flower. There are several named varieties such as Viscountess Byng and Mrs Hegarty which are paler than the true species. All are around 45 cm (1½ ft) tall and have grassy leaves.

Plant in spring, 8 cm (3 in) deep and as much apart. *Suitable for* warm and sunny borders at the foot of south- and west-facing walls. In cold districts protect with straw or bracken in winter. *Propagate* by division of mature clumps in spring.

Scilla   Squill

The two squills most commonly planted are *S. siberica*, 10 cm (4 in), and *S. bifolia*, 15 cm (6 in), both of which have rich blue, bell-like flowers in spring. The native British bluebell is strictly *Endymion non-scriptus* or, if you want to be slap-bang up-to-date, *Hyacinthoides non-scripta*, but it used to be a scilla and for convenience I'm including it here along with its heftier relation the Spanish bluebell *H. hispanica*. Both have variants with white and pink flowers but the Spanish bluebell is the more imposing plant at around 30 cm (1 ft) high with broader bells.

Plant all the bulbs in autumn to twice their depth. *Suitable for* bed and border edgings (in the case of the two true scillas) or for naturalizing in grass and woodland, in the case of the two bluebells. None of them needs to be disturbed once planted. *Propagate* by division after flowering.

Sternbergia

Lily of the Field, Winter Daffodil

Just like a vivid yellow crocus to look at, *S. lutea*, 10 cm (4 in), blooms in autumn and then sends up a neat fountain of lustrous green 'daffodil' leaves. Sometimes it's reluctant to flower but if planted deep enough and allowed a year or two to settle in it should oblige.

Plant in late summer, 15 cm (6 in) deep and 10 cm (4 in) apart. *Suitable for* sunny spots in well-drained soil, preferably at the foot of a warm wall where they will receive a welcome baking in summer. *Propagate* by division in late summer.

Tulipa   Tulip

As popular and as varied a race as *Narcissus* with almost as many variations. The hybrids are classified in different groups which vary in stature and time of flowering—it's possible to have tulips in bloom from late winter to late spring. Pick the hybrid types for bedding schemes (the Darwin hybrids have long stems and will bloom at the same time as wallflowers), and the smaller species for rock gardens. Colourful catalogues will give you more detailed information on varieties than I can hope to here, but let me urge you to have a bash with the miniatures like *T. clusiana*, 23 cm (9 in), white, flushed red outside, late April; *T. chrysantha*, 15 cm (6 in), red and yellow, mid-April, and *T. tarda*, 10 cm (4 in), yellow and white, April. The varieties of *T. kaufmanniana* and *T. greigii* are stocky, large-flowered and have leaves attractively streaked with maroon. At 23 cm (9 in) high they are the best types for container planting. There are many others that will delight you year in, year out.

Plant in October or November (no earlier), the deeper the better. Plant the miniatures 15 cm (6 in) deep, and the larger hybrids 23 cm (9 in) deep if you want to avoid lifting them every year. I've known them undisturbed at this depth for thirty years, flowering annually. Plant in pots at the same time, just covering the noses of the bulbs. Keep cool and dark for eight weeks, then bring into the light. Avoid a dramatic rise in temperatures. *Suitable for* bedding, naturalizing in beds and borders (where their foliage will not give offence), tubs, pots and windowboxes. Dwarf species look good on the rock garden. If tulips are used in a spring bedding scheme that has to be shifted to make way for summer flowers, lift the bulbs (leaving their top growth intact) and lay them in a trench on the vegetable plot, replacing some soil over the bulbs. When growth dies down, lift and strip the bulbs of their foliage before storing them in a cool, dry place. The small bulbs can be discarded and only the larger, flowering-sized bulbs retained for planting next year. Pot-grown bulbs can be allowed to dry out after flowering and be treated as for lifted bulbs. *Propagate* by dividing bulb clusters in summer and growing on the small bulbs.

FIND THE RIGHT BULB

Different bulbs are suited to different situations, though the majority of them will grow well in any ordinary well-drained soil. Almost all bulbs will rot in soggy earth, so it's always worth improving matters with grit, sharp sand and organic enrichment such as leafmould or peat—too much manure can cause leafy growth at the expense of flowers.

BULBS FOR GENTLE SHADE

Allium moly
Anemone blanda
Anemone nemorosa
Colchicum
Cyclamen
Eranthis
Erythronium
Fritillaria meleagris
Leucojum
Scilla

BULBS FOR BEDDING SCHEMES

Crocus
Dahlia
Gladiolus
Hyacinthus
Muscari
Narcissus
Tulipa

BULBS TO NATURALIZE IN GRASS

Crocus
Fritillaria meleagris
Galanthus
Narcissus
Scilla

BULBS FOR CONTAINERS

Anemone (some spp)
Chionodoxa
Crocus
Galtonia
Hyacinthus
Iris (dwarf spp)
Lilium
Muscari
Narcissus
Nerine
Ornithogalum
Tulipa

BULBS FOR ROCK GARDENS

Allium (dwarf spp)
Anemone
Crocus
Cyclamen
Eranthis
Erythronium
Galanthus
Iris (dwarf spp)
Leucojum autumnale
Muscari
Narcissus (dwarf spp)
Tulipa (dwarf spp)

11 Rock gardening

Every gardener has his favourite plants; alpines and rock plants happen to be mine (even though they are regularly rivalled by roses, shrubs, house plants, border plants . . .). If I do nothing else in this chapter I'd like to encourage you to grow alpines anywhere but on rock-studded mounds that look like large graves. Alpines mostly come from mountainous areas so it may seem natural to create mini-alps in the garden, but this is really not necessary. They are shown off and grow happily in rock beds (raised or flat), sinks and troughs as well as in properly constructed 'rock outcrops' that fit most naturally into banks or undulating ground.

WHERE TO MAKE YOUR ROCK GARDEN

Whatever the feature, the site should be open and sunny. There are one or two alpines that like a shady spot, but the vast majority need all the light they can get. Avoid a site that is overhung by trees or the plants will be dripped on all the year round and smothered with leaves in autumn.

Some shelter from strong winds is desirable and the patch of ground should not be in a frost pocket (a hollow that collects cold air). Most alpines flower in spring and will be damaged if badly frosted at that time.

As well as hating bad drainage, the plants hate winter wet. Most of them are protected in the wild by a thick, dry blanket of snow. In Britain they are more likely to be battered by distinctly soggy rain or sleet. Many alpines will reluctantly tolerate our winters; those that will not can be protected with panes of glass supported on wire legs, with cloches, or by being grown in a garden frame or (great luxury) an alpine house. Hairy-leaved plants in particular suffer from excessive damp in cold weather.

SOIL PREPARATION

Alpines like that seemingly impossible combination, rapid drainage in winter and adequate moisture retention in summer. You can usually achieve this happy state if you perk up your existing soil. Light earth will need the addition of coarse peat (alpines don't go a bundle on lashings of manure—well, actually they do but you'll get more foliage than flowers), and heavier soils can take both peat and sharp grit to improve their drainage.

A dusting of bonemeal before planting will set your alpines on the road to establishment.

The amount of lime your soil contains (its acidity or alkalinity) will affect the plants you can grow. Most rock plants will be happy in slightly acid earth, but there are dozens that can be grown on chalk (with the exception of some gentians, dwarf rhododendrons and others). Garden with your soil rather than against it and plant things that will be happy in your conditions.

Go to town when you prepare the soil. Dig or fork it over, working in the appropriate enrichment and pulling out any weeds. Make sure you eliminate every last bit or the blighters will be with you for ever once the rock garden is made. Let the soil settle for a while after cultivation; that way you can be sure it is firm and free of air pockets when construction of the rock garden begins. You'll also be able to spot any more weeds that emerge. Spring and autumn are the customary times to plant, though alpines from pots can be established quite happily in summer provided attention is paid to watering. It follows that construction of a rock garden can be carried out at almost any time of year except the middle of winter, when the soil will cling so fiercely to your spade and wellies as to make cultivation difficult.

WHICH ROCK?

You don't actually need any rock to grow rock plants; it's the state of the soil that matters most. But alpines do look good when displayed against a background of rock or when allowed to tumble over a boulder. This sets the gardener off on the road that leads to the rock-dotted mound. Steady now!

Decide which kind of rock would best fit into your garden. The answer is usually local stone which will also be cheaper thanks to its proximity. The two kinds of stone most frequently offered are limestone and sandstone. Waterworn Westmorland limestone is that beautifully runnelled and layered stone that, to many, typifies a traditional rock garden. It looks good in the right place but it's very expensive. Most plants will grow happily around it but one or two lime haters may curl up their toes. Sandstone hails from all sorts of regions and is a bland, mid-brown stone that looks good in most situations. Granite is sometimes available but is rather difficult to work with and not so easy to blend into the garden.

Tufa is formed from calcium carbonate deposits and is a soft, creamy-white rock that rapidly becomes coated with mosses. Use single lumps of it as features (chip out holes and plant them with cushion-forming alpines) rather than incorporating it into a rock garden. It's a bit too pricey for that anyway.

All rock costs money, so if you can't afford it, settle for just one or two pieces set into a flat bed to remind you of the nature of the plants. Most rock gardens are covered with a 2·5 cm (1 in) layer of gravel, stone chippings or even pea shingle once they've been planted up. This prevents the plants from being splashed by mud, it keeps their 'collars' dry, keeps down weeds, keeps in moisture and generally shows plants off to perfection.

ROCKY OUTCROPS

If you want to build a traditional rock garden the best place to do it is on a slight slope. Failing this you'll have to create a mound, but if this is the case for goodness sake make it sizeable and make the slope gradual. Try to construct an outcrop of rock that looks almost as if it is naturally occurring—pushing up through the soil in your garden.

Look at rocks in the wild and notice how their strata (layers) run in the same direction. Arrange your rocks similarly so that the layers run almost horizontal and the rocks tilt back slightly. Put large rocks in place first—100 kg (2 cwt) is about the largest a man can shift on his own; and position smaller ones around them. Leave pockets of firm soil for the plants both above and below the rocks. When rock was plentiful gardeners used to bury two-thirds of it in the soil. There's no need to be so extravagant nowadays; just make sure that the rocks sit firm and really ram the soil around them with your boot and an old spade handle. Jump from rock to rock and you should not detect any wobble.

Trample the soil to firm it when the job is finished so that no root-drying air pockets are left.

ROCK BEDS

In most gardens rock beds are easier to fit in than rocky outcrops. They're cheaper too. If your soil is sandy the bed can be made flat on the ground. On heavier soils it's a good idea to raise the bed up with two or three courses of brick or broken flagstone. There's no need to mortar this low wall, simply stack the bricks in a staggered fashion so that they slope inwards slightly for stability. Dry-mortar them with soil if you want to plant a few alpines in the crevices as you go.

Enrich the soil with peat and/or grit and add extra soil to bring the level up to within 2·5 cm (1 in) of the rim of a raised bed. One or two pieces of stone can be set in the surface of the bed to set the scene, but they are by no means essential. If your bed is too wide to lean across, lay some stepping stones for easy access.

Raised beds can also be built on patios but they will need to be about four bricks high and equipped with a drainage layer of rubble in the base before the soil is tipped in.

SCREE BEDS

Plants which insist on really sharp drainage are those that grow in almost pure rock chippings at the foot of mountain slopes. In the garden they can be catered for in a rock bed filled with a special sharp-draining mixture of 10 parts stone chippings, 1 part soil, 1 part peat or leafmould (sifted), 1 part sharp sand. They are really plants for the connoisseur and need a raised, rather than a flat bed which may act as a sump for all rainwater in the vicinity. Mind you, it's amazing how many rock plants will thrive in a bed containing a scree mixture, provided they are not allowed to dry out in summer (there are heavy showers even on alpine screes).

DRY WALLS

Where walls have to be constructed in the garden (to retain banks or divide off areas) consider making them 'dry' and packing either the cavity or the rear of the wall with soil as building progresses. Pack the joints, too, and as building progresses you'll be able to insert sempervivums (house leeks), encrusted saxifrages and other alpines that are happy in vertical crevices. The key to success with dry stone walls is watering, for the plants may bake before their roots become established if you forget to turn on the hosepipe occasionally.

PEAT BEDS

Peat beds are definitely for the connoisseur. They are made to accommodate a choice group of plants that relishes moist, acid soil and usually a modicum of shade. Site your peat bed against a north-facing wall and use coir-based compost if you would rather spare the peat bogs. On chalky soil you might as well forget the whole thing, for the plants insist on acidity and need a bed that has been so enriched that it contains as much peat as soil. The edges of the bed are usually raised up with peat blocks, but to conserve peat you can use logs.

The ground must be weed free from the outset and never allowed to dry out. Peat garden plants are mainly natives of woodland, so provide them with the shade and moisture they enjoy. The peat blocks, and the peat enrichment, must be moist from the very beginning. Soak them both in a tank or tin bath of water before constructing the bed.

Apply a dusting of blood, bone and fishmeal over the entire area, then a 5 cm (2 in) mulch of pure peat before planting. Stepping stones can be laid over wide beds (it's not a good idea to flatten the springy mixture with your size ten wellies) and a close watch must be kept at all times to prevent the medium from

Alpine pinks (dianthus) are especially useful for creating welcome rugs of colour on a rock garden.

Make a water garden and it will instantly become a magnet to all visitors, whether they're humans or other animals.

1. Lawn care In autumn any lawn will benefit from a really good scratch with a wire-toothed rake to remove dead grass or 'thatch'.

2. When you've scratched or scarified your lawn, aerate it with a fork to relieve compaction and to improve surface drainage.

3. Keen gardeners will follow up scarifying and spiking by topdressing with a mixture of leafmould, sand and soil, raked in well.

1. Sink garden Turn an old sink (this one is of the salt-glazed type found in old kitchens) into a garden. First put in a layer of drainage material.

2. Fill the sink to below the rim with a mixture of John Innes No.2 potting compost and sharp grit.

3. Space out the plants over the surface of the compost so they are roughly 15 cm (6 in) apart.

4. Remove the plant from the pot, scoop out a hole in the compost and lower it in. Firm down the compost.

5. When planting is completed, spread a 1-cm (½-in) deep layer of sharp grit over the surface of the compost.

1

2

3

4

5

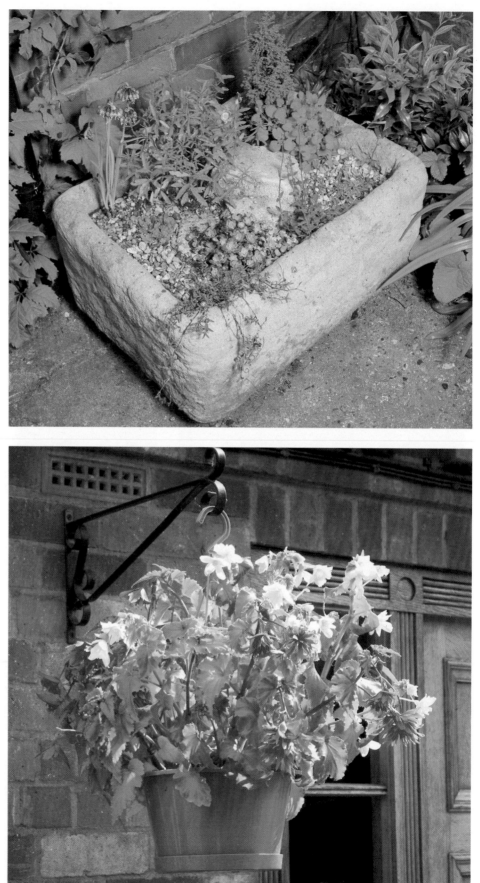

Old glazed, white sinks can be coated with an artificial stone mixture (see p. 133)

Some plants lend themselves to being planted in hanging baskets, and few are more brilliant than the pendulous begonia.

drying out. An additional top-dressing of peat should be applied each spring, and any weeds removed as soon as they are seen.

SINK GARDENS

Should you have the good fortune to come across an old porcelain sink, don't kick it out of the way or smash it up for use as hardcore; instead, turn it into a sink garden. No, not a shining white one, a stone one.

First clean it and remove the plug. Coat the outside with a bonding agent (an adhesive that's available from any hardware shop), and while this is tacky, pat on a moistened mixture of 2 parts coir, 1 part sand and 1 part cement. A 1 cm ($\frac{1}{2}$ in) thick layer all over the outside and 8 cm (3 in) over the lip inside is what's needed to transform the sink into a 'stone' one. The mixture is euphemistically called hypertufa (trust the alpine buffs to give it a fancy handle) and when it hardens it's as tough as cement itself.

Stand the sink in its final position before you coat it—afterwards it will be a weighty load. It will be best stood on bricks which keep it clear of the soil, so preventing frosting and faulty drainage. Alpines in sinks need sun just as much as those in the rock garden (unless you aim to grow one sink full of shade lovers).

Leave the sink to dry and harden for about two weeks, then place a layer of rubble in the base and fill with compost (John Innes No. 1 potting compost plus half its bulk of sharp sand is a good mixture). Plant your alpines (with a piece of rock and a dwarf conifer to add a bit of height and interest) and then water them in. About twenty plants will fit into the average sink if you sensibly choose those which are dwarf and slow growing. (See the list on p. 137.) Add a 1–2.5 cm (1–2 in) layer of stone chippings to the surface and the job is finished.

Keep a close eye on the sink during summer and soak it whenever the compost shows signs of drying out. Severe frosts may lift off parts of the 'stone' coating after a time but these can easily be patched. Replace any plants which succumb during the winter, rather than removing all the plants and starting again. Only when the sink has become really overgrown and unsightly need it be renovated and totally re-landscaped, but as a general rule age brings even greater beauty.

PLANTING

Now that alpines are almost entirely sold in pots, they can be planted with safety at any time between early spring and autumn. Water the plant well an hour or so before planting, tap it out of its pot and set it in a hole that is plenty large enough. Replace and re-firm the soil around its undisturbed rootball, spread the gravel mulch around it and then water it in. Don't plant too deeply.

Water thoroughly at the first sniff of drought. The plants are capable of coping with prolonged dry spells when they are established, but during their first year they will suffer greatly from drought.

PRUNING

As a general rule all faded flowerheads of alpines can be snipped off. Exceptions occur when you consider the seedheads to be decorative or when you want to collect seed for propagation. Spring is the best time for pruning dwarf shrubs and woody alpines, for then you can cut back to a bud that can be seen to be growing.

Dead leaves and rotting tissue can be removed at any time of year, as soon as they are seen.

LABELLING

If you can't remember what your plants are (and most of us have aberrations from time to time) label them. But don't stud your rock garden with white plastic markers that make it look like a miniature graveyard.

I find that those rigid plastic labels (written on in black indelible ink) can be pushed into the soil so that the top 1 cm ($\frac{1}{2}$ in) only is visible. This prevents the birds from pulling them out (they love doing that!) and lets you locate them when you need them without them being blatantly obvious at all times.

PLANT CARE

Rock gardens seldom need wholesale renovation; it is usually sufficient to replace worn-out plants either with new ones, or with their own divisions. Spring is the best time for this.

Weeds should be pulled up as soon as they are seen. Annuals will come out of the gravel layer with ease. Any perennial weeds can be spot-treated with a touchweeder containing a suitable herbicide (such as glyphosate).

Feed your rock plants once a year in spring. Scatter a light dusting of blood, bone and fishmeal over the surface of the gravel and let the rain wash it in.

PROPAGATION

Like border plants, alpines can be propagated by seed, cuttings or division. Details of these methods can be found in Chapter 20.

A–Z OF ROCK PLANTS

This is a brief alphabet of alpines, including only those plants which are easy to grow in a variety of situations. I have slipped in a couple of tricky customers just to tax you a little, but in the main you'll find them a bright and undemanding bunch.

Some of the plants that grow on rock gardens will also grow happily in beds and borders and may have been included in Chapters 4 and 8 on shrubs and border plants. I've indicated where this is the case.

Dwarf bulbs make a significant contribution to winter and spring colour on the rocks, and you'll find a list at the end of the chapter on garden bulbs which shows some species that look good with alpines. Remember though that all bulbs must be allowed to produce leaves after they have flowered, and these may be a bit of a nuisance if they swamp smaller plants.

Dwarf conifers offer year-round interest and add height and form to otherwise flat rock beds. Make sure, when you buy such conifers, that they are indeed dwarf or very slow growing, otherwise they'll quickly turn your rock garden into an arboretum.

Acaena   New Zealand Burr   Carpeting
Ferny-leaved plants with burr-like flowers in summer. *A. microphylla* is the tiniest and has bronze-green leaves; *A.* 'Blue Haze' has blue-grey leaves and pink-flushed stems. Both spread freely.   *Div.*

Aethionema   Stone Cress
15 × 60 cm (6 × 24 in)
A. 'Warley Rose' seems to be everybody's favourite variety. It makes a spreading shrublet and is smothered in pink flowers from late spring to early summer.   *Cutt.*

Ajuga, see Border Plants, Chapter 8

Alyssum   Gold Dust, Madwort
30 × 60 cm (1 × 2 ft)
It's popular and deservedly so. *A. saxatile* makes mounds of grey-green spatula-shaped leaves which are decorated with bright yellow flower clusters in spring. Brilliant with purple aubrieta, even if the combination isn't exactly subtle!   *Cutt.*

Androsace   Rock Jasmine
8 × 30 cm (3 × 12 in)
There are some lovely (and tricky) androsaces, but *A. sempervivoides* is not too difficult. It forms clumps of neat green rosettes over which rich pink flowers appear clustered on stalks in spring. The easiest of the cushion types is *A. cylindrica*, whose domes are smothered in white flowers early in May.   *Cutt. Seed.*

Anemone, see Garden Bulbs, Chapter 10

Arabis   Rock Cress   15 × 60 cm (6 × 24 in)
Always said in the same breath as aubrieta and alyssum. A cascading plant that tumbles happily down banks to show off masses of blue, pink or white flowers. There is also a variegated variety.   *Cutt.*

Armeria   Thrift, Sea Pink
8 × 23 cm (3 × 9 in)
Neat domes of needle-like leaves are topped in spring with drumstick tufts of rich pink, crimson or white flowers. *A. maritima* 'Dusseldorf Pride' (Düsseldorfer Stoltz) is the best red I've seen.   *Cutt.*

Aubrieta   Purple Rock Cress
10 × 60 cm (4 × 24 in)
Another cascader for banks and walls, *A. deltoidea* has a host of varieties with flowers of purple, mauve, lavender, crimson, pink and white, all set off well when they open against the grey-green leaves in spring.   *Cutt.*

Blechnum, see Border Plants, Chapter 8

Campanula   Bellflower   Various
There are literally dozens of dwarf campanulas suitable for the rock garden. Some of them are upright; others are sprawling. Avoid those which are very invasive. Bells of blue or white are produced from spring to autumn if you choose well.   *Div. Cutt.*

Cerastium   Snow in Summer
15 cm × 1·25 m (6 in × 4 ft)
Don't let this glorious, grey-leaved, white-flowered trailer loose anywhere near delicate plants—it will smother them. Find a sunny bank where it can romp rampantly and delight you in spring.   *Cutt.*

Chamaecyparis, see Shrubs, Chapter 4

Cytisus, see Shrubs, Chapter 4

Corydalis, see Border Plants, Chapter 8

Cyclamen, see Garden Bulbs, Chapter 10

Dianthus   Pink   5–15 cm × 60 cm
(2–6 in × 24 in)
The daintiest and most desirable rock pink is *D. alpinus* which makes a flat cushion topped with 5 cm (2 in) high wide-faced flowers of pale to deep pink. The hybrids of *D. deltoides* are taller at around 15 cm (6 in) but smaller flowered and perhaps best admired for their glowing colours at a distance.   *Cutt. Div.*

Diascia   23 × 100 cm (9 in × 3 ft)
As yet not widely grown, but it certainly should be. *D.* × 'Ruby Field' produces masses of spurred salmon pink flowers in dainty spires over low mats of foliage nearly all summer.   *Div. Cutt.*

Dicentra, see Border Plants, Chapter 8

Dryas   Mountain Avens   8 × 100 cm
(3 in × 3 ft)
Dark green, glossy, oak-shaped leaves make a dense carpet that is spattered with nodding white wood anemone flowers in early summer. There are two species commonly grown: *D. octopetala* and *D. suendermannii*.   *Div.*

Epimedium, see Border Plants, Chapter 8

Erigeron   Fleabane   23 × 30 cm (9 × 12 in)
Here's a bright alpine daisy with flowers of white or pink. *E. mucronatus* is an easy plant to grow and blooms sporadically from late spring to autumn.

Don't let it loose near dainty alpines or it will swamp them.   *Div.*

Erinus 10×15 cm (4×6 in)
A neat clump former with tiny saw-edged leaves and pretty pink flowers carried in clusters atop short stalks in late spring. *E. alpinus* is the true species but there is also a white variety.   *Div.*

Erodium   Heron's Bill 10×30 cm (4×12 in)
There are lots of erodiums valuable on the rock garden but *E. chamaedrioides* (syn. *E. reichardii*) is the most popular. White, pink-veined flowers are carried over low domes of leaves from early to late summer.   *Div. Cutt.*

Euphorbia   Spurge 15×60 cm (6×24 in)
The trailing *E. myrsinites* is a good plant to establish above a boulder or some steps where it can cast its grey-leaved stems downwards. Yellow-green flowers open at the stem tips in late spring.   *Cutt. Div.*

Festuca, see Border Plants, Chapter 8

Genista, see Shrubs, Chapter 4

Gentiana   Gentian 15×30 cm (6 in $\times 1$ ft)
The measurements I've given are for *G. septemfida*, a good-looking, summer-flowering, blue-trumpeted gentian that is easy to grow on any soil. Species from Asia generally hate lime; the European ones don't seem to mind it. Start with *G. septemfida* and progress to others.   *Div. Seed.*

Geranium   Cranesbill 8×60 cm (3×24 in)
You should grow as many geraniums as you can on your rock garden—they flower for such a long time. *G. sanguineum* 'Lancastriense' (now ssp. *striatum*) is one of the best—a sprawling mat with large, white, saucer-shaped flowers that are veined pink.   *Div.*

Heathers, see Shrubs, Chapter 4

Helianthemum   Rock Rose
23 cm $\times 1$ m (9 in $\times 3$ ft)
Sun loving summer bloomers making twiggy rugs of evergreen or evergrey leaves. The flowers may be yellow, orange, red, pink or white. 'Henfield Brilliant' is a striking mahogany orange. The doubles hold on to their flowers longer than the singles. Clip over lightly after flowering.   *Cutt.   Seed.*

Juniperus, see Shrubs, Chapter 4

Hypericum   St John's Wort
23×60 cm (9×24 in)
The dainty *H. polyphyllum* is a treasure that makes low domes of greyish leaves which are plastered in bright yellow, shaving-brush centred flowers during early to midsummer. 'Sulphureum' is a paler yellow. *Seed. Div. Cutt.*

Iberis   Perennial Candytuft
23×100 cm (9 in $\times 3$ ft)

Dark, evergreen leaves act as an effective backdrop to the dense heads of white flowers that *I. sempervirens* produces in spring. Needs room to spread.   *Div. Cutt.*

Leontopodium   Edelweiss
15×23 cm (6×9 in)
From tufts of greyish leaves the starry, white-felted flowers of *L. alpinum* rise up in early summer. Soggy soil kills it.   *Div.*

Lewisia 15×15 cm (6×6 in)
Some lewisias are the devil to grow. *L.* Cotyledon Hybrids are among the easiest. They make succu–lent rosettes from which rise branched flowerheads carrying salmon, pink or white flowers in summer. Lime-free soil is preferred, and walls and crevices are enjoyed.   *Div.*

Lithospermum   (now **Lithodora**)   Gromwell
8×60 cm (3×24 in)
A lime-hating trailer with narrow, hairy leaves and starry true-blue flowers in summer. It's the nearest blue to a gentian outside that family. *L. diffusum* 'Grace Ward' has replaced the old favourite 'Heavenly Blue', which is now rather lacking in vigour.   *Cutt.*

Nierembergia   Cup Flower
5×30 cm (2×12 in)
A low-growing plant with a little carpet of dark green leaves through which appear large, white, cup-shaped flowers in early to midsummer. *N. repens* (syn. *N. rivularis*) is the species offered.   *Div.*

Origanum   Dittany 30×30 cm (12×12 in)
Its time of flowering alone makes *O. laevigatum* worth growing—it carries tiny crimson-purple tubular flowers on branching stems in late summer and autumn. From a distance you'll see a purple haze mingled with grey-green leaves.   *Cutt. Div.*

Othonnopsis   (now **Othonna**)
30×30 cm (12×12 in)
O. cheirifolia has fans of grey, paddle-shaped leaves and yellow daisies, carried in late spring.   *Cutt.*

Oxalis   Wood Sorrel 5×23 cm (2×9 in)
Neatly pleated grey leaves rise from the tuberous root and are spiced with pale pink, darker-veined flowers in late spring and early summer. *O. adenophylla* is the species I describe; *O. enneaphylla* is more of a spreader.   *Div.*

Papaver   Alpine Poppy 15×15 cm (6×6 in)
Short-lived but self-seeding, *P. alpinum* has finely cut leaves and plenty of pink, white, orange or yellow poppy flowers from early summer onwards.   *Seed.*

Phlox 8×45 cm (3×18 in)
Thick mats of needle-like leaves and masses of bright, stemless flowers have made the varieties of *P. sub-*

ulata justifiably popular. They are easy to grow, too, and have blooms of violet, lavender, crimson, pink, lilac and white. 'Chattahoochee', lavender blue with a crimson eye, and 'Daniel's Cushion', large pink flowers, are two of the best modern hybrids.   *Cutt. Div.*

Polygonum   (now **Persicaria**)   Knotweed
8–15 × 100 cm (3-6 in × 3 ft)
There are two splendid polygonums for the rock garden: *P. affine*, which has pink 23 cm (9 in) high pokers in summer and autumn, and *P. vacciniifolium*, which is shorter with little pink mousetail flowers that persist right into the colder weather. Both are best when allowed to tumble over rocks.   *Div.*

Pratia   2·5 × 45 cm (1 × 18 in)
Not showy, but nevertheless valuable, *P. angulata* 'Treadwellii' makes a rug of green leaves decorated with tiny white flowers in summer. These are followed by crimson-purple berries to prolong the season of interest.   *Div.*

Primula, see Border Plants, Chapter 8

Pulsatilla   Pasque Flower
23 × 30 cm (9 × 12 in)
Early spring favourites with upturned bellflowers of purple, blue, crimson or white, centred with a boss of yellow stamens and swathed in silky hairs. *P. vulgaris* is the species most commonly grown. Carroty leaves follow the flowers. Loves chalk.   *Seed. Root Cutt.*

Salix, see Shrubs, Chapter 4

Saponaria   Soapwort   15 × 45 cm (6 × 18 in)
The old favourite *S. ocymoides* is a bright plant to put where it can tumble down a bank or boulder. It smothers itself in summer with plenty of pink flowers and as a result it can be rather short lived.   *Seed.*

Saxifraga   Saxifrage, Rockfoil   Various
You could plant up a rock garden with saxifrages and nothing else and still enjoy it for most of the year. The plants are divided into groups. Among the easiest (and the brightest) are the mossy saxifrages, with yellow, red, pink or white flowers carried in spring on 10 cm (4 in) stalks over cushions of bright green leaves. The encrusted saxifrages love crevices and have tough leaves decorated with lime deposits, and the kabschias make hard domes of leaves and usually produce short-stemmed flowers very early in spring. They like very gentle shade. Try any you can lay your hands on; they offer unparalleled value.   *Div.*

Sedum   Stonecrop   Various
The sedums are as varied as the saxifrages and even easier to grow. All have succulent leaves and flowers which are usually bright and starry. *S. kamtschaticum*

'Variegatum', 10 × 45 cm (4 × 18 in), is especially cheering with green and cream leaves and orange summer flowers.   *Cutt.*

Sempervivum   Houseleek
5 × 30 cm (2 × 12 in)
Rosette-forming succulents which are nevertheless quite hardy. They are available in assorted leaf colours—from green through to deep crimson—and have starry flowers of pink, crimson, yellow or white in summer. *S. arachnoideum* is the cobweb houseleek and is covered in silvery silky hairs.   *Div.*

Silene   Catchfly   15 × 45 cm (6 × 18 in)
The one catchfly that is easy and obliging on the rock garden is *S. schafta*, which produces plenty of pinkish-purple campion flowers in summer.   *Div. Cutt. Seed.*

Sisyrinchium   23 × 30 cm (9 × 12 in)
Among tufts of small, iris-like leaves, the yellow starry flowers of *S. brachypus* will appear from summer right through to autumn. Neat and pleasing when contrasted with carpeters.   *Seed. Div.*

Thymus   Thyme   Carpeting
Dense little rugs of aromatic foliage which are studded with pinkish lilac flowers in summer. There are colour variations in both flower and leaf, some plants having variegated or golden foliage.   *Cutt. Seed.*

Trillium   Wood Lily   23–30 × 30 cm
(9–12 × 12 in)
Choice woodlanders for shady, leafy pockets on the rock garden or for a peat bed. *T. grandiflorum* is the favourite species of most gardeners; its three leaves at the tip of a strong stalk set off to perfection the white, three-petalled flowers. For the patient.   *Div.*

Verbascum   Mullein   15 × 30 cm (6 × 12 in)
The neat *V.* 'Letitia' makes a mound of grey-felted leaves which is topped with spires of yellow flowers sporadically from early to late summer. It's a treasure that deserves a bit of protection from winter wet.   *Root cutt.*

Viola, see Border Plants, Chapter 8

Zauschneria   Californian Fuchsia
30 × 60 cm (12 × 24 in)
Tricky in the colder north but usually reliably perennial in the south, *Z. californica* makes a wiry shrublet with narrow greyish leaves and tubular flowers of burning scarlet. *Z.* 'Glasnevin' is a fraction taller and a better bet than the true species in colder areas. Both bloom from late summer into autumn.   *Seed. Cutt. Div.*

FIND THE RIGHT ROCK PLANT

Except where indicated, all the rock plants in the A–Z section are happy in an open, sunny spot in any well-drained soil, but the following are especially suited to the purposes indicated:

ROCK PLANTS FOR SINK GARDENS

Androsace
Armeria
Dianthus
Erinus
Gentiana
Juniperus communis 'Compressa'
Leontopodium
Lewisia
Oxalis
Saxifraga
Sempervivum
Thymus
Verbascum

ROCK PLANTS FOR GENTLE SHADE

Ajuga
Anemone
Blechnum
Epimedium
Lewisia
Pratia
Saxifraga (kabschia)
Trillium
Viola

ROCK PLANTS TO GROW IN WALLS

Arabis
Aubrieta
Campanula
Cerastium
Erigeron
Euphorbia

Genista
Helianthemum
Iberis
Lewisia
Lithospermum
Othonnopsis
Papaver
Polygonum
Saponaria
Saxifraga
Sedum
Sempervivum
Zauschneria

ROCK PLANTS FOR SCREE BEDS

Androsace
Erigeron
Erodium
Hypericum
Leontopodium
Nierembergia
Origanum
Papaver
Sedum
Sempervivum
Silene
Verbascum
Zauschneria

DWARF CONIFERS FOR ROCK GARDENS

Abies balsamea f. *hudsania*
Chamaecyparis lawsoniana 'Gimbornii'
Chamaecyparis lawsoniana 'Minima Aurea'
Chamaecyparis obtusa 'Nana'
Chamaecyparis pisifera 'Nana'
Cryptomeria japonica 'Vilmoriniana'
Juniperus communis 'Compressa'
Juniperus horizontalis 'Glauca'
Picea abies 'Gregoryana'
Picea glauca 'Albertiana Conica'
Picea mariana 'Nana'
Pinus mugo 'Gnom'
Thuja plicata 'Rogersii'

12 Water gardening

Picture, if you can, a still summer's day by a limpid pool. Sword-leafed irises and frothy lady's mantle decorate its edges, and a water lily flaunts its shiny pads and starry flowers in the warm light. Bright goldfish dart among the shadowy water while above the surface dragonflies and demoiselles buzz from plant to plant, courting in the sunshine. The plate glass surface is broken only by occasional ripples as a frog plops out of sight, or while the pond skaters dance like dervishes with a gift for walking on water. Now I know that gardening writers are incurable optimists but this really can be the scene if you play your cards right.

Even in the tiniest garden a sheet of water will provide spicy variety. You'll be able to grow a wider range of plants, both in the water and at its edges, and whether you like it or not you'll find that you've created a miniature nature reserve. You'll always have frogs, the occasional toad and newt, and an abundance of water-loving insects. If you don't like creepy-crawlies a pond is not for you. But before you try to expel the toad population, just think of all the slugs they'll eat.

If tiny tots are at large, then you'd better wait a few years before building the pond. Even a few inches of water are potentially dangerous. But there's nothing to stop you from laying a pool liner, filling it with about 15 cm (6 in) of soil, planting bog plants and then laying pebbles over the earth to produce a dry river bed effect. A hosepipe can be played into the liner occasionally to keep the soil moist. When the children are older it's a simple job to turn the river bed into a fully fledged pool—remove the bog plants, top up with water and treat the area as you would any other new water garden. But I'm racing ahead. If you want to build a simple pool that won't turn into a gigantic bowl of green pea soup, here's what to do.

THE RIGHT SPOT

Just as there's an ideal spot for every other garden feature, so there is for a pool. It should be open and sunny, not overhung by trees but sheltered at a distance from biting winds. Under trees the water will become a mass of soggy leafmould in autumn and your fish and aquatic plants will suffer.

If you insist on having a pool under a tree you'll have to be prepared for the task of stretching plastic net over it every autumn before leaves start to fall, and you'll also have to put up with spindly plants that don't grow or flower as well as those in the sun. Your pool won't be so much limpid as stagnant.

WHAT SHAPE?

Formal pools—circular, square or rectangular—are for formal gardens. In informal gardens (and most plots plunge headlong into that category) irregular shapes are better. Irregular doesn't mean fiddly. Make your pool as sweepingly curved as you can—don't go in for narrow necks and wiggly serpentine shapes.

Fit your pool into the general scheme of the garden so that its outline complements other beds and borders. Make it as large as possible—the bigger the stretch of water the more impact it will have and the easier it will be to keep in good condition (clear and not green).

HOW DEEP?

45 cm (1½ ft). Make your pool more than 60 cm (2 ft) deep and its bottom will become a stagnant mire of lifeless mud. Make it shallower than 30 cm (1 ft) and it will heat up like a pan of water on a summer's day, encouraging those algae that turn the water green. 45 cm (1½ ft) is the happy medium.

MATERIALS

Ancient ponds were made of puddled clay but the art of constructing them went out with button boots. Concrete came next, but the work involved in making a concrete pool is amazingly arduous and life is hell when a concrete pool starts to leak. Fibreglass or rigid plastic liners may look handy little jobs when you see them stacked in the garden centre, but they are iniquitously expensive and almost always useless in the garden. Most are too small, their shapes are weird and when filled with plant life and fish the water nearly always turns green.

By far the best bet are the flexible liners made of butyl—a sort of luxury rubber. Thick PVC liners are the next choice (provided they're not a nasty shade of turquoise) and finally, the cheapest liner, polythene. It's also the shortest lived, but where funds are lean it's worth using for it will almost always last for three years before it needs to be replaced. The other two liners will last for donkeys' years, and repair kits are available should they be encouraged to spring a leak by the clumsy placement of a garden fork.

For goodness sake calculate carefully the size of liner you'll need. Its length will be equal to the length of the pool, plus twice the depth, plus 60 cm (2 ft)—to allow it to be tucked under whatever edging material you decide on. The width will be equal to the width of the pool, plus twice the depth, plus 60 cm (2 ft). There's nothing worse than digging out a pool and putting the liner in place only to find that it's too small. The feeling compares with buying a fitted carpet that doesn't.

DIGGING THE HOLE

Once you've marked out the shape of your pool (either with a trail of sand or a curved hosepipe) you'll have to start excavating. April and May are the best months for pond making so start digging in March to allow for unexpected interruptions.

The more help you can get at this stage the better. You'll be surprised how many barrowloads of soil come out of a relatively small hole, leaving you with the problem of deciding what to do with the stuff. The usual solution is to build a rock garden mound at the side of the pool. Avoid it. It will always be patently obvious that the mound is a spoil heap, however hard you try to disguise it with well-placed pieces of rock.

Use the stuff to build a raised bed in another part of the garden or to make a terrace near the house or by a distant patio. It's the top 23–30 cm (9–12 in) of soil that's valuable as far as plants are concerned. In-

hospitable subsoil can be used for raising up hard areas of paving and the like or, as a last resort, it can be dumped in a hired skip and carted away.

The sides of the pool should slope gently at an angle of about 45°. Cut a step into the side if you like, just about half way up (Fig. 38). This will provide you with a shelf on which pots and baskets of marginal aquatic plants (those that like the shallows) can be stood.

It's tempting, at this stage, to get the liner in and fill it with water, but it might be a costly operation should any pieces of sharp stone or glass be protruding. First pat the exposed surfaces of the pool with a spade to knock any protuberances back into the soil, then spread a 2·5 cm (1 in) layer of sand over the whole area, including a 30 cm (1 ft) overlap at the pool edges. If you're hard up (or just plain mean) use several layers of newspaper instead of sand. With this buffering layer in place the liner can be laid.

FITTING THE LINER

Unpack the liner carefully and check it for holes (they have been known to exist even before the liner is laid). Stretch it over the hole (you'll need more than one pair of hands) and gently hold the edges down with smooth stones or bricks. Check that the material is evenly distributed so that when the water is in the hole the liner will overlap an equal amount all round.

Now the pool can be filled. Lay a hosepipe on the liner and turn on the tap. This is the exciting bit—as the water flows in you'll see your pool slowly taking

Fig. 38 The butyl liner is laid over a bed of sand to prevent puncturing, and the base of the pool is contoured to provide different water levels. Marginal aquatics stand on the shelf; submerged aquatics and water lilies rest on the bottom, and bog plants grow in the constantly moist earth at the pool's rim.

shape. Gradually the weight of the water will push the liner flat against the soil, but you'll have to help it to lay the material evenly by gently pulling and tucking in any overlaps to avoid a mass of creases which are potential leak areas. Turn off the hose when the pool is full to the brim. At this stage you'll be able to see the final level of the water and the level of your pool edging.

I usually incorporate a boggy area into a pool by excavating just 30 cm (1 ft) of topsoil at one end, running the liner over it and up to the surface level (Fig. 38). The soil is then replaced before the pool is filled. Here all sorts of bog plants are happy and they don't mind the fact that there's no drainage. Some gardeners insist on perforating the liner when it runs under a boggy area but this just isn't necessary. What's more, it means that you're for ever topping up the water level in the pool, and topping up encourages green scum.

The most popular way of edging a pool is to lay flagstones (crazy or sane) around it, tucking the liner under them. I know it's hackneyed but it is the most reliable method. Mind you, bricks will do just as good a job. Lay them (or the flags) so that they overlap the edge of the pool by 5 cm (2 in). There's nothing worse than having to look at a strip of pool liner around what should be a clean-edged stretch of water. Lay your edging very carefully, using the surface of the water as a straight-edge and making sure that the liner slopes upwards from the water just a fraction to prevent any leakage. Fine soil or sand can be used to bed your stones level, but don't consider cementing them into place or repairs and adjustments may be made difficult. Take your time over the edging and be meticulous—it will make or mar your pool.

Now comes the difficult bit. You've got to stand back and do nothing for about ten days. This will allow the water to settle down and disperse some of its undesirable chemical contents. After ten days you can introduce plants.

PLANTING

There are five basic kinds of plant that can be used in or around garden pools:

Submerged aquatics spend most of their time below the surface of the water and many of them are vital oxygenating plants. They keep fish happy and prevent the water from becoming stagnant by giving off little bubbles of oxygen as they grow. Some of them produce flowering shoots above the surface which makes them doubly valuable. No pool can become 'balanced' and clear without oxygenators, so make sure that you have at least two bunches of these plants for every square metre (sq yd) of the pool's surface area. You can always thin the plants out when they become overcrowded and give them away to pool owners anxious to clear their water.

Fixed-floating aquatics are anchored to the base of the pool (or to a basket of compost within the pool) but their leaves and flowers float on the surface. Water lilies come into this category.

Free-floating aquatics bob about merrily on the surface. Duckweed is a classic example, but fairy floating moss (*Azolla*) is a more desirable plant for it's less likely to swamp the pool.

Marginal aquatics like to grow in shallow water and are most at home on the shelf especially built for them just 23 cm (9 in) or so below the surface.

Bog plants are happy in soil that stays constantly moist. It doesn't need to be really muddy but most of the plants are quite tolerant of extreme conditions.

Fig. 39 (*a*) Water lilies are best planted in plastic baskets of garden soil lined with sacking. Cut off any really thick roots at planting time and firm the soil around the crown. (*b*) Spread gravel over the soil in the basket before you submerge it in the pool. Stand it on bricks for two weeks before lowering it to the bottom.

Free floaters require no 'planting' at all—just release them on the surface of the water. Bog plants can be planted with a trowel, like any garden plant, but take care not to perforate the liner. Submerged aquatics can be tied to pebbles with bits of fishing line and dropped to the bottom of the pool where they will soon take root in the sediment.

The marginal aquatics and the fixed-floating aquatics like water lilies are best planted in special plastic baskets that are made for the job (Fig. 39). Line the basket with a bit of old sacking (to prevent the compost from seeping out), and plant the lily or other aquatic plant in ordinary garden soil. This is the only occasion on which you'll hear me recommending garden soil for container-grown plants. Normally they are far better with a special potting compost, but in this case the chemical content of the compost will only help to foul the water.

Remove any tatty leaves or very long roots from the plants, then set them in the basket of soil so that their crown (junction of roots and shoots) is level with the surface. Firm the earth around their roots and cover its surface with gravel. This will prevent fish from disturbing the soil and muddying the water when the plant is in place.

When the basket is planted up, perfectionists will submerge it in a tank of water so that all air can be driven out (a process that can muddy the water). Only then will they transfer the basket to the pool, standing it on bricks at first so that it rests just 15 cm (6 in) below the surface. Marginal aquatics can go straight on to their shelves, but water lilies will appreciate this gentle introduction to the water. After a couple of weeks the bricks can be removed and the basket allowed to rest on the bottom of the pool.

Never be tempted to plant aquatics in mounds of soil at the bottom of the pool. Fish will forever create havoc down there, turning the water into grey soup as they ferret around for food. All planting up is best carried out in spring, during April and May.

GREEN WATER

This is your biggest pool problem, but if you make your stretch of water large enough and deep enough it will only be a temporary nuisance. All pools turn green shortly after they are made, but if plenty of oxygenating plants are present the water will eventually clear, though it may briefly turn pea-green each spring.

Don't be tempted to drain the pool and start again—the greening will only start again too. Leave the pool alone and only top it up with a hosepipe when it starts to get low. Excessive topping-up will exacerbate the problem.

Green blanket weed is easy to fish out with a wire-toothed lawn rake, but take care neither to disturb the sediment at the bottom of the pool nor to puncture the liner. Construct your pool properly and be patient—that way you're less likely to encounter long-term problems.

FISH AND OTHER WILDLIFE

No pool should be without its quota of wildlife (Fig. 40). You'll probably attract frogs and toads whether you want them or not; newts are not so easy to entice and you may not see them very frequently even if you take the trouble to introduce them.

Iridescent dragonflies and demoiselles, or damsel flies, will doubtless come uninvited, but they are a treat to watch as they perform aerobatics over the water in summer. Other insects will abound, especially pond skaters on the surface and water boatmen beneath. Don't worry about introducing water snails—they're not essential and if you end up with the wrong ones they'll spend all their time eating your water lily leaves instead of clearing up the sediment, for which they are renowned. I've never noticed that they make any difference at all to the state of the water.

Goldfish are a must. Most experienced pond makers recommend golden orfe as being the finest fish for a garden pond. I agree that they look good in shoals, but they're not so bright as your common-or-garden-pool goldfish which move around more slowly, giving you time to admire their vivid coats. I'd settle for a mixture of the two (Fig. 41), avoiding those expensive and revolting Koi carp which look like a fish-breeder's nightmare. Don't overstock your pool—allow at least 30 cm square (1 square ft) of surface area to each fish, and introduce your fish gently about two months after planting up the pond and establishing the oxygenators.

Always buy your fish from a reputable supplier, and avoid any fish that are listless or showing signs of white fungal growth. Suspend the container in which they are supplied over the edge of the pool for a few hours so that the water temperatures can equalize. Then the fish can be gently allowed to swim out of the bag or bowl into the pool.

There's much argument about feeding of fish. I've kept them going for years by dropping pelleted food into the pond once a week from April to September. Allow one pellet per fish. Drop too much food into the water and it will only cause the pool to become cloudy. Between October and March the fish will find all they need among the plants and sediment—they won't need any supplements to their diet.

Diseased or damaged fish are best removed and knocked on the head. Don't be shocked at this callousness. There are all manner of cures given for diseases, most of which involve immersing the fish in a bowl of water containing some thoroughly unpleasant solution. The fish will be miserable and is quite likely to infect the other members of the pool when he's re-introduced. I stand by my seemingly cruel solution.

Fig. 40 Whether you like it or not your pool will be a magnet for wildlife. Frogs and toads will probably appear uninvited, but they help to keep down plant pests. Newts can be introduced, and dragonflies and damselflies will flit over the glassy surface on warm summer days.

You'll also have to harden your heart if your fish are speared and stolen by herons. This stately grey bird cleared my pond of all but two fish a couple of years ago. All the fish had names and were won at assorted fairgrounds with well-aimed ping-pong balls (so much for reputable suppliers)—it was a heavy blow! Only plastic netting stretched over the pool will keep the big birds at bay, but who wants to look at a vista of plastic netting every day?

Fig. 41 Common or garden goldfish (*left*) are the brightest swimmers for your pool, but golden orfe (*right*) are the most social—swimming about the surface in shoals.

RENOVATION AND CLEANING
Just like other garden plants, aquatics and bog plants will need an annual clean-up in autumn and winter. Remove all faded leaves and chop back the stalks of deciduous kinds to within a few centimetres (inches) of soil level. Pull faded leaves from water lilies and remove any rotting vegetation from the water.

If your garden is a moving scene of fallen leaves in autumn it is definitely worthwhile covering the pool with plastic netting to catch the foliage before it falls in. Rotting leaves will cloud the water and poison the fish.

Don't clean the bottom of the pond every year; save the job up and do it when it's really necessary—say once every three years. Empty the pool and divide the plants at the same time, re-basketing those that need it. You'll have to catch and safely house your fish first.

In winter keep a patch of ice melted so that the fish can breathe. Don't clout it with a hammer—the sound waves will stun the fish—but pour a kettle of boiling water on the surface to make a hole. Extract a little water if you can to leave a greater surface area from which the fish can extract oxygen.

WATER FEATURES
I've said nothing about moving water—fountains, cascades and waterfalls—mainly because they seldom look attractive on a small scale, and also because plants seldom enjoy growing in moving water. If you insist on having a bit of movement (and I admit that on a large scale there's nothing more musical than a gurgling stream) then a specialist book will offer you advice, as will the manufacturers of submersible pumps, necessary for the circulation of water.

Pumps need electricity, always best installed by a professional electrician, as do pool lights, but these really do bring the water alive at night and are especially worth installing adjacent to a patio or picture window to illuminate the plants, water and fish. Make sure the correct lights are chosen for the job—again rely on your tame electrician.

TUB POOLS

Finally, for the gardener with no garden, there's the tub pool (Fig. 42). Half an oak beer cask that's soundly coopered and painted inside with water-proofing bitumen can be filled with water and used as a home for a pygmy water lily and three goldfish. If you can't lay your hands on a tub, find an old porcelain sink, treat it as described on p. 133, put the plug in and fill it with water. The plants and fish will do just as well as in a tub. The fish will need warmer quarters in winter (a friend's pond will do nicely) but in spring and summer the barrel or sink will bring life and interest to the tiniest patio.

Fig. 42 If space is short go for half a beer barrel. Well coopered and painted inside with bitumen it will hold a pygmy water lily and a couple of fish.

A–Z OF WATER PLANTS

The following lists include some of the most cheering water plants that are easy to grow in the right situation. They're a self-sufficient little bunch that give of their best in spring and summer.

SUBMERGED AQUATICS

Elodea canadensis Canadian Pondweed
This, and its larger relative *E. crispa* (syn. *Lagarosiphon major*), are the curly-leaved water plants that one was always given a sprig of with a petshop goldfish. Vital oxygenators.

Hottonia palustris Water Violet
Feathery underwater leaves and spikes of starry lilac flowers above water in spring.

Myriophyllum spp. Water Milfoil
Superbly dainty feathery leaves. Spikes of insignificant flowers in summer.

Potamogeton crispus Curled Pondweed
Narrow, wavy leaves. Insignificant flowers in summer.

Ranunculus aquatilis Water Crowfoot
Feathery leaves below water; buttercup leaves and white flowers above in late spring.

Utricularia vulgaris Bladderwort
A neat little insectivorous plant which catches its prey in minute bladders held among the feathery underwater leaves. Yellow snapdragon flowers appear above water in summer.

FIXED-FLOATING AQUATICS
Aponogeton distachyus Water Hawthorn
Oval leaves sit on the water and are decorated with scented clusters of white, black-anther-dotted flowers in summer.

Nuphar lutea Brandy Bottle;
Yellow Water Lily
Water-lily-like leaves and cup-shaped yellow flowers on stalks that hold them above the water in summer.

Nymphaea species and varieties Water Lily
The queen of the pool with those rounded, shiny pads of leaves and starry flowers of white, yellow, pink, crimson or violet blue. I offer a selection for ponds of different sizes. All bloom for most of the summer:
N. 'Carolinia' pale pink; small pools and tubs
'Escarboucle' rich rosy crimson; large pools
'Froebelii' rosy red; small pools
'Gladstoniana' white; large pools
'Gonnère' white; large pools
'James Brydon' rich rosy red; large or small pools
'Marliacea Chromatella' pale yellow; large pools
'Mrs Richmond' (*fabiola*) deep pink; large pools
N. 'Odorata Minor' tiny white flowers and leaves; small pools
N. 'Odorata Sulphurea' pale yellow; small pools
'Pygmaea Alba' minute white flowers and leaves; the best choice for tubs and sinks
'Rose Arey' rose pink; small pools

MARGINAL AQUATICS
Acorus calamus Sweet Flag 75 cm ($2\frac{1}{2}$ ft)
Sword-shaped leaves that are sweetly scented when crushed. The variety 'Variegatus' is cream-striped and more compact.

Butomus umbellatus Flowering Rush 90 cm
Grassy, green leaves and umbels of lovely pink flowers in summer.

Calla palustris Bog Arum 23 cm (9 in)
Glossy, green, heart-shaped leaves and miniature arum lily flowers of clear white in summer.

Caltha palustris Kingcup; Marsh Marigold
30 cm (1 ft)
Heart-shaped green leaves and bright yellow butter-

cup flowers in spring. The double variety 'Flore Pleno' is best.

Glyceria maxima 'Variegata'
Reed Meadow Grass   60 cm (2 ft)
A stunning variegated grass with leaves striped green and creamy white. Vigorous.

Houttuynia cordata 'Flore Pleno'   45 cm (1 $\frac{1}{2}$ ft)
Pointed, heart-shaped leaves make a dense clump that sports white, pyramidal flowers in summer. Very handsome.

Iris laevigata   Smooth Iris   75 cm (2$\frac{1}{2}$ ft)
Sword-shaped leaves and exceptionally handsome wide-petalled flowers of purple, blue, pink or white in early summer.

Iris pseudacorus   Yellow Flag   90 cm (3 ft)
Grey-green leaves and bright yellow iris flowers in early summer.

Juncus effusus 'Spiralis'
Corkscrew rush   45 cm (1$\frac{1}{2}$ ft)
A reed that has leaves spiralled just like corkscrews—a conversation piece if nothing else.

Mentha aquatica   Water Mint   45 cm (1$\frac{1}{2}$ ft)
Green leaves and the usual lilac summer flowers of mint. Equally as aromatic as garden mint and just as useful.

Menyanthes trifoliata   Bog Bean   30 cm (1 ft)
Three-lobed leaves and white early summer flowers with fringed edges.

Myosotis scorpioides   Water Forget-me-not
23 cm (9 in)
Clouds of pale blue flowers in late spring and early summer.

Orontium aquaticum   Golden Club   30 cm (1 ft)
Oval green leaves among which rise up golden-yellow flower spikes in early summer.

Pontederia cordata   Pickerel Weed
45 cm (1$\frac{1}{2}$ ft)
Arrow-shaped, glossy green leaves and spires of pale blue flowers in summer.

Sagittaria sagittifolia 'Flore Pleno'
Arrowhead   45 cm (1$\frac{1}{2}$ ft)
The handsome leaves give the plant its common name. The double white flowers are carried up tall stems.

Scirpus (syn. **Schoenoplectus**)
tabernaemontanus 'Zebrinus'   Zebra Rush
90 cm (3 ft)
Porcupine quills of green banded with creamy-yellow. Very handsome.

FREE-FLOATING AQUATICS
Azolla caroliniana   Fairy Floating Moss
A pale green, lacy-leaved floater that becomes pinky-red with the onset of cold weather. Overwinter indoors free of frost in a bowl of water.

Hydrocharis morsus-ranae   Frogbit
Miniature water-lily leaves and three-petalled white flowers in summer. Sinks to the bottom in winter.

Stratiotes aloides   Water Soldier
Bromeliad-like rosettes of green leaves float half in, half out of the water. White, three-petalled flowers open in summer.

Avoid duckweed (*Lemna* spp) like the plague. It will soon plaster your pool from end to end, totally masking its reflective properties, so that it looks like a sunken lawn. Woe betide the unobservant visitor who treads on it.

BOG PLANTS
The following plants are described in detail in Chapter 8 on *Border Plants*. They will all do well in a patch of moisture-retentive soil on the pond bank.

Aconitum
Ajuga
Alchemilla
Aruncus
Astilbe
Dicentra
Gunnera (massive bogs only!)
Hemerocallis
Hosta
Iris (some)
Lobelia
Lysimachia
Mimulus
Monarda
Rheum
Rodgersia
Trollius
Zantedeschia

13 Lawns

Every garden has a lawn—or something that passes for one. It's quite true that in tiny gardens the lawn brings with it a host of problems, but whatever the arguments against it, it has one unassailable advantage—it's cheap. It's all very well for the landscape architect to persuade you that what you really need is York stone paving, granite setts or brick paviors, but if you have to take on a second mortgage to cover the cost it's probably not worthwhile.

Mind you, he has a point about grass being a bad choice in confined spaces. It will be difficult to mow; the clippings might be difficult to dispose of; the grass is not an all-weather surface so you'll have to steer round it when it's muddy; and you'll likely as not have problems with wear and tear, moss and fungus diseases (but then so will any lawn owner).

Grown well, all the usual compliments levelled at a lawn have some truth in them. It sets off the rest of the garden; it shows off the plants a treat; when new-mown it makes the rest of the garden look tidy even if it isn't. And you can't play croquet on York stone paving.

THE NEW LAWN

If you're faced with the task of making a new lawn, get ready for a bit of hard graft. Whether you sow seed or lay turves the preparation of the ground is exactly the same. It should be cleared of debris, builders' rubble, long grass, all weeds and any piles of subsoil (if it's a new site) then forked or dug over. That's several weeks' work in just one sentence.

It does pay to take a bit of trouble at this stage. If you can dig out completely any tree stumps, for instance, you'll be saved the job of filling in the hole that appears years later when the stump rots. It's at this stage that fungi keep coming up on the lawn too.

A generous helping of moist peat dug into the soil during preliminary cultivations will give the grass some welcome organic matter into which it can sink its shallow roots and obtain a little resistance to drought.

Try to make the site as level as you can. Keen craftsmen will hammer pegs into the ground to the required level, and check them against one another with a straight edge and spirit level. To be honest, most gardeners needn't go to this length, but it's a good idea to rake the surface as level as possible, tramp it down with your feet and rake again, crouch-ing down and running your eye over the ground to spot any bumps and hollows which can be flattened or filled in.

When you've prepared the site it's a good idea to let it stand idle for at least a month before you sow or turf; that way any resident weeds you overlooked will come up and show themselves and you can remove them smartly.

You'll probably have little choice when it comes to siting your lawn, but remember that grass grows poorly in heavy shade under trees, and is likely to be out of bounds for much of the year on really sticky, boggy soil.

When it comes to shape, that's something for you to decide, but remember that twiddly bits are hard on the eye and hard to mow—make all your curves sweeping. Try to avoid making square or rectangular lawns—go for natural lines which will show off your plants better and look a little more romantic and restful.

Fiddle around with the shape of the lawn by laying a hosepipe on it to mark out the area. Go inside the house and check your design from windows both upstairs and down until you come upon the right shape. Mark this out on the soil with a trail of sand.

If you're being distinctly put off by the thought of going through all this rigmarole, there are a few shortcuts you can take in soil preparation. The weeds can be killed off with a herbicide such as Tumbleweed (glyphosate)—though you may need two or three applications—and the ground can then be rotavated. There are one or two disadvantages with this system. First, not all the weeds may have been killed and those that have survived will re-emerge later (probably chopped up into ten viable pieces). Secondly, the soil will be very fluffy and you'll have to make sure it's well firmed before sowing or turfing (shuffle around with your feet rather than using a roller which may just flatten the surface). You'll still have to take as much care over levelling as if you were using a fork or spade.

SEED OR TURF?

It's tempting to turf a lawn rather than seed it because the effect is instant, but consider the disadvantages of turf as well. It is ten times more expensive than seed; it varies in quality from supplier to supplier, and you'll still have to wait for a few weeks before you can walk on it or the un-knit turves will skid around. What's more, there's a darned sight more labour involved in laying turf evenly than there is in scattering grass seed and raking it in.

The advantages of turf? Well, apart from being almost instant, you can lay it at any time of year when the soil is moist, rather than dusty, frozen or muddy. Seed is best sown in September or April and May.

Finding good turf is not easy. Look through the Yellow Pages under Turf Supplies and ring around for a few quotes. Beware of firms who offer just one type of turf—it's probably mown meadow turf, and even if it's described as 'weed treated' you're likely to find that it's as varied in make-up as a patchwork quilt. Settle for a good, hard-wearing turf from a specialist supplier—don't be talked into having flashy 'sea-washed' stuff which is far too luxurious for a resilient lawn. Arrange for delivery on a day when you know you will be at home and ready to lay the stuff (weather permitting). Turf stacked for more than three days soon turns yellow and starts to die off. If you have to stack it yourself, remember to stack it grass to grass and soil to soil. Rolled turves can be left as they are, but do lay them quickly.

If you decide on seed, then you'll have to choose the kind of mixture you need. Don't get ideas above your station and sow a 'bowling green' type of mixture which looks good on the green-striped, pictorial packet. If you want a hard-wearing lawn that can tolerate children and picnics choose a mixture containing a dwarf variety of ryegrass. These mixtures make a dense, good-looking sward that wears well, and because the ryegrass is a dwarf strain it won't produce any of those long stems that refuse to be cut by the mower. The 'bowling green' mixtures are only suitable for lawns that won't be asked to take much wear. They don't contain ryegrass and need a much more comprehensive lawn care programme than those seed mixtures that do. They are likely to become overrun by alien grasses if not regularly mown, and fall prey to fungus diseases more easily. On the other hand, if you want to spend every waking hour producing a velvet lawn that's the envy of your neighbours, the fine mixture is the one to go for.

Slightly shady areas can be sown with grass seed mixtures that are made up from shade tolerant grasses—look for them in the garden centre.

Whether you choose seed or turf you'll still have to calculate how much you need. Turf is sold in square metres or yards, as a rule, and seed by weight. The recommended sowing rate is 40 g (about 1½ oz) per square metre or yard—that will allow the birds a few beakfuls without spoiling your lawn.

Laying turf

Once the turf is neatly stacked near the site of your lawn-to-be and the earth is waiting to receive it, scatter a light dusting of general fertilizer over the soil

(a handful to the square metre or yard will do) and lightly rake it in. Don't rake for hours or you'll find more stones than you know what to do with. The soil should be nicely moist—not dusty or so wet that it clings to your wellies.

You'll need a spade and a plank before you go any further: the spade for lifting and patting the turves into place (as well as adding and subtracting soil beneath them) and the plank to walk on.

Start at one end of the lawn-to-be and lay a row of turves overlapping the intended boundary. Lay them immediately in front of your plank (Fig. 43) so that you achieve a straight line right at the start. Butt them as close together as you can and pat them firm with the back of your spade (not so hard that they turn to mud). If any of them sit too far up or down, add or

subtract a little soil beneath them. If you find, as you're laying the turves, that they don't sit quite flush with one-another, take a bucket of soil with you and fill any cracks.

When the first row is laid, move your plank on top of them and lay the next row, staggering the joints like those of bricks in a wall. Continue like this, over-lapping the boundary of the lawn all the way round—you can trim it up later.

When the entire area is covered remove the plank and keep every member of the family off the lawn for at least ten days—that way the turf will have a chance to settle without being buffeted around.

If you're turfing in spring or summer, have a hosepipe and sprinkler handy and turn it on over the completed lawn at the slightest suspicion of dryness. Left to bake, the turf will turn brown, refuse to knit together and shrink, causing large gaps to appear.

With any luck the lawn will be ready to walk on after four to six weeks, depending on the time of year (sooner in spring and summer; later in winter). It's at this stage that you can trim the edges against a plank or a curved hosepipe. You can start to mow, too, but take it slowly and don't cut the grass too short—just remove the top cm ($\frac{1}{2}$ in) of grass once it has grown 5 cm (2 in) high.

Soon you can mow more regularly, but it's still a good idea to avoid giving the grass too much wear, and to make sure it never dries out. The kinder you are at this stage, the more quickly will your lawn establish itself.

Sowing seed

Soil preparation is exactly the same for sowing seeds as for laying turf—scatter a handful of general fertilizer over each square metre or yard of soil and lightly rake it in. Shuffle over the soil with your feet to firm it, then rake again. The soil should be moist, not dusty or muddy. Lawns sown in September stand the best chance of establishing quickly—there is less likely to be a sudden burst of weed growth than there is with the April and May sowings, and the earth will be nicely warmed up after the summer sunshine and gently moistened by early autumn rains. The grass will also be expected to put up with less wear and tear through autumn and winter than it would through summer, so it's likely to grow thicker more quickly.

The recommended sowing rate of 40 g (about $1\frac{1}{2}$ oz) per square metre or yard will allow the birds to have a nibble, so there's no need to be neurotic and rig up Heath Robinsonian devices using little metal bottle tops and steak-and-kidney pie dishes. Sparrows will only take dust baths on the soil if it's dusty, which as far as your grass seed is concerned is a bad thing—keep it moist with the aid of a sprinkler. The odd bit of disturbance won't really make any difference.

Don't go to the trouble of weighing out every 40 g ($1\frac{1}{2}$ oz) of the seed. Weigh one lot, put it into an old

Fig. 43 Turfing (a) Stand on a plank placed on the turves you have already laid. Work forwards and lay in a brick pattern. (b) Pat down the turves so that they are firmly in contact with the levelled earth. Don't bash them too hard or they'll turn to mud. (c) Adjust the level of uneven turves by adding or subtracting soil underneath them. (d) As the job progresses, brush fine soil (or a mixture of peat and sand) into any cracks between the turves. Soak the new lawn during dry spells. (e) 4–6 weeks after laying, the edges can be cut to the required shape with a spade or 'half moon' iron.

plastic yoghurt or cream carton and mark the side with a felt-tip pen. Use the measure for all subsequent work. I've never been conscientious enough to mark out the plot into square yards, but then I kid myself that I know what a yard looks like. If you don't, check up and chalk it out on a path or patio. When it's imprinted on your mind, start sowing—for goodness sake don't mark out the entire area into little squares with canes and string.

Scatter each measure of seed evenly over its allotted area and when the whole patch is sown go over it with a rake *lightly* raking the seed in. Don't roll it. If you've shuffled over the ground with your feet to firm it, that's all that's needed.

Turn a sprinkler on whenever the soil looks dry. It will seem ages before any grass shows, but after a few weeks, when you're bent double looking across the surface of the soil, you'll detect a faint green haze. That's the youngsters pushing their way up through the soil. Don't worry if the effect is patchy, even when the grass is a few centimetres or inches high. The seeds germinate erratically and may still come through a few weeks after the first ones showed.

When much of the grass is about 5 cm (2 in) high, go over the lawn either with a light roller (if you have one) or with a cylinder lawn mower that can be held so that only the back roller comes into contact with the soil. This rolling will make sure that the roots of the young plants are firmly anchored to the soil before they are pulled at by the mower.

The following day the lawn can receive its first mowing—take off just the top cm ($\frac{1}{2}$ in) of grass, which will encourage the plants to produce sideshoots lower down, so thickening up the lawn. Cut again when the lawn has put on another cm ($\frac{1}{2}$ in) of growth, and don't worry if there's a lot of weed growth present—most of it will be killed off by regular mowing, and any weeds that remain can be treated later with a lawn weed-killer. If you are committed to organic gardening, avoiding the use of weedkillers in particular, then you will have to settle for a weedy lawn. Some weeds, such as dandelions and plantains, can be removed by hand with an old dinner knife; others are difficult to eradicate by mechanical means.

Any bare patches that remain after eight weeks can be resown with seed. Rake them over, scatter the seed on and rake again.

Lawns sown in September will need few mowings before the onset of winter, but those sown in spring can be progressively mown more regularly until they are being cut once or twice a week. Keep off the area until the grass looks well established and quite thick. After about eight weeks you should be able to tread your verdant sward and park a deckchair on it, but wait a little longer before giving the go-ahead for vigorous games of football. It will be sometime before the roots of the young grass plants have explored deeply into the soil.

The idler's lawn

Any piece of ground that's fairly level and which has reasonable soil is a potential lawn. If you mow whatever grows on it—weeds, meadow- and weed-grasses—it will eventually turn into a lawn. The ironic thing is that after six or seven years you'll probably detect no difference between this type of lawn and one which was originally sown with a ryegrass mixture—unless the latter has been assiduously fed and treated against weeds. Where large areas of coarse turf are needed, under fruit trees and in paddocks, the mowing technique is well worth putting into practice.

LAWN CARE

Most of us are rotten to our lawns—we cut them and bash them around without ever giving them regular meals or a wash and brush-up. Expert gardeners have complicated lawn-care programmes, but the following are the basic tasks necessary to produce a decent patch of good-looking greensward.

Scarifying involves the removal of dead grass known as thatch. It also pulls out moss. Use a wire-toothed 'springbok' rake for the job, or one of those excellent new electrically powered lawn rakers. Don't worry that the lawn looks a bit bare and tatty afterwards; it will soon pull round and grow away with renewed vigour. *Timing* September.

Spiking the lawn with either a garden fork or a special 'hollow-tined aerator' relieves surface compaction and improves drainage and soil condition. Ram the fork in to a depth of at least 10 cm (4 in) and wiggle it around—you'll see the earth lift a little. Stab it in at intervals of 15 cm (6 in). *Timing* September (after scarifying).

Feeding is something that shouldn't be neglected. Apply a lawn fertilizer (or plain sulphate of ammonia at the rate of one clenched handful to the square metre or square yard) and water it in with a sprinkler if it doesn't rain within 24 hours. *Timing* May and (if you're really keen) July as well.

Watering will be beneficial during dry periods in spring and summer. Leave a sprinkler playing over the lawn for at least two hours. Oscillating sprinklers are better than the rotating type because they cover a sensible rectangular area rather than a circle, and they can be adjusted to throw just one way if you're having a picnic nearby. *Timing* Spring and summer.

Leaf sweeping is vital if your lawn is not to become patchy and brown. Remove all fallen leaves from the surface as soon as possible and compost them (see p. 13 for details). *Timing* Autumn.

Rolling can help to even out bumps on a new lawn if your mower does not possess a hefty rear roller, but it's not essential. *Timing* Spring.

Topdressing is really only for the keen gardener. Scatter a mixture of sieved leafmould and sand over the lawn and brush it in. One bucketful will do about six square metres (about seven square yards). *Timing* Autumn.

MOWING

Everybody mows, but some mow better than others. The secret is to avoid cutting the grass too close. Far too many lawns are shaved with the result that they wear badly and are susceptible to drought. Mowing is essential to encourage fine grasses and a thick carpet of growth, but it is far better for your grass (and for you) to mow regularly, taking off just a little, rather than to mow once a fortnight too close to the soil.

As a rule, mowing is necessary between March and October—more regularly at the height of the season than at each end. In June and July weekly or twice weekly mowing will be needed. I never mow closer than about 2 cm ($\frac{3}{4}$ in), and when the weather is really dry I prefer to leave on about 2·5 cm (1 in) of grass. Really rough areas can be left with about 4 cm (1$\frac{1}{2}$ in) of grass after cutting.

If you've masses of lawn and are bone idle, you can manage by mowing wide paths through it regularly, and cutting the long stuff occasionally. Not only will it save time, but it looks pleasant, too. If you don't treat your lawn with weedkiller you'll be surprised how many wild flowers it contains.

Take the clippings off the lawn when you mow, collect them in a grassbox fitted to the mower and compost them (taking care to mix them with other compost or they'll turn into a hot and smelly black gunge). If you can't be bothered to remove them, make sure you cut the grass regularly so that the clippings are small enough to be dried up by the sun and blown away by the wind. Left in large clods they'll kill out patches of grass and look very unsightly. Lawns from which the clippings are never removed will benefit from being scarified twice—once in June and once in September.

There's still plenty of controversy raging about the different types of mower (Fig. 44). Choose one that you find easy to work with and which cuts your grass adequately for your needs. Cylinder mowers give the finest results (the more blades there are in the cylinder the neater the finish) and are essential if you're out to make that bowling green lawn, in which case you can cut as low as 1 cm ($\frac{1}{2}$ in) or even 0·5 cm ($\frac{1}{4}$ in) if you irrigate it regularly and only walk on it occasionally. Rotary mowers are fine for most hard-wearing lawns, though it's a good idea to find a machine that is fitted with a grassbox. The rotary types won't give you the stripes you get from cylinder mowers, but they can cope with rougher, longer grass. Electric and petrol-driven versions are available.

Hover mowers are useful where the ground undulates too sharply for a wheeled mower, and on banks where they can be swung, pendulum fashion, to cut quite long grass.

Fig. 44 The cheapest cylinder mower (*a*) has side wheels and a rear grassbox. More expensive models have grass boxes on the front, large rear rollers and more blades to produce a finer cut. Petrol-driven rotary mowers (*b*) make light work of rougher grass, and hover mowers (*c*) float on a cushion of air which makes them easy to use on slopes and uneven ground.

If you've plenty of trees set in grass, a nylon cord trimmer might be useful (Fig. 45). This nifty little machine will cut off quite thick and rough grass right against the trunks with its whirling nylon thread.

Be guided by information sheets and salesmen when you're buying a mower, but try whenever possible to arrange for a demonstration of one or two machines. The mower is the one piece of equipment I would advise you to buy new, and you might as well know what you're in for before you part with your hard-earned cash. Pick one that's comfortable to use, looks sturdily made, and has as wide a cut as possible to lessen the time you need to spend cutting the grass.

When your lawn has had its last mow of the season, clean the mower and rub it down with an oily rag before you store it in a dry shed or garage. Winter is the time to have it repaired—not spring when every gardener is beating on the door of the workshop begging for attention.

EDGING

Cutting the frayed edges from your lawn is a time-consuming and back-aching business. Use a pair of long-handled edging shears if you have lots of vertical lawn edges, but if possible try to get rid of them to save labour. A single row of bricks laid flush with the soil at the edge of the lawn will mean that you can run

Fig. 45 Nylon cord trimmers are just the thing for cutting the parts that other mowers cannot reach—around trees and where lawn edges abut walls.

Fig. 46 A yearly trim with a half moon iron will keep lawn edges smart and firm. Cut against the solid edge of a plank or against a curved hosepipe.

the mower over them and so keep the grass in trim without resorting to shears. When the grass does start to creep over the brickwork you can give it a yearly cut back with a spade or a 'half-moon' iron sold especially for cutting new lawn edges (Fig. 46).

RENOVATION

If you take on an old lawn that's knee high in grass after months of neglect, don't start digging up the ground. Instead follow this course of action:

1 Clear away any bricks and debris.
2 Scythe or mow down the long grass with a rotary mower to a height of 5 cm (2 in).
3 Scarify to remove dead grass and thatch.
4 Mow to a height of 2·5 cm (1 in).
5 Apply a lawn fertilizer and weedkiller combined.
6 Mow regularly.
7 Treat as a normal lawn.

You don't have to do the lot in one day. Spread it over a period of seven weeks by doing one job each week.

WEEDS AND MOSS

I wish people didn't worry so much about weeds in lawns. If the turf stays green and looks fine enough from a distance then why worry that there's a bit of clover, dock or dandelion in it? If I banished all the daisies from my grass I'd be highly unpopular with both my daughters, so I'll continue to suffer the sideways glances of friends who think I ought to know better. If you feel you can't tolerate anything other than grass, then use a combined lawn weedkiller and fertilizer dressing in May, and again in August.

There are certain weeds resistant to all manner of herbicides, and those that you can't shift by means of special lawn weedkillers will have to be put up with unless you want to get down on all fours and grub them out with a knife.

Individual weeds are easy to bump off with 'touch-weeders'—aerosols or waxy sticks impregnated with herbicide that can be painted or sprayed on to isolated aliens. Before you use any weedkiller on a lawn do check that it won't kill the grass. It's surprising how many people think that 'Tumbleweed' (glyphosate) can be used as a lawn weedkiller. It can, but don't expect any grass to survive.

Moss is another *bête noir*. You can pour on as much moss killer as you want in spring and autumn, but unless you remedy the conditions that the moss finds favourable it will return and colonize the ground again after the initial killing off. Moss loves badly drained, poorly fed, acid soil, preferably with a bit of shade. Eliminate any of these problems and the moss will find it harder to survive. Scarifying helps to pull out the long, tufted mosses that give your lawn the springiness of a mattress, and I'd prefer to stick to this as a method of keeping it under relative control. Once again, if it's green and looks all right why worry what the neighbours think?

PESTS AND DISEASES

It's the fine lawn that is most troubled by disease—the coarser, more rugged grasses are seldom attacked by fungi apart from fairy rings. This fungus produces circles of dark green grass, often accompanied by toadstools. Only by digging out the infected turf and sterilizing the soil will you have any chance of eradicating it. Settle instead for mowing off the toadstools and telling the children about the fairies. The grass will come to no real harm.

Toadstools that arise from old tree stumps below the lawn are also a nuisance, but it's easier to mow them off than treat the area with a fungicide which may only retain its effectiveness for a few weeks. Removal of stumps at lawn-making time is the only permanent answer.

Brown areas may be caused by fungus diseases, but are more likely to occur as a result of fertilizer scorch (if you've applied it clumsily and too heavily) or bitch urine. In both cases a good soaking with a lawn sprinkler (or even a watering can in the case of the bitch) will help to alleviate the problem. The grass will green up later in the season.

Black or dark green areas of slime are caused by algae. If your lawn is well drained and well fed you should be able to stop them appearing. If you want to bump existing infestations on the head try watering each square metre (yard) with 7 g ($\frac{1}{4}$ oz) sulphate of iron in 2·25 litres ($\frac{1}{2}$ gal) of water.

Moles are a pain in the neck and in the lawn. You'll read of umpteen old wives' cures for them, but if they infest the land around your garden there's absolutely nothing you can do to stop them coming into your plot. Traps laid in their runs will catch the individuals, and there are nasty little fuses to poison them out, but if I were you I'd enlist the help of the local mole catcher or rodent officer and enjoy using the soil from the molehills in your potting compost—it's wonderful stuff!

Worms should be tolerated. I know you'll read about how essential it is to kill them in lawns, but a healthy worm population means a healthy soil. The lawn occupies such a large proportion of most small gardens that if you bump off the worms there you'll lose them from most of your garden. Few lawns are really plagued by worm casts and only on really fine turf are they a severe handicap. Just sweep them off before mowing.

You'll gather from all this that I'm not the possessor of a manicured lawn. While this is true, I can still boast a patch of good-looking, fresh green turf that co-exists with wild flowers, animals and insects and doesn't keep me occupied every waking hour. This is the kind of yearly calendar that will bring you such a lawn:

LAWN MINI-CARE CALENDAR

March Start to mow
April Roll a new lawn if necessary
May Apply fertilizer (and weedkiller if you must)
June
July } Water when necessary
August Apply fertilizer (and weedkiller if you must)
September Scarify and spike; topdress if you're keen
October
November } Stop mowing; sweep up leaves

14 Patio gardening

It's no use having a garden if you can't make time to sit in it, so cobble together a patio and you'll be able to sit outdoors at any time of year regardless of conditions under foot. Now the word 'patio' might conjure up an image of some Italian terrazzo, but it's lately come to mean any kind of stable surface on which a deckchair can be plonked. The sunniest part of the garden is the most obvious place to put your pleasure patch, but it's also a good idea to position it near the house; that way the chef won't have to stagger far with a heavy tray.

Reclining in the constant glare of summer sun palls after a while, so either allow room for a parasol, a good 2 m (6 ft) in diameter, or arrange for the sun to disappear behind a tree at a certain time of day. If you're no sun worshipper then there's nothing wrong with making a patio in the shade—surrounded by a leafy canopy—but remember that if it's really overhung you're likely to be dripped on in damp weather. (I speak as a gardener who eats out in any decent fine spell, winter or summer.)

At patio gardening the back-yard owner comes into his or her own, for it matters not a jot that there's no soil for miles; it can all be imported and put into assorted containers. But more of that later.

WHAT MATERIALS?

If you do possess a garden, what materials are you to use for your patio (Fig. 47) and how are you to lay them?

Gravel is by far the cheapest stuff of which patios are made. All you need to do is level and firm the soil before spreading over it a 2·5 cm (1 in) layer of washed pea shingle. Make the layer much thicker than this and you'll find that it's difficult to walk on and soon finds its way into the house. You'll always be sweeping the odd bit of gravel out anyway but that's the price you pay for doing things on the cheap! (My patio is made of gravel.)

Concrete is the next most economical surface but it involves more slave labour. You'll have to lay it over a 10 cm (4 in) layer of rubble or 'hard core' to give it

Fig. 47 Consider the texture of paving surfaces when you make a patio, but avoid using more than three different kinds. Flags, cobbles and gravel all show off plants.

stability, and large areas can look rather dull unless they're broken up by lines of brick or patches of cobbles.

Flagstones are pricey if you go for York stone or other natural materials; cheaper if they are reconstituted. Whatever you do, don't lay a patio of multicoloured pastel-shaded slabs; your sitting area should be a restful haven, not a Technicolor dream—the plants will provide the colour.

Bricks are pricey if new; quite cheap (and very good to look at) if they are mellowed second-hand stock. Lay both flagstones and bricks on an 8 cm (3 in) bed of sand spread over firmed and levelled soil. Use a straight edge and spirit level to make sure that your final surface is level (give it a slight 'fall' away from the house unless you want all the rain that lands on it to end up in your living room). Grout the bricks or slabs with a dry mortar mix (3 parts soft sand to 1 part cement) and allow the moisture which rises from below to set it. Don't turn a hosepipe on it or you'll splash cement everywhere and discolour your bricks or flagstones. A mate of mine spent every weekend of 1982 laying a brick patio and it nearly broke his heart when he washed in the grouting, only to find he had to spend days washing it out of his bricks again. If this disaster does befall you, try scattering damp coarse sand on the area and brushing it over the surface with a stiff broom (and no water). It should shift the cement deposit.

A change of texture on the patio is easy to provide if small beds are left for plants, but you can also incorporate patches of cobbles which have a similar effect. Don't overdo it though.

Whatever hard surface you decide on, buy your materials from a builders' merchant. In most cases this is a far cheaper source of supply than a garden centre.

Screens might be necessary in small gardens if you want your patio to be private (and not many of us relish being watched while we idle our time away, whatever our state of dress). Trellis is an attractive proposition because it's cheap, but it also looks good if painted white and held firmly between posts and battens. Victorian arbours are seldom seen today but they look delightful in shady or sunny parts of the garden where flowering climbers can be trained over them. Made out of white trellis they can be pleasant to sit in without being overpowering. Solid larch-lap fencing is certainly peep-proof but rather oppressive when it encapsulates a small area, and those concrete screening blocks always look, to me, as though they've been left off a boat to Greece. If you like them, use them and ignore my rude comments.

If wooden screening doesn't appeal, then use plants. There are plenty of climbers that can be trained up simple post and wire fences, or tall shrubs and hedges that can be planted densely enough to make an effective screen.

FURNITURE

I haven't the nerve to tell you what you should be sitting on! However, a few tips gleaned from practical experience might save you a few bob. For a start, make your patio as big as possible because furniture takes up more room that you'd think. Those beautifully upholstered recliners are the best things on earth to doze on, but they occupy a lot of space and you'll have to get them out and put them away (which may make for storage problems) every time you use them. Invest in a couple by all means, but also have a pair of all-weather chairs and a table that can be left out even in winter if necessary. That way you can nip out there in a quick burst of sunshine for your morning cup of coffee without having to spend half an hour getting the posh stuff out of mothballs.

A parasol is not just decorative, it's also functional—read a book in scorching sunshine and you'll then have a job to focus your eyes on anything else. If you do buy a parasol, go for one that's a plain colour rather than a floral print. Here I'm taking a liberty by inflicting my tastes on you, but it seems to me preferable that the flowers in the garden should not have to compete with those on a William Morris parasol. Suit yourself!

LIGHTING

An illuminated patio is definitely a luxury, but it becomes a bit of heaven on earth on summer evenings when you can sit out late and admire the leaves and flowers as they bask in a carefully placed spotlight. Your electrician will advise you on installation and the kind of lamps needed, but bear in mind that plants always look best when lit from the side or from below, rather than flat on. Even in winter you can enjoy patio lighting from indoors if the illuminated plants are within view of your windows. If you're the outdoor type, patio lighting is a luxury worth saving for.

PLACES FOR PLANTS

On many plots the garden will surround the patio, bringing plants right up to the edge. In back yards or on rooftops, where a patio is all you've got, your plants will have to be grown in containers. You can plant in anything (Fig. 48): wooden tubs, Greek urns, wall-mounted pots, large flower pots (small ones dry out too quickly), troughs, chimney pots (provided you remember they are bottomless and don't try to move them), growing bags and old porcelain sinks that have been treated to look like stone (p. 133).

Whatever your container, remember to place a layer of broken bricks, flowerpots or pebbles in the base to make for quick drainage (all containers should have drainage holes), and if the vessel is very large, stand it on a couple of bricks to keep it clear of the ground. With wooden tubs this helps to prevent rotting as well as allowing surplus water to escape unimpeded.

Fig. 48 There's no shortage of containers to choose from nowadays, from tubs and chimney pots to reproduction urns, troughs and the economical, but ugly, growing bag.

I would advise against the use of pots less than 23 cm (9 in) in diameter, simply because they dry out too quickly, and I would always use John Innes No. 2 potting compost in preference to the soilless types because, unlike them, if it should dry out it won't shrink from the sides of the container and be difficult to re-wet. However, on rooftop and balcony gardens peat-based composts have the advantage of being light-weight. (Always check with the appropriate authority before making a roof garden—it may save you a lot of heartache, and expense, later).

Leave a gap of a few centimetres (inches) between the compost and the rim of all containers to allow for watering.

WINDOWBOXES

Windows with outside sills lend themselves to being fitted with windowboxes that overflow with flowers all the year round. Spring and summer displays can be different (as with spring and summer bedding schemes) or some of the occupants can be permanent and a few bedders planted between them to vary the show from season to season.

Windowboxes are easy to make from old pieces of timber which have been screwed or nailed together with galvanized nails or brass screws. Treat them with preservative (such as Cuprinol—not toxic creosote which kills plants) and equip them with short legs and drainage holes (Fig. 49). Make sure they sit firmly on the sill. If you lack outdoor sills the boxes can be held on steel brackets screwed to the wall. Do make sure they're secure or you'll crown some unsuspecting passer-by, who won't be able to see your floral tribute for stars.

A drainage layer is as vital in a windowbox as in any other container, and the compost layer should be at least 15 cm (6 in) deep. Make your box large enough to allow for both.

HANGING BASKETS

These pendant floral features seem to have made a come-back in the last few years. Made of galvanized or plastic-covered wire they can be slung from stout hooks or angle brackets outside doors and on plain house walls to brighten your life in summer. They tend to get buffeted by the wind in winter and the plants suffer.

To plant up the basket stand it on a large flowerpot or bucket (Fig. 50). Line it with sphagnum moss (available from your florist) or old carpet underlay, or even three or four layers of newspaper cut to shape. Poke holes in the liner at intervals and insert suitable trailing plants from the outside (roots first), covering their roots with compost as soon as they appear inside the basket. When these are in place, plant up the top and then water the plants in. Bushy and trailing plants are naturally more suited to being grown in hanging baskets than are stiff and starchy plants.

Keep the basket under cover for a few weeks after planting to let its occupants establish themselves. Baskets are usually made up during late April and hung outdoors in late May or early June.

If a basket is to be hung directly over a door you'd do well to invest in the kind with a built-in plastic drip-tray, but you won't be able to plant anything in the sides—the plants will have to cascade over the rim.

The secret of success with hanging baskets is watering. You'll have to soak them twice a day in midsummer; once a day even in dull weather. Don't forget.

Fig. 49 Construct a simple windowbox from old pieces of floorboard, but make sure it's at least 15 cm (6 in) deep and treated with timber preservative.

PATIO PLANT CARE

Watering is certainly the most important job the patio gardener will undertake. All containers of compost dry out amazingly quickly on a sun-baked patch of hard standing, and plants that dry out soon die. Save your money and your temper (if not your time) by checking all containers morning and evening in summer. Daily or, at the very least, every other day, at other times of year.

Feed all container-grown plants once a fortnight in summer. Flowering plants love tomato fertilizer, which can be used at the same dilution as recommended for tomatoes.

Plants that are grown in pots for a number of years should either be potted on annually in spring, or topdressed. Both operations are described on p. 204 in Chapter 18.

The removal of dead and diseased plants and the controlling of pests and diseases is as vital on the patio as it is anywhere else in the garden, but at least if you're lounging on a sunbed you'll notice quite quickly if there are pests on an overhanging branch—especially if they drop into your gin and tonic. Which brings me to weeding. If you're as fidgety as I am you'll find that your patio beds and pots are the best-weeded parts of your garden. I'm forever leaping out of the chair to pull up a bit of groundsel or hairy bittercress!

PLANTS FOR PATIOS

I won't give you a long list of suitable patio plants, just a selection of those that I think are especially useful, because the truth of the matter is that you can grow almost anything in a pot for a limited period of

Fig. 50 Position a hanging basket on a bucket to plant it up. Line the basket with moss and push trailers through the sides before filling with compost and planting the top.

time. There are certain plants that will not like being baked in the reflected heat that comes off your patio—rhododendrons for instance—but on a shady patio they'll do well. Other trees will refuse to stay in a tub for more than five or ten years, but that's not a bad life for any pot plant.

The greatest boon of patio gardening is that you can try anything, and that your plants can be moved round to give different effects from week to week (if you feel strong enough).

In summer, house plants will benefit greatly from a holiday in the garden, and on the patio they will receive shelter as well as welcome sunshine. Summer showers will refresh them rather than doing them any harm.

To make your potted show interesting all the year round, some of the plants should be evergreen and a lot of them should be foliage plants. Roses and other flowering shrubs will give a grand show in their season, but the evergreens can be the backbone of the display just as they are in the garden.

Provided you and your patio can give a shrub, border plant, rose or any other plant the conditions it would appreciate elsewhere in the garden it will thrive.

PATIO FOLIAGE PLANTS

These are especially striking if grown in gravel- or cobble-covered beds in or around patios. The stone mulch (a single course in the case of cobbles or large pebbles, and a 5 cm (2 in) layer in the case of washed pea shingle or gravel) can be spread over the firmed soil after planting. It sets off the plants to perfection, keeps down weeds and keeps in moisture.

Border plants
Ajuga
Alchemilla
Artemisia
Asplenium
Ballota
Bergenia
Blechnum
Carex
Cynara
Dryopteris
Epimedium
Euphorbia
Festuca
Glyceria
Heuchera
Hosta
Iris
Liriope
Matteuccia
Milium
Phormium
Polygonatum

Polygonum (syn. Persicaria)
Rheum
Sedum
Stachys

Shrubs E = evergreen
Aralia
Arundinaria **E**
Aucuba **E**
Camellia **E**
Choisya **E**
Cistus **E**
Convolvulus **E**
Cotinus
Cotoneaster **E** (some)
Fatsia **E**
Heathers **E**
Hebe **E**
Hedera **E**
Ilex **E**
Juniperus **E**
Laurus **E**
Lavandula **E**
Lavatera
Mahonia **E**
Myrtus **E**
Paeonia
Pittosporum **E**
Rhus
Ruta **E**
Sambucus
Sarcococca **E**
Yucca **E**

Details of all these plants, and their likes and dislikes, can be found under *Shrubs* and *Border Plants* (Chapters 4 and 8).

PLANTS FOR WINDOWBOXES
Permanent residents
Festuca glauca (blue fescue grass)
Juniperus communis 'Compressa' (columnar dwarf conifer)
Hedera helix varieties (common ivy)
Heathers (*Erica* and *Calluna*—especially coloured-leafed varieties)
Euonymus 'Emerald 'n' Gold' (variegated evergreen leaves)
Hebe pinguifolia 'Pagei' (until it outgrows available space)
Buxus sempervirens 'Suffruticosa' (dwarf box)
Chamaecyparis obtusa 'Nana' (rounded dwarf conifer)
Thymus species (thyme—especially coloured-leafed forms)

Temporary residents are available in endless variety. Any spring or summer bedder that does not grow too tall will happily thrive, and dwarf bulbs will add to the spectacle in spring. Crocuses, dwarf irises and many of the compact narcissus varieties look superb, as do 'Universal' pansies which can flower right through the winter. Dig them out before you plant the summer occupants.

PLANTS FOR HANGING BASKETS
It's the summer-flowering plants that make up hanging baskets. Experiment with different combinations each year, but rely on bushy and trailing plants—not those that grow tall and stiff. These are all first class: ivy-leaf geranium (pelargonium), trailing lobelia, petunia, pendulous begonia, bush geraniums (zonal pelargoniums), *Senecio cineraria* (dusty miller), *Campanula isophylla* (Star of Bethlehem), *Begonia semperflorens*, mesembryanthemum (Livingstone daisy), ageratum, alyssum, *Centaurea gymnocarpa*, *Hedera helix* varieties (ivy), *Lysimachia nummularia* 'Aurea' (creeping Jenny), *Helichrysum petiolatum* nasturtium, verbena.

15 Fruit growing

There are few branches of gardening so confusing as fruit growing. True enough, the cultivation of raspberries and gooseberries presents few problems, but once you get on to apples and pears, cherries and peaches the pruning alone is enough to frighten you off. Here then, I've tried to simplify matters a little by not telling you too much. It's amazing how many gardeners grow tons of fruits without ever laying their hands on a pair of secateurs or loppers. The pruning techniques I've described are certainly necessary to make the best of your trees, but I defer to those gardeners with lofty apple trees coated with lichen which groan under the weight of a heavy harvest with amazing regularity.

I've dealt with most problems and operations under the individual fruit headings, but there are one or two general comments worth making.

First, remember that most fruits are expected to go on cropping year after year without being moved. Give them the best site and soil you can to help them achieve their aims.

Tree fruits generally need to be pollinated by another variety of the same fruit so that they can produce a good crop, but often you'll get by with a little help from your friends and neighbours. Try to persuade them to plant a tree that complements yours if you've no room for two.

Don't propagate your own tree fruits—they are grafted on to vigour-controlling rootstocks and are best increased by the nurseryman. Two- or three-year-old trees will cost a little more than one-year-old 'maidens' but they will come into cropping more quickly and will save you the complicated job of training them in the early stages.

When it comes to technical terms, fruit growing has its quota. The 'June drop' is the name given to the shedding of immature tree fruits when they are quite small. It's the tree's natural way of thinning out its crop so don't be alarmed. Just make sure that any thinning you do comes after this, otherwise you might find that the fruits you've left behind drop off too!

Gardeners are frequently frustrated by trees that come into flower but refuse to set fruit. The reason is usually lack of pollination, but it may also be due to frosting. Grow your trees in a sheltered spot that is not on low-lying ground.

When it's time for that terrifying job, pruning, use a sharp pair of secateurs to prevent diseases from gaining a foothold through torn tissue. Always prune to just above a bud—generally an outward facing one.

The branches themselves have technical names: leaders are the topmost, strongest-growing shoots; laterals are sideshoots. Sub-laterals are sideshoots that are growing from sideshoots.

Throughout this chapter I've referred you to Chapter 3 on trees for planting details. A fruit tree or bush is planted in exactly the same way as an ornamental tree or bush and it seemed a waste of space to keep repeating the instructions. Restricted forms of fruit trees (cordons and espaliers—see p. 159) are usually planted against stout post and wire fences. Make sure that they are indeed stout. The posts should protrude 2 m (6 ft) from the ground, be 10 cm (4 in) square in cross section, treated with a preservative other than creosote and buried to a depth of 60 cm (2 ft). They should occur every 2–2·5 m (6–8 ft) along the fence and the wire should be of a stout gauge. Spacings for the wires are recommended under individual fruits.

If your trees refuse to flower, suspect one of the following: bird damage, frost damage, an excess of nitrogen or a lack of food in general. Faulty or very hard pruning can produce growth buds at the expense of fruit buds.

Finally, if you intend to grow plenty of fruit it really is worth investing in a fruit cage—home-made or shop-bought. It is not much to look at and it will cost quite a few pounds to make or acquire, but it will make sure that you eat the fruits before the birds do.

APPLE

I've always fancied having an orchard full of old varieties of apple with quaint names like 'Norfolk Beefing', 'Devonshire Quarrenden' and 'Roundway Magnum Bonum'—the very sound of the names smacks of a bumper harvest. I've never yet got round to it; instead we have half a dozen hefty old trees scattered round the garden but even these provide us with more apples than we know what to do with.

If you're keen on apples then you'll want to grow a few varieties that not only taste good but which also supply you with fruit over as long a season as possible. If you grow trees in restricted forms such as cordons and espaliers you can fit quite a few varieties into a small space. Romanticism aside, these are the vari-

Table 7: Apples

Variety	In Season	Flowering time*
EATERS		
'George Cave'	Late August/early September	1
'Discovery'	Late August/early September	1
'Ellison's Orange'	September/October	2
'James Grieve'	September/October	2
'Egremont Russet'	October/December	1
'Sunset'	October/December	2
'Ribston Pippin'	November/February	1
'Rosemary Russet'	December/March	2
'Tydeman's Late Orange'	December/March	2
COOKERS		
'Arthur Turner'	August/October	2
'Grenadier'	August/October	2
'Bramley's Seedling'	November/March	2
'Annie Elizabeth'	December/June	2
'Howgate Wonder'	November/February	2
'Lane's Prince Albert'	January/March	2

* Varieties marked '1' will flower before those marked '2'. For effective pollination, varieties within the same group should be planted together.

eties with some of the tastiest fruits, even if they don't have the most euphonious names (Table 7).

The early varieties should be eaten as soon as possible after picking; the late varieties are the best keepers.

I'm afraid I've not included 'Cox's Orange Pippin'—it requires too much spraying to keep it in good condition. 'Ribston Pippin' is easier and just as crisp and tasty. Neither have I included 'Golden Delicious'. We get far too many of these apples from France, and while they may be uniform in shape and quality and crisp of flesh, they really do not possess a flavour that can rival a decent English pippin. Now there's prejudice for you!

Where to plant

Apples enjoy the classic situation: a site that's open and sunny but sheltered at a distance from strong winds. Avoid frost pockets where the blossom will be killed off. Good drainage is vital and adequate soil preparation essential; dig the ground as deeply as you can and work in plenty of compost or manure, plus a good dusting of blood, bone and fishmeal a day or two before planting. Different varieties suit different situations, and while those that I've recommended will thrive in most gardens it's a good idea to rely on the advice of your local nurseryman, who knows what thrives in your neck of the woods.

Rootstocks

Fruit trees are not grown from pips; they are propagated in the nursery by a technique known as grafting. This involves the joining together of a scion (piece of stem) from a branch of the required variety, and a rootstock. The rootstock is a plant which is especially grown to act as the root system for a chosen variety of fruit. If allowed to grow and crop itself it would have rather poor fruits because it's been selected, not for its own cropping ability, but for the effect it has on the vigour and cropping ability of the scion that is attached (grafted) to it. The two are spliced together in the nursery; a natural callus forms to glue them to one another, and the scion then forms the branch framework and the rootstock the roots.

There are hundreds of rootstocks—well, perhaps not hundreds but certainly enough to thoroughly confuse you. It's recommended that you ask for a tree on a particular rootstock number, so that you can be sure of getting a tree whose ultimate size is predictable; the trouble is that the numbers are easily confused. Here's all the average gardener needs to know:

The rootstock M.26 is the best one for general planting in small gardens. It is reasonably dwarfing and yet not so feeble that it needs to be staked all its life. Trees on M.26 grow 2·5–4 m (8–12 ft) high.

The rootstock M.9 is the dwarfest but it does need continuous staking and is a bit miffy on very poor or very heavy soils. Trees on M.9 grow to 2 or 3 m (6 or 10 ft).

The rootstock MM.106 is not quite so dwarfing as the previous two but it still keeps trees to a reasonable size. Trees on MM.106 grow 4–6 m (12–18 ft) high.

All three rootstocks will bring the trees into bearing quite early in their lives. Choose M.26 if you can; M.9 if you want a real midget and have good soil; MM.106 if you can't find M.26.

Tree forms

There's an added complication. You'll also have to decide what shape of tree you want. You can buy 'maidens' (one-year-old trees that consist of a single stem) and train them if you want, but it's easier (and not that much more expensive) to buy two- or three-year-old trained trees in one of several forms: standard, half-standard, bush, dwarf pyramid, cordon, espalier (Fig. 51).

Standards These trees have a branch framework at the top of a 2–2·25 m (6–7 ft) trunk. They are planted on vigorous rootstocks with numbers like M.2 and MM.111 and should really only be chosen if you want an ancient apple tree under which you can position a rustic seat for that cottage garden effect.

Half standards Here the trunk is 1·25–1·5 m (4–4½ ft) tall and the tree will also be vigorous. Both standards and half standards take longer to come into cropping than the dwarfer kinds.

Bushes Bush trees (although it sounds a contradiction) have a bare stem of around 60 cm (2 ft), often rather less if they are on the dwarfing M.9 rootstock. They are a good choice for general garden planting because all cultivation techniques—from spraying to picking—are made easy. The bush is usually grown so that its branches make a goblet shape—open in the centre to allow good air circulation and freedom from disease.

Dwarf pyramids Here the tree is grown into more of a conical shape and the central leading shoot is retained. The trunk is only 30 cm (1 ft) high and the tree is even more accessible than the bush.

Cordons These are restricted trees grown on M.9 or M.26 rootstocks and planted against a fence or post and wire framework. They are trained on a single stem that runs at an angle of 45°. Pruning is carried out in summer—the laterals are nipped back and the central leader allowed to extend slowly (further details are given below).

Espaliers These, too, are restricted trees; they are grown with one central stem rising vertically, and tiered pairs of branches trained at right angles from it. The yields of restricted trees are, not surprisingly, much lower than those of free-standing bushes.

If terror is struck into your heart by the thought of having to train or prune any fruit tree, then you can simply plant a bush, half-standard or standard tree and leave it to its own devices. You'll risk owning a tree that is not very shapely and which crops neither as heavily, nor as early in its life as a trained tree, but if you are happy to live with such a tree that's your affair and nobody else's.

Mind you; when you decide to prune it later you're in for a battle royal. Compromise by pruning it a little during its formative years to produce a good shape, then you can ignore it with less drastic results.

Planting distances

If you're growing more than one tree I suppose you can boast that you're planting an orchard (to an estate agent three trees constitute a small orchard). Plant

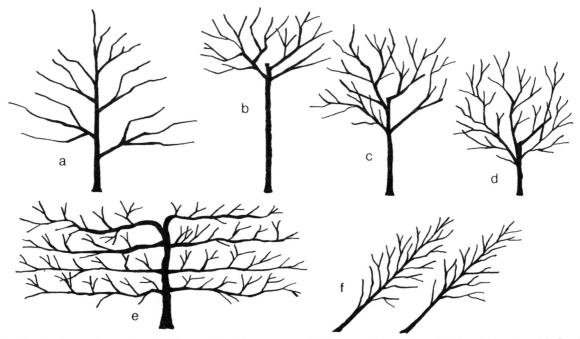

Fig. 51 Fruit tree forms (*a*) Dwarf pyramid. (*b*) Standard tree with 2 m (6 ft) of clear stem. (*c*) Half standard with 1·25 m (4 ft) stem. (*d*) Bush with 60 cm (2 ft) stem. (*e*) Espalier with tiered branches. (*f*) Cordon trees trained at an angle of 45°.

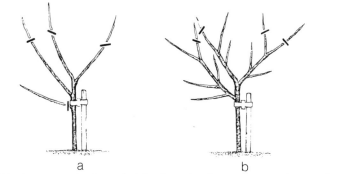

Fig. 52 Pruning a new bush apple (*a*) After planting a two-year-old bush (between November and March) shorten all the leading shoots by one half their length, cutting to just above an outward-facing bud. (*b*) The following winter, repeat the process, cutting back the newly grown leaders by half. (*c*) One year later the

bushes on M.9 and M.26 3 m (10 ft) apart; plant cordons 1 m (3 ft) apart with 2 m (6 ft) between rows; plant espaliers 3 m (10 ft) apart; dwarf pyramids 1 m (3 ft) apart in rows 2 m (6 ft) apart. You'll need to allow 6 m (20 ft) between standards and rather less between half standards.

Planting

Plant bare-root trees from November to March and container-grown trees at any time of year. Planting instructions are exactly as for ornamental trees (p. 24). Cordons and espaliers are planted against a strong, 2 m (6 ft) high post and wire fence with horizontal wires at 60 cm (2 ft) intervals.

During the spring after planting, scatter a good sprinkling of blood, bone and fishmeal around each tree and then lay a thick organic mulch. Make sure that the soil is not given a chance to dry out during establishment. Don't let grass grow up to the tree for

pruning can be restricted to lateral shoots—cut them back to about 10 cm (4 in). Those which grow outwards from the tree can be left if there's room for them to grow. It's a good idea to shorten some laterals every year.

at least three years. An annual spring feed with rose fertilizer is always appreciated.

Pollination

Apple pollination is complicated in theory but usually simple in practice—there are so many apple trees around that the bees can usually do a good job at cross-pollinating the flowers and ensuring a crop. Some apples won't set fruit with their own pollen, so to make sure of a good crop (without relying on your neighbours) it's a good idea to plant two or three trees, even if they are restricted forms. Make sure they flower at the same time (I've shown the flowering period of those varieties recommended on p. 158).

Pruning

This varies depending on the form of tree but basically aims to produce a healthy framework of branches and plenty of fruiting spurs. Proceed thus:

Fig. 53 Pruning to make a dwarf pyramid tree (*a*) Buy a partially trained tree and after planting (between November and March) cut back all leading shoots to 23 cm (9 in). (*b*) In July or August cut back all but the central leader to six leaves. Reduce all unwanted laterals to three leaves and cut back sublaterals to the leaf above

the lowest cluster. (*c*) The following winter cut the central leader back to 23 cm (9 in), and once the tree has reached a height of 2 m (7 ft) the central leader can be cut back into old wood. In succeeding years reduce overcrowding laterals and try to keep the pyramidal shape. This is a system for the patient and the keen!

Fig. 54 Pruning a new cordon apple (*a*) Maiden trees can be trained to form cordons. Plant at an angle of 45° (with the graft union uppermost) and prune the lateral shoots back to four buds between November and March. (*b*) Remove the flowers that form one year later. Allow the leader to continue growing undisturbed. (*c*) In subsequent years during late July and early August, cut back any lateral shoots emerging from the main stem to leave three leaves above the basal cluster. Sublaterals can be cut back to one leaf above the basal cluster. Further growth may occur in late summer and autumn, especially in wet areas. Cut back such shoots to two leaves. Cut out the leading shoot during spring when it reaches the topmost wire, and cut back to 2·5 cm (1 in) in summer any shoots which attempt to take over from it.

Bush After planting a two- or three-year-old bush, shorten all the leading shoots by one half their length, cutting back to an outward-facing bud (Fig. 52). The following winter do exactly the same but when the tree is in its fourth year only the laterals need be pruned—back to 10 cm (4 in). Leave plenty of unpruned laterals on 'Bramley's Seedling', which is a tip-bearing variety. Aim to produce a well-spaced framework of branches, and don't be afraid to cut out damaged, very old and badly placed stems completely if they are making a nuisance of themselves. But remember—the harder you prune the more growth you'll get and the fewer apples you'll harvest.

Standards and half standards Prune as for bush trees.

Dwarf pyramid Buy a partially trained dwarf pyramid tree and then you can slip into the routine of simple twice-yearly pruning. In winter prune back all the main, leading shoots to leave just 23 cm (9 in) of new growth. In July or August cut back all leaders except the central one, to six leaves. Any laterals not required as part of the branch framework can be reduced to three leaves, and sub-laterals (sideshoots that grow on sideshoots) can be cut to the leaf growing above the lowest cluster. Fig. 53 makes things a whole lot clearer than I can! The central leader can be cut back into old wood once the tree has reached a height of 2 m (7 ft). In subsequent years try to maintain the pyramidal shape of the tree; reduce overcrowded spurs and any vigorous shoots that sprout from within the framework.

Cordon Again, buy a partially trained cordon and concentrate on summer pruning—shortening any lateral shoots to three leaves to build up a spur system (Fig. 54). Prune the leader once it has reached the topmost wire. The cordon can then be lowered slightly to give it more room to grow.

Espalier Buy a trained tree and summer prune the branches as for cordons so that a system of spurs is built up on each 'arm'.

Fruit thinning

After the natural 'June drop', remove one or two fruitlets from each cluster if they look overcrowded. Always pull the central fruit out first. This is the 'king fruit' which has a deformed lump next to the stalk. Leave two fruits to each cluster.

Harvesting

Pick the fruits as soon as they will part easily from the tree without tearing. The earlies will be ready from late July through August, and the later varieties in September and October. Pick any remaining apples in October and store them.

Storing

The late varieties are the ones to store. It's a real fag wrapping them up in squares of greaseproof paper, so nip along to a friendly greengrocer and see if he can let you have some wooden 'Dutch trays' equipped with cardboard dividers (Fig. 55). Store only sound fruits, and check them once a week to remove any which show signs of rotting. A cool but frostproof shed or garage is the best fruit store you'll find, unless you happen to have a cellar, where conditions will be ideal.

If you've found in the past that apples and pears shrivel while they're in store, put 1·6–1·8 kg (3–4 lb) of them in a polythene bag with the corners cut off and lay the bags in the trays so that they can be stacked. The polythene will keep the atmosphere around the fruits pleasantly moist.

Sliced or puréed, the apples can also be frozen.

Pests and diseases

Aphids, sawfly, codling moth, winter moth, apple

Fig. 55 Apples can be stored easily in wooden tomato trays fitted with cardboard dividers to separate the fruits and prevent any rot spreading. Keep them cool and dark.

sucker, capsid bugs, red spider mites, bitter pit, mildew, canker, scab, brown rot.

So many problems does the apple have to contend with that many gardeners adopt a spray programme. Coping with children and dogs I've never felt that I could arrange for a comprehensive system of spraying. Idlers can spray with a tar oil wash such as Murphy Mortegg or ICI Clean Up in winter to remove hibernating eggs and bugs, and other infestations can be dealt with (or not) as they occur. It's not the perfectionist's way but you'll still manage to harvest good crops of apples.

A–Z OF FRUIT CROPS

Blackberry and Loganberry

For growing against fences and as productive screens against post and wire supports, these two fruits will produce a succulent harvest with very little bother. I'd choose 'Bedford Giant' or 'Oregon Thornless' when selecting blackberries; 'LY 59' or the thornless 'L 654' are by far the best of the loganberries. If you've never tried loganberries you're in for a treat. Mix them up with raspberries and smother them with cream! They crop in mid- to late summer.

Where to plant Blackberries will tolerate a little

Fig. 56 Space out the fruiting canes of blackberries and loganberries, training the new shoots up the centre as they grow. These can be spread out the following winter to replace the fruited stems which are cut out.

shade; loganberries will too but they definitely prefer full sun. The soil should be well dug, well drained and enriched with manure or compost. Fork in a dusting of blood, bone and fishmeal just before planting. *Supporting* Either equip a fence or wall with horizontal wires held in place by metal vine eyes at 45 cm (18 in) intervals, or make a 2 m (6 ft) post and wire fence with strands a similar distance apart (Fig. 56). Each plant needs about 4 m (12 ft) of lateral fence space. *Planting* Plant dormant canes between November and March—the earlier the better. Planting instructions are exactly the same as for ornamental trees and shrubs (p. 24). After planting, cut back the canes to 23 cm (9 in) above soil level, making your cuts just above a dormant bud. *Cultivation* Dust the soil with blood, bone and fishmeal in February and lay a thick organic mulch in March. Tie the new canes to the support system as they grow—space them out in a fan formation leaving a gap in the centre of the support system directly above the plant. Water well in dry weather. These canes will fruit in their second year while more new ones are growing. Train these up into the bare central area. *Pruning* When the canes have fruited, cut them out at ground level and then space out and tie in the new canes to replace them. Repeat the process in subsequent years. *Harvesting* Pick the fruits as soon as they are ripe. Hang old net curtains or muslin or closeweave plastic netting over them if birds are a problem. Pull the berries so that the 'plugs' are left behind. *Storing* Jam and freeze surplus fruits. *Pests and diseases* As for raspberries. *Propagation* During July, healthy shoot tips can be bent down and buried in the soil; hold them in place with a peg made from stout wire. Eventually a shoot will emerge and the new plant can be detached the

162

following spring (with its own roots) and planted out where it is to grow.

Blackcurrant

Just the thing for vitamin C fanatics. The trouble is that blackcurrants are a bit greedy when it comes to space, but 'Ben Sarek' is compact and a heavy cropper and so the best choice for small gardens. It's a flavoursome mid-season cropper yielding its bounty during late July. Try 'Mendip Cross' and 'Tor Cross' for slightly earlier crops and 'Ben Lomond' for an August harvest.

Where to plant Full sun or very gentle shade keeps blackcurrants happy but, like all fruits, they can be hammered by frost if they are planted in hollows. Lime acid soil in autumn and dig it over adding manure or compost during winter. Fork in a dusting of blood, bone and fishmeal just before planting. *Planting* Two-year-old certified bushes are the best kind to buy; that way you have a guarantee that they are not infected with yield-reducing virus diseases. Plant all the varieties I've mentioned 1·5 m (5 ft) apart on the square (I told you they were a bit greedy). Planting instructions are exactly the same as for ornamental trees and shrubs (p. 24). It's a good idea to set the bushes about 5 cm (2 in) deeper than they were planted in the nursery so that the stem bases are encouraged to form roots and so give the plant more support and nourishment. Now cut all the shoots back to within 5 cm (2 in) of soil level. Use the prunings as cuttings—trim them above a bud at the top and below a bud at the base so that they are 25 cm (10 in) long. Insert them on the vegetable plot so that all but the top 5 cm (2 in) is buried. They'll grow next year and can be transplanted the following autumn. *Cultivation* Mulch the soil around the plants with organic matter in spring. Don't let them go short of water during their first spring and summer. No fruits will be carried during the first year. Get into the habit of repeating the mulch each spring after scattering a little blood, bone and fishmeal over the soil. *Pruning* There's no need to prune after the first season's growth, but subsequently prune the bush each winter removing any spindly stems and a few old ones. Cut them all out at ground level. Never remove more than about one-third of the plant's shoots but aim to leave a well-spaced framework of branches. *Harvesting* Grow the bushes in a fruit cage or lay muslin or old net curtains over them when the fruits are coming to maturity—birds will enjoy them as much as you do. Cut off the strigs of fruit when they are ripe—black and tender to the touch. If you can use the fruits immediately (rather than in a few days' time) pull them straight from the stalks. You should get around 4·5 kg (10 lb) fruit from a single well-grown bush. *Storing* Currants freeze and jam well. *Pests and diseases* Birds, aphids, big bud mite, leaf spot, reversion virus, rust and American gooseberry mildew.

Propagation See above.

Red and White Currant

I wish more folk were willing to plant red and white currants—they make a bright show in the flower border and possess the richest of flavours. Both can be used in jelly making and wine making and they fill a plump fruit pie with promise. 'Red Lake' is the best red currant for most gardens, yielding in late July. 'Laxton's No. 1' is earlier and 'Rondom' later. No white currant is better than 'White Versailles', but you'll also find 'White Dutch' and 'White Grape' good value.

Where to plant Plant in the same kind of spot as blackcurrants, though these two are rather less tolerant of shade. *Planting* Plant one- or two-year-old plants between November and March. Buy from a reputable supplier—there is no certification scheme for red and white currants so they cannot be guaranteed free from virus diseases. Plant the bushes 1·5 m (5 ft) apart on the square and at the same level as they were growing in the nursery (look for the soil mark on the stem). Each bush should have a short trunk or 'leg' and at least three branches. Cut these back to half their length after planting, preferably to just above an outward-facing bud. *Cultivation* Dust the soil around the plants with blood, bone and fishmeal in February and then lay a mulch of organic matter. Repeat this operation annually. Do not let the soil dry out during the first spring and summer, and each May scatter a handful of sulphate of potash around each bush to encourage fruit formation. Birds can eat the buds in winter and the fruits in summer if the bushes are not netted or caged. *Pruning* The system is quite different from that adopted for blackcurrants. Aim to build up a goblet-shaped bush of six or eight branches—the older branches keep on fruiting for several years. Remove one or two of the most ancient branches each year in winter. Shorten all sideshoots to six leaves in summer. *Harvesting* Pick the fruits individually when they are ripe, or cut off the strigs if the fruits are to be kept for a few days before being used. Like blackcurrants, each bush should produce about 4·5 kg (10 lb) of fruit. *Storing* Use in jellies or freeze. *Pests and diseases* Aphids, birds, red currant blister aphid, capsid bug, currant sawfly, leaf spot and coral spot. *Propagation* As for gooseberries.

Cherry

Until recently the only cherry recommended for small gardens was 'Morello'—an acid cherry that makes the most delicious pies and jam. Sweet cherries tend to make towering trees that need to be planted at least 10 m (30 ft) apart and they are choosy as to how they perform. However, a new variety called 'Stella' has recently been introduced to gardens. Its main advantage is that, unlike other sweet cherries, it can set a good crop of fruits with its own pollen. 'Morello' is self-fertile, too.

Where to plant Although they're tolerant of positions in the open garden, cherries are usually grown as fan-trained trees against walls. 'Morello' is often recommended for a north wall where it enjoys the cool conditions. Avoid frost pockets at all costs, and dig over and manure the ground in the autumn before planting. *Supporting* Make sure that there are horizontal wires fastened at 30 cm (1 ft) intervals up the brickwork. The stems can then be tied in and spaced out as they grow. The tree will need about 6 m (20 ft) of lateral space. *Planting* To make life easier (if just a little more expensive), choose a tree that is already fan trained. It should be grafted onto a rootstock known as 'Colt', which is only semi-vigorous. Plant container-grown trees at any time of year; bare-root trees in November if possible. Planting is exactly as for trees and shrubs (p. 24). Set the tree about 30 cm (1 ft) from the wall and tilt its branches towards the surface, tying the stems loosely to the wire. Cut back the stems by about one-third of their length after planting, to encourage the production of sideshoots which will form the basic structure of the tree. Mulch the soil around the tree with organic matter in spring after dusting the soil with blood, bone and fishmeal. A dusting of rose or tomato fertilizer can be given each April. Never let the soil dry out. *Pruning* Prune cherries in spring or summer rather than winter. This lessens the likelihood of attack by silver leaf disease. Acid cherries flower on one-year-old wood and it is this that pruning aims to encourage. Thin out the shoots during spring and summer, cutting out any that grow directly away from the wall and any that are weak or overcrowding. The remaining shoots should be spaced about 15 cm (6 in) apart on the wall. After fruiting, cut out the cherry-bearing sideshoots, allowing them to be replaced by younger shoots which have arisen from their bases. If young growth is lacking as the tree matures, cut a few older branches back to young laterals so that new shoots are encouraged. At all times keep the framework well spaced and not overcrowded, and keep it young. Sweet cherries such as 'Stella' produce their fruit buds at the base of sideshoots that are one year old and which emerge from older wood. It follows that an older framework of branches is required on a sweet cherry than on an acid cherry which is constantly being required to produce new wood for cropping. Pinch out the shoot tips of the new sideshoots on sweet cherries during the summer so that they are left with just 5 leaves. Further shorten these shoots in autumn to 3 buds. These buds will carry blossom and fruits the following summer. *Harvesting* 'Morello' matures in August and September, 'Stella' in July. Pick the fruits when they come to ripeness. The birds may have a go so use a large sheet of plastic netting which can be draped right over the plant. The longer the cherries are left before they are harvested, the less acid they will be, but the more likelihood there is of them being pecked. There's no need to thin the fruits. *Storing* Pies can be frozen, as can the fruits themselves if they are stoned first. *Pests and diseases* Aphids, birds, slugworm, winter moth, bacterial canker, brown rot, dieback, and silver leaf disease.

Gooseberry

Gooseberries are not easy to prune, thanks to their thorns, but they're easy to eat in pies, jams, stewed and in that superb dessert gooseberry fool. There are culinary and dessert kinds and even dual-purpose varieties. I rate the following as some of the best:

Variety	Colour	Earliness of ripening	Culinary or dessert
'Careless'	white	2	C
'Golden Drop'	yellow	1	D
'Keepsake'	green	1	CD
'Lancashire Lad'	red	2	CD
'Langley Gage'	yellow	2	D
'Leveller'	yellow	2	CD
'May Duke'	red	1	CD
'Whitesmith'	green	3	CD

Where to plant Although they're tolerance of dappled shade, gooseberries grow best in full sun on ground that does not act as a frost pocket. Dig and manure the land in autumn before planting bare-root bushes between November and March. Scatter a dusting of blood, bone and fishmeal over the soil immediately before planting. *Planting* Plant to the same level as the old soil mark on the stem after removing any suckers (shoots arising from the roots or from the portion of stem that will be below ground). Like red currants, gooseberries are grown on a short 'leg'. For full planting details see the instructions on planting trees and shrubs (p. 24). Space plants 1·5 m (5 ft) from their neighbours, or plant them in flower beds and borders as shrubs. Cut back all the stems by half their length after planting, preferably to an outward-facing bud. Varieties that have a tendency to trail their stems can be cut back to an upward-facing bud. Cut out any overcrowding sideshoots—aim to produce a bush with six or eight main stems. *Cultivation* Dust the soil around the bushes with blood, bone and fishmeal in spring and then lay an organic mulch. Remove any suckers that form. Water well in dry spells. In succeeding years a little sulphate of potash can be scattered around each bush in February before the general fertilizer and mulch are applied. Keep down weeds during the summer. *Pruning* Prune twice: once in winter, cutting main shoots back by half and sideshoots back to three buds and removing one or two old stems completely; prune in summer, too, shortening sideshoots to about five leaves in early July. *Harvesting* The first pickings can be made in May when the fruits are thinned to leave them 5 cm (2 in) apart along the stems. Early pickings can be used in a pie. When the berries are fully fattened they will gradually soften and can then be harvested in one go. *Storing* All manner of preserves can be made; both pies and the fruits themselves can be frozen. *Pests and diseases* Aphids, birds, gooseberry sawfly, American gooseberry mildew. *Propagation* Take hardwood cuttings in September or October. Shoot tips 30 cm (12 in) long can be cut above a bud at the top and below a bud at the base and relieved of all but the top four buds, which will form the branch framework of the new plant. Insert the cuttings on the vegetable plot. The lowest bud on each cutting should be a few centimetres (inches) above ground level. Lift the rooted cuttings the following autumn and transplant them where they can be allowed to grow permanently.

Grape

We are now blest with a good number of grapes that can be grown outdoors, but most gardeners find greater satisfaction in growing one vine in a greenhouse or conservatory, so with that excuse I'm going to stay under glass.

For a start you'll need a greenhouse or conservatory at least 4 m (12 ft) long, otherwise your rampant vine will look like booting everything else out of the way.

Don't be tempted to try that aristocrat of grapes 'Muscat of Alexandria' unless you're prepared to take a gamble. It's a temperamental customer and not likely to perform as well as either 'Royal Muscadine' (if you want a green grape) or 'Black Hamburgh' (if you prefer black).

Preparing the soil and the house An Irishman once told me that the best thing to put under a grapevine was 'tree dead dogs', but failing the availability of a canine trio I should stick to a good load of manure. Traditionally vines were always planted outside the greenhouse and the stem taken in through a hole in the wall. Today it's considered better to plant inside the house where the soil is warmer and you will have far more control over watering and feeding.

Dig plenty of muck or compost into the border soil and a good sprinkling of general fertilizer. Fix training wires to the rafters of the house at 35 cm (15 in) intervals. The vine will be planted in the centre of one of the greenhouse borders and the stem or 'rod' led upwards to the eaves and then on to the ridge, which means that the growth will rest right against the glass. For this reason it's important to use 20–23 cm (8–9 in) long metal vine eyes to support the wire and allow maximum air circulation between the plant and the glass.

Planting Plant bare-root vines between November and December, container-grown vines at any time of year. Soak the soil thoroughly a few days before planting if it looks at all dry. Dig a hole large enough to take the roots of a bare-root vine, trim off any damaged roots with a sharp pair of secateurs, put the plant in the hole, spread out the roots and re-firm the soil with your feet. Set the plant 15 cm (6 in) from the greenhouse wall and make sure that the old soil mark on the stem is just level with the new surface. Container-grown vines should be tapped out of their pots but otherwise disturbed as little as possible (though any roots which are obviously trying to corkscrew themselves back into the rootball should

Fig. 57 Pruning and training a grape vine (*a*) Shorten the main rod to 60 cm (2 ft) and any sideshoots to one bud after planting a dormant vine. (*b*) Tie a cane to the wires and allow only the topmost bud to grow, fastening it to the cane as it extends. Sideshoots that emerge from this new stem should be thinned out so that one is allowed to remain for each wire. Train the shoots alternately right and left, pinching out their tips when they reach 1 , (3 ft). Pinch out any sideshoots on these stems so that just one leaf remains. (*c*) In the first winter after planting shorten the main sideshoots to leave just two buds. Cut back the leading shoot by two thirds. (*d*) Allow one shoot to grow from each stub or 'spur' in subsequent years, pinching out its tip three leaves after the flower cluster. Continue to pinch out sublaterals.

be teased out). Lower the rootball into the hole and firm back the soil. Water the plant well to settle the soil around the roots and apply a thick mulch of manure or compost.

Training and pruning There are lots of frighteningly complicated methods of training a vine but this is the simplest I know. Shorten the main rod (you'll have to get used to that word if you want to pass yourself off as an expert) to 60 cm (2 ft) and any lateral shoots to one bud after planting in December (Fig. 57). When the buds start to grow, nip off all but the topmost shoot and allow this to grow to a length of 3 m (10 ft), then pinch out its tip. The shoot is most easily supported by tying it to a cane which is, in turn, tied to the wires so that it runs up the side of the house; another cane can be tied to the roof section. Sideshoots will emerge from the new main stem. Thin them out to leave one shoot every 35 cm (15 in), to correspond with the training wires. The shoots should be trained alternately to right and left. Carefully fasten these shoots to the wires as they grow. Pinch out their tips when they are 1 m (3 ft) long, leaving five leaves on each. Pinch back any laterals which form on these major sideshoots to just one leaf.

In the first autumn after planting, cut back the main laterals to two buds and shorten the main rod by two thirds of its length. In the years that follow allow one lateral to grow from each stub or 'spur' and pinch out its tip two or three leaves after its flower cluster. Train the main rod as before, allowing it to retain an extra 60 cm (2 ft) each year until it is eventually pruned to just below the ridge.

Don't allow all the laterals to carry fruit in the second year—only the lower pair. Another tier can be allowed to fruit each year.

Cultivation Leave the house unheated and gently ventilated right through the winter until March. The rod is cleaned while it is dormant; lower it from the support wires and scrub it down with a stiff brush to remove flaking bark. Paint it with a winter wash to kill overwintering eggs of aphids, hibernating mealy bugs, red spider mites and scale insects. Heat can be applied as early as February but most folk are content to grow their grapes in an unheated greenhouse and settle for an August and September harvest. Close the ventilators in April and water the border soil well. Soon the buds will swell and training can begin. Leave the rod hanging down from the support system when you start it off, and tie it up again when the lower laterals have started to sprout.

Try to maintain a temperature of 16°C (60°F) gradually letting this rise to around 21°C (70°F) by late May (an automatic ventilating arm will be very useful here). Damp down daily in fine weather and spray the shoots with tepid rainwater once a day until the flowers open.

Shade when necessary from mid-May onwards. When the flowers open, dust over them with a fine paintbrush or a rabbit's tail to assist pollination. Try to maintain an average day temperature of 21°C (70°F) and a minimum night temperature of 13°C (55°F). Keep an eye on the border soil and really soak it before it has a chance to become dry. Apply a liquid feed (tomato fertilizer is best) every ten days once growth has started.

Thinning It's essential to thin out the fruit clusters if you want a healthy bunch of fat grapes. Thin the berries when they are pea sized. Work from the bottom of the bunch to the top so that 1 cm ($\frac{1}{2}$ in) is left between all the remaining fruits. Use fine-pointed scissors and keep your fingers off the grapes or the white 'bloom' will be marked.

Harvesting When the grapes start to ripen ease off watering and stop feeding or the fruits may over-expand and split. Snip off any that do. The grapes will be ready to cut in bunches about four weeks after they have changed colour. Once harvesting is completed, ventilate well and continue to ease off watering so that the vine gradually becomes dormant once more.

Pests and diseases Aphids, mealy bug, red spider mite, scale insects, scald, shanking.

Propagation Tricky and not necessary if you only need one vine.

Peach and Nectarine

Exotic-sounding though it may be, the nectarine is nothing more than a peach without the fur coat. Grow it in exactly the same way. Don't waste your time growing a peach from a stone—it may never come to much. Instead buy a plant of a proven variety that can be relied on to produce plenty of succulent fruits. 'Peregrine' is my first choice. It ripens in August and is a good doer both under glass and in the open. 'Early Rivers' and 'Lord Napier' are among the best of the nectarines, ripening in July and August. If you insist on having peaches in July you'd better pick 'Duke of York'.

Where to plant To keep them warm and in good order, peaches and nectarines are best trained as fan-shaped trees against a south- or west-facing wall or the rear wall of a lean-to greenhouse. Dig the soil deeply, working in plenty of manure or compost and improving drainage if necessary. Acid soil should be limed a few weeks after digging and a few weeks before planting. *Supporting* Horizontal wires should be fastened to the wall (or to a sunny fence if that's all you've got) to allow tying in. Arrange the wires at 30 cm (1 ft) intervals and hold them in place with metal vine eyes screwed into wall plugs.

Planting Plant a container-grown peach for preference. It can be planted at any time of year provided the soil against the wall is not allowed to dry out. It's easiest to plant a partially trained tree with the basis of the fan formation already established, but if you're mean, or just interested in doing the job yourself, you can buy a 'maiden' (a one-year-old tree) and start from scratch. Plant the tree (after watering it well) so that its rootball rests just below the surface of the soil. See under trees and shrubs for full planting details (p. 24). Set the plant 15–30 cm (6–12 in) away from the wall. Scatter a little blood, bone and fishmeal around it during February and then apply an organic mulch.

Training and pruning When your maiden tree is planted, wait until the shoots start to grow in spring then cut it back to 60 cm (2 ft) just above a sprouting shoot. When two healthy shoots are observed growing in opposite directions from the base of the tree (but above the graft union), cut back the central stem to just above them and remove all other shoots.

These two shoots will be taken up the wire framework in opposite directions at an angle of 45°. Fasten a cane to the wire to act as a marker and support for each shoot. Pinch out any sideshoots that form on these main laterals.

In winter, shorten the two laterals to about 1 m (3 ft) and allow four shoots to grow from each of them during the second summer. Make sure that these shoots are well spaced out on the framework, and at the end of the year cut them back to 1 m (3 ft), having pinched off their laterals during the summer.

During the third year shoots are allowed to grow from the established laterals at 23 cm (9 in) intervals, but only from the top sides of the shoots. Those growing out at other angles are removed. Pinch out the tips of these shoots when they are 45 cm (18 in) long. Allow the topmost bud that remains on each to grow on and extend the framework.

Peaches are carried on wood that is one year old and the aim should be to produce as much young wood on the mature framework as possible. Mature plants should have their fruiting sideshoots cut out as soon as the fruit is picked, and new ones tied in to replace them. Thin out overcrowding shoots in spring by simply pulling them off while they are soft and green.

Under glass There's no need to heat a peach under glass; it will have a head start simply by virtue of the fact that there's glass above it. Leave the ventilators open a little right through the winter, closing them in February and ventilating only when the temperature rises to 18°C (65°F). Ideally the plants want to be kept around 10°C (50°F) at night and 16°C (60°F) during the day, but in an unheated house you'll have to rely on the weather doing this for you (and in February she's not always kind). A good sprinkling of general fertilizer, followed by a thorough watering and mulching, will help to spur the plant into action, as will a daily spray with tepid water. Damp down the floor too. Soak the soil thoroughly whenever it shows signs of starting to dry out, and later in spring apply shading when there is a danger of sun scorch. Blinds are the best answer—they can be rolled up on dull days.

Pollination Peaches flower early, both in the open and under glass, and there are few bees around to do the job of pollinating for you. Use a soft paintbrush or

a rabbit's tail to dust the pollen from flower to flower. If frost threatens hang muslin or old net curtains over the flowering branches. When the fruitlets are the size of marbles, thin them out to leave one every 10 cm (4 in). Stop spraying the greenhouse plants with water now. When the fruits are as large as conkers, thin them to leave one every 23 cm (9 in).

Harvesting Pick the fruits as soon as they are ripe—the flesh will suddenly soften at the shoulder of the fruit (the end nearest the stalk). Once the fruits have been picked the plant can be sprayed daily with water once more.

Pests and diseases Aphids, scale insects, red spider mites, mildew, peach leaf curl. The latter rarely attacks peaches under glass but almost always attacks peaches in the open. For this reason it's a good idea to give preventive sprays each year before the buds open. See Table 10, pp. 225–8.

Pear

Perhaps the best all-round eating pear is 'Williams' Bon Chrétien', almost always known simply as Williams'. 'Doyenne du Comice' is certainly the juiciest and most succulent but it can be tricky in cold gardens. The long, slim 'Conference' is a good choice if you like your pears on the firm side, and if you want a good cooker try 'Catillac'.

Where to grow Warmth, sun and shelter are the keys to success with pears. Give them a well-cultivated, well-manured soil in a bright spot and they should do well. The flowers open earlier than those of the apple so keep the trees away from frost pockets at all costs or you'll lose your blossom. As well as being grown as free-standing trees, pears can also be trained as cordons, espaliers and fans (p. 159).

Rootstocks Like the apple, the pear is grafted on to a rootstock which controls its vigour. Quince A is the name of the stock most frequently used. It is relatively dwarfing and brings the tree into bearing quite quickly when it's only a few years old.

Pollination It's as well to think about pollination before you plant. If your pear tree, or trees, don't receive the right kind of pollen they'll fail to set a crop. In practice there are often trees in other gardens, and the bees are able to fly between them all doing a good job. If there are no other pears in the area you'd be well advised to plant two so that cross-pollination is ensured, but you'll have to plant pears that flower at the same time. 'Conference' will pollinate 'Williams', and vice versa; 'Doyenne du Comice' will pollinate 'Catillac' and that other favourite 'Beurre Hardy', and vice versa.

Planting If you are lucky enough to have room for a small orchard, plant bush trees 4 m (12 ft) apart on the square. Cordons should be planted 2 m (6 ft) apart on the support system; espaliers and fans 4·5 m (15 ft) apart.

Plant pears exactly as for ornamental trees (p.

24.) Scatter a good dusting of blood, bone and fishmeal over the soil during the spring after planting and then lay a thick mulch of organic matter on the soil. Don't let grass grow within 1 m (3 ft) of the tree for at least three years or the roots of the grass will rob the soil of nutrients the pear could use.

Training and pruning Pruning of established trees is similar to the pruning of apples (see p. 160 for fuller details). All the varieties I've mentioned carry their fruits on short sideshoots known as 'spurs'. To encourage the production of these the main shoots or 'leaders' are cut back by half their length during winter and the lateral shoots are shortened to three or four buds. Pears have a tendency to become overcrowded with fruiting spurs and the buds on these spurs can be reduced to three in number if you have the patience and determination. It's not the end of the world if you don't prune your tree every year but it does help to keep it in shape. A yearly feed with rose fertilizer gives the tree a boost, especially in the first five years of its life. Scatter half a dozen handfuls on the soil around the trunk and lightly hoe it in during March. Thin the young fruits in mid July to leave just two out of each cluster.

Harvesting A tricky operation. Many pears need to be picked before they are ripe and allowed to come to maturity in store:

Variety	Pick	Days to ripen
'Williams' Bon Chrétien'	September	7–14
'Doyenne du Comice'	October	7–28
'Conference'	October	7–28
'Beurre Hardy'	Late September	14–28
'Catillac'	October	Lasts until April

The general rule for picking is that the fruit should be removed as soon as it parts easily from the tree. 'Catillac' remains hard right through storage, softening when cooked.

Storing As for apples, but do not wrap the fruits. Keep an especially close eye on pears for they suddenly ripen and are likely to be past it if you only check them once a week. As soon as a fruit starts to soften, bring it in from the store and eat it within a day or two. The polythene bag method of storage is especially useful for pears—it stops them from shrivelling. The early varieties will not keep for long; the later varieties last better.

Pests and diseases Aphids, red spider mite, pear midge, pear leaf blister mite, birds, codling moth, slugworm, pear sucker, pear sawfly, winter moth, canker, mildew, scab, brown rot, blossom wilt and fireblight.

Plum, Damson and Gage

Luscious fruits that are really easy to grow. There's little to master in the way of pruning and, if you choose the right variety, you'll not need to worry about planting more than one, for the tree can set a good crop of fruits with its own pollen. If you're baffled by all the different varieties, the following are among the best: 'Victoria' is an unbeatable plum. Sometimes it's so anxious to please that the branches are snapped off by the weight of its fruits. If your penchant is for gages, try 'Early Transparent', a yellow fruit of incomparable sweetness. Both mature from mid- to late August. 'Czar' is a good culinary plum ripening earlier in the month, and 'Merryweather Damson' makes the most delectable dark red jam when it comes to maturity in September and October. Let your nurseryman tempt you with other goodies from his collection of varieties, but make sure you know whether they are dessert or culinary plums—the flavour of the culinary types is only appreciated after cooking.

Where to plant The plum is happy on deep soil; it will grow on chalky ground but seldom on really shallow stuff. Lime acid ground in the autumn before digging and manuring. The soil needs to be well cultivated to give the roots every chance to sink and establish themselves. Compared with other fruit trees plums are comparatively shallow rooting and an annual spring mulch of manure is especially welcome. Avoid frost pockets, and make sure the trees have plenty of sun.

Rootstocks Plums, damsons and gages are usually grafted on to one of two rootstocks—St Julien A or Myrobalan B. The latter is used for vigorous standard trees, the former for most others. In smaller gardens St Julien A is obviously a better choice, unless you have a craving for a tree seat in which case you'll plump for a standard. The new rootstock Pixy is more dwarfing than St Julien A but the trees are still quite large compared with bush apple trees.

Planting Having decided on a bush, pyramid, standard, half-standard or fan-shaped tree (see p. 159 for details) you can think about planting. Like all trees, plums can be planted from containers at any time of year or as bare-root plants from November to March. Choose two- or three-year-old trees and plant as for ornamental trees and shrubs (see p. 24). If you intend to plant them in an orchard, space bush trees 4 m (12 ft) apart, or 3 m (10 ft) apart if they are on Pixy rootstock; standards and half standards 5·5 m (18 ft) apart. Fans should be trained against tall house walls of a southerly or westerly aspect for preference. They'll need a wire framework as recommended for peaches and acid cherries. Scatter a general fertilizer on the soil around the tree in spring and then lay a thick organic mulch. Avoid growing grass right up to plum trees—they resent the competition. Pay attention to watering during establishment.

Pruning Prune your plums in spring or summer to lessen the risk of attack by silver leaf disease, which can enter wounds in winter. Newly planted trees should be pruned in March, just as the buds are starting to break. Cut all the shoots back by half their length. Remove completely any weak or overcrowding shoots. You can do this for a couple of years and then leave the tree to its own devices if you're really lazy. Prune when necessary in spring or summer to keep the tree shapely—cut back overlong leading shoots by one third of their length and snip the tips off laterals.

Start off a fan-trained plum tree as described for peaches (p. 166). Some lateral shoots are retained as part of the framework each year; those that are not required are pinched back to five leaves in summer to encourage the production of fruiting spurs. Cut out a portion of older wood each summer and replace it with strong, younger shoots. As with all fan-trained trees, cut out any shoots that grow directly away from the wall or towards it.

Pollination Most plums (and all those I've mentioned) will set a good crop of fruits with their own pollen, though the presence of another plum tree flowering at the same time will usually make for an even heavier crop. If frost threatens at blossom time, drape wall-trained trees with old net curtains or some other fabric to offer the blooms protection.

Thinning The tree will thin its own fruits to some extent in the 'June drop', but you can help out after this if you like by snipping off unwanted fruits to leave the remainder 5 or 8 cm (2 or 3 in) apart. If you don't thin 'Victoria' the boughs will often snap and can allow disease to enter. A tree that bears too heavily one year will often crop lightly the next. Prop up heavily laden branches with catapult-shaped poles.

Harvesting Pick dessert plums when they are fully ripe—bite in to one and see. Damsons and culinary plums can be picked with their stalks just before they are ripe and stored in a cool place while you see to jam and pie making. They'll freeze well if you remove the stones first. Try to harvest the fruits before birds and wasps eat their fill.

Pests and diseases Aphids, red spider mites, winter moth, pear leaf blister mite, plum sawfly, plum tortrix moth, mussel scale, wasps, silver leaf, bacterial canker, blossom wilt, brown rot.

Raspberry

It's a toss-up as to which is the more popular fruit in British gardens, the raspberry or the strawberry. The raspberry wins in mine. 'Malling Jewel' is easily the best flavoured of the summer fruiters, closely followed by the slightly earlier 'Malling Promise'. Make sure you try the autumn fruiters 'Autumn Bliss' (best) and 'Zeva', which extend the season well into October. Some folk claim that these autumn crops are not so fine flavoured as the summer harvest, but I wouldn't dream of complaining at that time of year.

Where to plant Best in full sun, though the summer fruiters can take dappled shade. Choose a sheltered site on well-drained soil that has been well dug and well manured. Scatter a good dusting of blood, bone and fishmeal over the soil a few days before planting. The plants can be used as a screen and then a 45 cm (18 in) wide trench can be prepared for them rather than an entire patch of soil. *Supporting* A 2 m (6 ft) high post and wire fence with stout horizontal wires at 45 cm (18 in) intervals is all that is necessary, or the plants can be trained against a fence fitted with wires at a similar spacing. *Planting* Buy only certified raspberry canes that are free of virus diseases which can cripple cropping. Plant from November to February. Soak the canes overnight in a bucket of water and then plant them at 45 cm (18 in) intervals along the foot of the support system, covering the roots with just 8 cm (3 in) of soil. Firm the earth well around the roots and then cut back the canes to 23 cm (9 in). *Cultivation* Scatter a dusting of blood, bone and fishmeal over the soil along the row in March and then lay an organic mulch. Tie in the canes as they grow, spacing them 10 cm (4 in) apart. Cut off the old stump at ground level when the new stems grow. When the canes grow taller than the topmost wire, bend them downwards and tie them in. Cut them off level with the top wire during the winter. Keep the plants well watered at all times during the first spring and summer. Hand weed among the plants and remove those that emerge too far away from the row. *Pruning* Summer fruiters will carry a crop in the second summer on the canes formed during their first year. The autumn fruiters will produce fruits in the first September after planting so pruning from now on is different. All the canes of the autumn fruiters are cut out at ground level in February. As soon as the summer fruiters have been picked, the canes which carried the fruits are cut out at ground level and the new ones (which will carry next year's crop) are thinned out if necessary and tied into the framework again at 10 cm (4 in) intervals. *Harvesting* Make sure it is you who get the harvest—not the birds, who will be fierce competition. Net or cage the crop if you can. Pick the berries, pulling them from their plugs, as soon as they are ripe. Check the canes every few days for ripening fruits. You should be able to harvest 900 g (2 lb) from every 30 cm (1 ft) run of row with summer-fruiting varieties; around 225 g (½ lb) with the autumn fruiters. *Storing* The fruits freeze well. *Pests and diseases* Aphids, raspberry beetle, cane spot, cane blight, spur blight, botrytis and viruses. *Propagation* Dig up and transplant suckers in autumn. Only propagate from healthy, virus-free plants. Replace raspberry rows every eight years or so.

Strawberry

The strawberry is more labour intensive than most fruits but that doesn't seem to put gardeners off growing it. Don't stick by the ancient varieties which are losing their vigour; go for some of the newcomers, but taste them before you commit yourself—I can heartily recommend the summer fruiters 'Tenira' and 'Pantagruella'. Varieties described as 'perpetual fruiting' crop late into the season; 'Aromel' and 'Rabunda' are both reliable even if they lack the full flavour of the first two varieties.

Where to plant An open, sunny spot in well-drained soil is what strawberries insist on. Don't whatever you do plant them in a frost pocket or you'll be lucky if you ever see a berry. Dig over the soil during spring and summer and add as much manure as you can spare. Scatter a general fertilizer over the soil a few days before planting and rake it into the surface. *Planting* Buy certified strawberry plants that are guaranteed free from virus diseases. Water them well (they are usually sold in pots) and plant while the soil is moist during July and August and certainly no later than September. These plants can then be allowed to crop the following year. Perpetual fruiters that are not planted until spring can still be allowed to fruit in late summer and autumn, but the earlier fruiting varieties should be relieved of their flowers if they are spring planted. Conserve their strength for a bumper crop in one year's time. Plant the strawberries 45 cm ($1\frac{1}{2}$ ft) apart in rows 75 cm ($2\frac{1}{2}$ ft) apart. The crown of each plant should rest at soil level—not below it, nor too far above it. Water the plants in thoroughly with a sprinkler. *Cultivation* Pay close attention to watering during the remainder of the summer and the following spring. I mulch my strawberry bed with pulverized bark immediately after planting. Pick off faded leaves and scatter tomato fertilizer among the plants in February at the rate of a handful to two plants; let the rain wash it in. Protect the plants from slugs and the fruits from birds—lay plastic netting over the rows or grow the plants in a fruit cage. Early in June push straw under the fruit clusters and around the plants to keep the crop clean. Bitumen strawberry mats and black plastic mulching are useful alternatives where straw is undesirable or in short supply. Remove any runners that form (unless you want to propagate from them). If you want to hasten fruit development and ripening, cover a row of strawberries with cloches in early February. Ventilate well when the flowers open, and remove the cloches when the crop has been picked. *Harvesting* Pick the fruits, with their stalks, as soon as they are ripe. When all the fruits have been picked, chop off all the foliage and burn it along with the straw to kill pests and diseases. The perpetual fruiters will be happier if you cut off just the older leaves and remove the straw. *Storing* Strawberries make good jam and the new variety 'Totem' freezes well, even if it's not A1 when it comes to flavour. *Pests and diseases* Aphids, birds, slugs, red spider mites, botrytis, viruses. *Propagation* To keep the plants in good condition, move the strawberry bed every three years. Allow runners to form during July and August in the third year (if the plants are still healthy and virus free) and peg these into 8 cm (3 in) pots of John Innes No. 1 potting compost sunk into the soil alongside the plants. Keep the compost moist and the plantlets will quickly send out roots. Sever them from their parents and plant them out individually six weeks later. If your plants have puckered or mottled leaves, burn them and buy in virus-free stock.

16 Vegetable growing

I wish I had a penny for every time I've been asked if it's really worth growing your own vegetables. If you're going to add up labour, the cost of seeds and fertilizers I doubt if it is. But how much do you allow for flavour, convenience, the thrill of the harvest and the fact that you can choose just what variety of vegetable you grow?

Gardeners who refuse to grow vegetables because it's easier to buy them from the shops must be desperately short of imagination as well as energy. Of course some crops fail, but isn't the magic moment of picking a good crop worth all that hassle? It is to me. So no more grumbling; on with the wellies and out with the spade!

WHERE TO PUT THE PLOT

In a tiny garden you might not have much choice; one patch alone will stand out as the obvious place for your vegetables. If you do have a choice, pick a spot that's well lit, sheltered at a distance from wind and within easy reach of the house. Avoid frost pockets—dips in the land which will collect cold air and make for a slow start and rapid finish to the growing season.

Paths around the plot will always make access easier, especially in wet weather, and it's not a bad idea to make them out of loose-laid flagstones which can be lifted and re-laid when necessary. I've divided my plot up with slabs laid on raked earth and it's easy to lift them for digging each winter. At just over £1 apiece they weren't too pricey, but I bought them a few at a time as the veg plot grew. It's no bad idea to start with a small plot and make it bigger as you need the space—that way you won't suddenly be faced with a massive patch of virgin soil to keep in trim.

Vegetables (more than any other plant) are dependent upon generous supplies of water in summer. Make sure the hosepipe will reach them. If they are allowed to dry out all development will stop and your yields will be down.

PLANNING

I always feel a killjoy when I tell folk to plan their plots before they sow anything—most want to be out on the soil bunging in seeds for all they're worth. But if you stop to take out a pencil and paper for a few minutes you can decide which crop should go where and what can follow it. Can it be grown between two other crops that will not need the space at that time? If it is positioned next to crops that need the same kind of soil preparation it will save you humping manure to all corners of the plot. Work out when the plant needs to be sown and when it is likely to be harvested and you'll know how it can be fitted into your cropping plan. This all sounds very grand, but a plan of campaign makes vegetable growing even more interesting.

Rotation The rotation of crops is an ancient practice based on sound common sense. Farmers change their crops from field to field each year so that specific crop diseases do not get a chance to build up in any one area and so that particular nutrients (which one crop might demand in quantity) do not become exhausted.

On the vegetable plot it is difficult to work out a really concrete rotation scheme (though I do try to divide my plot into three—liming one third, manuring another third and fertilizing the remainder) but it is sensible to put vegetables in a different place each year. Don't keep your runner beans at the same end, or your onions on one bed (even though some experts swear by this method). If disease does strike it will be years before you can grow onions again.

What you can do in practice is to group together on the plot those crops which enjoy roughly the same soil conditions. Those which like a freshly manured site (such as onions, leeks, peas and beans); those which need lime if the ground is acid (most brassicas); and those which just enjoy a little fertilizer (most root crops) can be kept to one section of the plot and that section moved yearly.

Manuring Those patches that need manuring every year can be enriched during digging in autumn, winter, or even spring (on light soils) with well-rotted manure or garden compost. If you can't get either (though you should always make your own compost—sorry to nag) use coarse peat laced with some general fertilizer. A bucketful to every running metre (yard) of trench will be fine (see p. 16 for digging instructions).

Liming Brassicas (members of the cabbage family) in particular grow best on a soil that is not too acid. Soil test kits will tell you the status quo (p. 13) and a dressing of lime can be applied during winter (at least one month after manure) when necessary.

Fertilizers All crops need fertilizer so I've not mentioned its application to individual crops in the A–Z of Vegetables. That's because without fail it should be scattered over the plot about one week before sowing any crop. Two handfuls of blood, bone and fishmeal or growmore can be scattered over each square metre (yard) and raked in. This is known as a base dressing.

Top dressings are given to boost growing crops. With leafy crops, fertilizers high in growth-promoting nitrogen are beneficial (sulphate of ammonia and nitrochalk, for instance). Others will prefer a more balanced fertilizer containing equal amounts of nitrogen, phosphates and potassium (such as blood, bone and fishmeal and growmore). I've indicated which crops like which.

Liquid feeds have the advantage of going straight into action and can give all crops a rapid boost.

Mulching In flower beds and borders mulching is a common practice, but few folk mulch on the vegetable plot. That's a shame, for many crops grow better if surrounded with an organic mat. Beans and peas are especially grateful for a mulch of compost or even grass mowings in summer. Apply the mulch while the soil is moist and it will keep in the moisture as well as keeping down weeds.

SEED SOWING
There are various ways of sowing seeds on the vegetable plot, and there are some vegetables that need to be sown in a greenhouse or on a windowsill before being introduced to the great outdoors. I've dealt with the techniques for both methods in Chapter 20, but here I want to mention a few wheezes that will enable you to get the best out of your plot.

Successional sowing This is the technique of sowing small quantities of one crop at intervals so that your harvest is spread. Don't sow three rows of lettuce or radish, for instance, all in one go. Sow half a row every fortnight. That way you'll have a steady succession of crops instead of an embarrassing glut.

Intercropping Here fast-growing crops such as radishes are sown between rows of slow-growing crops which will eventually need the space. The radishes will be mature by the time they are being jostled and you've managed to squeeze an extra harvest out of the soil.

Catch cropping Fast-growing vegetables are used again here (not just radishes but spring onions, turnips and non-hearting lettuce too). Sow them on land that will not be planted up with another crop until later in the year. Your first crop will have matured and been picked by then. Only with careful planning will you be able to manage catch cropping.

Thinning Here's a job that's more vital than you think. Even the obliging radish will not grow unless it's thinned quickly. Do the job as soon as you can to give the crops that remain room to grow. You don't have to pull up the unwanted seedlings; you can simply nip them off at ground level (unless you'd rather fork them up and carefully transplant them).

Planting and transplanting When you're mov-ing plants bear in mind a few golden rules: always water them well before transplanting, and 'puddle' them in afterwards. Plant firmly and plant youngsters, not gnarled grandads. Use a trowel for most plants; a thick spade-handle dibber for brassicas if you like. Plant to the same depth as the plant was growing in the nursery bed—no shallower, no deeper.

BED SYSTEMS
There's much fuss made of the modern technique of growing vegetables in beds rather than rows. It's a sensible scheme whereby several rows are spaced very close together (as close as the plants are spaced within the row) and a path left every 1 m (3 ft) or so between such blocks to allow weeding and other cultivations.

Deep bed system Here the soil within the beds is never walked on. It's double dug during the first year and enriched with compost and manure. In subsequent winters it is forked over and any additional enrichment worked in. A friend of mine swears by the method and I aim to try it myself. The first spell of double digging is hell on my flinty soil but I'm optimistic that the results will pay dividends.

WEED CONTROL
I'll speak only briefly of weed control but do remember that it is vital (see Chapter 22). If your crops have to compete with a forest of groundsel, chickweed, dandelions and couch grass they'll give up the ghost or at the very best become spindly and not worth harvesting. The Dutch hoe pushed between the rows on a dry day is the best means of control for most annual weeds, and that's all that should be left after your preliminary cultivations (except, perhaps, the odd persistent dandelion or nettle). Hand weeding between the plants is a bit of a chore but there's no finer method of getting to know your crops.

VEGETABLES IN THE FLOWER GARDEN
Where there's simply no room for a conventional vegetable patch you'll have to fit your vegetables among the flowers. It's not so funny as it sounds. The foliage of beetroot, Swiss chard, frilly 'Salad Bowl' lettuce, and even leeks, is good to look at and can show off flowers a treat. There are even ornamental cabbages with pink or white hearts that can be eaten. So if you're desperate to fit vegetables in, squeeze up the antirrhinums and dahlias and stick in a few runner beans and carrots, curly kale and globe artichokes—good in the border and in the pot.

CLOCHES
Those mini-greenhouses of glass or plastic that are used to give vegetable crops an early start or a late finish are called cloches. Think of them as umbrellas rather than hot-houses. They will shelter early sow-

Fig. 58 Cloches come in all shapes and sizes. The tent cloche (*a*) is the simplest. Here two panes of glass are held together by a clip. This barn cloche (*b*) is fitted with black plastic netting so that it will protect crops from birds when the glass has been removed. Polythene tunnels (*c*) can be made at home from lengths of polythene stretched over wire hoops and anchored to the ground with nylon twine and a peg at each end. Other cloches (*d*) are made of rigid corrugated plastic and should last for ten years or more.

ings from wind and rain, but should not be thought of as making sowing possible in really foul conditions. Seeds buried in cold, muddy earth under cloches will die almost as quickly as those buried in muddy earth in the open, so you'll still be governed to some degree by the weather.

Nevertheless, the greedy vegetable grower should not be without cloches. Fig. 58 shows the different types. All should be fitted with end pieces to prevent them from acting as wind tunnels, and for best results cloches should be put in place two or three weeks before the crop is sown to keep the soil in good condition.

Water can be applied over the top of the cloches when necessary (it will seep through the soil to the crop roots), and don't forget to ventilate both cloches and plastic tunnels in warm weather.

A–Z OF VEGETABLE CROPS

Globe Artichoke

Don't sow seeds which can yield variable plants. Instead plant rooted offshoots of a variety like 'Vert de Laon'. For patient gourmets only.

Where? Full sun and a very rich soil. A sheltered spot produces the biggest and best plants. *Plant* in spring spacing the youngsters 1 m (3 ft) apart both ways. *Cultivation* Topdress with compost or manure every May. Water well in dry spells. Remove all flowers during the first year. Cut the plants down to ground level in autumn and cover with straw or bracken. Scatter fertilizer around the plants in April and feed fortnightly in summer with liquid feed. Remove side buds to let only one flower develop on each head. Divide plants every four years. *Harvest* by cutting heads when firm and plump and when the scales are starting to expand. Don't wait until you can see the fuzzy flowerhead. In season July to September. *Store* by cutting with 30 cm (1 ft) long stalks and standing these in buckets of damp peat or sand. Will store for only a few days. *Problems* Blackfly and slugs.

Jerusalem Artichoke

'Fuseau' is a good, long, white variety that makes preparation a little easier. 'Boston Red' has ruddy skin. Both are dead easy to grow.

Where? Sunny spot on well-drained and preferably well-manured soil. A good screen or windbreak for more tender plants. *Plant* tubers either in November or February and March (plant those bought from a greengrocer if you like). Set the tubers 15 cm (6 in) deep and 30 cm (1 ft) apart allowing 1·25 m (4 ft) between rows or clumps. Label sites clearly. *Cultivation* Water well in dry spells and earth up with soil if tubers start to push through the surface. *Harvest* by chopping down dead stems in autumn and lifting the tubers as they are needed. Dig up and replant any that remain in March. *Problems* Slugs.

Asparagus

The show-off's vegetable. Previously popular varieties include 'Regal', 'Minerve' and 'Connover's Colossal', but now the all-male 'Lucullus' is proving a better cropper. Only for the very patient.

Where? In full sun and a sheltered spot on well-cultivated, well-manured soil. Make sure the spot is entirely weed free. Lime acid soil in the autumn before planting (but not at the same time as applying manure). *Plant* one-year-old crowns in April. Plant on slight ridges made in the bottom of 10 cm (4 in) deep and 30 cm (1 ft) wide trenches, spacing the crowns 30 cm (1 ft) apart (Fig. 59). Return and firm the soil. Allow 60–100 cm (2–3 ft) between rows. *Cultivation* Never let the bed dry out. Feed with liquid fertilizer monthly from June to September during the first year. Don't harvest any shoots for the first three years, but cut off all foliage in autumn when it yellows. Apply a general fertilizer each spring, keep the bed weed free and support the fern with canes and twine if necessary. In the third year, pull soil around the shoots as they start to grow; this will keep the bases white. *Harvest* by cutting all stems from the third year onwards. Harvest only from late April to late June, cutting the stems 8 cm (3 in) below ground level. Allow fern to grow after the final cutting date.

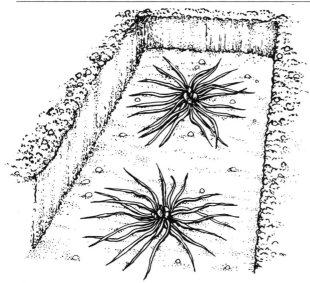

Fig. 59 Plant one-year-old asparagus crowns on slight ridges made in the bottom of trenches that are 10 cm (4 in) deep and 30 cm (1 ft) wide. Space them 30 cm (1 ft) apart.

Fig. 60 Runner beans are easy to cultivate and pick when grown up tent-shaped supports of tall bamboo canes. They are easy to clear in autumn, too.

Store by freezing if you have a surplus. *Problems* Slugs, earwigs, asparagus beetle, violet root rot.

Broad Bean
'The Sutton' and 'Bonny Lad' are good choices for spring and summer crops; 'Aquadulce' is for autumn sowing.

Where? Full sun and a rich, well-cultivated soil. Lime acid soils in autumn. *Sow* the seeds 5 cm (2 in) deep and 15 cm (6 in) apart in double rows 23 cm (9 in) apart. 'Bonny Lad' is a bush variety and can be sown in single rows. Sow 'Aquadulce' in November and cover with cloches if possible. Sow in spring from February to June. Can also sow under glass in peat pots during January and plant out in March under cloches. *Cultivation* Weed and water as necessary. Pinch out shoot tips to prevent blackfly infestation once five flower clusters have opened. Support with a cane and string enclosure if tall varieties are grown. Remove cloches when weather improves or when the beans hit the glass. *Harvest* regularly as soon as the beans can be seen to be swollen within the pods, or pick young pods and cook as for French beans. *Store* by freezing or drying beans. *Problems* Blackfly, pea and bean weevil and chocolate spot.

French Bean
The golden oldies 'The Prince' and 'Masterpiece' are still the most popular and reliable.

Where? A sunny, sheltered spot in well-manured soil. Lime very acid ground in autumn. *Sow* under cloches from mid-March to April; in the open from May to July. Sow the seeds at 8 cm (3 in) intervals along the bottom of a 5 cm (2 in) deep 'V'-shaped drill. Don't sow in cold weather or soggy soil. Thin to leave one plant every 15 cm (6 in). *Cultivation* Remove cloche coverings in May. Avoid drought at all costs, especially when the plants are flowering. If the plants flop, support them with brushwood. *Harvest* regularly from July to October. *Store* by freezing. *Problems* Red spider mites and blackfly.

Runner Bean
'Butler' is a good stringless variety; the oldies 'Enorma' and 'Scarlet Emperor' will produce very long beans. 'Pickwick' is dwarf and grown without supports like a French bean.

Where? A sunny, sheltered spot in very rich soil. During winter dig a trench along the line the plants will occupy and half fill it with compost before returning the earth. Moisture and food are vital. *Sow* at the foot of 2·25 m (7½ ft) high wigwams or ridge-tent-like supports (Fig. 60) in May and June, planting two seeds at each station. Thin to leave one plant if both seeds grow. The canes should be 30–38 cm (12–15 in) apart. Alternatively sow seeds individually in peat pots under glass in April and plant out (one to each cane) in late May. *Cultivation* A single twist-tie will make sure the shoots start to climb quickly. Weed regularly between plants and rows and really soak the soil in dry spells. Drought is detested. Mulch with manure or grass clippings or compost in June. *Harvest* regularly as soon as the beans are of a usable size (don't let them get too long and stringy). July to October is the runner bean season. *Store* by freezing. *Problems* Blackfly and birds (which nip off flowers).

Beetroot
'Boltardy' is best for early sowings until early April. The old favourite 'Detroit Little Ball' performs well if summer sown.

Where? Full sun and a patch of ground that is well worked but not stony or heavily manured. *Sow* seeds

8 cm (3 in) apart in drills 2·5 cm (1 in) deep and 30 cm (1 ft) apart. Sow from March to July but cover all sowings made before late March with cloches until mid-April. Thin to leave one seedling at each 8 cm (3 in) station with the early sowings; one seedling every 15 cm (6 in) with later sowings (each capsule contains several beetroot seeds). *Cultivation* Weed regularly and try to keep the soil evenly moist. Heavy watering during drought may split the roots. *Harvest* by pulling up the roots when they are large enough to be usable but before they reach tennis-ball size. Twist off leaves to prevent bleeding. Harvest between June and October. *Store* by pickling or by placing roots in boxes of dry peat or sand in a cool, dark, frostproof place. *Problems* Blackfly and birds (which may shred young plants).

Leaf Beet

Commonly known as Swiss chard, this is a space-saving dual-purpose vegetable. The broad leaf-stalks can be boiled for a few minutes and served with melted butter, and the leaves themselves make tasty spinach. There are white-stemmed (Swiss chard) and red-stemmed (Ruby chard) varieties, but the white is the better culinary proposition.

Where? Full sun and a rich soil. *Sow* the seeds 8 cm (3 in) apart in drills 2·5 cm (1 in) deep and 45 cm (1½ ft) apart in May and June. Thin to leave one plant every 30 cm (1 ft). *Cultivation* Keep weeded and watered. Cut out any seedheads if some of the plants bolt. *Harvest* by pulling off large, outer leaves as they are needed. Harvest from August onwards. *Store* under cloches or straw *in situ*. May last right through winter. *Problems* Slugs and snails.

Broccoli and Calabrese

Broccoli is the late winter and spring vegetable; calabrese the late summer and early autumn type, which is not reliably frost hardy. Try 'Early Purple' and 'Late White' broccoli; 'Express Corona' and 'Corvet' calabrese (which are the green ones).

Where? Full sun and a rich, well-cultivated yet firm soil. Apply lime in autumn if the ground is acid. *Sow* the seeds thinly in a seedbed 1 cm (½ in) deep in small rows 23 cm (9 in) apart. Thin to leave one seedling every 8 cm (3 in). Sow broccoli in April and May; calabrese from April to June. *Plant* out the youngsters when they are 8 cm (3 in) high. Space them 60 cm (2 ft) apart in rows 60 cm (2 ft) apart. Firm well and water in. *Cultivation* Earth up the stems if the plants lean. Weed and water as necessary. Scatter general fertilizer among the plants in July. *Harvest* calabrese from August to November (cut the central head first, then let side heads develop); broccoli from February to May. *Store* by freezing. *Problems* Exactly as for cabbages.

Brussels Sprout

Tangy winter vegetables. 'Peer Gynt' will be ready to pick from September onwards; 'Wellington' from December. 'Rampart' and 'Widgeon' are two excellent varieties for prolonging cropping well into the New Year, often as late as April.

Where? Full sun and a rich, well-cultivated and well-firmed soil. Lime in winter if the soil is acid. *Sow* in a seedbed under cloches during February; during March and April in an outdoor seedbed. Sow the seeds thinly in 1 cm (½ in) deep drills spaced 23 cm (9 in) apart. Thin to leave one seedling every 8 cm (3 in). *Plant* out when the youngsters are 8 cm (3 in) high. Space the plants 60 cm (2 ft) apart on the square. Firm well and water in. *Cultivation* Water and weed as necessary. Earth up the stems for stability as the plants grow. Stake them individually with canes in exposed areas. Scatter general fertilizer around the plants in summer and hoe it in. Remove yellow leaves in autumn. *Harvest* by pulling off the sprouts when large enough to eat. Start at the bottom and gradually work upwards. *Store* by leaving the sprouts on the plants through winter. End-of-season surpluses can be frozen. *Problems* Exactly as for cabbage. Loose sprouts will be produced as a result of soft ground or overfeeding.

Cabbage

A staple vegetable that can be harvested at any time of year, provided the sowings are planned. The chart below gives recommended varieties for a year-round supply of fat, firm hearts:

Sow	Variety	Plant	Harvest
Feb/Mar (frame)	'Hispi'; 'Golden Acre'	Apr/May	Jun/Jul
Mar/May	'Wiam'; 'Winnigstadt'	May/Jul	Aug/Oct
Apr/May	'Celtic'; 'Christmas Drumhead'	Jun/Jul	Nov/Jan
Apr/May	'January King' (savoy)	Jun/Jul	Oct/Mar
Jul/Aug	'April'; 'Harbinger'	Sep/Oct	Apr/May

Where? Full sun on a well-cultivated, well-firmed soil that was manured for a previous crop. Lime in winter if the soil is acid. *Sow* in 1 cm (½ in) deep drills on a prepared seedbed, spacing the drills 23 cm (9 in) apart. Thin to leave one seedling every 8 cm (3 in). *Plant* out the seedlings when they are 8 cm (3 in) high. Firm well and puddle in. Space the plants 45 cm (18 in) apart on the square. Spring cabbages ('April' and 'Harbinger') can be spaced 15 cm (6 in) apart in rows 30 cm (1 ft) apart and thinned to leave one plant every 30 cm (1 ft) as soon as their leaves touch. Use the thinnings as spring greens. *Cultivation* Water and weed as necessary. Guard against drought (which will cause growth to cease) and pigeons (which will do the same). Scatter a dusting of nitro-chalk among the plants in summer. Remove faded leaves. Feed spring cabbages with a dusting of general fertilizer in early April. *Harvest* the cabbages when they are large enough and firm enough to eat. For spring greens, cut a 'cross' shape in the stumps of harvested cabbages early in the year. Shoots will arise and can be harvested when of a decent size. *Store* all varieties mentioned by leaving *in situ*. *Problems* Aphids, caterpillars, cabbage root fly, flea beetles, pigeons, cabbage whitefly, clubroot, turnip gall weevil.

Carrot

A variety like 'Amsterdam Sweetheart' sown in a frame in March will give the earliest crops; 'Favourite' is certainly a favourite of most gardeners for April to June maincrop sowings. 'Autumn King', sown from May to early July, yields tasty late roots; the earlier you sow, the larger will be the carrots. 'Early French Frame' produces spherical roots that are easy to grow even on stony soil.

Where? Very well-worked soil that is not stony or well manured (both conditions can cause root forking). Full sun is essential. Add peat to open up heavy soil. If your soil is heavy or stony make a raised carrot bed in a 23 cm (9 in) high enclosure of old floorboards or timber. Fill the enclosure with sieved soil, sand and peat. *Sow* thinly in 1 cm ($\frac{1}{2}$ in) deep drills spaced 5 cm (2 in) apart. Five rows sown closely like this will produce plenty of roots while still allowing cultivations to take place. Avoid thinning the seedlings—it encourages carrot fly attack. Early crops sown in a frame or under cloches should be kept covered until mid-April. *Cultivation* Weed between rows and aim to keep the soil evenly moist. *Harvest* as soon as the carrots are of a usable size. *Store in situ* by covering with straw, or lift in October, trim off the tops and store the roots in boxes of dry peat or sand in a cool, dark, frostproof place. *Problems* Carrot fly, slugs, carrot willow aphid.

Cauliflower

Like cabbages, there are varieties to mature at different times of year:

Sow	Variety	Plant	Harvest
Feb (in heat)	'Andes'; 'Snowball'; 'All Year Round'	Mar	Jun/Jul
Mar/Apr	'F₁ Tulchan'; 'Snowball'; 'All Year Round'	Apr/May	Jul/Aug
L. Apr/May	'Wallaby'; 'Barrier Reef'; 'Autumn Glory'	Jun/Jul	Aug/Dec
L. Apr/May	'Asmer Pinnacle'; 'Walcheren Winter'	Jun/Jul	Aug/Jun

Where? Full sun and shelter from wind. Avoid frost pockets. The ground should be well cultivated but firm and enriched with well-rotted compost or manure. *Sow* in a seedbed as for cabbages (p. 175). *Plant* out when 8 cm (3 in) high, spacing the summer-maturing types 45 cm (1½ ft) apart in rows 60 cm (2 ft) apart, and the autumn- and winter-maturing types 60 cm (2 ft) apart in rows 75 cm (2½ ft) apart. Seeds sown in heat during February can be pricked out and hardened off before being planted out in April. Firm well and puddle in. *Cultivation* Weed and water copiously when necessary. Dryness at the roots will halt growth. A dusting of sulphate of ammonia will speed up the growth of slow plants in summer. Break two central leaves over developing curds (the white centre) to protect them from muck and weather. *Harvest* as soon as they are of a usable size. *Store* whole heads in boxes of straw; divided curds can be frozen. *Problems* As for cabbages. Failure to produce curds is usually caused by a check to growth—lack of water or food.

Celeriac

Try 'Balder', 'Tellus' or 'Iram'.

Where? In full sun only on very rich, moisture-retentive (but not soggy) soil. The roots won't fatten in poor earth. *Sow* in pots in a heated frame or greenhouse during March. Prick out the seedlings into trays as soon as they can be easily handled and harden them off before planting out. Alternatively sow outdoors under cloches in April, sowing the seeds thinly in 1 cm ($\frac{1}{2}$ in) deep drills. *Plant* out in late May or early June 30 cm (1 ft) apart in rows 45 cm (1½ ft) apart. Don't plant too deeply. Thin the outdoor-sown seedlings to a similar spacing. *Cultivation* Take care that the soil is not allowed to dry out. Feed with liquid fertilizer once a week. Remove a few leaves from the base of each plant as the roots start to swell; pull off sideshoots too. *Harvest* from September onwards as soon as the celeriac is fat enough to use. The turnip-like roots are celery flavoured and superb in soup or stew. *Store* all roots in boxes of dry peat or sand after trimming off leaves in October. Keep cool and dark but frost free. *Problems* As for celery but less likely.

Celery

Traditional 'trenched' celery is a labour-intensive crop. 'Giant White' is perhaps the most popular variety. Idlers can try self-blanching celery such as 'Golden Self-blanching' or 'Ivory Tower'. The self-blanchers won't stand frost.

Where? On really rich, well-manured and moisture-retentive soil in full sun. Avoid frost-pockets. Dig manure into the ground where self-blanching celery is to be grown; dig out a 38 cm (15 in) wide trench where traditional celery is to be grown and make it 30 cm (1 ft) deep. Spread plenty of compost or manure in the base and return the soil to within 10 cm (4 in) of the top, leaving the surplus at either side of the trench. *Sow* in a heated greenhouse or frame in late March or early April. Prick out into trays and harden off. *Plant* out in late May and early June. Plant the self-blanching types in blocks so that the plants are 23 cm (9 in) apart in both directions. Don't plant in rows (in blocks the plants will exclude light from one another and so stay crisp). Traditional

176

celery plants are set out in a single row at 15 cm (6 in) intervals along the trench. Water them in and never let the soil dry out from now on. *Cultivation* Remove any sideshoots from traditional celery and wrap the plants in 25 cm (10 in) high cylinders of cardboard when they are 30 cm (1 ft) high to keep the stems clean and in the dark (Fig. 61). Pull a little soil around the 'collars' and earth up gradually over the next few weeks until none of the card is visible. Self-blanching celery needs no such treatment, but a good wodge of straw can be spread around the outside plants early in July to exclude light even more. Both crops could do with a light dusting of general fertilizer (or a good liquid feed or two) in summer. *Harvest* as soon as the leaf stalks are fat and crisp enough to eat. Start at the outside of the block with self-blanching celery, and the end of the row with traditional types. The self-blanching celery should be harvestable from late July until October; the traditional from October to February. *Store* traditional celery *in situ* by piling straw over the green tops to give a little frost protection. Celery will freeze but can only be served cooked afterwards. *Problems* Celery fly, leaf spot and soft rot.

Kale

The tastiest of the greens, I reckon. Also known as borecole. 'Pentland Brig' is the most popular, but 'Fribor' is a compact newcomer just 30 cm (1 ft) high. 'Darkibor' is also very curly and is certainly well worth growing.

Where? Full sun and a moderately rich but well-drained soil. Lime in autumn if the ground is acid. *Sow* during April and May in a seedbed. Sow the seeds thinly in 1 cm (½ in) deep drills spaced 23 cm (9 in) apart. Thin to leave one seedling every 8 cm (3 in). *Plant* out from June to August when 10 cm (4 in) high, spacing the plants 38 cm (15 in) apart in rows 45 cm (18 in) apart. Firm well and puddle in. *Cultivation* Scatter a dusting of fertilizer around the plants during their second spring. Water and weed as necessary. Pull off faded foliage. *Harvest* leaves from late Autumn right through to the following May. 'Pentland Brig' produces edible flower clusters too. *Store in situ*. The plants are frost hardy and can be harvested on a cut-and-come-again basis. *Problems* As for cabbages.

Kohl Rabi

Odd but interesting. Turnip-shaped roots from which leaves arise. The taste is a cross between cabbage and turnip. Try the new varieties 'Rowel' and 'Lanro' for sowing between April and July.

Where? Sunny spot and a soil that's good but not freshly manured. Lime in autumn if the ground is acid. *Sow* thinly in drills 1 cm (½ in) deep and 30 cm (1 ft) apart. Thin to leave one plant every 15 cm (6 in). *Cultivation* Weed and water as necessary. An occasional liquid feed will be appreciated. *Harvest* from

Fig. 61 Wrap maturing celery plants in 25 cm (10 in) cardboard collars when they are 30 cm (1 ft) high. The protective layer keeps them clean and excludes light to blanch the leaf stalks.

June to December when the roots are slightly smaller than tennis balls. Larger roots are hard and unpalatable. Remove the leaves, boil the roots and serve them in white sauce. Lip-smacking good! The leaves will cook like spinach. *Storage* is not advisable—the roots quickly become wizened. *Problems* As for cabbages.

Leek

Wonderful winter vegetables. 'Musselburgh' and 'Lyon Prizetaker' are the old favourites; 'King Richard' is a long-stemmed newcomer.

Where? Full sun and a very rich, moisture-retentive soil. *Sow* thinly in March or April on a prepared seedbed in 1 cm (½ in) deep drills spaced 23 cm (9 in) apart. *Plant* out in June and July when the seedlings are 15 cm (6 in) or so high. Water them well a while before lifting. Select the largest seedlings and shorten their leaves by one-third and their roots back to 2·5 cm (1 in). Drop the plants into 15 cm (6 in) deep holes made with a piece of broomhandle at 10 cm (4 in) intervals along the row (Fig. 62). Make the rows 30 cm (1 ft) apart. Puddle the plants in and leave them to it. The soil will gradually fall back on its own to blanch the stem. *Cultivation* Never let the plants go short of water. Weed when necessary and apply occasional liquid feeds. *Harvest* from November to May as needed. *Store in situ*. Leeks are as tough as old boots. When the ground they occupy is needed

Fig. 62 Plant leeks by dropping them into 15 cm (6 in) deep holes made at 10 cm (4 in) intervals with a dibber. Puddle them in.

in spring, lift them and 'heel them in' on a corner of the plot (dig out a hole, lay the leeks in at an angle and cover their roots and the lower part of their stems with soil). *Problem* Leek rust.

Lettuce

Another hearty crop that can be harvested almost all the year round, with a bit of luck (assuming that you enjoy cold and crispy leaves in winter!). There are four basic types of lettuce: cos (with crispy upright leaves); butterhead (with soft leaves and spherical hearts); crisphead (similar but with crunchier leaves); and non-hearting (usually with frilly leaves that are cut-and-come-again). Here's a suggested cropping plan:

Variety	Sow	Harvest
'Tom Thumb' (butterhead) 'Little Gem' (cos)	E. Mar (under cloches)	E. Jun
'Webb's Wonderful' (crisphead) 'Salad Bowl' (non-hearting)	Mar/Jun	Jun/Aug
'Avondefiance' (butterhead) 'Avoncrisp' (crisphead)	Jun/Jul (cloche in Sep)	Sep/Dec
'Valdor' (crisphead) 'Winter Density' (cos)	L. Aug/E. Sep.	May/Jun
'Unrivalled' (butterhead) 'May Queen' (butterhead)	Oct (under cloches)	L. Mar/May

Where: Sun and a good but not heavily manured soil. Lime in autumn if ground is acid. Cos lettuces tolerate a little shade. *Sow* thinly in 1 cm (½ in) deep drills spaced 30 cm (1 ft) apart. Double rows under cloches can be 20 cm (8 in) apart. Sow sections of a row at fortnightly intervals for a succession. Thin gradually so that eventually the developing plants are about 23 cm (9 in) apart. 'Salad Bowl' can be closer and I've even got away without thinning it at all. *Cultivation* Keep the soil evenly moist to prevent 'bolting' (running to seed). Weed and control slugs regularly. Winter lettuces will enjoy a sprinkling of fertilizer in March. *Harvest* as soon as the plants are a reasonable size. *Store* they will not. *Problems* Aphids, birds, slugs, rabbits, mildew and botrytis (the diseases are a greater problem in winter than summer).

Marrow and Courgette

Courgettes are simply marrow pups, and if you grow a variety like 'Zucchini' you can make sure of having both—just leave the courgettes to mature into monsters. If you want only marrows, grow 'Green Bush' which is less space consuming than the trailing varieties.

Where? Prepare each planting site specially, working in masses of manure on the 45 cm (18 in) square patch which the plant will occupy. Some folk even plant on a mound of manure but I think that there's more danger of damaging drought if the spot is raised up. Marrows need full sun and shelter. *Sow* seeds individually in peat pots on a windowsill or in a greenhouse. Late April is the best time. Harden off before planting out. *Plant* in late June after watering the peat pot well. It should be just below the surface of the soil when planted. Water well. Allow 60 cm (2 ft) between plants. *Cultivation* Never let the plants go short of water. Mulch with compost or manure in June and then feed fortnightly with liquid tomato fertilizer. Manual pollination can boost fruit setting. Remove a male flower; tear off its petals and push it into the centre of a female flower (which will possess an immature marrow behind its petals). Put pieces of slate or wood under developing marrows to keep them clean and slug free. Lots of male flowers (and few females) are often produced early in the season or in cold weather. *Harvest* from July to September as soon as the fruits are large enough for use. *Store* marrows simply by standing them on shelves in a cool but frostproof shed or garage. *Problems* Slugs, mildew, botrytis, mosaic.

Onion

I reckon it won't be long before we have onions from the garden all the year round. This is the state of play at the moment:

Variety	Sow Seeds	Plant Sets	Harvest
'Ailsa Craig'; 'Bedfordshire Champion'	Mar/Apr	—	Aug onwards
'Sturon'; 'Stuttgarter Giant'	—	Mar/Apr	Aug onwards

Variety	Sow Seeds	Plant Sets	Harvest
'Express Yellow O–X'; 'Imai Early Yellow'	Aug	—	L. Jun
'Buffalo'	Aug	—	Jul
'White Lisbon' (spring onion)	Mar/Aug	—	May/Mar
'Unwin's First Early'	—	Sep/Nov	Jul onwards

Where? In full sun on soil that's as rich as can be. Some growers use the same rich soil on the bed every year but there's more likelihood of disease striking with this technique. Lime acid soil in autumn. *Sow* thinly in drills 1 cm (½ in) deep at the recommended time. Drills should be 30 cm (1 ft) apart; 23 cm (9 in) apart for spring onions. Thin bulb onions to 10 or 15 cm (4 or 6 in). Alternatively grow six rows of onions spaced 15 cm (6 in) apart and then leave wider paths from which to work. You'll save space but weeding may be more tricky. Autumn-sown onions should be thinned twice: once in autumn to 2·5 cm (1 in) and again in spring to 10 cm (4 in). *Plant* onion sets (small bulbs) with a trowel so that they almost disappear from view. Space them 10 cm (4 in) apart and leave the same distance between rows as with onions raised from seeds. They are a convenient means of growing onions but the bulbs are never quite as large as those grown from seeds. *Cultivation* Water and weed as necessary. Don't hoe too near the plants or you'll disturb the roots. Should a few bulbs run to seed, pull them up and use them at once—they won't store. When the leaves flop naturally in mid-summer, bend them all over in between the rows to allow the sun to ripen the bulbs. Fork up the bulbs in August and leave them on the soil to ripen (cover them with cloches if you can). Onions growing through the winter will appreciate any cloche protection you can give them. *Harvest* at the recommended times. Only well-ripened bulbs will store. Autumn-sown and Japanese onions must be used as soon as possible. *Store* by plaiting into ropes, or by hanging up in old pairs of tights (there's a novel use for them!). Keep the bulbs in the light or they'll sprout. *Problems* Onion fly, eelworm, mildew, neck rot and white rot.

Parsnip

'Avonresister' has small roots resistant to canker, and 'Gladiator' is longer but also resistant. Conservative gardeners almost always stick to 'Hollow Crown Improved' and 'True and Tender'.

Where? On well-worked but not well-manured ground that is stone free. Tolerant of just a little shade. Lime very acid soil in autumn. *Sow* three seeds at 10 cm (4 in) intervals in 2·5 cm (1 in) deep drills spaced 30 cm (1 ft) apart. Thin to leave one seedling at each station. The seeds are slow to come up. Sow from late February (in good years) to May. *Cultivation* Weed and water as necessary. *Harvest* as needed from September to March. *Store in situ.* Parsnips are as hard as nails. Mark the position of the rows for the tops die down. In frosty weather (when lifting is difficult) it is helpful to have some roots stored in boxes of sand or peat as for carrots. Lift any roots that remain when the land is needed for another crop and heel them in as for leeks. *Problems* Carrot fly, celery fly and parsnip canker.

Pea

If you've eaten only frozen peas since you can't remember when, it's time you tried some fresh ones. Here's how to arrange for a succession (or even just one crop to remind you of the good old days):

Variety	Sow	Harvest
'Hurst Beagle' 'Little Marvel'	L. Feb/Mar (under cloches)	L. May/Jun
'Hurst Green Shaft' 'Onward'	L. March/Jun	E. Jul/Sep
'Kelvedon Wonder'	L. Jun/Jul	Oct/Nov (cloche in September)
'Sugar Snap' (mangetout)	Mar/Jun	E. Jul/Sep
'Meteor'	Oct/Nov (under cloches)	May

The mangetout peas are especially recommended—harvest the pods while they're young, boil them whole for barely five minutes and serve them with melted butter; knock-out!

Where? For full sun on well-cultivated and well-manured soil that's not likely to dry out. Lime acid soil in autumn. *Sow* the seeds 5 cm (2 in) apart in the bottom of 5 cm (2 in) deep and 23 cm (9 in) wide flat-bottomed drills. Never sow in cold, wet soil. *Cultivation* Stake all peas with twiggy branches or cane and string enclosures when they are 10 cm (4 in) high. Water well in dry weather (copiously during flowering) and protect the plant with netting if bird damage is likely. Lawn-mowing mulches are appreciated in early summer. *Harvest* as soon as the pods are filled. Don't delay. *Store* by freezing. *Problems* Mice, slugs, pea and bean weevil, pea moth, birds, thrips, aphids, mildew and damping off.

Potato

Even if space is short a row of early potatoes is worth growing. Nothing matches that moment when the first tender spud of the year passes your lips! There are hundreds of varieties but these, I think, are some of the best:

First early: 'Maris Bard', 'Epicure'
Second early: 'Vanessa', 'Catriona'
Maincrop: 'Desiree', 'Golden Wonder'

Where? Full sun and a rich, well-cultivated soil. Spuds are often grown to break down virgin clay soils. Their roots do shatter the soil a bit but it's your earthing up that is mainly responsible. *Plant* first early varieties in mid- to late March; second early and maincrop varieties in April. Sprout or 'chit' the tubers before you plant them (Fig. 63). Stand them in egg boxes on a windowsill for six weeks prior to planting. The ends with the most buds should point upwards. When the shoots are 2·5 cm (1 in) or so long the tubers can be planted. Sprouted tubers tend to yield more heavily and rapidly than those planted with dormant 'eyes'. Plant with a trowel so that the tubers are 5 cm (2 in) below the surface with their buds pointing upwards. Plant first earlies 30 cm (1 ft) apart in rows 45 cm (1½ ft) apart; second earlies and maincrop varieties 45 cm (1½ ft) apart in rows 60 cm (2 ft) apart. *Cultivation* As soon as the shoots appear, pull some soil around them with a rake or draw hoe. Continue to earth up gently in cold weather until the ridges are 23 cm (9 in) high. If it's mild, one good earthing up can be given when the shoots have risen 15 cm (6 in) above their first earthing up. Irrigate in a prolonged dry spell. *Harvest* first earlies in June or July; second earlies and maincrop from August onwards. Maturity often coincides with flowering. *Store* in thick paper sacks in a cool, dark place as soon as the tubers are ready (if your land has a heavy slug population). If not, lift the tubers as you need them and lift the remainder for storing in October. *Problems* Slugs, wireworm, eelworm, blight, scab, virus.

Radish

The best vegetable for impatient gardeners. Ready in six weeks during summer. Try 'Cherry Belle' or 'Crystal Ball' if you like 'em round; 'French Breakfast' if you like 'em long.

Where? Full sun or very slight shade in a well-worked but not freshly manured soil. *Sow* sections of a row at fortnightly intervals from March to August (or from February if you can sow under cloches). Sow thinly in drills 1 cm (½ in) deep between other crops (to save space). Thin the seedlings to leave one every 2·5 cm (1 in). *Cultivation* Water well in dry spells and weed as necessary. Slow-growing, starved radishes will be as hard as bullets. *Harvest* as soon as of a usable size from April to September. *Storage* is not recommended. *Problem* Flea beetle.

Rhubarb

Yes, it is a vegetable and not a fruit. The newly developed varieties 'Cawood Castle' and 'Cawood Delight' are the ones to plant nowadays.

Where? In full sun and a really rich soil that's been well manured. Plant in early spring (though on light soils autumn planting is often successful). Set the clumps or 'crowns' 5 cm (2 in) below the surface of the soil and 1 m (3 ft) apart. Firm the soil well. *Cultivation* Don't cut anything during the first year

Fig. 63 Stand seed potato tubers in good light for six weeks before they are planted to encourage the shoots to grow. They'll crop better as a result.

except any flower spikes (which should always be removed as soon as they are seen). Mulch with manure every spring. Dig up and divide the plants every few years. For really early sticks, cover one plant with a bucket stuffed with straw in January. Tender pickings should be yours in March. Feed the plant well during the summer and don't force it again for a few years. *Harvest* from April to July, then let the plants build up their strength. *Store* by freezing. *Problems* Honey fungus and crown rot.

Spinach

You'll love or loathe spinach. If you love it you can enjoy it all the year round with a bit of thoughtful sowing:

Variety	Sow	Harvest
'Norvak'; 'Longstanding Round'	Mar/May	May/Nov
'Broad-leaved Prickly'	Aug/Sep (can cloche in Oct)	Nov/Mar
Perpetual spinach	Mar/Apr	Jun/Jan
Perpetual spinach	Jul/Aug	Nov/May

Where? Full sun and a rich soil. Perpetual spinach doesn't mind a bit of shade. Lime very acid ground in autumn. *Sow* seeds at 8 cm (3 in) intervals in 2·5 cm (1 in) deep drills at the recommended time. If you're growing more than one row allow 30 cm (1 ft) between rows. Thin to 23 cm (9 in) for winter spinach; 30 cm (1 ft) for summer. *Cultivation* Weed and water as necessary. Drought causes bolting (remove any flowerheads). *Harvest* as soon as leaves are large enough to use. *Store* by cooking and freezing. *Problems* Birds, slugs, downy mildew.

Swede

There's nothing like a few mangels for warming you up in winter! I think 'Marian' is the best variety; it's tasty and resistant to clubroot and mildew.

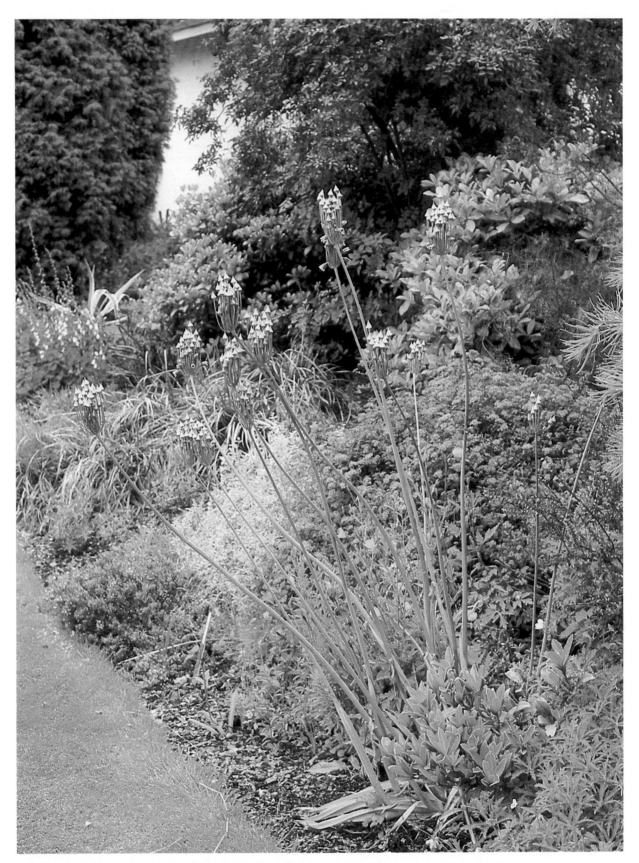

This border in Beth Chatto's garden at White Barn House, near Colchester, shows how plants with differing forms can be used to complement one another. The tall seed heads are *Allium bulgaricum*, shown off well in front of *Rosa rubrifolia*.

2. Drop in the plant and push back the earth as firmly as you can.

1. Cabbage planting Use an old spade handle as a dibber and make a hole in the prepared soil.

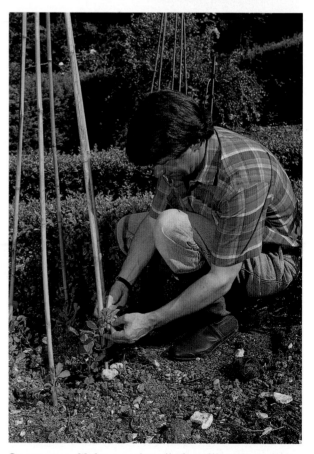

3. 'Puddle' the plant with a watering can that's not fitted with a sprinkler head.

Sweet peas Make sure that climbers like sweet peas and runner beans are tied to supports early in their life.

Left: In summer move house plants outdoors to a sheltered spot and clean glossy leaves with kitchen roll dipped in a mixture of milk and water.

Below: Connoisseurs of alpines can grow the choosy sorts in pots which can be overwintered in a cold frame or greenhouse. They make a fascinating spring show.

1. Potting up Plants obtained by mail order should be unpacked immediately on arrival and placed in good light.

2. Choose a suitable soilless potting compost, or John Innes No.1 potting compost, and a pot large enough to hold the roots with a little room to spare.

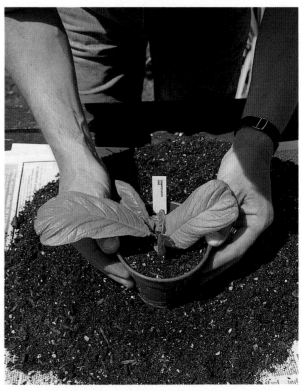

3. Feed in the compost and then gently firm it with the fingertips to make sure there are no air pockets.

4. When potting is complete the crown of the plant should be level with the surface of the compost which should be slightly below the rim of the pot.

Where? Full sun a good but not freshly manured soil. Lime acid soils in autumn. *Sow* in May and June thinly in 1 cm ($\frac{1}{2}$ in) deep drills spaced 38 cm (15 in) apart. Thin to 23 cm (9 in) in stages. *Cultivation* Weed and water as necessary—if the ground becomes dry swelling will stop. *Harvest* from October onwards as soon as large enough to use. The roots should last until early spring. *Store in situ*; the roots are quite hardy. If frosty weather looks like making harvesting difficult, lift and store a few roots as for carrots. *Problems* Clubroot, brown heart and flea beetle.

Sweet Corn

Dicey everywhere but more reliable in the sunny south. Try 'Sundance' as the best all-rounder; 'Candle' is a 'supersweet' variety, best in the south.

Where? In full sun on a rich soil in a sheltered spot. Poor, dry soils are useless. *Sow* individually in peat pots under glass during April. Harden off before planting out. *Plant* in late May or early June after watering the pots thoroughly. Space the plants 45 cm (18 in) apart on the square (blocks of sweet corn, rather than rows, are pollinated better and so yield better). Water the plants well. *Cultivation* Water copiously in dry spells and hoe between the plants to keep down weeds. The male spires of bloom open at the top of the plants and should be regularly knocked to discharge their pollen on to the ladies below (Fig. 64). Poor pollination makes for partly filled cobs. Give a dilute liquid feed once a month in summer. *Harvest* when the cobs are fat and ripe. The tassels above them will turn brown and the cob will become angled away from the stem. Pull away the sheaths to see if the grains are fat and yellow. The old test of sticking a fingernail into a grain to see if it exudes milky, rather than clear, sap can obviously disfigure the cob. *Store* by freezing. *Problems* Fruit fly and slugs.

Tomato

There are many bush varieties for outdoor growing. 'Tornado' crops well in poor summers; 'Gardeners' Delight' is tops for flavour.

Where? A sheltered spot in full sun on well-cultivated and rich, but not freshly manured, soil. *Sow* as for greenhouse tomatoes (p. 200). *Plant* in late May or early June after hardening the plants off. Space the plants 45 cm (18 in) apart and sink a flowerpot into the soil alongside each one to make watering easy. *Cultivation* Water regularly in summer (daily if necessary) and feed fortnightly with dilute liquid tomato fertilizer once the fruits have set. Do not remove the sideshoots from bush varieties. Spread dry straw underneath them in June to keep the fruits clean. *Harvest* as soon as ripe. Stand cloches over laid down plants in September to prolong the harvest. *Store* unripened fruits in October and discard the plants. Ripen the fruits in a cool place (in a drawer or on a shelf, not necessarily in bright sun).

Fig. 64 The female sweet corn flowers that grow from the leaf axils will produce the cobs. Tap the pollen from the male flower at the top to ensure fat, fully developed cobs.

Green fruits can be used in chutney. *Problems* as for tomatoes under glass (p. 200).

Turnip

An underrated vegetable. 'Snowball' and 'Golden Ball' are my recommendations.

Where? Full sun and good but not freshly manured soil. Lime acid soil in winter. *Sow* thinly in 1 cm ($\frac{1}{2}$ in) deep drills from March to September. February sowings can be made under cloches. Use 'Snowball' for February to May sowings, 'Golden Ball' for later sowings. Space the rows 23 cm (9 in) apart for early crops; 30 cm (1 ft) apart for later crops. Thin early crops to 10 cm (4 in), later ones to 23 cm (9 in). *Cultivation* Water when necessary and weed to relieve competition. *Harvest* the early sown crops as young as possible and before they are tennis ball sized. Late sowings can be left in the ground and pulled as needed. *Store* as for carrots if you want a few winter roots handy. *Problems* Clubroot, mildew, soft rot and flea beetle.

HERBS

Nobody should be without a handful of herbs to add flavour and aroma to their cooking. Grow them on the vegetable plot if you like, but most are quite handsome plants for the flower border or as edges to paths where they'll release their fragrance when brushed against (Fig. 65). Almost all herbs relish a warm sunny spot; this helps bring out their full flavour.

Basil

The sweet aniseed flavour of basil is at its best in our kitchen on baked tomatoes and buttered carrots. Plant it in late June and pick and dry it for winter use (it will be killed by frost). Raise new plants from seed indoors in March or outdoors in May. Pinch out the shoot tips regularly and pick off any flowers.

Chives

A little clump of reed-shaped, onion-flavoured leaves. Happy in gentle shade if that's all you have to offer. Plant in spring or autumn—mature plants can be divided at that time and tired old plants cut down to ground level in early summer. Don't remove the flowers—they're lilac-pink and quite pretty. The plant is perennial.

Fennel

A hefty herb with 1·5 m (5 ft) stems of delicate feathery leaves. It tastes of aniseed and is usually used in fish dishes. Plant in spring and divide mature clumps at the same time. The plant dies down in winter and does not store very well.

Marjoram

Pot marjoram is the desirable perennial kind with a thyme-like flavour. Plant in spring and clip with shears when very untidy. Divide clumps in spring to propagate. Freeze or dry for winter use.

Mint

Every gardener's bane if it gets loose. Plant it in a bottomless bucket sunk into the ground but with the rim protruding—that will halt its spread. Plant in spring or autumn and propagate by division at those times. Dies down in winter. Dry or freeze for winter use. Make your own mint sauce with the stuff in summer and store a few bottles for winter. Can be frozen in ice cubes for use in fruit cups.

Parsley

Sow annually outdoors in April but be patient—seeds are slow to germinate. Cut off any flowers that form and protect with cloches in winter if you want to go on harvesting. The plant will perk up at the start of its second year but will gradually wear out. Can freeze for winter use.

Rosemary

A 1·5 m (5 ft) evergreen shrub that's very useful because it can be harvested at any time of year. The leaves have a warm, savoury flavour. Plant in spring and propagate by cuttings in a propagator at the same time. Severe winters will cause die-back. Essential in stuffings and with roast lamb.

Sage

Another evergreen bush but this time it's not so hefty at around 30 cm (1 ft). Plant in spring and prune in summer to encourage fresh growth. There's not

Fig. 65 Herbs. 1. Rosemary. 2. Mint. 3. Basil. 4. Sage. 5. Chives. 6. Fennel. 7. Parsley. 8. Thyme.

much leaf in winter but sometimes enough to harvest. The variegated varieties are prettiest and just as tasty. Cuttings can be rooted in a propagator in summer.

Tarragon

It's the French variety that has the best flavour. Plant it in spring in a warm, sheltered spot. Protect with cloches or straw in winter. Propagate by division in spring. Freeze for winter use. Severe winters may see it off.

Thyme

Evergreen carpeter with savoury aromatic leaves. Grow against paths and in patios. Plant in autumn or spring. Cut back in spring to promote new growth and use the clippings as cuttings. Can be gathered fresh all the year round.

Drying herbs

Herbs tend to have their maximum flavour just before they flower, so cut and dry them at that time for winter use—those that dry well, that is. Put the shoots in brown paper bags and store them in a warm, dark place. Crush them when they are dry and put them in airtight containers from which the light can be excluded. That way they'll keep as much of their flavour as possible.

Freezing herbs

Herbs that lose their flavour when dried can often be successfully frozen. Sprigs of mint and parsley can be frozen in ice cubes for fruit cups; sprigs of herbs can be placed in polythene bags and put in a freezer compartment of a fridge. Although they won't keep their shape when defrosted they will often keep their flavour.

17 Greenhouse gardening

Having a greenhouse is like having a dog; you might not want to be without one but it does tie you down. You'll need to visit it every day, morning and evening, during the growing season, and you'll not be the most popular person in the household when you dive out to water your tomatoes just as dinner is being served.

But set against all this is the pleasure you'll get from growing a wider range of plants (and the frustration of a few failures), and the fact that you'll regularly be able to make a sizeable contribution to the meal you're about to eat. You'll be able to raise potfuls of flowers nearly all the year round (if your greenhouse is kept frost free), and a few crops can be forced out of season to yield their bounty when shop prices are sky high.

So if you think you can risk the wrath of your spouse, or that you can placate it with out-of-season offerings for the table, take up the challenge and go in for gardening under cover.

THE RIGHT SPOT

The ideal spot for a greenhouse probably doesn't exist in a small garden, but bear these points in mind when you're trying to shoe-horn it into the scheme:

1 Choose a spot which is well lit and not overshadowed by trees or buildings.

2 The site should be sheltered at a distance from strong winds which will send heating bills soaring.

3 Avoid frost pockets—those dips in the land where cold air collects.

4 Avoid badly-drained ground or your greenhouse crops that are grown in the soil will always have a late start.

5 Try to find a level site; it makes foundation laying easier.

6 Site the greenhouse where water and electricity can easily be laid on.

I don't happen to subscribe to the idea that your greenhouse must run either north/south or east/west. It makes a difference where large commercial glasshouses are concerned, but not in your average back garden.

One final point: check with your local authority to see if planning permission is required before you erect the greenhouse.

WHICH GREENHOUSE?

You'll find that there are dozens of greenhouses to choose from, all of which are capable of growing plants well. Two factors in particular will whittle down a few of the choices: price and design. You'll have to pick a greenhouse you can afford, and you're quite right to pick one that has an appealing shape. Whatever the practical qualities of a greenhouse, if you can't stand the sight of it there's not much point in owning it. Practical points are nevertheless important, so make sure that your chosen design can fulfil the following requirements:

1 Good light transmission.
2 Stability
3 Good ventilation (one side and one ridge ventilator for every 2 m (6 ft) of the greenhouse's length).
4 Easily accessible (a wide enough door to allow in a wheelbarrow if you feel this is necessary).

The most important consideration of all should be the use to which the house will be put. Pot plants are best in a house that has half-timbered sides, for then the 'understage' area can be hidden from view. Plants grown in the border soil will need a glass-to-ground greenhouse so that they receive plenty of light.

If you're intent on growing food crops, a glass-to-ground model is for you; if you aim to grow both tomatoes and pot plants then how about a house that's half glass-to-ground and half 'half timbered'? Some manufacturers are making the decision even easier by supplying timber panels for their glass-to-ground greenhouses so that they can be transformed within minutes.

Wood or alloy? Timber houses are the romantic gardener's favourite (and that includes me). They are usually made of western red cedar, which is amazingly light, amazingly durable and very handsome. They have to be painted with a preservative every two or three years to prolong their life but they look good in the garden and blend beautifully with plants.

Cedar is not cheap, and wooden houses are now more expensive to buy than those made of alloy. Greenhouses made of Baltic pine are less pricey but I can't recommend them because they have nothing like the durability of their cedar relations.

Aluminium alloy greenhouses score because of their reasonable price, the fact that they need no maintenance other than the oiling of hinges, and because they are easy to glaze; the glass is held in position with clips or rubber strips. If you don't like the look of aluminium you can choose a model that's been coated with acrylic paint which stops the formation of that white powdery deposit too.

Both timber and alloy houses will outlast you if they are treated well, so pay your money and take your choice.

Glass or plastic? If you want a permanent greenhouse the answer has to be glass. It lasts virtually for ever, a fact which should counteract the initial expense. It allows in more light than plastic and allows heat to escape much more slowly. When it comes to cleaning it takes little time to restore grimy glass to its former crystal-clear state, even if it has been painted with shading compounds to cut down summer glare.

Plastic has two great advantages—cheapness and safety where children are concerned—but the fact that it has to be replaced after a few years will often step up the cost. Certain plastics are now guaranteed a life of fifteen years, but that's only a fraction of the time you can expect glass to last.

In time all plastic becomes opaque and allows in less light; it loses heat rapidly, allows rapid temperature fluctuations and produces much condensation. In plastic tunnels ventilation is difficult, and even though plastic houses may be easy to erect they can be equally quickly dismantled by a gale if not securely anchored to the ground.

After all that, you could be forgiven for thinking that plastic houses are useless! They're not, and they do have a lot to recommend them where temporary and easily movable forms of protection are needed.

WHICH DESIGN?

Buy the largest greenhouse you can possibly afford or accommodate—you'll soon find that it's bursting at the seams.

Span roof This is the traditional greenhouse with vertical sides and two roof sections that slope down at an angle of roughly 45°. Glass-to-ground and half-timbered models are available, as are models with curved eaves. Remember that the curved sections are plastic, not glass, and they will become opaque and need replacement in time. Span-roof greenhouses with a dividing partition are especially useful for then only a portion of the house need be heated in winter to protect frost-tender plants.

Dutch house This design has been around for many years. The panes are very large—roughly 1·5 m by 60 cm (5 ft by 2 ft)—and the sides slope outwards from the eaves (Fig. 66). Light transmission is good but breakages are expensive.

Octagonal Rather more ornamental (Fig. 67) than useful, except to the disabled gardener who will find that many plants can be easily tended from a wheelchair. Make sure that ventilation is adequate—on

some models ventilation is inadequate.

Dome Space-age in appearance, this is a strong house with good light transmission. It is also very expensive (Fig. 68).

Lean-to Designed to fit against the wall of a house, the lean-to has the advantages of being easily accessible (Fig. 69), well insulated on one side and good to look at from inside the home if it is erected over a window. The installation of electricity and water (as well as an additional radiator from the central heating system) can be easily accomplished. This design is now becoming very popular—the conservatory is making a deserved come-back. Glass-to-ground and half-timbered models are available, as well as mini-lean-tos which can be stood on patios and in back yards. A lean-to may affect your rates but it can make sure that you get to the greenhouse in the foulest weather without getting your feet wet.

Plastic tunnel This is the type of house to invest in if cheapness and portability are important (Fig. 70). Access and ventilation are achieved via the doors at either end, and a tubular steel framework supports the replaceable polythene envelope. The edges are well buried in the soil to ensure stability even in high winds.

FOUNDATIONS

Laying foundations is a real fag. Most gardeners are anxious to get cracking with putting up their greenhouse and all that trench digging and concrete humping is a sizeable fly in the ointment.

By far the best solution is to buy a greenhouse for which tailor-made concrete kerb foundations can be bought. All you need to do then is lay the kerbs on firmed and levelled ground (checking that they themselves are level and square) and erect the greenhouse on top of them. Bolts will attach the base of the house to the prefabricated foundation, giving it stability in wind.

Some greenhouses come equipped with an integral base-plate, which means that they can be erected straight on to firmed and levelled earth. Metal 'ground anchors' can be driven in at strategic points to offer wind resistance.

If no alternatives are available you'll just have to get out the pick and shovel. Dig a 23 cm (9 in) deep trench along the line of the foundation, ram 10 cm (4 in) of hardcore into the base and then top it with a layer of concrete shuttered between boards. A mix of 6 parts aggregate, 1 part sand and 1 part cement, mixed to a sticky consistency with water, should be tamped down between the boards which have been checked for level and squareness. Coach bolts can be sunk into the concrete (threads uppermost) so that later the base of the house can be drilled to fit over them and the nuts screwed down to anchor the structure. It's all a real chore—you'd be better off with purpose-made foundations!

Fig. 66 The so-called 'Dutch' greenhouse has large panes and sloping sides. It admits plenty of light right down to the ground but replacement panes are costly.

Fig. 67 Octagonal greenhouses are good to look at and useful for disabled gardeners who tend their plants from a wheelchair. Make sure that ventilation is adequate.

Fig. 68 Dome-shaped greenhouses are for lovers of space-age designs. They are costly but allow exceptionally good light transmission. Check that there are plenty of vents.

Fig. 69 As a conservatory, a lean-to greenhouse comes into its own. Heating can be piped in from the system used in the home.

Fig. 70 Plastic 'tunnel' houses are cheap but nothing like so durable as their glass counterparts. Anchor the edges firmly for stability by burying them 30 cm (1 ft) deep in the soil.

ERECTING THE GREENHOUSE

Almost all greenhouses come with detailed instructions on erection, though the instructions very considerably in their degree of lucidity. Usually the structure is glazed after erection, though some manufacturers supply ready-glazed sections. This is a mixed blessing; it saves you the job of glazing but it makes erection a more nail-biting job, for there's always the risk of breakage.

Certain manufacturers offer an erection service—if you let them construct the house on site it can be bought free of V.A.T. which may offer a considerable saving of money and effort.

Greenhouses that can be glazed with clips or rubber strips make glazing a doddle, but some houses still come with a large bag of putty and a smaller bag of glazing sprigs.

It's always a good idea to have somebody around to help you glaze the greenhouse—especially if putty is involved. You'll become more proficient as you progress, but at first the putty gets everywhere except in the channels for which it is intended. Try to glaze the house in one day—if it's part-glazed and a wind gets up you could be in for a hefty bill for glass replacement.

If you do have to use putty, start by glazing the roof, strip by strip. Work putty into the rebates along the glazing bars (don't be too generous with it), and then insert the glass, starting at the bottom and leaving each pane overlapping the one below it by about 2·5 cm (1 in). Fasten the glass in position with glazing sprigs (making sure you put one under each side of the lower edge to prevent the glass from slipping) and then clean off the excess putty. Rub the glass immediately with a dry cloth to remove finger marks. You'll have a devil of a job to shift them once they're dry. When the house is glazed you can move in without delay.

WHERE TO GROW THE PLANTS

If you plan to raise tomatoes, cucumbers, peppers and aubergines you can grow the crops in the soil within the greenhouse for a few years. Dig it well first and work in some well-rotted compost or manure. Don't grow the same crop in the same place year after year. Practise a small rotation scheme and you should be able to grow good plants in the earth for three or four years. After this length of time the soil often becomes 'sick' or exhausted and it's a good idea to move over the growing in pots, growing bags or, where tomatoes are concerned, ring culture.

Some experts would have you ignore the border soil from the outset—I'd rather enjoy its cheapness and convenience for a couple of years before moving over the containers. You can always dig up and replace tired border soil with fresh, but it's an expensive and labour-intensive job.

Ring culture If it's tomatoes you're growing, and the border soil becomes tired of them, turn to ring culture.

Lay a 15 cm (6 in) deep bed of washed pea shingle over a strip of polythene and retain it with boards at the edges. Alternatively, excavate a 15 cm (6 in) deep trench and lay the polythene and shingle in it. The gravel bed can stretch right down one side, or both sides, of the greenhouse.

Remove the bottoms from some 23 cm (9 in) plastic plant pots (a hacksaw will do the job), or buy special 'whalehide' rings which are bottomless. (Conservationists please note: whalehide pots are made from bituminous paper.)

Sit the rings on the shingle, spacing them 45 cm (18 in) apart. Fill them with John Innes No. 3 potting compost and plant the young tomatoes in them. Water them well in and apply all subsequent waterings to the shingle. Only liquid fertilizer should be applied to the compost in the pot.

The plant will develop two root systems, one for absorbing water and one for absorbing food. At the end of the season the plants can be removed and the gravel thoroughly washed so that it is fit to use the following year.

A path down the centre of the greenhouse is a must whether you grow plants in pots or on the floor. Stone slabs are easy to lay and comfortable to walk on; gravel is cheaper and where plants are to be grown in pots on the staging it can be laid over the entire floor area to a depth of 2·5 cm (1 in). It looks good, keeps down weeds and holds moisture in summer when humidity is important. Buy the stuff from a builders' merchant, where it is described as 'washed pea shingle'.

Staging Pot plants need to be grown on shelves or on benches which the greenhouse gardener calls staging. The most luxurious staging is made from timber or alloy and supports plastic trays which can be filled with gravel. During spring and summer the moisture evaporating from the gravel keeps the air around the plants pleasantly humid and conducive to growth. In winter it can harbour too much moisture and lead to fungus attack, but it's a time consuming job to remove all the gravel every autumn and replace it each spring. For this reason I always spread gravel on the floor of the greenhouse and have plain slatted wooden staging which can be easily and relatively cheaply built from 5 × 2·5 cm (2 × 1 in) deal and painted with a red cedar timber preservative to match a cedar greenhouse. The gravel on the floor provides sufficient buoyancy in summer without being over-poweringly moisture retentive in winter.

For ease of working, make the staging waist high and no more than 1 m (3 ft) deep so that all plants can be reached from the front. If the house is very wide or intended to display flowering pot plants the staging can be lower and tiered to present a bank of floral colour to the spectator. Any staging should be strong. Pots full of compost may not feel very heavy on their own but collectively the weigh a 'ton'.

Don't let the area underneath the staging lie idle. Shade-loving ferns and foliage plants will enjoy growing there.

Shelves fixed above the staging down the sides and at the end of the greenhouse provide more valuable space for growing pot plants. Fix them to metal angle brackets but make sure that they don't cast too much shade on the staging below. Shelves about 15 cm (6 in) wide should not cause much of a problem.

Fig. 71 shows a well equipped home greenhouse.

HEATING

To overwinter frost-tender plants and to make an early start with seed-raising in spring your greenhouse will need heating. Certainly an unheated structure is valuable during the warmer months of the year and for growing winter lettuce, but a little heat

Fig. 71 A greenhouse designed and kitted out to cope with pot plants on staging and tomatoes and the like in soil borders or on the ring culture system. Roller blinds provide shading; an automatic ventilating arm prevents dramatic temperature fluctuations; thermostatically controlled tubular heaters keep out frost; gravel-filled benches maintain humidity in summer and a propagating frame allows new plants to be raised all the year round.

will spread its usefulness over twelve months.

I'm not going to take up pages by going over all the forms of heating; instead I'll tell you quite simply that nothing beats electricity for efficiency or economy. Gone are the days when coal and paraffin offered cheap heat; thermostatically controlled electric heaters beat them hands down nowadays.

You'll have to enlist the help of an electrician to equip your greenhouse with the juice and to fit special waterproof plugs for safety. I use tubular heaters, which are slung underneath the staging and wired up to a rod-type thermostat set at 7°C (45°F) in winter (to keep my geraniums frost free) and a little higher in spring. The thermostat is the key to economy. It switches the electricity off when the required temperature is reached—a feature lacking in paraffin and solid fuel heating systems where burning continues regardless of temperature.

The other big advantage of electricity is that it produces dry heat. This is especially important in winter when excess humidity encourages fungus diseases. Paraffin heaters give out gallons of water every day and can also cause leaf scorch. Use them as emergency measures during winter power cuts, and try to apply a little ventilation at all times so that poisonous fumes can escape. Use only those paraffin heaters expressly designed for greenhouses.

Tubular heaters are just one form of electrical air warmer; fan heaters (designed for greenhouse use) and air-warming cables can also be used (though the latter are really at their best in small structures where they can be clipped to the wall beneath the staging). Both types again should be fitted with a thermostat for economy. Don't let a fan heater blow directly on to plants or it may brown their foliage.

Heaters running from natural gas might seem to be desirable, but they need to be connected up to the gas supply, which may be even more difficult than laying on electricity. They also produce water vapour and poisonous fumes and so cannot really compete with clean electricity.

Manufacturers will advise you on the size of heater needed for your structure. Make sure that the equipment you buy is capable of giving you the heat you need. A maximum and minimum thermometer should hang in every greenhouse to check that your heater is functioning properly.

LIGHTING

If you're investing in electrical heating you might as well have lighting fitted too. A single fluorescent strip fastened to the ridge will provide plenty of working light on dark evenings (and mornings, too, in winter). If you simply want enough light to check that no one's run off with your plants then an ordinary lamp socket will do.

Lean-to greenhouses that are positioned over house windows can be lit for pleasure rather than practicality. A spot light fitted to the back wall can be angled to shine on to the plants and provide colourful evening scenery.

INSULATION

In winter, every step you take to prevent heat loss will save money. For a start check that doors and ventilators fit snugly. Stick-on household draught excluder can be used to plug any gaps. Mend all broken panes of glass before the bad weather arrives.

Keep all the glass clean so that every ray of sunlight can be utilized, and if your greenhouse is heated to a temperature of 10°C (50°F) or more, rig up some form of plastic insulation inside. Polythene sheeting or, better still, bubble polythene with built-in air pockets, should be fixed to the roof and sides of the house so that it creates an insulating layer of air. It's the 2·5 cm (1 in) gap between the polythene and the glass that does the insulating, rather than the polythene itself. Put up the insulating material in November and take it down in April. Don't cover the vents with the stuff—you'll still need them on warm days.

Double-glazed greenhouses are now on the market; they're efficient and amazingly strong but they're rather expensive too.

VENTILATION

In a stagnant atmosphere fungus diseases are rife so try to provide plants with a little fresh air at all times except in really cold or severe weather. In summer the ventilators are vital in letting in air to lower temperatures and prevent the plants from baking, so when you buy a greenhouse do make sure that plenty of ventilators are present. As a rule of thumb look for one ridge ventilator and one side ventilator for every 2 m (6 ft) of the greenhouse's length. If there are fewer than this, ask if more can be fitted; if they can't then shop elsewhere.

Ventilators on both sides of the house will allow you to vent on the leeward and prevent howling draughts. Louvre vents are efficient but not always draughtproof; ordinary hinged vents fitted with casement stays can usually be made to fit snugly.

The one piece of equipment you should not be without is an automatic ventilating arm. These devices are fastened to a ventilator and set to open and close it at a given temperature. If you have to be out at work during the day the arm will efficiently prevent your plants from being baked alive. The automatic ventilator is not expensive and needs no power supply; it is activated by the expansion and contraction of a substance confined in a special rod-shaped chamber.

HUMIDITY

During winter high humidity in the greenhouse will bring problems in the shape of diseases. In spring and summer it is essential to keep the plants in good health. The easiest way of maintaining a buoyant atmosphere is to 'damp down' the floor of the greenhouse both morning and evening, and the staging too if it is covered with gravel. The moisture will evaporate into the atmosphere and keep the plants perky. Don't damp down after late summer. From autumn until late spring the atmosphere wants to be on the dry side.

SHADING

In summer additional measures have to be taken to lower temperatures and prevent plants from being scorched by the sun. Shading is the solution. The cheapest form comes in a bottle; dilute it in water and paint it on so that a white film coats the glass. There are various products: one has the advantage of being easily removed with a dry duster and yet it stays firmly in place regardless of summer downpours. Another becomes translucent when wet, so allowing in more light on dingy summer days. Shading compounds such as these cannot be used effectively on all plastics—on some they will refuse to shift however hard you wash and scrub them in autumn.

Blinds are more expensive but more versatile, for they can be raised and lowered according to the weather. External blinds are preferable to those fixed inside the house for they will intercept the sun's rays before they have a chance to heat up the greenhouse atmosphere.

If you can't afford blinds, invest in some green plastic close-weave netting which can be pinned or otherwise fixed to the outside of the greenhouse. Put it up in May and take it down in September.

WATERING

When I first worked in a nursery we had to water all the plants with a can. There were thousands of them. Eventually hosepipes were fitted, but the boss watched us like a hawk and came down like a ton of bricks if the hosepipe was running too fast. Whether you use a can (a long-spouted one is best) or a hosepipe, that's the secret—don't let it run too fast or the compost will be efficiently flushed out of the pot and splashed round to make a breeding ground for disease.

Tapwater does most plants no harm at all. Only if it's very hard and the plants are very sensitive will you encounter problems. In this case you can collect rainwater in a large tank, but make sure that leaves and other debris can be prevented from falling into it or it will turn into a bacterial broth. Rainwater that runs off the greenhouse roof can be channelled via the guttering into a tank sunk below the staging inside the house. Fasten a piece of nylon stocking over the inlet to keep out rubbish and empty it regularly to prevent blockages. Some gardeners consider that water which is collected and stored in this way is full of disease.

I've never found this to be the case. You can't grow plants in a sterile atmosphere and if they can't cope with a few germs in the rainwater then they are of a pretty sour constitution.

Automatic watering saves a lot of time. It also takes some of the skill out of growing plants, but if you're busy it's worth the candle. Capillary benches are perhaps the best form of automatic watering. They are level and consist of waterproof trays on which is laid special nylon matting. This is kept constantly moist (from a reservoir or drip-feed system) and plants that are stood on it can take up just the water they need. Plastic pots with plenty of drainage holes are essential. Clay pots (unless they are fitted with a wick of the nylon material) cannot absorb the water because of the gap between the compost and the bottom of the pot. Various proprietary systems are available.

The 'spaghetti-tube' watering system consists of a large Alkathene pipe from which small-bore 'spaghetti' tubes emerge at intervals. Each tube is pegged into a plant pot and when the tap is turned on, water is delivered. The trouble with this system is that it is unselective—every plant is watered when the tap is turned on and there is consequently a risk of overwatering.

When to water If you're watering by hand the time to water any pot plant is when the surface of the compost in the pot feels dry. You can also tell by lifting the pot up and testing its weight (the drier it is the lighter it will be). Most plants suffer no more from being allowed to dry out occasionally than we do from being thirsty, but regular drought will cause leaf browning and flower drop and overwatering will cause the plants to go into a wilt from which they will seldom recover.

A final tip on watering plants in the greenhouse border soil. Sink a flowerpot into the earth alongside each plant at planting time. Subsequent waterings can be applied into the pot and will get straight to the roots without running off the surface.

COMPOSTS

Pot plants won't grow in garden soil. In such a confined space it is neither well drained enough nor nutritious enough to support them. For this reason gardeners have developed a range of composts for different purposes. Originally there was a different mix for each plant, but nowadays we have just a handful of recipes that can keep most plants happy.

The John Innes composts were developed in the 1930s at a research institute carrying that man's name. They are now manufactured to the original formulae by many firms (look for the seal of the John Innes Manufacturers' Association on the bag to be sure that the compost is genuine). If you want to make them up at home, here are the recipes for the five different types of composts:

John Innes Seed Compost
A mixture in which all seeds can be sown.
2 parts by volume partially sterilized loam
1 part by volume granulated peat
1 part by volume coarse sand
+
40 g (1½ oz) superphospate of lime
20 g (¾ oz) ground limestone or chalk } per 36.1* (1 bushel)

John Innes No. 1 Potting Compost (JIP 1)
Prick out bedding plants into this mixture and use it when potting up rooted cuttings.
7 parts by volume partially sterilized loam
3 parts by volume granulated peat
2 parts by volume coarse sand
+
110 g (4 oz) John Innes base fertilizer
20 g (¾ oz) ground limestone or chalk } per 36.1* (1 bushel)

John Innes No. 2 Potting Compost (JIP 2)
Suitable for most pot plants.
Loam, peat and sand as for John Innes No. 1 potting compost
+
225 g (8 oz) John Innes base fertilizer
40 g (1½ oz) ground limestone or chalk } per 36.1* (1 bushel)

John Innes No. 3 Potting Compost (JIP 3)
Suitable for vigorous plants including tomatoes, chrysanthemums, cucumbers and melons.
Loam, peat and sand as for John Innes No. 1 potting compost
+
340 (12 oz) John Innes base fertilizer
60 g (2¼ oz) ground limestone or chalk } per 36.1* (1 bushel)

John Innes Ericaceous Compost
Suitable for lime-hating plants such as rhododendrons, azaleas and heathers.
Loam, peat and sand as for John Innes No. 1 potting compost
+ 4 oz John Innes base fertilizer per 36 1* (1 bushel)

* 1 = litres

Loam

Kettering loam was originally prescribed, but by now Kettering must be in a gigantic valley. Good garden soil or, better still, soil derived from stacked turves, will do but it should really be partially sterilized to kill harmful bacteria and weed seeds.

Proprietary electric soil sterilizers are easy to use but pricey. The soil in them should be sterilized for 10 minutes at a temperature of 82°C (180°F). If you can't afford the equipment, find a large, old saucepan and boil 1 cm (½ in) water in the base before filling it to the brim with sieved soil and letting it simmer for 15 minutes. Tip out the soil afterwards and let it cool.

Peat

Granulated peat should be used and before it is mixed in it must be moist. Pass it through a 1 cm (½ in) sieve. Peat is difficult to replace in potting compost.

Sand

Don't use bright yellow builder's sand. Coarse river sand is what is needed to make for good drainage.

Bushel measure

A box 25 × 25 × 55 cm (10 × 10 × 22 in) contains one bushel when filled to the brim.

Fertilizer

John Innes base fertilizer is available ready mixed from most garden shops or nurseries. It contains:
2 parts by weight hoof and horn
2 parts by weight superphosphate of lime
1 part by weight sulphate of potash

Mixing and storing

Measure out the ingredients and tip them into a heap. Turn the heap three or four times with a shovel until the compost is well mixed. Store the compost in black plastic sacks or dustbins, but try to use it within two months. After this time it starts to turn sour. Mind you, I've used old John Innes compost on many occasions with no ill effects, but there's always a chance that some plants might not like it.

Peat- and coir-based composts

There are dozens of proprietary soilless composts which at one time were based almost exclusively on peat with the addition of fertilizers. Now, due to a need to conserve our peat resources, other renewable organic resources are being experimented with. Many soilless composts today are based on coir — the fibres from coconut husks. Much has been written about the advantages and disadvantages of such composts. Only continuous experience will show us how they can best be managed, and which plants will and will not grow well in them. What all soilless composts have in common is an inability to hold on to nutrients for as long as loam-based composts, which means they need feeding regularly six weeks after potting. Heavy plants may overbalance in them, and they are best kept gently moist at all times — never let them dry out. Firm them only gently at potting time.

Compost for cuttings

One of the simplest and most effective composts for cuttings is 1 part granulated peat or coir to 1 part coarse river sand. Use it in pots or a propagator where it will provide a well-drained medium capable of inducing root formation. Information on propagators is given on p. 218. Don't be without one in your greenhouse. Details of seed sowing and other propagation techniques are given on pp. 215–221.

POTTING

Plants in the greenhouse grow rapidly and frequently need to be given larger containers of fresh compost. There are several different techniques:

Potting up Here a rooted cutting or seedling is put in its first pot. A container 9–10 cm (3½–4 in) is usually large enough. Some compost is placed in the bottom of the pot (over a layer of crocks or other drainage material if a loam-based compost is being used in a clay pot) and the plant is then dug out of its seed tray or propagator with as much compost adhering to its roots as possible.

The plant is seated on the compost in the new pot, and more compost fed round it and lightly firmed with the fingers. When potting up is completed the plant should sit at the same level at which it grew in its previous container, and there should be a gap of about 2 cm (¾ in) between the surface of the compost and the pot rim.

Water the plant in either by standing it in a shallow trough of water and allowing it to take up what it needs, or by gently soaking it with a can fitted with a fine rose.

Potting on Plants which have outgrown their existing container are moved on to a larger one (Fig. 72). The technique is described on p. 204. Plants growing in the greenhouse may require more than one new container each year if they are growing strongly prior to making flowers. Perennials that are kept for several years will usually be happy with one new pot a year, or maybe even one every second year. As a rule, pot on only during spring and summer when plants are growing actively.

Repotting A term that is often loosely used for any type of potting but which really indicates that a plant in a large pot is being knocked out, some of the compost removed from its rootball and replaced with fresh when the plant is returned to the same container.

Topdressing Equally useful where plants are growing in large pots. Scrape away the top 5 or 8 cm (2 or 3 in) of compost and replace it with fresh.

FEEDING

Greenhouse plants have what you might call a high metabolic rate, thanks to good light and relatively high temperatures. For this reason they enjoy regular feeding during the growing season. Use dilute liquid fertilizers and apply them once every ten days during the growing season. Newly potted plants need not be fed for eight weeks, if they are growing in loam-based compost such as John Innes, or for six weeks if they are in a peat-based compost.

SUPPORT AND TRAINING

Just like house plants, greenhouse plants need pinching out from time to time to keep them bushy. Simply nip out the shoot tips between your forefinger and thumbnail to encourage the production of more sideshoots. Very dwarf plants won't need pinching, nor will plants being grown on a single stem.

Fuchsias and other plants being trained as 'standards' on a tall, single stem, should have their

Fig. 72 Once a plant has completely filled its container with roots it should be 'potted on' to a pot which is about 5 cm (2 in) larger in diameter.

sideshoots removed so that the main stem is encouraged to grow to the required height. Then it can be pinched out and the bushy head developed at the top.

Support single-stemmed plants with individual canes to which the stem can be loosely tied with soft twine. Multi-stemmed plants can be held up either with a few twiggy sticks pushed into the compost among them, or by an enclosure made from split green canes and twine. All supports should be put in place before they are needed so that the plant can grow up and mask them.

Don't be frightened to cut old and straggly plants back quite hard in spring. They will often sprout vigorously and take on a new lease of life.

HYGIENE

Tidiness pays dividends in the greenhouse by keeping the risk of pest and disease attack to a minimum. Never leave dead or diseased plants among healthy ones, and always pick off faded leaves and flowers immediately you spot them.

Remove any weeds that sprout from the greenhouse floor, and act immediately when you spot a pest or disease outbreak by fumigating the house.

Once a year (in spring for preference) give the inside and outside of the house a good scrub down with horticultural disinfectant, which is sold especially for the purpose. It will remove dirt and grime as well as killing overwintering pests and their eggs. Keep the plants out of the way during the clean up—stand them under the staging and cover them with a sheet of polythene.

Permanganate of potash, or one of the new algicides, will shift green algal deposits from paths if a stiff brush and elbow grease are used as well.

If gravel is present on the staging, put it in a sieve and swill it clean with a hosepipe bit by bit.

GREENHOUSE FLOWERS

There's no reason why your greenhouse needs to be heated to tropical temperatures to keep you in flowers during winter. A minimum temperature of 7°C (45°F) at night, and just a fraction more during the day, will keep plenty of temperate plants blooming. Even this bit of heat will cost you money, but with thermostatically controlled heating you can keep the bills as low as possible.

I've drawn up a chart (Table 8) of flowering pot plants that can be grown from seeds to give year-round colour in a cool greenhouse, but the following plants are such confirmed favourites that they need individual treatment:

CARNATION

Perpetual-flowering carnations are those that you buy from the florist for wedding buttonholes. There are dozens of varieties with blooms of red, orange, yellow, pink, white and magenta; most of them are called something-or-other Sim—'White Sim', 'Ar-

thur Sim', 'Tangerine Sim' and so on.

Pot up young rooted cuttings into 8 cm (3 in) pots of JIP 1 in January, February or March. Specialist nurserymen will supply them at this time.

Cultivation Grow on in a temperature of 4–7°C (40–45°F)—the plants insist on cool temperatures. Pot on into 13 cm (5 in) pots of JIP 2 when the plants have outgrown their previous containers, and stand them outdoors during the summer. Pot on into 20 cm (8 in) pots when necessary. Pinch out the central shoot when ten pairs of leaves have been formed, and pinch out sideshoots after eight pairs of leaves. 'Stop' the plants (pinch them out) at different times to stagger flowering. If you want winter flowers, don't stop the plants after June. Bring the pots into the greenhouse during September. The plants will grow to at least 1 m (3 ft) and will need some support. Canes and string are used by most gardeners, but special carnation supports are also available. Feed fortnightly with tomato fertilizer when the plants have been in their final pots for six or eight weeks. When the flower buds form, remove all but the large central one. Cut the blooms with a good length of stem just before they are fully open.

Propagation Replace the plants with newly rooted cuttings every two years. Propagate them yourself by taking cuttings of sideshoots during December, January and February and rooting them in a propagator heated to 16°C (60°F).

CHRYSANTHEMUM

The early-flowering chrysanthemums that bloom in September can be grown outdoors, but October- and

Table 8: Greenhouse Pot Plants to Grow from Seeds

Plant	Height	Description
Begonia semperflorens	15 cm (6 in)	Round, glossy leaves of green or brown; red, pink, salmon or white flowers
Browallia 'Blue Troll'	20 cm (8 in)	Starry flowers of sky blue on very compact, green-leafed plants
Calceolaria hybrids	23 cm (9 in)	Soft green leaves and pouch-like flowers, often with contrasting spotting
Celosia 'Fairy Fountains'	30 cm (12 in)	Plumes of orange, red or yellow flowers like waxy feathers
Cineraria hybrids (now Pericallis)	30 cm (12 in)	Daisy flowers of white, pink, blue, magenta or purple; often two-tone
Cobaea scandens	Climber	Bells of pale blue and white on a vigorous, vine-like plant
Coleus blumei (now Solenostemon)	30 cm (12 in)	Colourful leaves splashed with red, yellow, orange, green and purple
Cuphea ignea	15 cm (6 in)	Tiny, tubular red flowers tipped with purple and white
Didiscus caeruleus (now Trachymene)	45 cm (18 in)	Pale blue scabious flowers on tall stems
Exacum affine	15 cm (6 in)	Tiny lilac-blue flowers on a neat, glossy-leaved plant
Gomphrena globosa 'Buddy'	23 cm (9 in)	Globular, crispy flowerheads of rich crimson-magenta on compact plants
Hypoestes phyllostachya	23 cm (9 in)	Dark green leaves spotted with bright pink
Mimulus 'Calypso'	15 cm (6 in)	Trumpet-shaped blooms of red, orange and yellow covered in contrasting spots
Primula malacoides	30 cm (12 in)	Toothed leaves held in a rosette from which rise tiered heads of pink, blue or white flowers
Schizanthus 'Hit Parade'	30 cm (12 in)	'Poor man's orchid' flowers beautifully painted atop ferny green leaves
Streptocarpus hybrids	20 cm (8 in)	Long, downy leaves and elegant trumpet flowers of blue, white, pink or magenta
Thunbergia 'Orange Wonder'	Climber	Vine-like stems clothed in green leaves and decorated with orange, black-eyed blooms
Torenia fournieri	30 cm (12 in)	Much-branched plants with pale blue and dark blue trumpets
Vinca 'Dwarf Mixed'	30 cm (12 in)	Tender periwinkles with flowers of pink or white, often with a contrasting eye

late-flowering varieties are grown in pots so that they can be given greenhouse cover. Buy from a specialist grower who will offer a wide choice of varieties.

Pot up rooted cuttings in March or April—one plant to an 8 cm (3 in) pot of JIP 1. Grow on at a temperature of 10°C (50°F)—the plants must be kept cool.

Cultivation Pot on the plants as they grow, first into 13 cm (5 in) pots and then into 20 cm (8 in) pots of JIP 3. Give each plant a 1·25 m (4 ft) cane when it is in its final pot. Pinch out the main shoot when it is 20 cm (8 in) tall and pinch out subsequent sideshoots when they, too, are 20 cm (8 in) long. Specialist nurseries will recommend precise stopping dates for each of their varieties if you want to time your blooms for a flower show. The fewer stems you leave to develop, the larger will be the individual blooms. Lightly tie the stems to the cane with soft twine as they grow. Stand the plants outdoors on a path, patio, gravel or ash bed from late May onwards when there is no danger of frost. They should be sheltered from winds which will blow them over, or else tied to a horizontal wire strained between two posts. Feed weekly eight weeks after planting the chrysanths in their final pots. If you want large, single blooms, remove all but the central bud on each stem. If you want sprays of flower, remove the central bud and let the rest develop. In late September bring the plants into the greenhouse, keeping them cool but frost-free and in good light. Nip off any extra sideshoots and dead leaves. Either cut the open blooms with long stems, or bring the entire pot into the house if you want colour in the home. Chrysanthemum leaf miner may be a problem (see Chapter 21 on pests and diseases).

Propagation is easy from cuttings. Cut the plants down to within 5 cm (2 in) of the compost after flowering and box up these 'stools' in trays of JIP 1 (having shaken most of the old compost from the roots). Keep the stools in a cool, well-lit greenhouse and they will eventually produce tough little shoots which can be taken as cuttings during January and February. Make them 5 or 8 cm (2 or 3 in) long and root them in a propagator in a temperature of 16°C (60°F).

FUCHSIA

Hardy fuchsias are shrubs that can be grown permanently in the garden, even though frost might cut them to the ground each winter. Tender fuchsias need frost protection and so are grown as greenhouse plants or bedded out in summer and brought under cover in autumn. There are hundreds of varieties. Some are suited to being grown as 'standards' on a single stem; others make good hanging basket plants due to their pendulous habit; but the majority make shapely bushes.

Pot up rooted cuttings in spring or early summer in 8 cm (3 in) pots of JIP 1 or a peat-based equivalent.

Cultivation Pinch the shoot tips and subsequent sideshoots to encourage bushiness. Flowering will usually commence about six or eight weeks after pinching. To produce a standard fuchsia, first check that the variety is suitable, then remove all sideshoots and fasten the main stem to a cane as it grows. When the required height is reached, pinch out the shoot tip and keep pinching the terminal sideshoots to encourage the development of a bushy head. Pot on the

Jan	Feb	Mar	Apr	May	Jun	Jul	Aug	Sep	Oct	Nov	Dec	Key
	⌞20°⌟	⌞⌟	⌞10⌟		✿	✿	✿	✿	✿			✿ = flowering season
✿	✿	✿			⌞18°⌟	⌞10⌟		✿	✿	✿		
			✿	⌞15°⌟✿	⌞⌟✿	⌞8⌟	⌞13⌟					⌞16°⌟ = sow in this temperature (°C)
	⌞20°⌟	⌞⌟	⌞10⌟		✿	✿	✿	✿				
✿	✿		⌞16°⌟	⌞⌟	⌞8⌟	⌞13⌟			✿	✿		⌞⌟ = prick out into trays
		⌞18°⌟	⌞8⌟	⌞15⌟			✿	✿	✿			
		⌞16°⌟	⌞8⌟	⌞13⌟								⌞15⌟ = pot up into this size container (cm)
		⌞18°⌟	⌞8⌟	⌞13⌟	✿	✿	✿	✿	✿			
		⌞18°⌟	⌞8⌟	⌞13⌟	✿	✿	✿					
✿	✿	✿	⌞18°⌟	⌞8⌟	⌞13⌟		✿	✿	✿	✿		
		⌞18°⌟	⌞⌟	⌞10⌟	✿	✿	✿	✿	✿			
		⌞18°⌟	⌞8⌟	⌞13⌟								
		⌞18°⌟	⌞10⌟	✿	✿	✿						
	✿	✿	✿			⌞18°⌟	⌞8⌟	⌞13⌟				*Footnote*
		⌞16°⌟	⌞8⌟	⌞13⌟	✿	✿	✿					All these plants can be grown in a cool
⌞18°⌟		⌞8⌟		⌞10⌟			✿	✿	✿	✿	✿	greenhouse—minimum temperature 7°C (45°F).
		⌞18°⌟	⌞8⌟	⌞13⌟	✿	✿	✿	✿				Supplement this selection with plants included in
		⌞16°⌟	⌞8⌟	⌞13⌟	✿	✿	✿	✿				Chapter 18 on House Plants, and with pot-grown
		⌞16°⌟	⌞⌟	⌞10⌟	✿	✿	✿	✿	✿			bulbs (for details see Chapter 10 on Garden Bulbs).

plants in JIP 3 or a peat-based equivalent as necessary. They are usually happy in 15 cm (6 in) pots. Plant pendant types in a hanging basket. The plants will flower continuously during summer and autumn. Stand them or hang them outdoors between June and September if you wish, but bring them back inside before frosts threaten. Feed fortnightly when in flower or bud. Keep the plants on the dry side in winter. Cut the shoots back to within a few centimetres or inches of compost level in spring to encourage shoots which can be used in propagation or pinched to produce a shapely plant once more. Repot in fresh compost at the same time. The plants will need a winter minimum temperature of 7°C (45°F); 10°C (50°F) if they are to be kept growing rather than ticking over.

Propagation is by shoot tip cuttings which can be removed and rooted in a propagator at any time during spring and summer. Maintain a temperature of 16–18°C (60–65°F) to induce rooting.

PELARGONIUM

'Geraniums' are real favourites with any gardener who appreciates brilliance and value for money. The 'Zonal' types are the commonest, with their attractively marked leaves and bright blooms; the miniature varieties are especially good because large numbers of them can be fitted into a small greenhouse to provide almost year-round colour. Scented-leaved pelargoniums should be tried too; their foliage may be scented of anything from peppermint to pineapples and is often finely cut.

Pot up rooted cuttings of named varieties obtained from specialist nurseries in February or March. Put them in 12 cm (4½ in) pots of JIP 2.

Cultivation Pelargoniums, more than most plants, prefer to dry out just a little between waterings, so don't keep them soggy. Pinch out the shoot tip of each plant when it is 10 cm (4 in) high. The miniatures will grow well without pinching. Pinch again later on to keep plants bushy. Feed fortnightly from May to September, and keep the plants in brilliant light. Pick off faded flowers and leaves as soon as they are seen. Stand the plants outdoors in summer if you wish, or plant them in bedding schemes. Bring them back under cover in September before the frosts. Keep the plants very much on the dry side in winter; singles may continue to flower (especially if they are disbudded during summer to save their energy), but doubles are less likely to do so. Maintain a minimum winter temperature of 7°C (45°F), though the plants can stand anything down to freezing point and still survive. Plants to be kept for a second year can be potted on into 13 or 15 cm (5 or 6 in) pots in their second spring, but most are best replaced annually from cuttings.

Propagation Take shoot tip cuttings at any time between April and September. Make each cutting 8

to 10 cm (3 to 4 in) long and root cuttings around the edge of a 10 cm (4 in) pot of peat and sand. Maintain a temperature of 16–18°C (60–65°F) for rooting. Pot up as soon as roots are well developed. Hybrid pelargoniums can be raised from seeds sown in a temperature of 18–21°C (65–70°F) between January and March. The plants will flower from July onwards (old seed-raised types would seldom bloom before September).

GREENHOUSE FOOD CROPS

You can grow all sorts of fruit and vegetables in a greenhouse, but here I want to include just the big five: tomatoes, cucumbers, aubergines, sweet peppers and melons. Grapes and peaches are included in Chapter 15 on fruit, and crops which can be forced to produce their goodies early are dealt with on pp. 200–1.

AUBERGINE

'Long Purple', 'Moneymaker' and 'Slice Rite' are three reliable and dark-purple-skinned varieties.

Sow thinly in a pot of seed compost in January or February and germinate in a temperature of 16–18°C (60–65°F). Prick out individually into 8 cm (3 in) pots of peat-based compost or JIP 1.

Cultivation Pot on into 13 cm (5 in) pots of JIP 3 or a peat-based compost when the plants are 15 cm (6 in) high. Water well when necessary. Pinch out the shoot tip one week after potting on. Transfer to 20 cm (8 in) pots when the plants have outgrown their 13 cm (5 in) containers. Spray open flowers with tepid water, and give a fortnightly liquid feed of tomato fertilizer from this stage on. Allow six to eight fruits to remain on each plant. Pinch out any sideshoots. Stake if necessary.

Harvest the fruits when they are a good size and while they are still shiny (they'll become tough when they turn dull). Watch out for the thorns!

Store by freezing.

Problems Aphids, red spider mites and whitefly.

CUCUMBER

The 'all-female' varieties which produce very few male flowers are well worth growing. They save you the annoyance of bitter, misshapen cucumbers if you happen to miss just one masculine bloom (they should always be pinched off to prevent fertilization). 'Femspot', 'Femdan' and 'Pepinex' are all good.

Sow two seeds to an 8 cm (3 in) peat pot full of peat-based compost in March or April. Push the seeds 2·5 cm (1 in) deep and germinate them in a temperature of 18°C (65°F). Should both seeds germinate, remove the weaker and grow the remaining one on in a temperature of 18°C (65°F).

Cultivation Plant in growing bags or large pots of JIP 3 or a peat-based equivalent as soon as the young

female

male

Fig. 73 The simplest way of training a cucumber plant is to pinch out sideshoots after three leaves have formed and subsequent sideshoots after two leaves. That way the plant takes up little space but crops well.

plants are 23 cm (9 in) high. Equip the sides and roof of the greenhouse with horizontal wires at 30 cm (1 ft) intervals immediately above the site where the cucumbers are growing. Two plants will fit in a growing bag (Fig. 73). Water well before planting and plant so that the rim of the peat pot is just fractionally below the surface of the compost. Water in and keep the compost constantly moist (but never soggy) from now on. Place a cane alongside each plant and train the main stem upwards, pinching out sideshoots after three leaves have formed and subsequent sideshoots after two leaves. Pinch out the tip of the main shoot when it reaches the ridge of the greenhouse. Spray daily with tepid water and keep the atmosphere moist by damping down. Pinch off any male flowers which do occur (female flowers have immature cucumbers behind them; males do not). Keep the plants shaded from bright sun. As soon as roots appear above the compost apply a topdressing. Feed fortnightly with dilute tomato fertilizer as soon as the fruits start to swell.

Harvest the fruits as soon as they are of a decent size. The plant may continue to crop for many weeks if fruits are not allowed to mature fully.

Problems Whitefly, red spider mite, aphids, mildew, stem rot and mosaic virus.

MELON

The canteloupe melons 'Charantais' and 'Sweet-heart' are old favourites; I rather like the earlier maturing 'Early Sweet', which is mouthwateringly succulent.

Sow exactly as for cucumbers.

Cultivation In the early stages the same instructions apply as for cucumbers, with regard to pinching and training, but *do not* remove the male flowers. As soon as four or five female flowers are open at the same time (the females have miniature melons behind them), remove a male flower and push it into the centre of the females to assist pollination and subsequent fertilization. Do the job around midday when the humidity is high. If all four (or even five) fruits start to form, all well and good. If they don't, remove all the remaining females that were fertilized and wait for another batch of four to come along. Melons need to develop simultaneously because far less water must be given to them as they reach maturity. If some fruits were just starting to swell when others were almost ripe, it would be difficult to give the swelling fruits the water they required without causing the mature fruits to split. Feed weekly with liquid tomato fertilizer once the fruits have set. Pinch off subsequent female flowers. Topdress the compost when roots appear above the surface. When the fruits are tennis-ball-sized, support them in string bags slung from the framework of the greenhouse. Shade them from bright sunshine.

Harvest the fruits as soon as the end furthest from

the stalk gives a little when pressed. Just before this happens the fruits will start to exude that long-awaited melon aroma. This is the signal to cut down on the watering and let the compost become drier. Overwatering now will cause fruit split.

Problems Aphids, whitefly, red spider mite and stem rot.

SWEET PEPPER

Also known as capsicums. 'Canape' and 'World-beater' are old favourites; the new 'Bellboy' is good too.

Sow seeds in a pot in March and germinate in a temperature of 16°C (60°F). Prick out individually into 8 cm (3 in) pots of JIP 1 or a peat-based equivalent. Grow on in a temperature of 16–18°C (60–65°F).

Cultivation Pot on into 15 cm (6 in) pots of JIP 3 or a peat-based equivalent when the plants are 15 cm (6 in) high. Pinch out the shoot tips at the same time. Try to keep the compost gently moist at all times and shade the plants from bright sun. Spray the flowers with tepid water daily once they have opened, and feed weekly with dilute tomato fertilizer once the fruits have set.

Harvest the fruits as soon as they are of a usable size and while they are still shiny and green. If left to turn red they will slow down the plant's growth rate and fewer fruits will come to maturity.

Problems Aphids and red spider mite.

TOMATO

Everybody has their own favour tomato variety; mostly 'Moneymaker'. Try 'Alicante' or 'Ailsa Craig' for a change, or the hefty-fruited 'Big Boy' if you like beefsteak tomatoes. 'Golden Boy' is a bright yellow tomato with an exquisite flavour. More folk should grow it.

Sow seeds in a pot during March and germinate in a temperature of 18°C (65°F). Prick out the seedlings individually into 8 cm (3 in) pots of JIP 1 or a peat-based equivalent.

Cultivation Grow on the plants in a temperature of around 18°C (65°F). When they are 23 cm (9 in) high, plant them out either into the border soil (spacing them 45 cm (18 in) apart), into 23 cm (9 in) diameter pots of JIP 3 or a peat-based equivalent, into growing bags or into rings (for ring culture see p. 190). Water the plants well after planting and provide each one with a support—a stout cane or a string running up to the roof of the house. Remove any side-shoots as soon as they are seen. Tie the stem to the cane as it grows, or twist it carefully around the string. Try to keep the compost gently moist at all times. Sink a flowerpot into the soil alongside each border-grown plant and pour water into that instead of on to the surface of the soil. You'll prevent your tomatoes from becoming mud-spattered and the water will get straight to the roots. Spray open flowers with tepid water to en-

courage fruit setting. Feed weekly with diluted tomato fertilizer once the first fruits start to swell. Shade and ventilate as necessary. Pinch out the main shoot tip when six flower clusters or 'trusses' have been formed. Cut away one or two leaves around each developing truss. Do *not* remove all the lower leaves as some growers do. It's not necessary and it weakens the plant.

Harvest the fruits just as soon as they are ripe. Don't leave them on the plant too long or cropping will slow down.

Store all remaining fruits in October. Strip the plants of their bounty and uproot them. The unripe fruits will slowly ripen if stored in a cool place. Put them in a drawer with a ripe banana if you want to speed up the process. Green tomatoes that refuse to blush can be used for chutney.

Problems Mindboggling, but you won't get them all: Whitefly, red spider mite, blossom end rot (especially on plants in growing bags), blotchy ripening, greenback, eelworm, leafmould, stem rot, root rot, potato blight, verticillium wilt, virus.

FOOD CROPS TO FORCE

It sounds a bit cruel, but it's not really. You're just providing plants with favourable conditions which *allow* them rather than *force* them to start growing early, yielding their crops while prices are high.

FRENCH BEAN

Use our old friends 'The Prince' and 'Masterpiece'.

Sow four seeds 2·5 cm (1 in) deep in a 15 cm (6 in) pot of JIP 1 during December, January or February. Keep the compost moist and maintain a temperature of 16°C (60°F). Stake with a cane and string enclosure or short twiggy pea sticks as the plants grow. Feed fortnightly with tomato fertilizer once the flowers have opened.

Harvest between ten and twelve weeks after sowing. Pick the young pods regularly.

POTATO

'Epicure' is about the best choice for forcing, but 'Sharpe's Express' is also good.

Pot in January. Half fill a 20 cm (8 in) pot with JIP 3 and peat-based compost mixed in equal parts. Plant three tubers 5 cm (2 in) deep in the mixture. Keep the compost moist and maintain a temperature of 10°C (50°F). Topdress with more compost as the shoots grow until the pot is nearly full.

Harvest during April. Deliciously early!

RHUBARB

'Timperley Early' and 'Champagne' are both good.

Plant the crowns close together in a 20 cm (8 in) deep box of moist peat at any time during November or December. The crowns should have been dug up a week before planting and left on the surface of the soil exposed to frost. Keep the boxes in the dark (blacked out with sacking or black polythene) in a temperature of 13–17°C (55–60°F). Check regularly and keep the compost moist.

Harvest during January and February, cutting the pink sticks when they are about 30 cm (12 in) long. Discard the crowns after cropping, unless you want to grow them on and rest them for a year before picking again.

STRAWBERRY

'Tamella' and 'Cambridge Favourite' are both good forcers.

Plant three rooted runners to a 20 cm (8 in) pot of JIP 3 in August. Stand the plants outdoors during the autumn and early winter, watching them carefully for dryness (or, more likely, waterlogging). Bring the pots in during January. Try to maintain a temperature of 10°C (50°F) at first, gradually raising this to 16°C (60°F) during February. Feed fortnightly with liquid fertilizer once the plants come into flower. Limit the number of fruits on each plant to twelve.

Harvest during April and May. Discard the plants after fruiting, or grow them on in the garden if you are soft-hearted.

18 House plants

What makes a good house plant grower? Skill? Luck? Green fingers? Usually it's a smattering of all three and a hefty helping of common sense. No plants are more at your mercy than house plants: you control the amount of heat, water and light they receive and so you're directly responsible for their state of health.

Too many house plants are killed with kindness and a few are murdered by neglect, but if you choose the right plant for your particular situation and learn what it likes and loathes then it will grow happily. A plant that's put in the kind of light it enjoys and at a temperature which suits it can only be killed by faulty watering. Master all three techniques and you'll win.

FINDING THE RIGHT PLANT

All too often the house plant comes as a present, which means that you're stuck with it whether it likes your conditions or not. You'll have to do your best to find it a suitable spot. If you're buying a plant, make sure you know exactly what it likes, dislikes and tolerates, and what it is supposed to do.

There are three basic kinds of house plant: the foliage types which last almost for ever and which are grown especially for their leaves; the flowering pot plants which are perennial and which keep growing after blooming; and the short-term flowering pot plants that die once their blooms have faded. Most folk like a good number of foliage pot plants which offer year-round interest, plus a few flowering ones to brighten life at intervals.

Don't think of pot plants as single pieces of furniture—often they look good and feel more at home when grouped together, provided they all have the same heat and light requirements.

PLANTS SUITABLE FOR VARYING CONDITIONS

It makes sense to find out which plants are suitable for your house before you go out to buy them. The following plants are suitable for the conditions indicated:

PLANTS THAT ARE HARD TO KILL

Aspidistra, Billbergia, Chlorophytum, Cissus, Cyperus, Fatshedera, Fatsia, Impatiens, Philodendron, Rhoicissus, Sansevieria, Tradescantia, Zebrina.

PLANTS FOR CENTRALLY HEATED ROOMS

Aechmea, Aphelandra, Begonia, Codiaeum, Dieffenbachia, Dracaena, Euphorbia, Ficus, Howea, Monstera, Peperomia, Philodendron, Pilea, Rhoicissus, Saintpaulia, Sansevieria, Schefflera, Siningia, Stephanotis, Yucca.

PLANTS FOR UNHEATED ROOMS

Calceolaria, Chrysanthemum, Cordyline, Cyclamen, Erica, Fatshedera, Fatsia, Hedera, Primula, Rhododendron, Saxifraga, Senecio.

PLANTS FOR SHADY CORNERS

Adiantum, Asparagus, Aspidistra, Asplenium, Cissus, Fatshedera, Fatsia, Maranta, Peperomia, Philodendron, Pilea, Platycerium, Rhoicissus, Sansevieria.

PLANTS FOR WINDOWSILLS

Capsicum, Cyclamen, Dionaea, Erica, Fuchsia, Hedera, Impatiens, Pelargonium, Primula, Rhododendron, Saintpaulia, Sansevieria, Saxifraga, Schlumbergera, Senecio, Solanum, Solenostemon, Tradescantia.

PLANTS FOR WARM BATHROOMS

Adiantum, Aechmea, Aphelandra, Asparagus, Asplenium, Begonia, Cyperus, Dieffenbachia, Dionaea, Maranta, Nephrolepis, Peperomia, Pilea, Platycerium, Saintpaulia, Tradescantia.

BUYING HOUSE PLANTS

Spring and summer are the best times to buy house plants; at these times they can be transferred to your home with little check and should carry on growing happily in a suitable environment. Christmas-flowering pot plants will obviously have to be bought in winter. Make sure they are wrapped up well for their journey home, and don't leave them in an icy car while you complete your shopping.

Buy in preference from the nursery where the plant was grown, or from a garden centre where it has been kept in the conditions it likes. Buy from chain stores and supermarkets only when the plants are known to be fresh in, and buy from greengrocers' pavement displays at your peril. Most of the plants will have been chilled and blasted by icy winds. They may be cheaper but they'll suffer as a result of their ill treatment.

Look for a healthy, shapely plant which has plenty of stems (unless it is purposely grown on a single stem). Avoid plants that are wilting, leafless at the base (unless this is part of their charm), brown at the leaf tips or showing signs of pest and disease attack. Flowering pot plants are best bought with a few blooms fully open and a few in bud. Plants in tight bud may not develop properly in the home; those in full flower will not last so long.

If there is a gap between the compost and the sides of the pot, leave the plant alone. It has been allowed to dry out too much and may suffer when you get it home.

STARTING THEM OFF

When you get the plant home, unwrap it and stand it in the room where it is to be grown. A spot that's not in full sun is best at first—even for those plants that like bright sunlight. Keep a sun-loving plant in its temporary position for two or three days before moving it into a window. Most plants prefer a spot in good, indirect light and these can be stood immediately in their final positions; as can those plants which tolerate shade.

Check the plant immediately for water. If the rootball is drier than a wrung-out flannel then water it thoroughly (see below for full details on watering).

DEATH TRAPS

No house plant likes to grow directly above a radiator or other heat source, in a cold draught, or sandwiched between the curtains and the window on a winter's night. Plants placed where they are constantly brushed against will soon turn brown at the edges. Spiny plants placed where they are brushed against will soon bring forth bad language and blood.

TEMPERATURES

There's no need to alter your central heating thermostat to suit your plants; buy instead those that can cope with your way of life. Most plants like to be warmer during the day than they are at night, and most houses fit conveniently into this pattern.

Plants recommended for unheated rooms will grow well in temperatures around 10–15°C (50–60°F), and can sometimes tolerate a chilly 5°C (40°F), but they'll stop growing. Those recommended for centrally heated rooms will be happy in 18–24°C (65–75°F).

LIGHT

That mystical thing called 'good, indirect light' is the kind of brightness encountered a few feet from a window. Here the plants receive plenty of light but not the direct rays of the sun. This is the situation that most of them enjoy.

Those plants that like full sun can be stood right against a window, but take care that they are not scorched by brilliant sunshine at the height of summer. Plants recommended for shade will not grow in a pitch dark corner. If you can't read small print at arm's length in such a spot it's too dark even for shade lovers.

HUMIDITY

It's amazing what a bit of atmospheric moisture can do. House plant owners who are used to their leaves turning brown at the edges can take heart; the problem is often solved if the pot is stood on a tray or saucer of gravel that is kept constantly moist. The water evaporates around the plant and creates an environment that's much more conducive to growth than hot, dry air. Ferns especially will appreciate such treatment.

If you're making a plant group, try standing the pots on a large tray or bowl of moist peat—part plunging them in the stuff. Not only will the humidity be improved, but the compost in the pots will dry out more slowly.

Large, glossy-leaved plants can be sprayed with rainwater from a hand mister. Don't do this to hairy-leaved plants; they'll probably rot.

WATERING

Don't overdo it. Ninety-nine per cent of all household plants are killed by overwatering. Rhododendrons (Christmas azaleas), cyperus and ferns should be kept very moist at all times. All other plants need a good soak when they start to feel dry on the surface. Not before. If the compost feels like a wrung-out flannel it is still moist.

Nearly all pot plants are happy being watered from above. Fill the pot to the brim with water and let it soak into the compost. When water runs out of the base of the pot the plant has had enough (unless it's been allowed to dry out so much that the compost has shrunk from the sides of the pot and is letting the water run straight through).

A plant will recover from wilting if it is dry. If it wilts because it's too wet you can wave it goodbye.

Plants like saintpaulias (African violets) and cyclamen may have such a tight dome of leaves that you can neither get your finger in to feel the compost, nor penetrate the rosette with a watering can or jug. Water these from below by standing them in a shallow container for half an hour and letting them take up what they want. Check for watering by weighing the pot in your hand. You'll soon become as efficient at predicting dryness as are those ladies at church bazaars who can guess the weight of a cake to the nearest ounce.

Check the plants daily in summer; weekly in winter. They'll need much less water during the darker months of the year.

Fig. 74 A hydroculture unit consists of a plastic reservoir fitted with a water depth indicator. The plant grows in a perforated plastic pot of gravelly granules, taking up the water it needs.

If you still fail (and I can't really believe you can be so unlucky), invest in a plant that is growing in a hydroculture unit (Fig. 74). Its roots will delve through a plastic basket of gravelly granules which sits over a water reservoir. All you have to do is keep the reservoir topped up with water. There's even a little indicator to help you out. Don't mistake a compost-filled self-watering pot for a hydroculture unit. Self-watering pots simply draw water through the compost from a reservoir below. They are difficult to manage and I've yet to see one that's full of happy plants.

FEEDING

Give all pot plants a few square meals while they are growing actively. This is usually in spring and summer, but winter-flowering plants can be fed at that time too. Most vigorous plants will appreciate a fortnightly summer feed of diluted liquid pot plant fertilizer; slow-growers can be fed monthly. Flowering pot plants thrive on diluted liquid tomato fertilizer and it's just the thing to coax shy saintpaulias (African violets) into bloom.

POTTING ON

It's surprising how long a pot plant can carry on growing in the same container, but as we're in the business of growing plants well (rather than just keeping them alive) it's a good idea to give them a new pot of compost every year. Spring is the best time to move them—just before growth begins with the warmer weather and improved light.

Pot on into a container that is 5 cm (2 in) larger in diameter than the existing one. Use a loam-based compost such as John Innes No. 2 or one of the proprietary soilless composts. Plastic pots have many holes in the base; clay pots only one, so it's a good idea to lay a few pebbles in the bottom of a clay pot to prevent the hole becoming blocked by a plug of compost.

Water the plant well an hour before potting on. Place some moist compost in the bottom of the new pot (on top of the drainage layer if it is needed) and then tap the plant from its old pot so that the rootball comes out in one piece. Sit it on top of the compost in the new pot and check that the surface of the rootball rests 2·5 cm (1 in) or so below the rim. When potting is completed it should be fractionally below the surface of the new compost, yet there should still be a gap between the surface and the rim to allow for watering.

Fill in compost around the rootball, firming it lightly with your fingers. One rap with the palms of your hands on the sides of the pot will level the compost surface. Now all you need to do is water the plant well. At this stage the job is best done by standing the pot in a bowl of water; the compost can be easily displaced if it is soaked from above.

There are exceptions to all rules. A few house plants do not need repotting every year because they grow very slowly and prefer to be a little 'rootbound'. Large palms such as howeas, aspidistras and sansevieria (mother-in-law's tongue) are three such examples, but as a general rule a plant needs a new pot when its roots are wrapped around the inside of the old one. Knock out the plant to see.

Never use garden soil when repotting plants. It's just not good enough for them.

Hefty pot plants that are already in 30 cm (12 in) containers should not be repotted. Instead they can be topdressed. Scrape away the top 5 cm (2 in) of compost in spring and replace it with fresh.

TAKING CARE

When you're dusting the furniture don't forget the plants. They collect just as much grime, and a leaf that's dirty can't manufacture food very well.

Clean hairy-leaved plants with a dry paintbrush. Glossy leaves can be wiped clean with kitchen roll dipped in tepid rainwater (or with a mixture of rainwater and milk if you insist on giving them a shine). Leafshine products may damage sensitive plants, but the new tissue 'leaf-shine wipes' seem to do a good job without causing any leaf burn.

Pinch out the shoot tips of bushy plants to keep

them that way, and stake any plants that need support. Single canes and string will keep up single stems; moss-covered sticks will keep vine-like plants with aerial roots happy, and small trellis or wire supports will hold up other climbers and scramblers.

Remove any wayward or unwanted shoots at any time of year if you're desperate to be rid of them. From the plant's point of view spring is the best time.

If you're due to go away on holiday, try to enlist the help of a neighbour and leave precise instructions on watering. If this isn't possible, plunge them in seed trays of moist peat in a shady room. They'll stay in reasonable condition for a fortnight like this.

During summer all house plants except ferns will appreciate a summer break outdoors on a sheltered patio. Bring them indoors early in September.

BOTTLE GARDENS

Small plants fond of high humidity can be grown really well in bottle gardens made in sweet jars, cider flagons, carboys and even goldfish bowls.

Clean the bottle thoroughly, then spread 2·5 cm (1 in) of gravel in the base followed by 2·5 cm (1 in) of charcoal, which will prevent the compost from becoming sour. An 8 cm (3 in) layer of peat- or loam-based potting compost will keep the plants happy. Feed all three layers in through a homemade cardboard funnel if the neck of the container is narrow (Fig. 75).

Nurseries and garden centres usually have a good selection of plants for bottle gardens, ready established in tiny pots. I'd recommend Chamaedorea, Dionaea, *Ficus pumila*, *Hedera helix* varieties, Maranta, Peperomia, Pilea and Saxifraga. Don't introduce anything too rampant or slower growers will soon be swamped in a miniature jungle.

Tap the plants from their pots after watering them and plant them in the compost. If the neck of the bottle is narrow, scoop out a hole in the compost with a spoon fastened to a cane. Drop the plant into the hole (tilting the bottle to line it up if necessary) and re-firm the soil with a cotton reel pushed on the other end of the cane. Plant at a sufficient spacing to allow a little growth.

Water the plants in by running water down the inside of the bottle (this will clean the glass too). For best results bottle gardens are best placed where there's good but (you've guessed it) indirect light. That way they won't steam up too much. Leave the top off altogether if you like (I always do), or put it in place after a few days.

Stoppered bottles will need hardly any watering at all; unstoppered bottles should be checked once a month, but it's doubtful that they'll need watering every time.

HANGING POTS AND BASKETS

Trailing plants look particularly good when planted in suspended containers so that their stems can cascade into the air. Plant in soilless compost (rather

a   b   c   d   e

Fig. 75 Bottle gardening (*a*) A layer of gravel and a layer of charcoal are fed into the bottle through a cardboard funnel before the compost layer is inserted. (*b*) A teaspoon fastened firmly to the end of a bamboo cane acts as a hole digger. (*c*) The plant is watered before being knocked from its pot and dropped into the hole. (*d*) A cotton reel pushed on to the other end of the cane is used to firm back the soil. (*e*) Settle the plants in by running water down the inside of the bottle—not too much!

than the heavier soil-based types) and make sure that the pot or basket is securely fastened to the wall or ceiling. Built-in drip trays will prevent damage to furniture.

If you're short of inspiration when it comes to choosing plants try: Asparagus, Chlorophytum, Fuchsia, Hedera, Justica, Nephrolepis, *Philodendron scandens*, Saxifraga, Schlumbergera and Tradescantia.

All plants in suspended pots and baskets tend to dry out more quickly than most pot plants. Check them regularly. They'll also go a bundle on extra humidity—spray them daily with tepid rainwater, but watch the furniture!

PROPAGATION

I've indicated in the A–Z section how each plant can best be increased. You'll find fuller details in Chapter 20 on propagation.

PESTS AND DISEASES

Relatively few pests and diseases attack house plants, but those that do make an amazing impact both on your temper and on the plant's health. I've dealt with them in Chapter 21 on pests and diseases, but for the record these are the beasts and blights most likely to attack:

Pests

Aphids (greenfly), caterpillars, earwigs, leafminers, mealy bug, red spider mite, scale insects, vine weevil, whitefly.

Diseases

Botrytis (grey mould), damping off, mildew, rust, sooty mould, viruses.

Table 9: House Plants

Plant	Common name	Height	Spread	Features	Position
Adiantum capillus-veneris	Maidenhair fern	30 cm	45 cm	Foliage	◐
Aechmea fasciata	Urn plant	45 cm	45 cm	Foliage/flowers	◐
Aphelandra squarrosa	Zebra plant	30 cm	30 cm	Foliage/flowers	◐
Asparagus densiflorus	Asparagus fern	30 cm	45 cm	Foliage	◐ ●
Asparagus setaceus (syn. *A. plumosus*)	Asparagus fern	30 cm	30 cm	Foliage	◐ ●
Aspidistra elatior	Cast iron plant	45 cm	45 cm	Foliage	◐ ●
Asplenium nidus	Bird's nest fern	60 cm	60 cm	Foliage	●
Begonia maculata	Spotted begonia	1·25 m	1 m	Foliage/flowers	◐
Begonia rex	Rex begonia	45 cm	1 m	Foliage	◐
Begonia semperflorens	Bedding begonia	15 cm	15 cm	Flowers	◐ ○
Begonia × tuberhybrida	Tuberous begonia	60 cm	60 cm	Flowers	◐
Beloperone guttata (now *Justicia*)	Shrimp plant	60 cm	60 cm	Flowers	○
Billbergia nutans	Queen's tears	60 cm	60 cm	Flowers	◐
Calceolaria hybrids	Slipper flower	30 cm	30 cm	Flowers	◐
Capsicum annuum	Ornamental pepper	30 cm	15 cm	Fruits	○
Chamaedorea elegans	Parlour palm	60 cm	45 cm	Foliage	◐
Chlorophytum comosum	Spider plant	45 cm	60 cm	Foliage	◐
Chrysanthemum × morifolium (now *Dendranthema*)	Pot chrysanthemum	23 cm	30 cm	Flowers	○
Cissus antarctica	Kangaroo vine	1 m	60 cm	Foliage	◐ ●
Citrus × microcarpa	Calamondin orange	1 m	1 m	Foliage/flowers/fruits	○

Disorders

These are caused by you. They occur as a result of unfavourable growing conditions, so take the necessary remedial action to put matters right. The most common disorders are:

Bud drop Caused by dry air, draughts, dry compost, poor light or movement of the plant during bud formation.

Failure to flower Caused by underfeeding, lack of light, unsuitable temperatures or too large a pot of compost (the plant is busy growing roots).

Leaf fall Caused by dry air, draughts, dryness at the roots or fluctuating temperatures.

Leaf spot Caused by sun scorch, splashed water, too much or too little water.

Leaf yellowing Caused particularly by overwatering and also by draughts, lack of light or nutrients. Remember that old leaves at the bottom of the plant naturally turn yellow before they fall.

Spindly shoots Caused by lack of light.

Stem rot Caused by soggy compost.

Variegation fading Caused by lack of light.

Wilting Caused by overwatering, underwatering, excessively high temperatures, vine weevil attack.

A–Z OF HOUSE PLANTS

I've given the information on house plants in tabular form (Table 9) so that you can quickly spot the conditions your plant requires. Almost always the sight of it in the shop or nursery is what persuades you to buy it, rather than a glowing description. What you do with it when you get it home is what matters, so try to follow the guidelines given for your particular treasure.

Temp.	Season	Compost	Humidity is important	Propagate	Pot on: Frequency in years	Special information
Cool	AYR	Loam	H	Div.	1	Fronds brown if air or compost dry. Cut back dead fronds.
Warm	AYR	Soilless	H	Offsets.	2	'Vase' dies after flowering. Others replace it.
Warm	AYR	Loam	H	Cutt.	1	Cut off faded flowers. Cut back in spring.
Cool/Warm	AYR	Loam/s'less	H	Div.	1	Good in hanging baskets and pots.
Cool/Warm	AYR	Loam Soilless	H	Div.	1	Dry air or compost will cause leaf drop.
Cool	AYR	Loam		Div.	3	Repot only when absolutely pot bound. Don't overwater.
Warm	AYR	Soilless	H	–	1	Dry air, bright sun and draughts cause leaf scorch.
Warm	AYR	Loam	H	Cutt.	1	Cut back hard in spring when spindly.
Warm	AYR	Loam	H	L. cutt.	1	May be short lived and may not grow very large.
Cool/warm	AYR	Loam		Cutt.	1	On sunny windowsill will bloom through winter.
Warm	Summer	Loam	H	Div.	1	Start dry tubers in February. Flowers fall if compost dry.
Cool/Warm	AYR	Loam Soilless	H	Cutt.	1	Cut back hard and repot every spring.
Cool/Warm	Late winter	Soilless	H	Div.	2	Dry atmosphere causes brown leaf tips.
Cool	Spring/summer	Soilless	H	Seed	–	Sow early summer for spring flowering. Discard after blooming.
Cool	Winter	Soilless	H	Seed	–	Sow in spring. Discard after winter fruiting.
Cool/warm	AYR	Loam	H	Seed	2	Good in bottle gardens.
Cool/warm	AYR	Loam		Plantlets	1	Starved or dry plants develop brown leaf tips.
Cool	Any season	Soilless		Cutt.	–	Plant in garden after blooming. Will then grow taller.
Cool	AYR	Loam/S'less		Cutt.	1	Train over a trellis or wire framework.
Cool	AYR	Loam		Seed. Cutt.	1	Flowers in summer; fruits follow.

Plant	Common name	Height	Spread	Features	Position
Codiaeum variegatum	Croton; Joseph's coat	1 m	45 cm	Foliage	◐
Coleus blumei (now *Solenostemon*)	Flame nettle	60 cm	60 cm	Foliage	☼
Cordyline australis	Cabbage tree; ti tree	1 m	60 cm	Foliage	☼
Cordyline indivisa	Mountain cabbage tree	1 m	60 cm	Foliage	☼
Cordyline terminalis vars	Dragon tree; ti tree	1 m	45 cm	Foliage	◐
Cycas revoluta	Sago palm	1 m	1 m	Foliage	◐
Cyclamen hybrids	Cyclamen	30 cm	30 cm	Flowers	☼
Cyperus albostriatus	Cyperus	45 cm	45 cm	Foliage	◐ ☀
Cyperus alternifolius (syn. *C. involucratus*)	Umbrella grass	1·25 m	60 cm	Foliage	◐ ☀
Dieffenbachia 'Amoena'	Dumb cane	1 m+	45 cm	Foliage	◐ ☀
Dieffenbachia seguine vars	Dumb cane	1 m+	45 cm	Foliage	◐ ☼
Dionaea muscipula	Venus fly trap	10 cm	10 cm	Foliage	☼
Dizygotheca elegantissima (now *Schefflera*)	Finger aralia	2 m	60 cm	Foliage	☀
Dracaena species and vars	Dragon tree	1 m	45 cm	Foliage	◐
Erica 'Hyemalis'	Cape heath	30 cm	23 cm	Flowers	☼
Euphorbia pulcherrima	Poinsettia	1 m	1 m	Bracts	◐ ☼
× *Fatshedera lizei*	*Ivy tree*	*2 m*	*1 m*	*Foliage*	◐ ☀
Fatsia japonica	False castor oil palm	1 m	1 m	Foliage	◐ ☀
Ficus benjamina	Weeping fig	2 m	1 m	Foliage	◐
Ficus elastica vars	Rubber plant	3 m+	1 m+	Foliage	◐
Ficus pumila	Creeping fig	5 cm	50 cm	Foliage	☀
Fuchsia hybrids	Fuchsia	60 cm+	60 cm+	Flowers	☼
Hedera helix vars	Ivy	Climber/trailer		Foliage	◐ ☼
Hippeastrum hybrids	Amaryllis	60 cm	30 cm	Flowers	◐ ☼
Howea belmoreana	Kentia palm	2 m	1 m	Foliage	◐ ☀
Howea forsteriana	Kentia palm	2 m	1 m	Foliage	◐ ☀
Hoya carnosa	Wax plant	Climber	—	Foliage/flower	☼
Impatiens hybrids	Busy lizzie; balsam	60 cm	60 cm	Flower	☼
Maranta species	Prayer plant	15 cm	30 cm	Foliage	☀
Monstera deliciosa	Swiss cheese plant	2 m+	2 m+	Foliage	◐ ☀

Temp.	Season	Compost	Humidity is important	Propagate	Pot on: Frequency in years	Special information
Warm	AYR	Loam	H	Cutt.	2	Leaves fall if food, light, warmth or humidity in short supply.
Warm	AYR	Loam Soilless		Cutt.	1	Tatty if poor light in winter. Chop back and repot in spring.
Cool	AYR	Loam		Seed	1	Good outside in summer.
Warm	AYR	Loam		Seed. Air L.	1	Dry air and draughts cause leaf browning. Cut off flower spikes.
Cool/warm	AYR	Loam	H	Seed	2/3	Mealy bug and scale are common pests.
V. Cool	Winter	Loam		Seed. Tuber	1	Must be kept cool. Dry off after flowering. Repot late summer.
Cool/warm	AYR	Loam		Div.	1	Stand in a saucer of water that is always kept topped up.
Cool/warm	AYR	Loam		Div.	1	Stand in a saucer of water that is always kept topped up.
Warm	AYR	Soilless	H	Cutt.	1/2	Chop back when leggy. Pull off yellow leaves.
Warm	AYR	Soilless	H	Cutt.	1/2	Need more light than green-leaved types.
Cool/warm	AYR	Moss/S'less	H	Div.	2/3	Grown in live sphagnum moss under a transparent dome.
Warm	AYR	Soilless	H	Seed	2	Draughts, dry air, wet or dry compost will cause leaf fall.
Warm	AYR	Loam		Seed. Air L.	1	Dry air and draughts cause leaf browning. Cut off flower spikes.
Cool	Winter	Peat	H	Cutt.	1	Cut back and repot after flowering. Stand outside in summer.
Warm	Winter/spring	Loam Soilless		Cutt.	1	Cut back after flowering and repot. Long nights induce bract formation.
Cool	AYR	Loam Soilless		Cutt.	1	Needs a moss-covered stick or frame up which to climb.
Cool	AYR	Loam Soilless		Seed. Cutt.	1	Plant out in the garden when too large for rooms.
Warm	AYR	Loam	H	Cutt.	2	A few leaves yellow and fall when first bought.
Cool/warm	AYR	Loam	H	L. Cutt. Air L.	2/3	Easy to overwater. Tolerant of dryness.
Warm	AYR	Soilless	H	Cutt.	1	Good in bottle gardens and suspended pots.
Cool	Summer	Loam		Cutt.	1	Don't move in flower or buds drop. Cut back and repot in spring.
Cool	AYR	Loam Soilless	H	Cutt.	1	Dry air brings red spider. Shade causes loss of variegation.
Warm	Winter/spring	Loam Soilless		Seed	1	Pot in autumn and water gingerly at first. Dry off after flowering.
Warm	AYR	Loam/S'less	H	Seed	2/3	Leaves brown in dry air or draughts.
Warm	AYR	Loam/S'less	H	Seed	2/3	Leaves not so curly as previous species. Equally sensitive.
Warm	Spring/autumn	Loam	H	Cutt. Layer.	2/3	Needs a support system. Leave on old flower stalks—bloom again.
Cool/Warm	AYR	Loam Soilless		Cutt.	1	Cut back and repot in spring. Plenty of food needed.
Warm	AYR	Soilless	H	Div. Cutt.	2	Good in bottle gardens. Hate soggy compost.
Warm	AYR	Loam Soilless	H	Cutt. Air L.	2	Only leaves of older, well-fed plants are perforated.

Plant	Common name	Height	Spread	Features	Position
Nephrolepis exaltata	Ladder fern	60 cm	60 cm	Foliage	◐ ●
Nephrolepis exaltata 'Bostoniensis'	Boston fern	60 cm	1 m	Foliage	◐ ●
Pelargonium hybrids	Geranium	60 cm	30 cm	Flowers	☼
Peperomia species	Peperomia	15 cm	15 cm	Foliage/flowers	◐ ●
Philodendron scandens	Sweetheart plant	Climber	—	Foliage	◐ ●
Pilea cadierei 'Minima'	Aluminium plant	15 cm	23 cm	Foliage	◐ ●
Platycerium bifurcatum	Stag's horn fern	45 cm	45 cm	Foliage	●
Primula obconica	German primrose	30 cm	30 cm	Flowers	☼
Rhododendron simsii	Azalea	30 cm	45 cm	Flowers	☼
Rhoicissus rhomboidea (now *Cissus*)	Grape ivy	Climber	—	Foliage	● ◑
Saintpaulia ionantha vars	African violet	10 cm	30 cm	Flowers	☼
Sansevieria trifasciata 'Laurentii'	Mother-in-law's tongue	1 m	30 cm	Foliage	☼ ◐ ●
Saxifraga stolonifera vars	Mother-of-thousands	5 cm	Trailing	Foliage	◑ ☼
Schefflera arboricola	Heptapleurum; umbrella tree	2 m+	45 cm+	Foliage	◑
Schlumbergera × buckleyi	Christmas cactus	Trailing	—	Flowers	◑
Senecio cruentus (now *Pericallis × hybrida*)	Cineraria	30 cm	30 cm	Flowers	☼
Sinningia speciosa	Gloxinia	23 cm	30 cm	Flowers	☼
Solanum capsicastrum	Winter cherry	30 cm	30 cm	Fruits	☼
Stephanotis floribunda	Clustered wax flower	1 m	1 m	Flowers	◑
Tradescantia species	Wandering Jew	Trailing	—	Foliage	☼
Yucca aloifolia	Spanish bayonet; ti tree	2 m	60 cm	Foliage	☼
Zebrina pendula (now *Tradescantia zebrina*)	Inch plant	Trailing	—	Foliage	☼

Temp.	Season	Compost	Humidity is important	Propagate	Pot on: Frequency in years	Special information
Warm	AYR	Soilless	H	Div.	1/2	Humidity is vital. Dry air and draughts cause leaf browning.
Warm	AYR	Soilless	H	Div.	1/2	As above. This variety is good in hanging baskets provided it can be kept moist.
Cool	Spring/autumn	Loam Soilless		Cut. Seed	1	Bright light is vital. Leaves yellow in shade. Singles bloom in winter.
Warm	AYR	Loam	H	L. Cutt.	1/2	Good in bottle gardens. Hate soggy compost.
Cool/Warm	AYR	Soilless		Cutt.	1/2	Needs a large support system. Thrives on neglect.
Warm	AYR	Loam	H	Cutt.	1	Good in bottle gardens. Renew regularly from cuttings.
Warm	AYR	Soilless	H	–	1/2	Can grow in a wad of moss wired to a piece of bark.
Cool	AYR	Loam/S'less		Seed. Div.	1	Can cause a rash on sensitive skin.
V. Cool	Winter	Soilless	H	Cutt.	1	Never let the rootball dry out. Water with rainwater.
Cool/Warm	AYR	Loam Soilless		Cutt.	1/2	Provide a large support system. Bomb-proof.
Warm	Spring/autumn	Soilless	H	L. Cutt.	1/2	Dilute tomato fertilizer encourages flowering. Don't overpot.
Cool/warm	AYR	Loam		Div.	3/4	Only overwatering and overpotting kill this plant.
Cool	AYR	Loam	H	Plantlets	1	Good in hanging pots. Dry air turns stems brown.
Warm	AYR	Loam/S'less	H	Seed	2	Variegated kind needs good light.
Cool	Winter	Loam	H.	Cutt.	1/2	Superb in hanging baskets. Stand outside in summer.
V. Cool	Winter/spring	Loam		Seed	—	Easily overwatered. Discard after flowering. Loved by greenfly.
Warm	Summer	Soilless	H	Seed. Tuber	1	Dry off after flowering. Repot tubers in spring.
Cool	Winter	Loam	H	Seed. Cutt.	1	Cut back and repot after fruiting. 1 tsp Epsom salts in 1 pint water prevents leaf yellowing.
Warm	Spring/autumn	Loam Soilless		Cutt.	2	Train over a support system. Watch out for mealy bug.
Cool	AYR	Soilless		Cutt.	1	Replace regularly from cuttings. Feed well.
Cool/warm	AYR	Loam		Cutt.	2	Stand outdoors in summer. Peel off faded leaves.
Cool/warm	AYR	Soilless		Cutt.	1	Replace regularly from cuttings.

19 Wildlife in the garden

A garden without animals and birds, butterflies and bees is as dead as a doornail and as dull as ditchwater. Ever since I was a lad I've been just as interested in the wildlife to be found in a garden as in the plants. Serried ranks of lobelia and alyssum, salvias and French marigolds hold no joy for me, but a bank of billowing summer flowers that's perhaps a bit too overgrown for the neat-and-tidy-minded gardener offers great excitement when it's alive with butterflies and abuzz with bees.

I don't carry my love of nature to extremes though—snails and slugs have to be ruthlessly expelled from the rock garden and the vegetable plot (the places where they seem to do most damage), and I can't stand greenfly on roses. So how is a gardener to live with these conflicting ideas? It's not so difficult as it sounds.

The first rule is one that all lazy gardeners will enjoy putting into practice: don't be too tidy. That's not an excuse for letting all parts of the plot lie fallow for the rest of your life, it's simply a matter of selecting certain areas of the garden that can be left relatively undisturbed and where the right weeds can be encouraged to grow. (There's planning to be done, even in a wilderness.)

BUTTERFLIES AND MOTHS

Most of us admire butterflies, and a few of us like moths as well. Both can be encouraged to make themselves at home in the garden if the right food plants are present. There are two distinct kinds of food plant: those that nourish the larvae or caterpillars, and those from which the adults drink nectar. You'll need patches of both so that you have vital egg-laying sites for the propagation of the species, and insect pubs where the adults can drink their fill from spring to autumn.

In a large garden it's easy to let a sunny and sheltered corner run wild with nettles, thistles, grasses and other food-supplying weeds for egglaying; in a small garden it's more difficult to squeeze them in, but a patch of nettles alone (always in a sunny spot) will bring you a surprisingly rich harvest.

The following butterflies have all been seen in my Hampshire garden during our first summer here. Those starred were also spotted in our minute garden at Sunningdale which was at the back of a tiny terraced cottage. Against each butterfly is shown the plant on which the eggs are laid and the caterpillars feed.

* Small tortoiseshell – nettle
  Red admiral – nettle; occasionally thistle
* Small white – cabbages (unfortunately!) and their relations
* Large white – as small white; plus nasturtium (more bad news!)
* Brimstone – buckthorn (*Rhamnus*)
* Peacock – nettle
* Orange tip – lady's smock, hedge mustard
* Painted lady – nettle, thistle
  Small skipper – grasses
  Speckled wood – couch grass (the only good thing about couch)
  Meadow brown – annual meadow grass (joy again) and others
* Gatekeeper – as meadow brown
  Green-veined white – members of cabbage family
  Common blue – clover, trefoil and vetch
  Ringlet – grasses
* Comma – nettle, willow, hop and others
  Wall brown -- grasses

The moths have an equally varied diet from privet to various weeds, cabbages and lettuces. Most of them are nocturnal but they are often disturbed during the day if you brush past their resting sites among plants. In our garden we are plagued with large yellow underwings, but the occasional maiden's blush, magpie moth and hawk moth come to light too.

To watch adult butterflies feeding by day you'll be pleased to hear that there are plenty of ornamental garden plants whose nectar they love. Your entire plot does not have to be converted to (or allowed to remain) a flowerless jungle. Plants with purple or yellow flowers are apparently the favourites, but in my own garden these are the ones that have been as well patronized as any real-ale pub by the butterfly population:

Buddleia, sedum, liatris, phuopsis, lavatera, eryngium, agrostemma, caryopteris, Michaelmas daisy, alyssum, aubrieta, hebe, centranthus, nepeta, phlox, scabious, echinops, honesty, lavender, thyme, nicotiana, ageratum, petunia (single). Single flowers are always better than doubles for they have large nectaries.

Finally, remember that a little shelter in the garden—in the form of a thick coat of ivy on a garage or outbuilding, or a thicket of brambles in a corner—will allow hibernating butterflies and moths to shelter through the winter and carry on their good work the following season.

BEES

If you wave your arms around and do an impersonation of a windmill every time a bee comes near you the last thing you'll want to do is attract them to your garden. But if you like all forms of wildlife, then the following plants will persuade the bees that your garden really is the place to visit:
Lupins, nepeta, lavender, scabious, monarda, lavatera, eryngium, erica, fuchsia, echinops, lime trees, buddleia, borage, godetia, nigella, phacelia, nasturtium and many, many more (see also the list at the end of Chapter 8).

BIRDS

Faded seedheads on all manner of plants from thistles to sunflowers and Michaelmas daisies will keep seed-eating birds such as goldfinches busy for hours, and berrying shrubs like berberis, pyracantha and symphoricarpos will feed other species in winter. That's the time at which you should be making a special effort to supplement the diet of all wild birds (Fig. 76). Outside my study and our sitting-room windows wire netting bird feeders hang from November to March, filled with bits of fat and peanuts. After years of squirrels destroying flimsy models, I now have sturdy, squirrel-proof ones. The feeder is filled every morning and by evening it's almost empty, proving that the birds have a powerful hunger. The bird bath is patronized too (and kept thawed in winter) and mixed wild bird food is scattered on the lawn for those species that have no head for heights (though they seem happy enough when flying). The centre of the lawn is the place for bird food; scatter it near beds and borders and cats will stealthily sneak through the undergrowth to wreak havoc.

Coconuts we never bother with (they seem to dry up before the birds can really get stuck in) and pieces of bacon rind are ignored too—it's the softer fat or suet that goes down best. Coal tits, blue tits, great tits, nuthatches and greenfinches are regularly in evidence, and a great spotted woodpecker sometimes turns up too. So far, after 11 years of living here, 47 species of bird have appeared at one time or another.

Stop feeding the birds as soon as spring arrives—if their young are fed a diet of peanuts they'll suffer. By egg-hatching time you should be encouraging the adults to help you out with pest-control in the garden—there will be plenty of caterpillars and grubs to devour.

Some birds are irritating pests at certain times of year. Sparrows and bullfinches will strip fruit trees of their buds, often as soon as the leaves fall in autumn. Netting is really the only successful long-term deterrent. Blackbirds will adore your raspberries, but mostly the depredations can be lived with, and both

Fig. 76 A selection of the various types of bird feeders on the market that will attract tits, nuthatches, greenfinches and other birds fond of winter snacks of suet, fat and peanuts.

you and the birds will have a substantial diet.

It's always fun to put up nestboxes (Fig. 77). But do the job properly. Tits need a box with a hole just 3 cm (1⅛ in) in diameter; make it any larger and sparrows will take over. Robins and spotted flycatchers need open-fronted boxes, and there are all manner of different permutations that can be made at home or bought from specialist firms. They're well made from tough plywood and highly successful in persuading birds to nest.

The secret is to find the right place for the box. I'm no expert here, but have put all my boxes at a height of around 2 m (7 ft)—out of the way of our marauding cat. I've yet to try them in woodland, but they've lured blue tits with ease on walls facing east and south. Put your boxes up in autumn. That gives the birds a chance to do plenty of prospecting right

Fig. 77 Bird boxes fitted with 3 cm (1⅛ in) holes (a) will attract blue tits more often than not. Open-fronted boxes (b) suit robins and spotted flycatchers.

through the winter. Sometimes they'll roost in the boxes rather than nesting in them; other years they'll ignore them completely. As well as being skilful in placing your boxes, you'll also have to rely on luck.

Don't forget that birds like the cover and nesting sites provided by shrubs, hedges and brambles. Provide these hiding places and you're bound to get more birds.

WILD ANIMALS

I've no room to launch into a comprehensive natural history of the back garden, but I will remind you of the joys to be had from hedgehogs (who slurp saucers of milk more quickly and noisily than a cat), and the mixed feelings you'll have about foxes, rabbits and deer.

There's nothing so romantic as the sight of a few deer at the top of our garden in summer or winter, but I go up the hill with a sinking feeling whenever they've been, wondering what they've eaten this time. Once they've ring-barked a pine tree or another favourite it's curtains (for the tree, not the deer). Plastic rabbit guards are a bit of a help, but not much.

A garden pool is less of a worry and more of a magnet for all sorts of creatures from frogs and toads (valuable slug eaters) to dragonflies and damsel flies. You might be lucky enough to have newts, and you'll certainly have pond skaters whose acrobatics defy the laws of gravity. With frog spawning sites disappearing every year, the back garden pond is playing a vital role in their continued wellbeing. There are further details in Chapter 12 on water gardening.

WILD FLOWERS

Finally, don't forget the wild flowers. Only where there's space to spare for such luxuries will you want to make a patch of natural 'wild garden' or grassland where the rarer wild flowers can feel safe. But such a patch dovetails into other forms of wildlife encouragement because butterflies, moths, bees and other insects will relish the opportunity to feed in these mini-reserves. To keep the patch as grassland you'll still have to mow, but only three times a year—in early to mid-July, late August and finally October.

There's just one problem with this type of gardening, and that's the use, or non-use, of chemicals. It's a thorny old problem and I don't want to preach about the wonders of organic gardening, but if you're out to create a reserve that will replace the natural habitats decimated by modern farming methods and pesticides you'll have to take extra care. If your plants need feeding, try to use organic fertilizers such as blood, bone and fishmeal that will encourage bacterial activity (inorganic fertilizers like sulphate of ammonia and superphosphate supply nutrients in a readily accepted form as far as plants are concerned, but they give the bacteria—vital to soil wellbeing—nothing to break down). Avoid using herbicides altogether (except on paths and drives) and learn to live with a weedy lawn—I have! When really severe outbreaks of pests appear most gardeners feel that they have to take action with a chemical. If this is necessary, do the job in the evening when there are few butterflies and bees around. Choose a still, windless day and a chemical that is known to be fairly specific. There is one chemical at least that will kill aphids (greenfly and blackfly) while leaving beneficial insects such as bees, ladybirds and lacewings unharmed. Any chemical that has these advantages is to be preferred to a lethal insecticidal potion that kills everything and anything, or to a supposedly harmless concoction made from rhubarb leaves which is equally toxic to other forms of insect life. The choice is yours.

20 Propagation

Most of us are compelled to propagate plants simply to save money, but the compulsion soon becomes an addiction when we find out how easy it is, and how satisfying, to raise a large number of plants with little effort and expense. Putting aside the failures, that is. After centuries of gardening there are still a few plants that readily defy attempts at propagation, or which are extremely difficult to multiply in large numbers. This accounts for the relatively high price of certain trees and shrubs. Fortunately, most of the plant kingdom is more obliging and, provided the right conditions are created, most trees, shrubs, flowers and vegetables will increase happily.

There are two basic methods of increase: sexual reproduction (by seeds) and asexual reproduction (by vegetative means such as cuttings and divisions). Seed is a cheap and easy method for many plants (especially vegetables) and is the only way of increasing many annuals (plants that live for just one year before setting seed and dying). Seed-raised plants are almost always vigorous and disease free.

Vegetative means of propagation must be used where no seed is set, or where such seed will not produce offspring identical to the parent (which is the case with many plant varieties and hybrids). Always take special care to ensure that plants from which cuttings are taken are healthy and disease free or the problems will be inherited by the offspring.

SEEDS

Rather like the lady who thought that beans only came out of tins, some folk seem to think that seeds only come out of packets. Don't forget that good seed can often be collected from many plants in the garden. Collected when fully ripe (the pods or capsules usually split at this stage so you'll have to beat them to it) and stored in a cool, dry place the seeds will often germinate well the following spring. Keep them in the fridge in an airtight container with a sachet of silica gel to absorb any moisture.

If you're buying seeds always go to a reputable seedsman. There are plenty of them about so it's not difficult. Nowadays all firms are bound by law to test their seeds and guarantee a high viability rate (percentage of germination). If the seeds don't come up when they've been bought from a reputable supplier the chances are that either you've stored them in too warm a place or you've not given them the conditions

they need. Don't rush to blame the seedsman before you check your own treatment.

F_1 hybrid seeds are becoming more popular year by year. The first thing you'll notice about them is their price—they cost a bomb! The reason for this is that the seeds have been specially produced by crossing two selected plants which are known to produce a seed that yields vigorous and uniform offspring with certain desirable qualities—massive flowers or (in the case of a vegetable) whopping roots or leaves.

For the home gardener F_1 hybrid flowers are almost always a good buy. F_1 vegetables may not be. They tend to come to maturity with amazing uniformity, providing you with a glut which might be embarrassing unless you have a freezer!

Don't save seeds from plants which are F_1 hybrids—all the characteristics they possess will be distributed unevenly in their offspring and you'll have a varied and probably inferior group of plants on your hands.

Pelleted seeds are simply ordinary seeds encased in a coating of clay (sometimes with a fungicide added to aid germination). They make space sowing easy (so cutting out the need for thinning) but they are pricey and if the soil dries out in the slightest they may fail to germinate. I never use them, preferring to pay less for a greater number of plain seeds which are not so finicky.

Germination requirements

All seeds need air, moisture and a suitable temperature to trigger off germination. Some also need light (primulas for instance) and should be sown on the compost surface rather than being given the usual burial. Many seeds need exposure to cold before they will germinate (a lot of hardy plants fall into this category) so autumn sowing is practised and the seeds are left in a cold frame during winter.

Some seeds have such tough coats that they have to be chipped a little to allow water to be absorbed (sweet peas are sometimes reluctant to come up unless you 'nick' them, but I've never found them to be difficult provided the compost is kept sufficiently moist).

Berries are usually 'stratified' before being sown to yield plants. Spread them in alternate layers with sharp sand in a flowerpot during autumn and stand the container outdoors to be frosted all winter. Turn it out into a frame in spring, sift a little compost over the mixture and wait for germination. Some tricky blighters take several years to come up.

'How deep do I sow?' is a regular question. The answer is almost always 'to one-and-a-half times the diameter of the seed'. Dust-fine seeds need no covering at all; large seeds such as beans and nasturtiums can actually be pushed down into the soil with your fingers. Always sow in moist soil but never in cold, soggy earth where the seeds will rot. Seeds sown late in warm soil will always overtake those put in earlier during unfavourable conditions.

Sowing in drills

Most vegetables are sown in straight lines in little 'V'-shaped channels known as drills. The best way to create such drills is to fasten a taut garden line across the soil (resting on the surface) and to draw the soil away from the edge of it using a Dutch or draw hoe. Stand on the line to keep it firm (Fig. 78a). Sow the seeds thinly in the drill—by thinly I mean at least 0·5 cm (¼ in) apart—and then carefully return the soil to the drill with a rake. Label the row with the name and variety of the crop as well as the date of sowing.

Fig. 78 (*a*) Drills for vegetable seeds can be taken out with a Dutch hoe or a draw hoe. Stand on the line to keep it firm while you pull away the soil. (*b*) Seed sowing in tray.

Sowing broadcast

In the flower border hardy annual flower seeds can be sown broadcast in irregular-shaped areas known as drifts. Rake the soil so that tiny furrows are left by the rake and then scatter the seeds over the surface before raking once more in the opposite direction to cover them up.

Don't underestimate the value of thinning out seedlings—do it as soon as possible to give the chosen plants enough light and air to develop.

Sowing under glass

Under any kind of cover, be it greenhouse, frame or windowsill, seeds must be sown in pots of seed compost, not garden soil. However good your soil it will not be open or well drained enough for plants in pots. Any proprietary seed compost can be used and it should be lightly firmed within the container before sowing so that it rests about 1 cm (½ in) below the rim to allow for a covering of compost and subsequent watering. Make sure the compost is moist before you sow.

Now read the seed packet. Can you provide the right temperature for germination? The majority of plants you sow under protection will need a temperature of around 18–21°C (65–70°F), though one or two may need a little more heat.

Take the seeds out of the packet and place them in the palm of one hand. Tap the edge of this hand with the other so that the seeds are dislodged a few centimetres (inches) above the compost (Fig. 78b). They will fall and bounce on the surface, so becoming more evenly distributed. Don't sow too thickly. When you think you've sown enough seeds, return the rest to the packet and lightly sieve compost over those you have sown. Use a 0·3 mm (⅛ in) sieve and stop sieving as soon as the seeds disappear from view. Very fine seeds (like lobelia, gloxinia, begonia, petunia and calceolaria) need not be covered at all, except with a sheet of paper followed by a sheet of glass (which is a covering recommended for all seeds). The glass helps to keep the compost moist and the paper cuts down the sun's glare (and mops up condensation if it is put over the pots first).

Label the containers (with variety and date) and stand them in a warm place—ideally a propagator (Fig. 79). These mini-greenhouses can be obtained in all shapes and sizes and at reasonable cost. If you're going in for a bit of propagating you'll find that the kind that utilizes a plastic seed tray with a transparent dome and a heated baseplate will suit you nicely without breaking the bank. Alternatively you can always stick to the airing cupboard if you don't mind compost-covered washing.

Check the pots every day and as soon as the first seedling in each container breaks the surface, remove the pot and stand it in a warm, well-lit place. Should the compost dry out, water it with a watering can

Fig. 79 The cheapest propagator consists of a seed tray covered with a transparent dome which is fitted with small vents (*a*). An electrically heated panel can be positioned beneath the tray to provide 'bottom heat'.

More elaborate structures can be made at home and fitted with thermostatically controlled soil warming cables (*b*). A polythene shroud maintains humidity.

fitted with a fine rose.

Seeds of hardy plants can be sown in pots of compost which are then stood outdoors in a garden frame. Spring is the usual time to sow, though many seeds are often best sown as soon as they are ripe—in summer or autumn. A cold winter may be just what they need to spur them into growth.

Pricking out

As soon as the seedlings are large enough to handle they should be transplanted into seed trays where they will have more room to develop (Fig. 80). Lever them from the compost in the pot with a pencil or small dibber (keeping as much compost around their roots as possible). Hold each seedling by one of its seed leaves (not its fragile stem) and lower its roots into a hole made in the compost with the point of the pencil. Firm the compost around the roots so that the seedling stands upright. Space the seedlings about 5 cm (2 in) apart on the square. Water them in when the tray is fully planted up. Grow the seedlings on until they are ready to be hardened off for planting out or potted up into individual containers. Pot plants such as geraniums (pelargoniums) can be pricked out straight into 8 cm (3 in) pots to save time.

DIVISION

This is one of the easiest means of propagating plants. Simple division (best carried out in autumn or spring where hardy border plants are concerned) involves the digging up and prising apart of established clumps. It sounds cruel but it does most plants the world of good. When you've dug up the clump, chop it into coconut-sized pieces with a spade, discarding the dead central portion (most perennials spread outwards and the old centre gradually dies). Make sure you replant the new plants at the same level as before.

Water them well in times of drought. Autumn dividing pays dividends on any well-drained soil for the plants are ready to grow away eagerly, come the spring, outstripping spring-divided plants by leaps and bounds. On clay soils, though, they may sit and sulk through the winter.

Irises and other plants which make rhizomes (fat stems at or just below ground level) can also be divided. Irises are best split after flowering and fat, healthy rhizomes can be cut into individual portions, each bearing a fan of leaves. Replant these (shortening the leaves by half) so that the rhizomes sit just beneath the new soil surface.

Fig. 80 Pricking out. Lever seedlings from the compost in which they are growing, holding each one by a seed leaf. Lower it into a pencil-hole made in the new compost and firm it in. Water carefully but well.

It is always a good idea to clean up and enrich the soil before replanting your divisions (and it's a good idea to replant in a different spot, too).

Plants which produce suckers (shoots from the roots) can be propagated by severing the new shoot in autumn or spring, with a few roots, and replanting it where it is wanted. Plants grafted on to a different rootstock will, of course, produce suckers inferior to themselves and these should be removed and discarded.

Tubers (which have been mentioned in Chapter 10 on bulbs) can also be divided, provided that each division has a portion of tuber plus a bud.

Any kind of plantlet (be it a strawberry runner or an offset of a sempervivum) makes propagation easy. The youngster can simply be detached and encouraged to make roots of its own in a pot of compost or a bed of soil before being planted out independently. Alternatively it can be encouraged to form roots while still attached to its parent and then removed and transplanted afterwards.

CUTTINGS

There are three basic types of cutting: stem, root and leaf. All three are removed from the plant and then encouraged to form either roots or shoots, whichever is lacking.

Stem cuttings

These fall into three categories, depending on the time of year at which they are taken and the consequent hardness of the wood.

Softwood cuttings These are taken in spring and early summer and consist of healthy, vigorous shoot tips that are soft and pliable. The finished cutting should be 5–8 cm (2–3 in) long with two or three leaves at the top. The lower leaves should have been removed and the basal cut made just below a leaf joint or 'node'. Insert the cuttings to half their depth in a propagator filled with a half and half peat/sand mix, or around the edge of 10 cm (4 in) pots of the same medium. 'Bottom heat' is helpful in rooting the cuttings quickly. This can be applied via a heated base plate below the propagator or with special soil-warming cables. Some cuttings (such as impatiens) can even be rooted in jars of water stood on a windowsill. Only tricky cuttings need have their bases lightly dipped in hormone rooting powder before insertion.

Keep the cuttings shaded from brilliant sunshine (but not in the dark) while they root. Humidity is vital in preventing dehydration, hence the desirability of an enclosed propagator or a polythene bag over the pot. Most softwood cuttings root readily in a temperature of around 18°C (65°F). Growth of the shoots is a good indication of rooting and at this stage the plants should be knocked out of their containers and potted up individually. Keep them out of bright

sunlight for a few days until their roots are established in the new potting compost.

Half-ripe cuttings During July and August the shoots of many plants (especially shrubs) begin to harden. At this stage (but while they are still relatively pliable) they are said to be half-ripe or semi-ripe. Cuttings taken at this time should be about 10 cm (4 in) long and prepared and inserted as for softwood cuttings. Half-ripe cuttings of hardy shrubs may also be inserted in a well-drained medium within a cold frame outdoors. Here they can stay until the following spring when they can be removed and potted up or planted out. Those rooted in a propagator can be potted up and overwintered in a garden frame before being planted out the following year.

Some half-ripe cuttings are found to root better if

Fig. 81 Hardwood cuttings of plants such as roses and gooseberries should be taken in autumn. Make them 20 cm (8 in) long and trim them above a bud at the top and below a bud at the base. Insert them to two thirds their depth in narrow trenches into which sand has been trickled and firm back the soil.

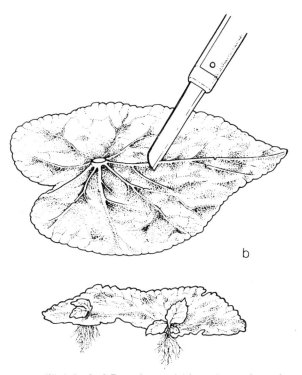

Fig. 82 (a) Single leaves of African violets (saintpaulias) taken with a stalk, can easily be rooted in pots containing a mixture of peat and sand. Keep them warm. (b) A leaf of *Begonia rex*, laid on the surface of moist compost and slit at the main veins, may produce a young plant at each of the slits.

removed from the parent plant with a 'heel' of older wood. Tear them from the main stem and trim the heel to a length of 1 cm (½ in) before insertion. Many conifers root better with a heel.

Hardwood cuttings These need no protection at all and they provide an easy means of increasing many deciduous shrubs including roses. Hardwood cuttings are taken just as the leaves fall in autumn. Young, healthy shoots of pencil thickness should be selected. Trim them above a bud at the top and below a bud at the base so that they are about 20 cm (8 in) long. Roses can be left with two leaves at the top, should these still be present.

Insert the cuttings to two-thirds their depth in narrow slit trenches (Fig. 81) into which a little coarse sand has been trickled. (The vegetable plot may be the most convenient spot for them.) Firm back the earth with your feet. The cuttings should root and grow during the following spring and summer and may be lifted and transplanted the following autumn.

Leaf cuttings

Some plants can be propagated from leaves without any vestige of stem at all. Those of African violets (saintpaulias) and others are removed from the plant (with their leaf stalks intact) and dibbed into sand and peat (Fig. 82a) in a propagator. I've even rooted them in jars of water with the leaf blade supported over the water; the stalk is pushed through a piece of transparent cling-film fastened over the top of the jar.

Leaves of *Begonia rex* can be cut up into postage-stamp-sized pieces and inserted into the rooting medium like gravestones (provided they are the right way up) where they will root and send up youngsters from their bases. The entire leaf of the plant may be laid on the surface of the compost, slit at the main veins and kept moist (Fig. 82b). Plantlets will arise at the cuts with any luck.

Leaf bud cuttings include a small portion of stem and a bud (Fig. 82c). Camellias, ficus (rubber plant) and even clematis can be propagated from them. Early summer is generally the best time for this type of propagation.

Root cuttings

These are best taken during the plant's dormant season. Lift the plant to be propagated, wash its roots free of soil and then cut suitable roots (between knitting needle and pencil thickness) into 5 cm (2 in) long sections (Fig. 83). To make sure that the roots are the right way up, make a flat cut at the top (the end which was nearer the parent) and a slanting cut at the base. Insert the cuttings in pots of seed compost, planting them vertically with the aid of a dibber. The top of the cutting should be level with the surface of the compost. Scatter a little sharp sand over the

Fig. 83 Some plants can be propagated from sections of root which are removed and inserted in pots of compost. Keep them the right way up.

surface, label the pot and stand it in a garden frame (or propagator if the plant is tender). If the compost is moist and the pot is kept lightly shaded, no water should be given until more roots are produced, probably after the shoots appear in early spring.

Not all plants are capable of being propagated by root cuttings; I have indicated in the A–Z sections those which are.

LAYERING

Ordinary stems of garden plants can sometimes be encouraged to form roots if they are bent down and partly buried in the soil. The operation is usually carried out in early spring.

Find a conveniently long and supple stem which can be bent down to the ground. Trim off any leaves that occur between 15 and 38 cm (6 and 15 in) below the shoot tip so that a healthy cluster is left at the end of the shoot with a bare length of stem behind (Fig. 84). Bend the stem to the soil and make a slight wound in the bark at the point of contact—slit the stem with a knife to make a 'tongue'. Work peat and sand into the soil immediately below the cut and then scoop out a 5–8 cm (2–3 in) hole and lay the cut portion in position. Pin it down with a piece of wire if necessary. Replace the soil and do not let it dry out.

Cut the new plant from its parent in the autumn and leave it for a few weeks before attempting to lift and transplant it. Alternatively wait until spring.

Tip layering can be carried out with plants such as the blackberry. Here the shoot is bent down to the ground and the top 10 cm (4 in) is completely buried. Once a new plant arises it can be transplanted.

Many tall house plants (and shrubs) can be air layered. At a suitable point in the stem—usually about 45 cm (18 in) from the shoot tip and a few

Fig. 84 Plants with suitably low-growing stems can often be propagated by layering. Make an incision in the shoot then bend it down and bury it in the soil, holding

it firm with a peg. Sever the stem and detach the new plant when it is well rooted.

Fig. 85 (*Left*) Rubber plants that have outgrown their welcome (*A*) can be reduced in size by air layering. Make an upward cut in the stem (*B*) and fill it with moist sphagnum moss from a florist (*C*). Wrap the area with polythene (*D*) and tie or tape the covering firmly at the bottom (*E*). Fill the rest of the polythene with more moist moss and seal the top (*F*). Keep the moss moist. When roots are established the top part of the plant can be removed and potted up.

Fig. 86 Bulbils that form up the stems of certain lilies can be removed and grown on to flowering-sized bulbs. All you need is patience.

centimetres below a healthy leaf—an upward incision is made (as for ordinary or simple layering). Sphagnum moss (available from florists) is moistened and pushed into the incision then padded around it (Fig. 85). Polythene is bandaged around the moss and fastened top and bottom with sticky tape. Keep the moss moist and be patient. Roots are likely to be slow in coming (though the higher the temperature the more quickly they will emerge). In most cases you may have to wait a year before the top half of the plant can be severed from the bottom and potted up on its own. Cherish it for a few months until it becomes established. The bottom part should grow away and become pleasingly bushy.

Plants such as heathers can be propagated by 'dropping'. Dig them up in spring, plant them again more deeply so that only the shoot tips can be seen. In autumn dig up the plants and cut off the shoot tips, which will have formed roots. Replant your new heathers in peat-enriched soil.

BULBS AND CORMS

Most bulbs and corms reproduce themselves naturally, though their rates of multiplication vary. I have no room here to delve deeply into the technicalities of 'scooping' and 'scoring' bulbs which some aficionados may consider. It's a painfully slow job for use on bulbs which are otherwise hard to propagate in large numbers.

Where most gardeners can cash in is by growing on the smaller bulblets or cormlets produced around the base of larger flowering bulbs. A piece of good soil in full sun should be selected and, at the appropriate planting time, the babies should be set in the soil to twice their depth and allowed to grow on for another

year or more until they reach flowering size.

Bulbils (the tiny bulbs produced in the stems of some lilies and one or two other bulbs) can be similarly grown on in pots of sandy compost placed in a garden frame (Fig. 86). Remove the bulbils from the plants as soon as they are ripe (they are usually black and plump) and press them into the surface of the pot of prepared compost, sifting a little sharp sand over them. Stand them in a garden frame for about a year and then transfer them to their flowering positions in the garden where they may need to grow on for at least another year. It's a job for the patient, but a rewarding one. If your plants don't produce bulbils you may be able to induce them to do so artificially by nipping the flower buds from the stem before they open. Are you prepared to make the sacrifice?

For more detailed information on propagation than I am able to include here, see *The Complete Book of Plant Propagation* by Robert Wright and Alan Titchmarsh, Ward Lock, 1981.

21 Pests, diseases and disorders

The last thing I want to do is turn you into a hypochondriac, but sooner or later your plants will be attacked by a beast or blight and it's as well to know just how you can nurse them back to health.

There are two schools of chemical thought on pests and diseases: one is that you spray immediately at the first sign of attack; the other is that you spray as a preventive measure before the pest or disease has a chance to raise its ugly thorax. As I said in the Preface to this book, I no longer use sprays, dusts and other chemical applications, preferring instead to find biological means of control.

Surprisingly, my garden has not become a haven for pests and diseases because all the plants are mixed up and an epidemic cannot find sufficient concentration of any one thing to sustain it. I am a gardener who enjoys seeing the mullein moth eating my verbascums and Solomon's seal sawfly munching my polygonatums. But I'm an oddity and you may not feel the same way about pests and diseases.

For those of you who *do* wish to use sprays, then the charts that follow will at least guide you in the right direction.

Where really severe problems occur, and there are plenty of them, you should know exactly what is available to effect a control and when to take steps. That's where the charts come in. They shouldn't encourage you to be forever rushing out with a sprayer—let's face it, you'll seldom have more than a handful of pest and disease problems at any one time—but they should help you to identify the problem and take the appropriate action.

Bear in mind at all times that healthy, well-grown plants are more resistant to attacks than feeble weaklings, and some varieties have been bred for their resistance to particular diseases—these are always worth buying. Try to use specific chemicals where possible; there's now a specific aphicide that kills greenfly yet leaves bees, ladybirds and beneficial lacewings unharmed. I've shown it in the chart.

Always buy plants from a reputable supplier, and with fruit bushes, try to buy stock that is certified disease free. Viruses are crippling, crop-reducing diseases that are transmitted by aphids and you'd do well to make sure that the bushes you buy at the outset are not infected with them. There's no cure once the plants are under attack.

Crop rotation is something that farmers have practised for ages, and it follows that even in the garden it's risky to grow one type of plant in the same spot year after year, except where trees and shrubs are concerned.

Some plant problems are caused neither by pests (mainly insects) nor by diseases (fungi, bacteria and viruses). They are caused by you, or by the faulty growing conditions you have provided for the plant. They are known as disorders and can usually be put right if your cultivation techniques are adjusted.

SAFETY

Table 10 should help you over the major hurdle of finding the right spray for the job. When you've found it, apply it safely, whether it's a dust, a spray, an aerosol, a fumigant or granules that are scattered on the soil.

Store all chemicals in carefully labelled containers out of the reach of pets and children, and dispose of any surplus mixture down the lavatory. Wear rubber gloves when mixing up the solution or scattering granules, and wash your hands and the sprayer thoroughly afterwards. It seems a bit of a bind but it's only sensible; something that kills an insect is likely to give you stomach ache. Spray any product on a still evening, rather than during the day when bees are active, and do not spray open flowers if you can avoid it. Keep children and pets indoors.

Use hand sprayers that you can keep especially for insecticides and fungicides, and always allow the recommended interval between spraying and harvesting. However safe a product may be, always wash fruits and vegetables before eating them.

Follow the instructions on the container to the letter. NEVER add more solution than is recommended.

It's all a bit terrifying, but rest assured that much research work has been carried out on chemicals, and you're more likely to do damage to wildlife if you start spraying with home-made concoctions of nettle leaves, rhubarb leaves and age-old quassia chips than with many of the new and more specific chemical preparations. Now and again we have legitimate safety scares with chemicals, but by and large most of them are reliable and safe if used wisely. It's easy to rant and rail at the chemists for poisoning our atmosphere, but chemicals keep many folk alive who would otherwise have perished.

Table 10: Pest, diseases and disorders

VEGETABLES

Pest	Crops Attacked	Damage/Symptoms	Control
Aphid (greenfly, blackfly)	Wide range	Small insects suck sap, weaken plant, transmit viruses, secrete honeydew.	Spray with specific aphicide: Rapid Greenfly Killer.
Birds (sparrows, pigeons)	Wide range	Leaves, pods and flowers torn.	**Netting is only reliable long-term control.**
Cabbage root fly	Brassicas	Leaves wilt and turn blue; roots eaten away by white maggots.	**Place black felt 'collars' around plants to prevent egg laying.**
Cabbage whitefly	Brassicas	Small, white, 'V'-shaped flies suck sap and soil leaves.	Spray with Picket or Bio Flydown.
Carrot fly	Carrot, parsnip	Leaves turn reddish and wilt; roots tunnelled by grubs.	Avoid by not thinning. Protect with horticultural fleece.
Caterpillar	Wide range, especially brassicas	Leaves eaten; caterpillars or green droppings visible.	Pick off small infestations. Spray with ICI Picket; Bio Flydown.
Celery fly	Celery	Leaves tunnelled and blistered by maggots	**Spray with Malathion.**
Eelworm	Onion	Leaves distorted and bloated; bulbs soft and deformed.	Destroy crops. Prevent by rotation. Keep onions, beans, parsnips and carrots off site for three years.
Eelworm (root-knot)	Tomato	Lower leaves yellow and wilting; galls on roots.	Destroy plants. Replace border soil or grow in containers.
Flea beetle	Radishes and other seedlings	Tiny spots and holes in leaves.	Dust with derris at first sign of attack.
Frit fly	Sweet corn	Young plants twisted and distorted; leaves ragged.	Prevent by sowing seeds in greenhouse (not outdoors). Dust with Murphy Gamma-BHC Dust.
Gall weevil	Brassicas, swedes and turnips	Roots swollen and pierced by maggots; plants stunted.	Dust soil around young plants with Sybol Dust.
Leek moth	Onion, leek	Leaves tunnelled.	**Spray with pbi Fenitrothion.**
Mealy cabbage aphid	Brassicas	Leaves turn yellow; grey-coloured insects on undersides.	**Spray with pbi Fenitrothion.**
Onion fly	Onion	Leaves wilt and turn yellowish; grubs eating roots.	Prevent by crop rotation. Drench with spray-strength Sybol.
Pea and bean weevil	Pea, broad bean	Leaf edges scalloped by chewing action of small, brown weevils.	**Tolerate if mild. Spray severe attacks with pbi Fenitrothion.**
Pea moth	Pea	Peas within pod found to be maggoty.	**Prevent by spraying with pbi Fenitrothion one week after flowers have opened. Spray in evening.**
Pea thrips	Pea	Pods blotched and spotted silvery grey.	Spray with pbi Fenitrothion.
Potato cyst eelworm	Potato	Plants stunted; lower leaves brown and shrivelled; tiny nodules but few few potatoes on roots.	Grow resistant varieties. Do not replant infected soil with spuds for eight years.
Red spider mites	French and runner beans	Leaves greyish or yellow; fine webs and tiny mites observed.	Spray with derris, Murphy Liquid Malathion, Murphy Systemic Action Insecticide.
Root aphid	Lettuce	Stunted, wilting, yellow leaves; insects on roots.	Grow resistant varieties. Drench with spray-strength Malathion.
Slugs and snails	Wide range	Leaves and stems eaten; silvery trails visible.	Sink yogurt carton into soil and fill up with beer to trap. Surround susceptible plants with sharp grit.
Tomato moth	Tomato	Leaves and fruits eaten by fat caterpillars.	**Prevent by weeding. Hand pick if few, or spray pbi Fenitrothion.**
Wireworm	Potato	Narrow tunnels made in tubers.	Harvest tubers quickly. Rake in Murphy's Gamma-BHC Dust.

Disease	Crops Attacked	Damage/Symptoms	Control
Anthracnose	French and runner bean	Leaves, stems and pods blotched brown.	**Burn all infected plants. Buy seeds from a reputable source.**
Beet leaf miner	Beetroot	Yellow or brown tunnels and blisters on leaves.	Spray with Sybol or Doff Systemic insecticide.

Table 10: Pests, diseases and disorders—*continued*

Pest	Crops Attacked	Damage/Symptoms	Control
Apple sawfly	Apple	Fruitlets fall; tunnels visible. Remaining fruits possess ribbon-like scars.	Spray with pbi Fenitrothion when most of petals have fallen.
Apple sucker	Apple	Flowers turn brown; green, aphid-like insects observed among them.	Spray trees in winter as for aphids. Spray with a systemic insecticide before flowers open.
Big bud mite	Blackcurrant	Dormant buds fat and spherical.	Prune out and burn infected shoots. Spray with Pbi Supercarb as flowers open.
Birds (*sparrows, bullfinches, pigeons*)	Wide range	Fruits pecked or wholly eaten.	Invest in a fruit cage or try 'Scoot' and 'Stay Off' sprays.
Blossom weevil	Strawberry	Unopened flowers wither and turn brown; stalks eaten through.	Pick off and burn any infected flowers.
Brown scale	Peach, grape and gooseberry	Stems covered with small, brown, limpet-like scales.	Spray in winter as for aphids. Spray in summer with Malathion.
Capsid bug	Wide range	Leaves punctured with tiny brown holes; fruits develop raised brown areas.	Spray with pbi Fenitrothion.
Caterpillar	Wide range	Leaves eaten; caterpillars or droppings visible.	Spray with Picket.
Cherry fruit moth	Cherry	Small green caterpillars eat buds and flowers and green fruits.	Spray trees in winter with Murphy Mortegg.
Codling moth	Apple, pear	Fruits are maggoty when harvested.	Spray with pbi Fenitrothion. Once in June; once in July.
Currant blister aphid	Red and white currant	Upper leaves twisted and blistered; often tinged red.	Spray in winter as for aphids. Spray in summer with systemic insecticide.
Currant sawfly	Currants	Leaves eaten, and only veins left.	Spray with Derris (if fruits near maturity); pbi Fenitrothion.
Gooseberry sawfly	Gooseberry	Leaves eaten, and only veins left.	Spray with Derris (if fruits near maturity); pbi Fenitrothion.
Leaf and bud mite	Raspberry	Leaves blotched yellow on upper surface; no reduction in vigour or cropping.	None. Do not confuse with mosaic virus—accompanied by distortion and poor cropping.
Leaf midge	Currant	Shoot tips distorted and withered.	Spray with systemic insecticide immediately before flowers open.
Mealy bug	Grape and occasionally other crops	Small, white, mealy insects visible on stems; suck sap; secrete honeydew.	Spray with Malathion. Brush down rods in winter and spray with Murphy Mortegg.
Mussel scale	Plum	Tiny, mussel-shaped scales plastered on stems.	Spray with Malathion. Spray in winter with Murphy Mortegg.
Pear leaf blister mite	Pear and sometimes plum	Spots—pale green, then pink, then black—appear on leaves.	Pick off and burn infected leaves if possible. Keep tree well fed and watered.
Pear midge	Pear	Fruits fall when small. Lots of small yellow maggots inside.	Destroy infected fruitlets. Spray with pbi Fenitrothion just before flowers open.
Pear sawfly	Pear	Fruitlets fall and are tunnelled by one maggot. Ribbon-like scars on remaining fruits.	Spray with pbi Fenitrothion when most of petals have fallen.
Pear sucker	Pear	Flowers turn brown; green, aphid-like insects among them.	Spray trees in winter as for aphids. Spray with systemic insecticide before flowers open.
Plum sawfly	Plum	Fruitlets fall before fully developed; and they are tunnelled.	Spray with pbi Fenitrothion one week after petals have fallen.
Plum tortrix moth	Plum	Leaves woven together with silken web; caterpillars inside.	Spray in winter as for aphids. Spray in summer with pbi Fenitrothion.
Rabbits/deer	Wide range	Leaves or bark gnawed away.	Difficult. Plastic tree guards help. Try 'Scoot' and 'Stay Off'.
Raspberry beetle	Raspberry	Fruits eaten by small maggots.	Spray with Derris when fruits turn pink.
Red spider mite	Apple, plum, peach,	Leaves bleached and mottled; webs spun; tiny yellow, green or brown mites visible.	Spray in winter as for aphids. Spray in summer with systemic insecticide.

Pest	Crops Attacked	Damage/Symptoms	Control
Slugworm	Pear, cherry	Small, slimy, black, slug-like creatures eating leaf surfaces.	Spray only very severe infestations with Derris; otherwise ignore.
Tortrix moth	Apple	Surface of fruit eaten; leaf stuck over damage; caterpillar may be seen.	Spray in winter as for aphids. Spray at fruitlet stage with pbi Fenitrothion.
Wasp	Wide range, especially plum	Fruits eaten as they approach ripeness.	Tolerate. Drape wall-trained trees with old net curtains to keep wasps out.
Winter moth	Apple, pear, plum, cherry	Young leaves and open flowers eaten by small, green caterpillars.	Fasten grease bands around trees from September to March. Spray in spring with pbi Fenitrothion.
Woolly aphid	Wide range	Stems covered in colonies of greyish-white, wool-covered insects.	Spray with systemic insecticide. Insect causes canker on apple and pear.

Disease	Crops Attacked	Damage/Symptoms	Control
American gooseberry mildew	Gooseberry, blackcurrant	Leaves, shoots and fruits covered in white powder which turns to light brown felt.	Prevent by pruning well. Don't apply too much nitrogen. Spray with Pbi Supercarb.
Bacterial canker	Cherry, plum	Gum oozes from flattened cankers on stem; leaves full of holes; tree weak.	Cut out and burn infected wood and treat wounds with special paint. Spray with Vitax Bordeaux Mixture.
Blossom wilt	Apple, pear, cherry, plum	Flowers wilt and turn brown; leaves may die.	Cut out infected wood. Spray before flowers open with pbi Supercarb.
Botrytis (grey mould)	Raspberry, strawberry	Fruits covered with fluffy grey mould.	Pick off infected fruits. Spray open flowers with Pbi Supercarb.
Brown rot	Apple, pear, plum, cherry	Fruits become brown and rotten; develop concentric rings of buff pustules.	Dispose of infected fruits (do not compost). Store only undamaged fruits.
Cane blight	Raspberry	Leaves wither; dark areas on canes at ground level; canes become brittle.	Cut out and burn infected canes. Sterilize secateurs. Spray with Murphy Traditional Copper Fungicide.
Cane spot	Raspberry	Small purple spots on canes; eventually turn grey; fruits and leaves spotted later.	Cut out and burn infected canes. Spray new ones with Benlate.
Canker	Apple, pear	Shoots wounded and, in winter, filled with reddish fruiting bodies.	Prune out infected wood. Control woolly aphid.
Coral spot	Wide range, especially currants	Orange pustules appear on stems which are dead or dying.	Cut out infected wood.
Crown gall	Blackberry, loganberry	Swollen galls visible on stems at soil level or higher.	Cut out and burn. Replant on uninfected soil.
Fireblight	Apple, pear, cherry and others	Shoots wither and turn brown; leaves do not fall; wounds visible at stem bases.	Cut out damaged wood well back into healthy wood that is not stained brown.
Honey fungus (Armillaria)	Wide range	Trees die back; honey-coloured toadstools may appear; white fungal threads in soil; black 'bootlaces' in soil on occasions.	Dig up and burn badly infected plants. Manure others to maintain vigour.
Leaf spot	Currants	Small brown spots on leaves coagulate; leaves eventually fall.	Spray with Benlate. Gather up and burn fallen leaves.
Peach leaf curl	Peach, apricot, nectarine	Leaves become puckered and bright pink in colour.	Spray with Vitax Bordeaux Mixture or a Liquid Copper Fungicide before buds open in January and as they burst. Destroy infected leaves.
Powdery mildew	Wide range	Leaves and shoots covered in white powder.	Spray with Benlate.
Reversion disease	Blackcurrants	Leaves distorted with fewer lobes; flowers pinkish purple.	Dig up and burn. Control big bud mite which spreads this virus disease.
Rust	Plum, currants	Leaves spotted yellow on undersides; may fall early.	Keep tree well fed and watered. Gather fallen leaves. Spray with pbi Dithane 945.
Shot hole	Cherry, plum	Leaves full of small holes and spotted brown. No gummosis visible.	Feed tree well and apply water. If gum oozing from bark: see Bacterial canker.
Silver leaf	Plum and sometimes cherry, peach, nectarine	Leaves silvery in appearance on one or more branches; wood stained brown within.	Cut out infected branches back to healthy tissue. Burn them. (See false silver leaf.)

Disease	Crops Attacked	Damage/Symptoms	Control
Blackleg	Potato	Stem bases black; leaves yellow and wilting.	Dig up and destroy. Store only healthy tubers.
Black rot	Turnip, swede	Leaf edges yellow; black veins; sliced root black round perimeter.	Destroy infected plants. Prevent by improving drainage and crop rotation.
Buckeye rot	Tomato	Grey or reddish areas on fruit, overlaid with brown concentric rings.	Pick off and destroy. Water compost with Cheshunt compound.
Canker	Parsnip	Upper areas of root turn soft and brown.	Sow resistant varieties. Avoid over manuring. Lime acid soils. Rotate crops.
Chocolate spot	Broad bean	Leaves blotched with brown; leaves may die.	Avoid applying too much nitrogen. Spray with Benlate.
Clubroot	Brassicas	Plants stunted and weak. Roots swollen and foul smelling.	Lime acid soil. Improve drainage. Dip roots of young plants in Pbi Liquid Clubroot Control.
Crown rot	Rhubarb	Buds and centre of plant brown and rotten.	Dig up and burn. Improve drainage. Don't replant rhubarb on infected soil.
Downy mildew	Brassicas, lettuce, spinach, onion, pea, beetroot	Leaves yellow above, whitish or purplish-felted below.	Spray with pbi Dithane 945; Grow resistant varieties.
Dry rot	Potato	Tubers in store wrinkle at one end; white or pink fungus visible.	Prevent by lifting and storing carefully. Destroy infected tubers.
Foot rot	French bean, pea, runner bean	Leaves yellow; stem bases black and rotten.	Prevent by rotating crops. Water seedlings with Cheshunt compound.
Gangrene	Potato	Stored tubers develop sunken brown areas and flesh rots.	Prevent by storing healthy tubers in ideal conditions.
Ghost spot	Tomato	Fruits develop white, circular spots centred with brown.	Caused by grey mould. Prevent by ventilating well and watering carefully.
Grey mould	Wide range	Brown, rotting areas are covered with grey fur.	Prevent as for Ghost Spot. Spray with Pbi Supercarb. Pull off affected leaves.
Halo blight	French and runner bean	Brown, yellow-edged blotches on leaves; soggy blotches on pods.	Prevent by buying seeds from a reputable supplier. Destroy infected plants.
Heart rot	Celery	Centre of plant brown and rotton.	Avoid damaging plants or applying too much nitrogen. Practise crop rotation.
Honey fungus	Rhubarb	Plant dies; white fungus found on roots; black 'bootlaces' may be in soil.	Dig up and burn. Replant new crowns on uninfected soil.
Leaf mould	Tomato	Leaves yellowish above; purplish mould visible below.	Prevent by growing resistant varieties. Ventilate well. Spray with Pbi Supercarb.
Leaf spot	Rhubarb, spinach, celery	Leaves spotted with brown—centres of spots fall out. Spots on celery develop black 'pinheads'.	Pull off infected leaves. Spray celery with pbi Dithane 945
Leek rust	Leek and occasionally onion	Leaves spotted with orange.	Destroy infected foliage. Other parts still edible. Practise crop rotation.
Neck rot	Onion	Stored bulbs become mouldy on upper surface.	Prevent by storing ripe, well-dried onions.
Potato blight	Potato, tomato	Leaves curled inwards and blotched brown. White mould on undersides. Tomato leaves brown at tips.	Spray with pbi Dithane 945 from July onwards. Grow resistant varieties of potato.
Powdery mildew	Wide range	White powdery deposit visible on leaves, shoots and pods.	Sow resistant varieties. Space adequately. Spray with Nimrod-T.
Powdery scab	Potato	Circular, dark brown scabs with raised edges found on tubers.	Destroy infected bulbs. Prevent by ensuring good drainage and practising rotation.
Rust	Broad bean	Raised orange spots on undersides of leaves.	Spray only severe outbreaks with pbi Dithane 945.
Scab	Potato	Tubers marred by rough brown scabs.	Prevent by avoiding over-liming. Grow resistent varieties. Infected tubers still edible.
Shanking	Onion	Central leaves turn yellow and wilt. Bulbs foul smelling when sliced.	Destroy infected plants. Prevent by practising crop rotation.

Disease	Crops Attacked	Damage/Symptoms	Control
Smut	Onion, sweetcorn	On onion: leaves and bulbs spotted with black; on sweetcorn: white outgrowths on cobs and stems.	Destroy infected plants. Keep onions off infected ground for eight years.
Soft rot	Carrot, swede, turnip	Stored or growing roots brown and rotten in centre.	Destroy infected roots. Prevent by ensuring good drainage and avoiding over-manuring.
Spinach blight	Spinach	Leaves roll inwards and turn yellowish.	A virus disease. Destroy infected plants. Control aphids which transmit viruses.
Spraing	Potato	Tubers marked with red semi-circles when cut open.	A virus disease. Prevent by rotating crops and planting certified potatoes. Infected roots still edible.
Stem rot (didymella)	Tomato	Black areas on stem bases; fruits may also become brown.	Dig up and burn. Spray healthy plants with Pbi Supercarb.
Verticillium wilt	Tomato	Lower leaves yellow; plant wilts in sun.	Topdress plants and water with Pbi Supercarb. Grow resistant varieties.
Violet root rot	Carrot	Roots felted with purple mould.	Destroy infected roots. Practise rotation. Keep carrots off infected ground for four years.
Virus	Wide range	Leaves puckered, distorted and mottled with yellow.	Destroy infected plants. Keep down aphids which transmit the diseases.
Wart disease	Potato	Black, warty outgrowths appear on tubers of old varieties.	Ministry of Agriculture must be informed. Grow new varieties which are immune. Destroy infected tubers.

Disorder	Crops Attacked	Damage Symptoms	Control
Blossom end rot	Tomato	Black, sunken areas on undersides of fruits.	Caused by erratic watering. Aim to keep compost evenly moist.
Blotchy ripening	Tomato	Fruits ripen unevenly.	Ventilate and shade well. Ensure adequate supplies of food and water.
Bolting	Wide range	Plants form flowers and 'run to seed' prematurely.	Prevent dryness at the roots. Do not transplant large plants.
Brown heart	Turnip, swede	When sliced open, roots reveal brown centre.	Caused by boron deficiency. Apply balanced fertilizer before sowing.
Fanging	Carrot, parsnip, beetroot	Roots forked and distorted.	Caused by stony or over-manured soil.
Greenback	Tomato	Upper part of fruit remains green.	Shade from bright sun. Feed well. Do not defoliate. Plant resistant varieties.
Green tubers	Potato	Tubers green both outside and inside.	Caused by sunlight. Earth up tubers adequately.
Hearts (lack of)	Cabbage	Plants remain leafy and open—no solid heart formed.	Plant in firm, well-manured soil which does not dry out.
Hollow heart	Potato	Tubers undamaged outside but hollow inside.	Caused by heavy rain or irrigation after drought. Keep evenly moist.
Root split	Carrot	Roots split longitudinally.	Caused by heavy rain or irrigation after drought. Keep evenly moist.
Scald	Tomato	Sunken, straw-coloured patches on fruits or leaves.	Shade from bright sunshine.
Split fruit	Tomato	Fruits split open when ripe.	Caused by heavy watering after dryness. Keep evenly moist.
Tip burn	Lettuce	Leaf edges marked with brown.	Caused by dryness at the roots.
Weedkiller damage	Tomato	Leaves narrow and distorted; stems twisted; fruits oval and hollow.	Keep all weedkillers away from tomatoes and use a separate watering can.
Whiptail	Brassicas	Leaves reduced to just the midrib. No pest damage visible.	Water with 28 g sodium molybdate in 9 litres (2 gal) water to each 8·3 sq m (10 sq. yd.) of soil.

FRUIT

Pest	Crops Attacked	Damage/Symptoms	Control
Aphid	Wide range	Sap sucked; plant weakened; viruses transmitted; honeydew secreted.	Spray trees in winter with Murphy Mortegg to kill eggs. Spray in summer with Rapid Greenfly Killer.

Table 10: Pests, diseases and disorders—*continued*

Disease	Crops Attacked	Damage/Symptoms	Control
Spur blight	Raspberry, loganberry	Purplish areas develop around buds; buds fail to grow or soon wilt.	Cut out and burn infected canes. Spray others with Pbi Supercarb.
Stem rot (collar rot)	Melon	Stem base turns brown and rots.	Prevent by not planting too deeply and by using sterilized compost.
Strawberry mildew	Strawberry	Leaves purple blotched above, white beneath.	Dust fortnightly with sulphur from flower bud formation onwards.
Virus	Raspberry, strawberry and others	Leaves distorted, twisted and often mottled yellow; yields down and vigour reduced.	Dig up and burn. Control aphids which spread the disease.

Disorder	Crops Attacked	Damage/Symptoms	Control
Bitter pit	Apple	Fruits spotted dark brown; flesh affected too.	Keep trees well watered. Spray with calcium nitrate—28 g (1 oz) in 9 litres (2 gal) water—in mid-June and twice more at fortnightly intervals.
False silver leaf	Cherry, plum	Leaves on entire tree turn silvery; no die-back.	Water well and spray with foliar feed.
Frost damage	Strawberry	Centres of flowers turn black.	Cover flowering plants with straw, newspaper or cloches if frost threatens.
Fruit drop	Apple, pear, plum	Fruitlets fall early; no sign of insect damage.	There is a natural 'June drop' in which the tree thins out its fruits. If they all drop suspect lack of food, water or suitable pollinator.
Fruit not forming	Wide range	Flowers appear but no fruit follows.	Check that a suitable pollinator is present. Frost damage may produce the same symptoms.
Gummosis	Cherry, plum	Clear gum oozing from trunk or main branch; no other symptoms.	Cut off hardened gum. Feed tree with general fertilizer.
Nutrient deficiency	Wide range	Areas between veins on leaves become yellow. No distorting.	Enrich surrounding soil with general fertilizer.
Scald	Grape	Berries scorched on one side—nearest glass.	Shade and ventilate as necessary. Cut out affected fruits.
Shanking	Grape	Fruit stalks wither and berries fail to develop; turn brown.	Remove affected grapes. Keep soil evenly moist. Thin grape bunches.

ORNAMENTAL PLANTS

Pest	Crops Attacked	Damage/Symptoms	Control
Aphid	Wide range	Suck sap, weaken plant, secrete honeydew, transmit viruses.	Spray with a specific aphicide: Rapid Greenfly Killer.
Birds	Wide range	Leaves, shoots, flowers and fruits pecked.	Netting is the only real solution. Spray with 'Scoot' or 'Stay Off'.
Broom gall mite	Broom (Cytisus)	Green or grey-brown, lumpy outgrowths appear on stems.	Cut off and burn galls. Destroy badly infected plants.
Bulb scale mite	Narcissus	Bulbs in store are soft, lightweight and brown; slice open and specks are visible in tissue.	Destroy infected bulbs.
Capsid bug	Wide range, especially rose	Leaves punctured with brown holes and distorted.	Spray with systemic insecticide as the leaves unfold.
Carnation fly	Carnation	Maggots tunnel into stems, leaves, roots.	Spray with Derris dust.
Caterpillars	Wide range	Leaves eaten; caterpillars or droppings visible.	Pick off small infestations. Spray larger outbreaks with Sybol.
Chrysanthemum eelworm	Chrysanthemum	Leaves turn dark brown between the veins; eventually entirely brown.	Burn infected plants and buy in new stock. Plant in sterilized compost.
Cuckoo spit (froghopper)	Wide range	Green insect shelters in blob of spittle on stem.	**Rub off or spray with pbi Fenitrothion.**
Earwig	Dahlia and others	Flowers and leaves eaten.	Trap in flowerpots stuffed with straw and inverted on garden canes. Tip into boiling water. Apply Bio Flydown or Picket at dusk.

Pest	Crops Attacked	Damage/Symptoms	Control
Leaf cutter bee	Rose	Large pieces cut from leaf to leave scalloped effect.	None, You'll just have to lump it!
Leaf miner	Chrysanthemum, cineraria, holly	Leaves tunnelled by small grubs.	Spray with Sybol where practicable, or pick off infected leaves.
Leaf rolling sawfly	Rose	Leaves curled under like scrolls; caterpillars may be inside.	Pick off isolated leaves, Spray with pbi Fenitrothion in May and again in June before attack.
Lily beetle	Lily and relations	Leaves eaten; scarlet beetles observed.	Spray with Sybol. Only found in Surrey, Berkshire, Hampshire.
Narcissus fly	Narcissus	No flowers produced, only weak, grassy leaves. Cut bulbs reveal maggot.	Destroy infested bulbs. Buy from reputable supplier. Dust naturalized bulbs with Murphy Gamma-BHC Dust after flowering
Rhododendron bug	Rhododendron	Leaves mottled yellow above, brown beneath.	Spray undersides of leaves with Sybol.
Slugs and snails	Wide range	Leaves and flowers eaten; silvery trails observed.	As for slugs on vegetable crops.
Stem and bulb eelworm	Narcissus	Leaves distorted and yellow mottled; lack of flowers; brown rings within bulbs.	Destroy infected bulbs. Buy from reputable supplier.
Stem eelworm	Phlox	Leaves narrow and distorted; stems split; growth stunted.	Dig up and burn infected plants.
Thrips	Rose, gladiolus	Flowers and leaves spotted with silvery grey.	Spray with pbi Fenitrothion.
Vine weevil	Rhododendron	Lower leaves eaten and shredded.	Dust lower leaves and soil with Murphy Gamma-BHC Dust.

Disease	Crops Attacked	Damage/Symptoms	Control
Azalea gall	Azalea	Green, red and eventually white swellings appear on leaves.	Remove and burn galls. Spray with Murphy Traditional Copper Fungicide.
Blackleg	Pelargonium (geranium)	Base of stem becomes black and soft; grey fur develops.	Prevent by using sterile compost and by ventilating well. Pull off dead leaves.
Black slime	Hyacinth	Leaves turn yellow and collapse. Black resting bodies found between outer scales of bulb.	Destroy infected bulbs. Do not replant in infected area. Use sterile composts.
Blackspot	Rose	Large black spots appear on leaves; leaves eventually fall.	Pick off and burn infected leaves. Gather all fallen leaves. Spray with Nimrod-T from April onwards.
Botrytis	Wide range	Parts of plant rotting and covered with grey fur.	Pick off infected parts. Spray with Pbi Supercarb.
Bud blast	Rhododendron	Buds turn brown and do not open; black 'pinheads' appear on them.	Cut off and burn infected buds. Spray in late summer with pbi Fenitrothion to control leaf hoppers which spread the disease.
Canker	Rose	Rough, Brown, sunken areas appear on stem.	Cut out and burn infected stems. Spray with Synchemicals Bordeaux Mixture.
Carnation leaf spot	Carnation	Purplish brown spots appear on leaves.	Pull off and burn badly infected leaves. Spray with pbi Dithane 945.
Clematis wilt	Clematis	One or more stems wilt, then collapse completely.	Prune out infected shoots at ground level. Drench plant and soil with Pbi Supercarb. Be patient.
Clubroot	Wallflower	Plants wilt and looked stunted; roots swollen and knobbly.	Dip roots in Liquid Pbi Clubroot Control. Lime acid soil.
Dutch elm disease	Elm	Trees look burned; branches and eventually whole tree will die.	None. Fell, then strip off the bark and burn it. Timber unaffected.
Grey bulb rot	Hyacinth	Top of bulb becomes dry and grey; black fungal resting bodies found.	Burn infected plants. Do not plant bulbs in soil known to be infected.
Honey fungus (Armillaria)	Wide range, especially trees and shrubs	Trees or shrubs die back; honey-coloured toadstools may appear; white fungal threads and black 'bootlaces' in soil.	Dig up and burn badly infected plants. Manure to improve vigour.
Ink disease	Bulbous irises	Black patches develop on bulb and on leaves and flowers in wet weather.	Burn infected bulbs. Prevent by spraying emerging leaves with pbi Dithane 945.

Disease	Crops Attacked	Damage/Symptoms	Control
Leaf blight	Lily	Leaves covered with brown blotches.	**Remove and destroy infected growth. Spray with Vitax Bordeaux Mixture in wet weather.**
Leaf spot	Dahlia, rhizomatous iris	Brown spots appear on leaves and eventually coalesce.	Pull off and destroy infected leaves.
Powdery mildew	Rose, chrysanthemum and others	Leaves and shoots covered in white powder.	Spray roses with ICI Nimrod-T; other plants with pbi Benlate.
Rhizome rot	Rhizomatous irises	Leaves turn brown from tips backwards; rhizomes rot and become slimy.	**Dig up and burn. Control slugs. Spray with Vitax Bordeaux Mixture. Improve drainage.**
Rust	Rose, pelargonium, antirrhinum, hollyhock	Rusty brown marks appear on underside of leaves.	Pick off badly infected leaves. Spray with pbi Dithane 945.
Scab	Gladiolus	Red-brown spots on leaves; growth may topple; black areas on corm.	Destroy infected plants. Keep gladioli off infected ground.
Smoulder	Narcissus	Stored bulbs rot; growing leaves spotted and rotten in wet springs; black resting bodies on bulb.	**Destroy stored bulbs that are infected. Spray growing ones with Benlate.**
Tulip fire	Tulip	Leaf tips scorched; straw-coloured streaks on leaves and flowers.	**Burn infected bulbs. Do not plant tulips in infected soil. Prevent by spraying with pbi Dithane 945.**
Virus	Wide range	Leaves mottled with yellow and distorted.	Destroy infected plants. Control aphids which spread virus diseases.
Wilt	Michaelmas diasy	Leaves at stem bases wilt and shrivel; effect spreads up stem.	Destroy infected plants. Do not replant on infected soil.

Disorder	Crops Attacked	Damage/Symptoms	Control
Blind shoots	Narcissus	Leaves produced but flowers fail to appear.	Make sure bulbs do not dry out in spring. Feed after flowering.
Bud drop	Camellia and others	Flower buds fall before they have a chance to open.	Caused by dryness at roots—keep evenly moist and mulch.
Chlorosis	Wide range	Leaves yellow between veins. No distortion.	Caused by food shortage. Feed well. Water plants on chalky soil with Iron Sequestrene.
Oedema	Pelargonium	Blisters form on undersides of leaves; eventually burst.	Caused by overwatering and high humidity.
Peony wilt	Peony	Tree peony: unopened buds turn grey and rot. Herbaceous peony: leaf bases turn brown and collapse.	Cut out infected growth.

GREENHOUSE AND HOUSE PLANTS
(see also under Ornamental Plants)

Pest	Crops Attacked	Damage/Symptoms	Control
Aphid	Wide range	Sap sucked; plant weakened; honeydew secreted; viruses transmitted.	Spray with a specific aphicide: ICI Rapid Greenfly Killer.
Caterpillars	Wide range	Leaves eaten; caterpillars or green droppings visible.	Fumigate greenhouse with Murphy Permethrin Whitefly Smoke; hand pick from house plants.
Earwig	Wide range	Young leaves and flowers eaten.	Fumigate greenhouse with pest smoke. Scrub down greenhouse in winter.
Mealy bug	Wide range	Oval bugs covered in white wax suck sap and secrete honeydew.	Spray with Bio Flydown.
Red spider mite	Wide range	Leaves bleached; webs spun; tiny mites visible on foliage.	Discourage by maintaining a humid atmosphere. Spray with pbi Fenitrothion; Malathion. Fumigate with Murphy Pest and Disease Smoke.
Root aphid	Small range	Plant wilts and looks stunted; aphids found among roots.	Destroy isolated infections. Water compost with diluted Malathion.
Scale insect	Wide range	Brown, limpet-like scales on stems and leaves; honeydew secreted.	Spray with Bio Flydown.
Slugs and snails	Wide range	Leaves and flowers eaten; silvery trails visible.	Pick off pot plants. Use beer traps in greenhouse borders.

Pest	Crops Attacked	Damage/Symptoms	Control
Symphilid	Small range	Plants wilt and look stunted and blue-grey; tiny, white grubs with 12 pairs of legs can be found among roots.	Treat affected plants with diluted Murphy Soil Pests Killer.
Thrips	Wide range	Leaves and flowers speckled with white.	Spray with Bio Sprayday or fumigate with Murphy Permethrin Whitefly Smoke.
Vine weevil	Small range including cyclamen	Plants wilt and look sick. Fat, 1 cm (½ in) long creamy white grubs found among eaten roots.	Destroy infected plants. Use sterile compost. Water healthy plants with diluted Hexyl.
Whitefly	Wide range	White, 'V'-shaped flies on undersides of leaves; honeydew secreted.	Spray with Bio Flydown or Sprayday. Fumigate as for thrips.

Disease	Crops Attacked	Damage/Symptoms	Control
Algae	—	Green, slimy growth on paths, pots and compost surface.	Scrub off paths. Add sharp grit to improve surface drainage of compost.
Blackleg	Pelargonium (geranium)	See under Ornamental Plants.	
Damping off	Wide range of seedlings	Seedlings keel over at stem bases and die off.	Prevent by sowing thinly, ventilating well and watering with Cheshunt Compound.
Sooty mould	Wide range	Black felt appears on leaves and stems.	Grows on honeydew secreted by aphids etc. Control the pest; sponge off the mould.

LAWNS

Pest	Damage/Symptoms	Control
Ants	A nuisance where picnics are popular. Fine soil brought to surface to provide a spot for weeds and moss.	Dust nests with Fison's Ant Killer.
Birds	Only a nuisance when lawns are being sown—they eat the seeds. They also eat lawn pests.	Sow enough seeds for the lawn and the birds.
Dogs	Bitches in season have strong urine which burns off the grass.	Spike area with a fork and water immediately to reduce caustic effect.
Leatherjackets	Patches of grass turn yellow. If watered and covered with polythene overnight grey grubs will be found on the surface in the morning.	Water turf in autumn with Murphy Lawn Pest Killer.
Moles	Molehills appear.	Set traps in runs to catch offending mole—release him where he can do no harm. If adjacent to farmland there's no way of controlling moles.
Worms	Wormcasts appear on surface.	Brush them off. Worms should be tolerated on all except bowling green lawns, where they can be controlled with Murphy Lawn Pest Killer.

Diseases	Damage/Symptoms	Control
Algae	Dark green slimy areas appear, usually in damp, shady spots.	Spike and aerate lawn. Treat with Bio Mosskiller; Murphy Tumblemoss.
Damping off	Newly germinated grass seedlings wilt, turn brown and die—especially in humid weather.	Water with Cheshunt Compound at first sign of disease.
Dollar spot	Straw-coloured patches 2·5–5 cm (1–2 in) across appear on lawn in late summer; enlarge and join together.	Prevent by keeping lawn well fed. Water each sq m of infected lawn with 7 g sulphate of iron diluted in 2·25 litres water.
Fairy rings	Dark green rings appear on lawn, often accompanied by toadstools.	Water with 448 g (1 lb) sulphate of iron in 6·8 litres (1½ gallons) water—enough for 3 sq m.
Fusarium patch	Grass turns yellow in patches, then brown before dying off. White or pink fungus strands visible.	As for dollar spot.
Moss	Moss colonizes areas of soil between grass—especially under trees and in shade.	Improve drainage, do not mow so close, feed lawn well, relieve shady conditions, relieve acidity. Moss killers will kill existing moss but will not remove cause.
Red thread	Patches of pink fungal growth appear in summer and autumn; 'stag's horn' fruiting bodies are produced.	Spike lawn regularly and feed well to prevent attack. Scatter 14 g sulphate of ammonia over each sq m of affected lawn. Water in.

22 Weed control

The battle against the weeds is never ending but it need not be so arduous as many folk assume. The cynic who is convinced that he'll have to spend most of his time in the garden bent double pulling up nettles and dandelions probably does just that. The sensible or idle gardener will look for measures that help to prevent the weeds re-emerging once the ground has been cleaned up. Fig. 87 shows some of the common types of weed that you are likely to encounter.

When you start to cultivate the soil try to eradicate weeds at the outset. There are two basic kinds: the annuals which have small root systems but copious amounts of seed; and the perennials which are often thick-rooted and persistent. The annuals may not last long as individuals, but the old saying 'One year's seed, seven years' weed' shows that they can be as much of a pain as the longer-lived perennial kinds. Always try to eradicate annual weeds before they flower. That way they'll have no chance to regenerate. The oldest and most obvious way of weeding is to pull or fork the plants from the soil. It's a practical proposition where ground is being dug or forked over, even though it might be arduous. Where annual weeds are a problem you can use a Dutch hoe. Push it over the soil so that it skims just fractionally below the surface to sever the top half of the plant from the roots. Carried out in dry weather it will leave the weeds to turn crisp on the surface. It's a useful technique on the vegetable plot.

Perennial weeds that are hoed will simply re-emerge from their fat roots, so you'll have to eradicate the underground parts too. If you can't do this by forking or digging you might be tempted to tackle them with a weedkiller.

There are three basic types of weedkiller: those which kill only green parts of the plant that they touch (contact weedkillers); those that are absorbed by the foliage and transported around inside the plant so that they infect the entire sapstream (translocated or systemic weedkillers); and those that can be watered on to clean soil to prevent weed growth from emerging (residual weedkillers). There are also combination weedkillers that can kill off any existing green growth *and* stop more weeds emerging.

Remember too that there are selective and total weedkillers. Those that can be used on lawns are selective in that they kill broad-leaved weeds but not grass. Others are designed to kill couch grass but to leave broad-leaved ornamentals unharmed.

I'm always reluctant to use weedkillers or 'herbicides' among cultivated plants; it's too easy to let the solution stray on to a plant you want to keep. On paths and drives, though, weedkillers with both a contact and a residual action are useful, for they'll kill off any existing growth and prevent its re-emergence for almost twelve months. Choose a herbicide that contains paraquat, diquat and simazine in the form of soluble granules.

Among cultivated plants the best thing to do is to weed the soil properly during preliminary cultivations—with the spade or fork—and then immediately after planting (when the soil is moist) lay a 5–8 cm (2–3 in) thick mulch of moist leafmould, peat, pulverized bark or other organic matter over the surface. Some of these materials may give rise to a few weed seedlings of their own, but such weeds are easy to pull up compared with heavy infestations on bare soil. Top up the mulch when necessary each spring. A closely planted bed or border will be less likely to support weed growth than one which is sparsely filled. The benefits of ground-cover planting coupled with regular mulching will save you hours of unnecessary hard graft.

Among certain vegetable and fruit crops (strawberries, for instance) you can lay a surface mulch of black polythene, pulling the plants through small holes made at the required intervals. This kind of mulch is an effective weed suppressor, but it won't win any prizes in the garden for its good looks.

If you refuse to clean up your land by these mechanical means in the first place, you can adopt a system which is euphemistically called the 'scorched earth policy'. The entire area is treated with a total weedkiller and the application repeated at intervals until nothing else emerges. Then the soil can be rotavated. Do this, though, and your soil will not be the most hospitable place for plant growth for quite some time. Specific instructions can be found on the containers of all total weedkillers. There are many to choose from, but avoid sodium chlorate if you can. It stays active in the soil for six months or more; it is highly inflammable; it corrodes metal; and it moves sideways in the soil, often attacking plants that you didn't intend to harm. Others are equally efficient and less lethal.

Fig. 87 Weeds. These are among the worst: 1. Bindweed. 2. Couch grass. 3. Ground elder. 4. Marestail.

Fig. 88 Herbicides are safely applied with a watering can fitted with a dribble bar. The danger of spray 'drift' is avoided.

Where specific weeds are a problem on uncultivated land and you want to use a herbicide to banish them, try to choose the right chemical. The following table will give you some idea of the products that are likely to be effective in particular cases:

The recommended herbicides are available under

Weed	Recommended herbicide
Bracken	Murphy Tumbleweed (regular cutting back of young growths will eventually wipe out the plant)
Brambles	Vitax New Formula SBK Brushwood Killer; Boots Nettle & Bramble Killer
Convolvulus (bindweed)	Murphy Tumbleweed
Couch grass	Murphy Tumbleweed on uncultivated ground; wipe leafblades with Tumbleweed gel among plants
Creeping buttercup	Murphy Tumbleweed
Creeping thistle	Murphy Tumbleweed
Dock	Murphy Tumbleweed (two applications)
Ground elder	Murphy Tumbleweed (two applications)
Japanese knotweed	Murphy Tumbleweed (two applications)
Marestail (horsetail)	Murphy Tumbleweed on uncultivated land; Casoron G4 among shrubs and roses
Mind-your-own-business	Murphy Tumbleweed
Oxalis	Murphy Tumbleweed
Pearlwort	Murphy Tumbleweed
Plantain	Murphy Tumbleweed
Speedwell	Tar oil winter wash
Stinging nettle	Murphy Tumbleweed (two applications)

many trade names; the names I have used are their active ingredients, which will be found in the small print on the packet.

SAFETY

Please use all herbicides with care, and store them in their clearly labelled containers out of reach of children and animals. Dispose of any container that has lost its label (put it, tightly capped, into the dustbin after flushing its contents down the lavatory). Keep a watering can for weedkiller application and use it for nothing else. Fitted with a dribble bar (Fig. 88) it will apply the solution effectively without it drifting on to nearby cultivated plants. Some herbicides have to be sprayed on to weed foliage, in which case they should be applied on a still day to prevent spray drift.

Always wear wellingtons and rubber gloves when dealing with weedkillers, and wash thoroughly afterwards, taking care to rinse the watering can too.

Keep children and animals off treated areas until the solution has dried up. After that it should not harm them.

Think carefully before you use any herbicide. All other means of control involve less risk to you, your plants and wildlife.

233

Index